D1242152

Robert Bierstedt

Professor and Chairman, Department of Sociology and Anthropology
The City College of New York
Advisory Editor to Dodd, Mead & Company

Marriage and the American Ideal

Floyd M. Martinson

**Head of the Department
of Sociology and
Social Work
Gustavus Adolphus College**

Dodd, Mead & Company

New York   Toronto

1960

 *Marriage and the American Ideal*

Editor's Introduction

It is difficult for a number of reasons to do a book on marriage and the family. In the first place, although marriage and the family are surely the most pervasive and permanent of all social institutions, they have only recently—in the long course of intellectual history—received a thoroughgoing investigation and analysis. In the second place, the family is as intimate as it is pervasive, and it is always difficult to write with candor about a phenomenon that is so close to most of us. In the third place, marriage is a subject that easily lends itself to sentimentality and sentimentality, in turn, is inconsistent with the sociological discipline. And finally, the family has such close affiliations with other institutions of society—most notably the state and the church, both of which compete for its control and make sometimes contradictory demands upon it—that a writer in this field has to contend with the pitfalls of political and religious prejudice.

If for these reasons, among others, it is difficult to do a book about marriage and the family, it is even more difficult to do it well. One takes pleasure, therefore, in introducing a book whose author has done it not only well but with genuine distinction. As will immediately become apparent to the reader, Floyd Martinson exhibits in the pages that follow a combination of competence and style that one welcomes

v

especially in writers in this field. He has avoided excessive sentiment on the one side and excessive sophistication on the other. His sentences are lucid and straightforward. He knows what he is talking about. He knows also how to present his materials in an attractive and instructive form. From the background of an extensive scholarship he discusses the various attitudes toward marriage that have appeared in recent history and, eschewing a bland and empty impartiality, clearly indicates his preference for one of them. He is convinced himself—and his conviction will impress the reader as well—that the American family in its ideal representation reflects the virtues of the American civilization.

Dr. Martinson's book, in short, has many merits. Not least of these is the judicious and altogether sensible idealism with which he regards his subject. Those who are depressed by the divorce rate or by gloomy predictions about the future of the family will find reasons for a renewed optimism in the pages of this book. The students who use it as an undergraduate text will discover that Dr. Martinson is a good guide and counsellor. They have here a book that is as wise in its prescriptions as it is sound in its scholarship. They have a book, finally, that they can use with confidence as they think about, and plan, their own future roles as marital partners and as parents.

Robert Bierstedt

Preface

Anyone who sets out to write a functional textbook in the marriage and family field—that is, a book designed to facilitate human action—is forced by the nature of the assignment to accept some basic assumptions about the nature of man and the nature of marriage and the family. Regarding the nature of man, the author writing on marriage and family accepts the assumption that the personality of the reader is not "set" and that he is capable of personality growth and can benefit from new experience. If this were not the assumption of the author, he would not write the book.

Secondly, the author assumes that people are not mere pawns at the mercy of forces outside themselves, but that they have the capacity to make decisions and to choose values and goals for living. If this were not so, a book designed to facilitate human action would be useless.

Thirdly, the author assumes that people are at least in part rational creatures and that they choose values and goals for living on the basis of knowledge and insights available to them—knowledge and insights of the kind presented in this book.

Regarding the nature of marriage and the family, the author accepts the assumption that there are things about marriage and the family which can be known and transmitted to others and that the discipline or disciplines the author represents possess such data. It is the asumption of this text that the empirical social sciences possess knowledge and insights about marriage and the family which are worthy of the reader's time and attention.

All of the above assumptions are basic. Their truthfulness cannot be absolutely demonstrated, as is the case with all basic assumptions. They must be accepted on faith. The writer accepts them for the purposes of his task, either implicitly or explicitly. In this book they are made explicit.

But apparently these are the assumptions of most authors of books on marriage and family. What is it that makes this book different from the other marriage and family books on the market? This is a fair question, and we will attempt to answer it.

No marriage and family text adequately covers its subject matter unless both the importance of values and the findings of empirical science are taken into account. Only the conviction that no text to date had adequately dealt with the first of these—the importance of values in the marriage and family decisions of individuals—called for adding another text to the array already available.

Hence there are "firsts" in the text which will be apparent to the person familiar with other texts in the field, and the major "first" is the conscious and explicit attempt to give place to values consistent with their place in the lives of people. The primary purpose of this book is to show how the major value themes in American culture and the findings of social science relate to problems and decisions of marriage and family living.

In books on marriage and family it is customary to concentrate on the family life cycle, beginning with dating and progressing through the stages of marriage, parenthood, and family living. The present book is no exception. However, in choosing to follow this pattern, the author would not appear to approve of the myopic view that one's dating, marriage, and family life are so important that all other goals and activities in life pale before them. Statements such as, "Choosing a mate is the most important decision you will make in your lifetime" or "Marriage is the most important vocation that a young person can choose" are evidence of this narrow view. It may be true for one person that to marry will be the most important decision in life. For another the most important event in life may be his decision to embrace one philosophy of life rather than another. Another person may regard his calling or profession as most important in his life. Hence no exaggerated claims should be made for the importance of marriage and the family. Marriage is one of life's important areas. This is all that should be claimed for it, but this is enough to merit its serious consideration in the pages that follow.

Though the concentration of interest in this book is on the marriage and family aspects of life, the discerning reader will note a conscious attempt to maintain a broader perspective on the individual and his total involvement in society.

We assume only a very limited background in social science on the part of the reader. For this reason the first chapter deals with the basic concepts—society, culture, and personality. Despite the attempt to write a book that is readable and understandable to undergraduates, the concepts and the analysis of data are more in the category of knowledge and insights to be taught to rather than to be read by the college undergraduate. The book is more than a functional text. In the analysis of social systems—dating, marriage, and family—a number of contributions are made to the analysis of social systems per se.

If I were to list the names of all persons to whom I am consciously aware of owing intellectual debts, the list would be excessively long for a preface. Only a few whose intellectual stimulation has been particularly pertinent to the present endeavor can be included. These include my former teachers,

F. Stuart Chapin, Clifford Kirkpatrick, William L. Kolb, and Paul Popenoe, and a number of persons who have influenced me through their writings, Derrick Sherwin Bailey, Ernest W. Burgess, J. V. Langmead Casserley, Emile Durkheim, Nelson N. Foote, Reuben Hill, Alfred C. Kinsey, William L. Kolb, Talcott Parsons, J. H. W. Stuckenberg, Carle C. Zimmerman, and Max Weber.

For their careful reading of the manuscript in whole or in part and their encouragement as well as their criticisms, I am deeply indebted to Robert Bierstedt, Lee Burchinal, William L. Kolb, Peter P. Klassen, William Oman, and Beatrice Awes Martinson.

For a year's leave of absence in which to complete the project, I am indebted to President Edgar M. Carlson, Dean Albert G. Swanson, and the Board of Trustees of Gustavus Adolphus College. For providing pleasant and stimulating surroundings in which to spend that year, I am indebted to Tulane University, and especially to Dean Robert M. Lumiansky and Professor William L. Kolb.

My wife, Beatrice Awes Martinson, has been a constant source of encouragement and my support—in a very tangible way—during the year. Our children—John, Anne, Stephen, and Peter—have perhaps contributed little, but their interruptions have kept me close to the realities of family living throughout the entire project.

Floyd M. Martinson

Contents

iii *Marriage*

iv *The Family*

Marriage and the American Ideal

The nature of man and marriage

I Man, Society, and Culture

i

This is a book about human beings. It does not deal with all of human life, but it does deal with an important part of it—namely the processes and decisions involved in falling in love, getting married, and raising a family. It deals with the person as he passes from stage to stage in the family life cycle.

But before we talk about dating—this is the point at which we enter the cycle—we must set the stage by discussing briefly the nature of man, his "way of life," and the nature of relationships between men.

There are distinct views on these three subjects in the Western world, all based on beliefs about the nature of man. Unless one understands what man means to Americans he cannot understand American family life. This view of man is basic to our whole system of dating, marriage, and the family.

In America we place man on a pedestal. Ideally, we treat man as worthy of awe and respect. In fact, this view has become so commonplace that we regard it as natural and right to treat ourselves and others in this way.

But it has not always been so in human history, nor is it so at this time in all societies around the world. In other times and places the state or the nation has been regarded as the entity most worthy of man's adulation. This has happened as recently as the 1930's, 1940's, and 1950's with Naziism, fascism, and communism holding sway over the minds of men. In other times and places the objects of adoration have been ancestors or the kinship group, a malicious or capricious hierarchy of spirits, or a god of vengeance, wrath, or love. All of these and more have from time to time captured the imagination of man or filled him with fear. Hence they became dominant objects of awe, reverence, and respect.

Not so in America. Here man holds the center of the stage and all things revolve about him. Scholars who have studied values generally agree that the shared ultimate value or the shared core of ultimate values underlying the development of Western culture centers in this belief in the dignity, freedom, and equality of men—in the sacredness of human personality.

> . . . the Hellenic-Judaic-Christian tradition of Western European society . . . places the human individual, as the child of God, at its core. This complex of values measures the validity of institutions and social groups by their contribution to personal growth and expanding experience through freedom, for in this system society and the group exist for the sake of the individual.[1]

Ideally, in American secular culture man is the measure of all things. If it is good for man, it is good. If it is bad for man, it is bad.

[1] William L. Kolb, "Family Sociology, Marriage Education, and the Romantic Complex: A Critique," *Social Forces*, Vol. 29, October 1950, p. 65.

In ideal form the basic values that order individual and societal life in America can be stated as follows:

1. *The dignity and worth of man.* No other object on earth, animate or inanimate, is of equal worth to man. His relation to other creatures and things can only be one of superordination-subordination; he is the master of all. Even his own creations—ideas, institutions, groups—must serve his ends or be subject to change or abandonment.

2. *The freedom of man.* Since man is not subordinate to any other object on earth, he is and must be free. No other objects can be given greater latitude than man, even those that have been objects of veneration in other times and places—the state, the kinship group, etc. Free man is regarded as capable of almost limitless growth and personality development. He is regarded as capable of acting responsibly—even though free—for he is a rational creature able to distinguish between right and wrong.

3. *The equality of men.* The only object on earth sharing man's exalted position is another man. This is the reason why there must be order in society—the rights of *all* men must be protected and insured.

In referring to this common core of ultimate values in American culture, scholars have frequently used the terms, the American dream, the American ideal, or the American creed. It is fair to ask if this core of values is uniquely American or if it is a core of democratic values inherent in Western civilization and hence manifest in the culture of the English, Swiss, and Scandinavians, as well as in America.

It is true that the roots of this common core of values are historically grounded in value premises common to Western civilization. In fact, the roots go back to Hebrew, Greek, Roman, and Christian origins. Be that as it may, many strains in the American core of values are uniquely American in origin, and the combination of beliefs, values, and norms made up of the various strains results in a peculiar American ethos. There is also a unique *élan* to the American core of values not characteristic in other Western societies.[2]

This common core of values in American culture is firmly grounded, historically, in a number of documents and records which continue to be a source of inspiration for each new generation of Americans. Some of the major repositories of the American ideal are the Declaration of Independence; the Preamble to the Constitution of the United States; the Bill of Rights; legal statutes; documents and pronouncements of American Jewish, American Protestant, and American Roman Catholic institutions and groups; the pronouncements of American presidents—Wilson's fourteen points, Roosevelt's four freedoms; and others.

But the historic American ideal does not merely repose in these documents. It is constantly being brought to the attention of the American people and the world by various protagonists and role specialists who are the keepers and the interpreters of the documents containing the ideal. It is variously interpreted and expounded by statesmen, politicians, judges, and lawyers; rabbis, priests, ministers, and theologians; teachers of American history, political science, economics, and social studies. Out of conviction or because of the requirements of the offices they hold, these specialists and others teach, preach, or pronounce regarding aspects of the common belief in the dignity, freedom, and equality of all men.

The American ideal is more than a static set of values and norms. Though grounded in the historical record, this common core of values continues to be freshly interpreted, to change, and to grow. These core values referred to as "creed" or "dream" are less static and dogmatic than a creed and more concrete and real than a dream; hence the label, the American ideal.

Needless to say, it is difficult to maintain a proper balance between the best interests of the group and the needs and desires of each individual. A number of writers have

[2] Myrdal, Gunnar, *An American Dilemma*, New York: Harper and Brothers, 1944, Ch. 1.

observed that the balance has shifted in the present decade toward an emphasis on the importance of the group and that the individual is not being treated as a creature of dignity, worth, and responsibility in the way that the American ideal prescribes. William H. Whyte, for instance, suggests that a social ideal or ethic has replaced the traditional individual ethic—a belief that the group (togetherness) is the source of creativity, that to belong to groups is the ultimate need of the individual. Riesman similarly notes a trend toward acceptance of other-directedness as a value. "What is common to all other-directeds is that their contemporaries are the source of direction for the individual—either those known to him or those with whom he is indirectly acquainted, through friends and through the mass media." [3] The goal of the other-directed individual is to conform, and conformity is the one stable element in his personality. What he conforms to will vary with the demands made by the group to which he desires to belong. Other-directedness then becomes a goal or a value in society because it tends to insure order and efficiency in human thought and action. Both Whyte and Riesman view the trend toward acceptance of this social ethic with some concern and misgiving.

However, to emphasize the importance of the group is not necessarily to belittle the individual. One of the finest, most constructive apologies for the importance of the group in the self-realization of the individual is that of Foote and Cottrell in their book, *Identity and Interpersonal Competence.* They develop some new directions in social research in the hope that discoveries will provide not "hidden persuaders" for the manipulation of the individual by the group but "a mean for everyone to explore new possibilities of self-development" through more meaningful group experiences.

It is not our place here to evaluate the merits of this recently emerged emphasis on the importance of the group in the life of the individual either in terms of the desirability of

[3] David Riesman, *The Lonely Crowd*, New Haven: Yale University Press, 1950.

conformity or in terms of its relationship to self-development. We have used it instead as an example of a significant new interpretation on the general theme of the American ideal.

To summarize, the American ideal has deep roots in Western civilization; yet it is uniquely American. The historic formulations of the ideal have been preserved in a variety of documents and records, and these formulations are kept alive in contemporary American culture through the efforts of role specialists in various fields of human relations. Nevertheless, the American ideal is not essentially historic or static in nature; it is constantly growing and changing as the recent emergence of the strong emphasis on group life, group creativity, and conformity attests.

It is only against this background of beliefs and values— which we will hereafter refer to as the American ideal—that the American dating, marriage, and family systems can be understood and appreciated.

The Nature of Man

What is the nature of this creature around whom—in the American value structure—the whole world of other creatures and creations revolves?

One thing is certain: man is an extremely complex creature only partially understood by himself. This is not a book on the nature of man in all his biological, psychological, sociological, philosophical, and theological aspects, but there are some things we must know about man in order to understand him, even partially, in his love, marriage, and family living.

Man is able to learn and to evaluate symbols and objects, including himself. Herein lies a large part of his uniqueness. Herein also lies the complexity of human life.

If it were correct to assume the existence of given needs and their necessary satisfaction, then at any given time, if these needs were not met, the individual would perish. While this is true of a person's organism, each person is more than a mere organism. If a person as a self-conscious personality does not sufficiently and intelligently value his organism, he will let it perish; his organism is his servant, not his master. A person wants not only survival but many other satisfactions as well, the nature of which cannot be deduced from his organism. He wants optimal satisfaction of these wants also.[4]

Man, when properly motivated, has a highly developed psychic nature. He is capable of knowing and desiring an ever increasing number of possible satisfactions as his experiences increase. For instance, man desires food to satisfy his tissue needs, but he also receives psychic satisfaction from the experience of eating if the food carries prestige as well as nutrition—if it is T-bone steak, not hamburger, if it is eaten at Antoine's, not at the corner drugstore. Or, in the area of sex, he may feel the physiological urge for sex outlet, but his pleasure is increased if he and his spouse carry out sexual intercourse in an atmosphere of love and affection rather than one of duty or obligation. It is quite evident that even the physiological needs have social and psychological overtones for man, whereas other of man's desires are largely psychic in nature and far removed from the realm of physiological needs. The latter would include the enjoyment he receives in visiting with friends, in watching a TV program, or in listening to a piece of music.

The point is that man's capacity for wanting many satisfactions is all out of proportion to his ability or opportunity to satisfy all of them.

To add to the complications, as well as to the satisfactions, of being human, man is aware of himself and capable of knowing right from wrong. He is aware of his finiteness, of the possibilities of suffering and death. Questions about existence, and the rightness or wrongness of it, universally plague man: Where did I come from? Why am I here? What shall I do

[4] Nelson N. Foote and Leonard S. Cottrell, Jr., *Identity and Interpersonal Competence*, Chicago: University of Chicago Press, 1955, p. 98. Copyright 1955 by the University of Chicago.

with my life? Will I succeed? When and how will I die? Is there any life after death? These universal questions of man—man's existential anxiety—cause him to inquire into his nature and the nature of his world "not as a casual spectator, but as a passionate seeker."

When added together, the needs, interests, and desires of man become limitless—his physiological needs, his psychic needs, his social needs, and his need for meaning as he con-

*"I think the whole idea of living makes
Bradley uneasy."*
Reproduced courtesy of Stan Hunt.

templates the mysteries of life. And when we consider that each need or goal can be met in a variety of ways, we see further the extreme complexity of human life and the need for order if man's tremendous potential is to be turned to satisfying pursuits rather than end in bewilderment and frustration.

> The need of a system of orientation and devotion is an intrinsic part of human existence. . . . Indeed, there is no other more powerful source of energy in man. Man is not free to choose between having or not having "ideals."

. . . All men are "idealists" and are striving for something beyond the attainment of physical satisfactions.[5]

How does man bring this order into his life? He must balance the satisfactions of these many wants as they increase in number and in complexity against each other. He must constantly evaluate. He must accept from others or set up for himself standards of judgment for organizing his actions. These are his values.

Society

We must not give the impression, however, that each individual sets up categories and standards of judgment unaided by other persons in the society. During his formative years the child spends his life in the close company of a small group of persons, known as his family of orientation. In fact, it is here that he first has his life ordered for him. During these formative years someone else surrounds him with the right answers to life's problems and shields him from many anxiety-creating situations. It is only gradually that he becomes aware of choices and dilemmas in life. By the time he is ready to launch out on his own as a free and independent individual he has accepted from his parents, childhood companions, and school associates many of the values that he will utilize in ordering his affairs throughout the remainder of his life. It is probably a minority of people who question or reject all the orientations received as "givens" in childhood. These early associations provide the setting in which the dependent and undisciplined child is shaped and molded into a social being with interests and goals somewhat unique, but, nevertheless, enough like those of others so that he can live in a cooperative and harmonious way with his fellow men. We

[5] Erich Fromm, *Man for Himself*, New York: Rinehart & Company, Inc., 1947, p. 49.

call this process of learning to act in a socially responsible way the socialization process.

The individual lives most of his life in association with others in groups—occupational groups, family groups, recreational groups, educational groups, religious groups. Each of these groups in turn gives some direction and order to life. Only the hermit chooses to withdraw completely from such involvements. So from birth to death most persons are immersed in group life. This provides satisfactions and helps give direction to individual and group activity.

Culture

Just as each individual does not create his own order, so the groups of which he is a part in the society do not create their own rules for living. For there is in every society a backlog of accumulated patterns of thought and action which give meaning and direction to life. This backlog of "proper" patterns of thought and behavior we commonly refer to as culture. Culture is the "way of life" of a people.

The actions of individuals as well as the actions of groups take on meaning and order when goals for living are selected and arranged in a way that is generally consistent with the culture and when the means of achieving these goals have been spelled out in accordance with the shared ultimate values pertinent to the culture.

We do not decide what we want from life all at one time, of course; we make decisions every day. Most of these do not give us trouble. Shall I have corn flakes or puffed rice for breakfast? Shall I skip English class today and work on my overdue term paper in history? These are the kinds of daily decisions we make. But some decisions are more important, and we are relieved when we have made a choice. Shall I go to work immediately upon graduating from high school or shall I go to college? Shall I get married immediately upon graduating from college or shall I work a year or two? In all our decisions we try to do what seems best to us. We apply values in an attempt to narrow down and simplify the choices to be made.

To live with any degree of confidence in himself and in his decisions, the individual must feel that his goals in life have been selected in accordance with values that are "right" and worthy of respect. In other words, he must feel a greater loyalty to the value than to the need which called it forth. It is like the boy who craves a piece of candy but does not steal it because of a prior conviction that it is not right to steal.

> Value-orientation refers to those aspects of the actor's orientation which commit him to the observation of certain norms, standards, criteria of selection, whenever he is in a contingent situation which allows (and requires) him to make a choice. Whenever an actor . . . is forced to make any choice whatever—his *value-orientations* may commit him to certain norms that will guide him in his choices. The value-orientations which commit a man to the observance of certain rules in making selections from available alternatives are not random but tend to form a system of value-orientations which commit the individual to some organized set of rules (so that the rules themselves do not contradict one another).[6]

Individual behavior and societal life are, in other words, guided by "taken values rather than given needs." Sometimes these values become so important and compelling that the individual is willing to give up personal comfort and profitable career because of deep conviction and loyalty to a set of values. "To act in accord with such demands frequently requires of the individual that he give up all his interests except his interest in the ultimate value itself and in the nonempirical realm in which the value is anchored."[7] The mis-

[6] Talcott Parsons and Edward A. Shils, *Toward a General Theory of Action*, Cambridge: Harvard University Press, 1951, p. 59.
[7] William L. Kolb, "Urbanization and Urbanism" (Mimeographed), pp. 16–17.

sionary and the martyr are not uncommon types in human history.

Values and Marriage

As individuals turn from the childhood world in which many values and norms for action are given to a more independent adult life, they begin to assess the values and norms they have been given and either accept or discard them, modify them, or take new ones. In American society high value is placed on marriage as a lifelong partnership; therefore, careful planning makes sense, and young people anticipating marriage look for values to guide them in choosing a mate and in arranging family life. Since social scientists have prestige as students of man and group life, young people often turn to them for help. In fact, it is generally conceded that student demand is in large part responsible for the great number of course offerings in marriage and the family in high schools and colleges today.

Social scientists, particularly family sociologists, have accepted the challenge and are offering preparation-for-marriage courses. But herein lies a problem. What values or norms, if any, should the sociologist-turned-marriage-educator transmit to students? According to William L. Kolb, "Sociologists of the family . . . view [their work] as an aid for those who are about to establish a marriage relation or those who are disturbed by the conflicts of their family relations. In so doing these workers discard whatever protection is derived from engaging in non-value oriented research. They actively enter the field of value discrimination and judgment, and their work must be judged on that basis, as well as by the criteria of scientific method." [8] This problem becomes a real

[8] William L. Kolb, "Sociologically Established Family Norms and Democratic Values," *Social Forces*, Vol. 26, May 1948, p. 451.

stumbling block for sociologists who have sought to discover empirically the shared ultimate values guiding the destinies of Americans have not been encouraged by what they have found. Our broad, nonspecific value orientation—belief in the dignity, freedom, and equality of man (the American ideal)—lends itself to many conflicting interpretations. Sociologists have concluded that our "cultural blueprint lacks unity and consistency," and that "the chief distinguishing characteristic of our society is precisely its lack of any sovereign culture pattern."

In view of this lack of specific norms that can be presented to all young people in preparation-for-marriage courses, several courses of action are open to the marriage educator. He can attempt, as some have done, to present the findings of science—the facts—without any interpretation. It is generally agreed that this attempt has not been successful. Facts do not speak for themselves. Someone must interpret facts before they can be used as values and norms to live by.

Or the marriage educator can present to the student the findings from studies of marriages that have been "happy" or "adjusted"—by their own definition or the definition of their acquaintances—and recommend the factors associated with happiness as guides for young people today. The problem with this approach is that only a small and nonrepresentative sample of marriages have been studied, and presenting the findings as patterns for living has resulted in values being taught that are quite out of keeping with our basic belief in the freedom of man, as we point out in our discussion of the rationalistic marriage model in Chapter 4.

There is a third alternative. The marriage educator can use the American ideal—belief in the dignity, freedom, and equality of man—as the core value complex against which to judge the efficacy of choices which young people make and must make in dating, choosing a mate, marriage, and family living. This third method of dealing with values is the one used in this book.

There are difficulties in this approach as in the others. First, we have already pointed out that this core value complex is extremely vague and that it lends itself to a variety of interpretations. We will illuminate the core value complex by utilizing the findings of science, but here additional problems present themselves. First, there are gaps in the scientific knowledge. Some problems have been almost overinvestigated, whereas others have been slighted almost entirely. Secondly, some of the findings of science are not applicable to analysis when we use the American ideal as our ultimate value complex, for most of the research on man and the family has been designed in support of a view that man does not possess either dignity or freedom but that his life is determined by the various forces that play upon him. However, valuable empirical data have been gathered even when the scientist has, from the point of view adopted here, been proceeding according to false or inadequate assumptions about the nature of man and society.

In summary, what values to teach continues to plague the marriage educator. That some values must be taught, most scholars will agree. "Facts cannot be said to be fundamental, for they are variously seen and so are subject to interpretation. The teacher cannot avoid the traffic in viewpoints, since without them there may be nothing to teach." [9]

The student is interested in values; he takes a marriage course precisely because he hopes that it will shed some light on decisions and choices he is soon to make, or is in the process of making, some of which may be as important as anything he does or will do in life. To make these decisions and choices, he must sort out and take a new look at many values. Glover found in a study of 218 young people counseled on difficulties by teachers of marriage and the family that the problems about which they were most concerned involved their beliefs, values, attitudes, and ethical and

[9] Forest K. Davis, "Teaching Ethical Values Through the Marriage Course: A Debate—A Listener's Reaction," *Marriage and Family Living*, Vol. XIX, November 1957, p. 335.

moral concepts. Foote and Cottrell make a more general observation that is in line with this.

> As suggested by David Riesman in *The Lonely Crowd*, millions seem to occupy a limbo between values indoctrinated in them by their parents and values freely chosen by themselves. Without commitment to past or future, they are rudderless, other-directed, unable to design and organize a style of life which can in any determinative sense be termed a personality.[10]

Summary

Man is a valuing creature, and his actions are informed by sets of beliefs or value orientations. In the belief systems informing action in the Western world, man is highly regarded. Each man is regarded as worthy of respect and freedom and as the equal of all other men. An understanding of this view of man in its uniquely American formulations is basic to an understanding of the American systems of dating, marriage, and family life.

If the chapters to follow remove any of the uncertainty by clarifying and making precise the American ideal as it applies to marriage and the family when illuminated by the findings of empirical science, then the mission of this book will have been accomplished.

QUESTIONS AND PROJECTS

1. When man is made the object of ultimate value, what roles do the institutions and groups in society play in relation to him?
2. State the American ideal in your own words. Why is it called an "ideal" rather than a "dream" or a "creed"?
3. Why does the individual need values? What are the sources of his values?

[10] Foote and Cottrell, *op. cit.*, p. 166.

4. Why is it essential that the marriage educator relate empirical facts to some set of values in his teaching?
5. In your judgment, what are the primary reasons why students take marriage and family courses?

SUGGESTED READINGS

Bailey, Derrick S., *The Mystery of Love and Marriage*, New York: Harper & Brothers, 1952.

Bowman, Henry, *et al.*, "Teaching Ethical Values Through the Marriage Course: A Debate," *Marriage and Family Living*, Vol. XIX, November 1957, pp. 325–339.

Casserley, J. V. Langmead, *Morals and Man in the Social Sciences*, London: Longmans, Green & Co., Inc., 1951.

Clarke, W. Norris, S.J., "Christian Humanism for Today," *Social Order*, Vol. III, May–June 1953, pp. 269–288.

Ditzion, Sidney, *Marriage, Morals and Sex in America*, New York: Bookman Associates, Inc., 1953.

Foote, Nelson N., and Leonard S. Cottrell, Jr., *Identity and Interpersonal Competence*, Chicago: University of Chicago Press, 1955, Chapter IV.

Kolb, William L., "The Changing Prominence of Values in Modern Sociological Theory," in Howard Becker and Alvin Boskoff (eds.), *Modern Sociological Theory*, New York: The Dryden Press, 1957, pp. 93–132.

———, "Family Sociology, Marriage Education, and the Romantic Complex: A Critique," *Social Forces*, Vol. 29, October 1950, pp. 65–72.

———, "A Social-Psychological Conception of Human Freedom," *Ethics*, Vol. LXIII, April 1953, pp. 180–189.

———, "Sociologically Established Family Norms and Democratic Values," *Social Forces*, Vol. 26, May 1948, pp. 451–456.

Myrdal, Gunnar, *An American Dilemma*, New York: Harper & Brothers, 1944, Chapter 1.

Parsons, Talcott, and Edward A. Shils (eds.), *Toward a General Theory of Action*, Cambridge: Harvard University Press, 1951, Parts 1 and 2.

Sirjamaki, John, "Culture Configurations in the American Family," *American Journal of Sociology*, Vol. 53, 1948, pp. 450–456.

Williams, Robin M., Jr., *American Society*, New York: Alfred A. Knopf, Inc., 1951, Chapter 11.

Zimmerman, Carle C., and Lucius F. Cervantes, *Marriage and the Family*, Chicago: Henry Regnery Co., 1956, The Present Crisis.

2 *Men and Women*

i

"Male and female created he them. . . . And God saw everything that he had made, and behold, it was very good." Mankind has been debating the latter point—"it was very good"—ever since. And it is an important debate, for the beliefs and values one holds regarding the similarities and differences between men and women will color one's whole attitude toward marriage and the family.

The argument boils down to this: If men and women are inherently different, their roles in marriage (and in society generally) should be different. The saying, "A woman's place is in the home," is characteristic of such a view. If men and women are essentially the same, their roles might well be interchangeable—women holding "masculine" careers and men helping with the housework, for instance. If they are different but complementary, their roles might complement each other in such a way that marriage would be the most complete state in life—more complete than the life of even the best adjusted single person. If two things (or creatures) are complementary, neither is complete in and of itself; each mutually supplies the other's lack. Although the incompleteness of the individual—as though the unmarried adult were only one half of a whole—is a very old notion in human thought, it is inconsistent with a cherished American conception, namely, the perfectibility of each person regardless of sex.

In America we cannot decide what it is we want to believe about men and women. Our basic acceptance of the American ideal makes us reluctant to accept any view that emphasizes differences between the sexes, particularly if it carries the slightest suggestion of a superordinate-subordinate relationship between them.

The belief in the dignity, freedom, and equality of man has provided fertile ground for a number of interpretations of sex that de-emphasize differences. One interpretation is that of behavioral psychology; another is found in feminism. Behavioral psychology minimizes the extent of the fixed or given differences between the sexes and attributes the apparent differences between individuals to differences in conditioning or socialization. Feminism also de-emphasizes the differences between men and women. The feminist sees women as inherently the equals of men, as does the behavioral psychologist, but the feminist goes a step beyond this and attributes to women a lower status in our society due to the prejudice, suppression, and discrimination they have been subjected to in a male-dominated society.

Since one's attitudes and actions in marriage will reflect one's convictions about the similarities and differences between the sexes, it will be worth while to examine the issue with insights based on the empirical researches of the social sciences.

Sex Similarities and Differences As Seen by the Social Scientist

It is a universal observation in anthropology and sociology that in human society the roles of men and women are different.

In no society do the same norms apply with equal force to these two groups. In all societies there are different norms and different statuses for the two sexes. No society treats its men and its women exactly alike. In no society do they indulge in identical activities, share identical aspirations, or pursue identical goals in identical ways. In all societies they think differently, dress differently, and do different kinds of work.

One could argue, therefore, with perhaps only a slight exaggeration, that all societies have two cultures, a male culture and a female culture, and that these two cultures are quite different. More precisely, perhaps, one might say that each society has at least three cultures—one male, one female, and one shared by the two sexes. In any event, it is certain that the biological fact of sexual differentiation has manifold social consequences. . . .[1]

In American society, as in all other societies, the roles of men and women are differentiated. The thing which distinguishes our society, however, is a trend toward sameness in the roles of the sexes. Historically, the breadwinning role has been that of the man whereas the woman has been the homemaker and the one who cares for the children. We would not be misunderstood, however; these roles are still largely sex-differentiated. The point is that they are less so today than in earlier times.

[1] By permission from *The Social Order* by Robert Bierstedt. Copyright 1957. McGraw-Hill Book Company, Inc., p. 313.

It is obvious to all that the roles of women have been changing drastically.

Probably the most obvious change in the general social position of women has been a blurring of the feminine sex role in the masculine direction. Some specific evidence may be briefly enumerated:

1. *Legal rights:* women vote, hold public office, practice professions, hold and dispose of property, etc.

2. *Occupational role:* women participate in paid work outside the home on a large scale; they have entered traditionally male occupations.

3. *Educational participation:* there are coeducational school systems, colleges, and universities. . . .

4. *Recreational patterns:* women participate in active sports, patronize drinking places, etc.

5. *Courtship behavior:* women have a kind and degree of freedom and initiative in courtship not before sanctioned.

6. *"Symbolic" evidence:* women emulate men's clothes in their slacks, tailored suits, etc.[2]

These changes in women's roles have been dramatic and have received a great deal of attention from the "man in the street," the teacher, the preacher, and the scholar, partly because some of the changes were marked changes and partly because some of the changes were interpreted as degrading to women. But the changes also commanded attention because of the dramatic way in which they were brought about. The reformation of women's roles—women's suffrage, for instance—has been one of the most dramatic crusades in American history.

Less dramatic and less well documented are the changes in the roles of men in our society. The changes are as real and in many ways as important as the changes in the roles of women. In fact, it would be impossible to have as great changes in women's roles as we have had without having concomitant changes in the roles of men.

[2] Robin M. Williams, Jr., *American Society*, New York: Alfred A. Knopf, Inc., 1951, pp. 57–58.

The changes in women's roles are partly due to various situational changes—industrialization and war being prominent. But more is involved than situational changes. The changes in women's roles have been more than adaptations to changing conditions; they have also been brought about because of convictions. Those who crusaded for women's rights made it painfully clear that discriminations against women were clearly out of line with our shared belief in the American ideal. Hence, the changes in the status of women were in part a matter of women "winning" their freedom, but they were also in part a matter of the society collectively attempting to implement the American ideal by "giving" women equal rights. In other words, a change in the attitudes of men as well as a change in the attitudes of women has preceded and accompanied the emancipation of women.

While women's roles have been changing in the male direction there has been a blurring of the masculine sex roles in the feminine direction. The exact nature of the changes in masculine roles and the reasons for the changes have not been carefully documented. There are, no doubt, some situational changes that account for the changes in the status of men and in their roles: brute strength has become obsolete in many kinds of work formerly handled exclusively by men; when the wife works the husband may almost be forced to help with the home work (concomitant variation); the commuting father in our urban and industrial society leaves boys at home to be brought up and perhaps "feminized" as a result of the large measure of maternal supervision and control; men have abandoned the teaching profession at the elementary levels, leaving young boys to be taught almost exclusively by women. So men and women have been victims of circumstances in our ever-changing society and have been forced or strongly pressured into changing their patterns of action.

But of equal, and perhaps greater, importance is not that men have been forced to change their roles, but rather that the dominant values regarding the roles of men, the roles of women, and the nature of associations between the sexes have undergone change. The changes are clearly in the direction of emphasis on the sameness of the sexes and the sameness of sex roles and away from an emphasis on differences. The whole emphasis in our dating system, for instance, is upon the view that social and recreational affairs are more fun in the company of someone of the other sex than they are with those of one's own sex. The notion of dating as an end in itself is based on this value.

The idea of sameness and companionship carries through mate selection and marriage, too. One is expected to marry only when he finds someone who is "a real pal" and companion, and marriage is a comradely existence. Also, women are to have equal opportunities in occupational, social, and recreational activities and men are expected to appreciate the "feminine" interests—art, music, home decorating, the culinary arts.

Woman has become less the "delicate flower" in the process of masculinization, but, on the other hand, man has become less the boor in the process of feminization. The man pays attention to grooming and to the social niceties; he wears more colorful clothing—matching husband and wife sports outfits are not uncommon. The greater similarities in men's and women's attire in recent years have not all been due to the adoption of masculine attire by women. Hence, the blending of sex roles resulting from conditions and convictions is well on the way with both sexes involved in the give-and-take process.

This blending of sex roles has not been an unmixed blessing. It has led to confusion and misunderstanding of statuses and roles, as is true in periods of change in any aspect of life. However, the blending of roles has not and need not lead to disaster as some prophets of doom would suggest. The effect of the blending can be a salutary one if married part-

ners are sensitive to the capacities and interests of each and
proper allowance is made for freedom of expression.

The Subcultures of Men and Women

Even with the blending of sex roles subcultures remain
within American society. A person planning to enter one

"*You don't know my bridge club.*"
Reproduced courtesy of Ed Dahlin.

of our intimate, companionship type of marriages should
understand and appreciate these subcultures if he is to
understand and appreciate his spouse.

Having been brought up in a family with parents and siblings of both sexes does not necessarily prepare one to understand the other sex or the subculture of the other sex, though it may help. Dating and marriage, but especially marriage, mark the beginning of intimate knowledge of the other sex and of the subculture of the other sex. It is imperative as a prospective spouse that one understand not only himself but the other sex as well.

As LeMasters points out, men and women continue to participate in their own subcultures even after marriage. We do not always appreciate this, and we create some tensions and problems by insisting on complete sharing of activities in the companionship marriage. Each partner must recognize that the subcultures of the sexes are in fact different. Each must try to understand and appreciate the social roles of the other.

But the problem of understanding the other sex—and in particular one's own spouse—runs even deeper than differences in subcultures of the sexes. One does not understand and appreciate the social roles of the other sex unless he understands something about the other sex per se. Scholars are impressed by the fact that sex differences are more than a matter of socialization in different subcultures. Amram Sheinfeld makes this point in the preface of his book, *Women and Men.*

I had expected to devote myself mainly to the social factors, past and present, as they have served to influence the relationships between the sexes, and to give only passing attention to biological sex differences. . . . But as intensive research proceeded, as pertinent facts were brought together and new avenues explored, it began to appear that the original premise had many weaknesses. The basic sex differences, I was forced to conclude, were far more extensive, and had far more to do with the behavior patterns, capacities and activities of the sexes, than most persons in professional circles had suspected or conceded.[3]

[3] Amram Scheinfeld, *Women and Men,* New York: Harcourt, Brace & Co., 1943, p. ix.

We turn to the empirical sciences of biology and differential psychology to find what evidence there is in support of the view that the roles of men and women are based on inherent differences between the sexes—differences which are not entirely erased but perhaps even enhanced in the process of socialization.

Sex Similarities and Differences As Seen by the Biologist and the Psychologist

"From head to toe, in every cell of the body the male and female are different." Some of the differences are relatively insignificant. Others are quite important in determining the roles of men and women. Some of the differences are obvious—differential rate of growth, curvature of the body, facial and body hair, pitch of voice, physical stature, and strength. Physical stature and strength were very important to status before the invention of power machinery, but in a highly mechanized society brute strength becomes obsolete, although it is still handy to have a man around the house to reach high shelves and to lift heavy things!

Persons who would like to believe that the roles of men and women should and must be clearly distinguished and not overlapping—that woman's place is in the home, for instance—will find less support than they might hope in the empirical findings of biology and psychology. But neither will those who insist that the differences between the sexes are apparent rather than real find conclusive evidence.

It seems now that it is possible for any degree of "masculinity" or "femininity" to occur in an individual of either sex, but that a girl growing up does find certain attitudes, interests, and personality traits more congenial than others and tends to acquire them, whereas a boy is likely to acquire another set. This slanting, this difference in tendency to acquire differential characteristics, is the factor that may have a biological basis.[4]

THE REPRODUCTIVE PROCESS

One physiological difference determinative of social roles is the difference in reproductive functions of the sexes. If the human race is to continue to inhabit the earth, women must continue to bear the babies—at least for the present. This fact has far-flung social consequences.

Consider for a moment that man's part in the reproductive process, physiologically speaking, is a momentary involvement. When he has deposited the sperm during coitus, his function in procreation is at an end. On the other hand, for women, once conception—the joining of the male and female sex cells—has taken place, social activity is markedly affected by the physiological fact of pregnancy. The woman carries the growing fetus within her body for nine months—months in which changes take place physiologically, psychologically, and socially. Parturition is also a physiologically determined significant event in her life.

After the birth of the baby the involvement of the mother with the child can end only if the baby is placed with a mother substitute. The human infant is the most dependent of all creatures and his prolonged infancy requires constant vigilance and ministration by some adult. If he is to be suckled, only mother can suckle him. Father cannot and the profession of the wet nurse is not popular in our society.

The reproductive function with its potential involvements is the single greatest factor causing role differentiation between the sexes. But there are other important differences between the sexes.

[4] From *The Psychology of Human Differences*, Second Edition, by Leona E. Tyler. Copyright 1956. Appleton-Century-Crofts, Inc., p. 272.

THE NATURE OF MAN AND MARRIAGE

THE WEAKER SEX

The term "weaker sex" has generally been applied to women. The reasons are obvious; woman's strength is more subtle and not as readily observable as that of man. In dramatic physical achievements man clearly holds the advantage. Man shows his superiority in contact sports such as football and hockey, weight lifting, distance running, etc.

Recent empirical findings, however, would lead one to suspect that we have misplaced the label "weaker sex," for in more subtle but nevertheless striking ways woman must be regarded as stronger than man. Geneticists tell us that somewhere between 120 and 150 males are conceived for every 100 females conceived; yet the sex ratio at birth is roughly 105 boy babies born to every 100 girl babies born. This means that larger numbers of males succumb during the gestation period. The difference in death rate favoring the female continues throughout the entire life span of the sexes. Generally speaking, more males than females die at every age of life. For the wife to outlive her husband must be regarded as "normal." Even if they are the same age at marriage, the wife can expect to outlive her husband by a few years.

To increase the disparity in longevity, as standards in hygiene, sanitation, and preventive medicine improve, the life expectancy rates of both men and women improve but the differential favoring women becomes greater rather than smaller. In other words, it is the female of the species, not the male, who is most responsive to improved health practices. Women are ill more often than men, but they survive; men are less often ill, but they succumb. Diabetes is the only important disease to which women are more susceptible than are men. "If there is any lesson in these statistics for females, it is that they should take good care of the men in their lives—they should wait upon them, serve them diligently, never let them exert themselves, and nurse them carefully at the slightest sign of indisposition." [5]

SEX AND INTELLIGENCE

Intelligence tests do not give the information we would like to have regarding differences in intelligence between

"*That big thing on top is the air filter. But how does it get from there down to the tires?*"

Reprinted from *This Week* magazine. Copyright 1958 by the United Newspapers Magazine Corporation.

the sexes. The tests were not designed to show sex differences and have not been employed for that purpose. They were designed to meet a bisexual need in a coeducational school system. Hence, the tests are deliberately structured to minimize differences and to test intelligence without regard to sex. In the Bellevue intelligence tests, for instance, boys did better in cube analysis, and the cube analysis questions were consequently dropped from the test.

But in spite of the attempt to make the tests serve a

[5] Bierstedt, *op. cit.*, pp. 319–320.

bisexual purpose, some differences in performance have been noted. Boys, as a group, receive higher scores in science, mathematics (especially mathematical reasoning), judgment, manipulation of spatial relations, and other areas of abstract thought. Girls, as a group, show superiority in social items, esthetic responses, color perception, hand skills, verbal fluency, memory, perceptual speed, and in observation of details. Girls are better coordinated in speech and less likely to be color-blind.

We must bear in mind, however, that these are group differences, not individual differences. Group differences between the sexes are so small, and differences between individuals of the same sex show such a wide range, that any given individual of either sex may show any degree of these intellectual capacities.

INTERESTS AND MOTIVATION

In inquiring into the differences between the sexes we must go beyond intellectual differences to the important matter of motivation. Intelligence is one thing; motivation to use one's intelligence is another. The question regarding motivation and interest might be posed as follows: Are men and women motivated to action by the same or different stimuli, and do they seek the same or different ends? As pointed out in Chapter 1, one's socialization through the family and other groups greatly influences one's actions. But here we are interested in investigating whether these differences are inherent in the make-up of the person.

There is fairly conclusive evidence that this is the case. Psychologists tell us that "it is when we move into the area of non-intellectual traits that we begin to find psychological differences between males and females."

What are some of these sex-linked personality differences?

When we turn . . . to evaluations of emotionality or "neuroticism" by means of pencil-and-paper questionnaires, we find that there is a consistent tendency for women's averages to be closer to the maladjusted end of the scale than men's are. On the Bernreuter Personality Inventory, for example, the norms show that women are more neurotic, less self-sufficient, more introverted, less dominant, less self-confident, and more socially dependent than men. . . . Some other investigations of children by non-questionnaire methods—fear response, nervous habits, and so forth—suggest also that females may really be somewhat more unstable emotionally than males. . . .

If there is some evidence that females tend to be more neurotic, there is no doubt whatever that males tend to be more aggressive. This is one of the sex differences most universally found and shows up as clearly in preschool children as in adults. . . .

Although the "ascendance" or "dominance" evaluated by personality inventories is not the same thing as aggressiveness, it probably bears some relationship to it. Here too, males characteristically score significantly higher. . . . Studies of young children by a variety of methods agree that quarrelsome behavior occurs more often in boys than in girls.[6]

Additional evidence of differences in personality traits between the sexes can be drawn from the work of Terman and his associates. We must caution the reader, however, that the following summary is based on a study designed to highlight differences between the sexes by eliminating from consideration characteristics in which the sexes do not show differences.

From whatever angle we have examined them the males included in the standardization groups evinced a distinctive interest in exploit and adventure, in outdoor and physically strenuous occupations, in machinery and tools, in science, physical phenomena, and inventions; and, from rather occasional evidence, in business and commerce. On the other hand, the females of our groups

[6] Tyler, *op. cit.*, pp. 262–263.

evinced a distinctive interest in domestic affairs and in aesthetic objects and occupations; they have distinctively preferred more sedentary and indoor occupations, and occupations more directly ministrative, particularly to the young, the helpless, the distressed. Supporting and supplementing these are the more subjective differences—those in emotional disposition and direction. The males directly or indirectly manifest the greater self-assertion and aggressiveness; they express more hardihood and fearlessness, and more roughness of manner, language, and sentiments. The females express themselves as more compassionate and sympathetic, more timid, more fastidious and aesthetically sensitive, more emotional in general (or at least more expressive of the four emotions considered), severer moralists, yet admit in themselves more weaknesses in emotional control and (less noticeably) in physique.

But we must define some of our terms more precisely, for instance, "aggressiveness" and "self-assertion." The evidence is for initiative, enterprise, vigorous activity, outdoor adventure; "aggressiveness" need not imply selfishness or tyranny or unfair attack. The compassion and sympathy of the female, again, appears from the evidence personal rather than abstract, less a principled humanitarianism than an active sympathy for palpable misfortune or distress. In disgust, in aesthetic judgment, and in moral censure, the evidence is rather for the influence of fashion and of feeling than of principle or reason. Our evidence need not imply the possession of a "truer" taste or a more discerning conscience.[7]

Regarding motivation, persons whose job it is to counsel young persons report that many girls do not seem to aspire to the positions their abilities would make possible, whereas boys more likely make vocational choices in the professional areas whether or not their level of intelligence and academic success warrants such choices. Rather than having a lower general need for achievement, however, psychological experiments have shown that women are motivated by differ-

[7] By permission from *Sex and Personality* by Lewis M. Terman, and Catharine Cox Miles. Copyright 1936. McGraw-Hill Book Company, Inc., pp. 447–448.

ent stimuli. Women show greater motivation toward doing the things that are socially acceptable. Perhaps this reflects a greater sensitivity to dependence on others among women and a greater independence of others on the part of men.

Summary

In any society there is a core of common beliefs, values, and behavior patterns that is shared by men and women alike. This makes for ease in communication and a measure of consensus in thought and action within the society.

Beyond these shared norms there are norms outlining the major roles expected for each sex. These sex-differentiated norms give direction to the behavior of each sex in relation to the other sex, in relation to children, and in relation to the innumerable other demands of group life. These male and female subcultures develop in part in response to inherent differences between the sexes. In this chapter we have highlighted some of these subtle but nevertheless important differences. They have been presented to inform the reader and to encourage him further to gain knowledge and insight concerning inherent and culturally induced similarities and differences of men and women within his own society. No individual is merely the "statistical average" of his sex; awareness of group differences is significant in understanding individual behavior.

The data presented in this chapter will be reflected in our discussion of roles of men and women in dating, marriage, and family living.

Vive la différence!

QUESTIONS AND PROJECTS

1. What changes have taken place in the social roles of women? Of men?

2. What has brought about changes in the roles of the sexes?
3. List some of the major aspects of the subcultures of men and women in American society.
4. Elaborate on the statement, "Man is the weaker sex."
5. To what extent are the differences in subcultures of the man and the woman attributable to personality differences?

SUGGESTED READINGS

Kinsey, Alfred C., Wardell B. Pomeroy, Clyde E. Martin, and Paul H. Gebhard, *Sexual Behavior in the Human Female*, Philadelphia: W. B. Saunders Co., 1953.

————, Wardell B. Pomeroy, and Clyde E. Martin, *Sexual Behavior in the Human Male*, Philadelphia: W. B. Saunders Co., 1948.

Kirkpatrick, Clifford, *The Family: As Process and Institution*, New York: The Ronald Press Company, 1955, Chapters 2, 3.

Krich, A. M. (ed.), *Men*, New York: Dell Publishing Co., 1954.

————, *Women*, New York: Dell Publishing Co., 1953.

Landis, Paul H., *Making the Most of Marriage*, New York: Appleton-Century-Crofts, Inc., 1955, Chapter 3.

LeMasters, E. E., *Modern Courtship and Marriage*, New York: The Macmillan Co., 1957, Chapters XXII, XXIII.

Mead, Margaret, *Male and Female*, New York: William Morrow & Co., Inc., 1949.

Scheinfeld, Amram, *Women and Men*, New York: Harcourt, Brace & Co., 1943.

Shuttleworth, Frank K., "A Bio-Social and Developmental Theory of Male and Female Sexuality," *Marriage and Family Living*, XXI, May 1959, pp. 163–170.

Tyler, Leona E., *The Psychology of Human Differences*, 2nd ed., New York: Appleton-Century-Crofts, Inc., 1956.

Williams, Robin M., Jr., *American Society*, New York: Alfred A. Knopf, Inc., 1951, Chapter 4.

Zimmerman, Carle C., and Lucius F. Cervantes, *Marriage and the Family*, Chicago: Henry Regnery Co., 1956, Differences of the Sexes.

3 Models for Marriage I

i

Young couples pattern their marriages after some marriage model, or combination of marriage models, acceptable to themselves and to the society in which they live. But in America there are three basic marriage models, greatly complicating the problem of young lovers as they seek a pattern for married life. There are the historic Judaic-Christian marriage model, the romantic marriage model, and the rationalistic marriage model.

The model a couple chooses as a pattern for marriage, or the elements which they choose out of the several models, will go a long way in determining the nature of their life together. Therefore, it is important to look at each of the models in terms of the values supporting each and the structure and functions of marriage prescribed in the norms of each model.

The Judaic-Christian Marriage Model

In the historic Judaic-Christian model, with its deep roots in the Jewish tradition, the institution of marriage is regarded not simply as a pragmatically devised creation of man but as a God-given order—a creation of God to be accepted and used by man and not to be abused, abandoned, or destroyed by him. Marriage is viewed as one of God's good gifts to man. This gift of God is to be utilized by man for man's benefit. Also through using it in the way in which God intended, man serves God and his fellow men by acting responsibly—in the area of sex expression, for instance—and by taking responsibility for his spouse and offspring.

According to the Judaic-Christian model, marriage binds the partners together in a mysterious union also through an act of God. "Therefore a man leaves his father and his mother and cleaves to his wife and they become one flesh" (Genesis 2:24).

The older of the two Genesis creation myths describes how God took one of Adam's ribs and built it into a woman. (Gen. 2:21f.) Male and female are thus shown to have a common origin; they are not independent but complementary and individually incomplete until they have achieved the union in which each integrates and is integrated by the other.

Although the union in "one flesh" is a physical union established by sexual intercourse (the conjunction of the sexual organs) it involves at the same time the whole being, and affects the personality at the deepest level. It is a union of the entire man and the entire woman. In it they become a new and distinct unity, wholly different from and set over against other human relational unities, such as the family or the race; to bring into existence the "one flesh" a man must leave his father and his mother.[1]

[1] Derrick S. Bailey, *The Mystery of Love and Marriage*, New York: Harper & Brothers, 1952, p. 44.

Because of the nature of this "one-flesh" union, Christian marriage is commonly referred to as a sacrament—an outward visible sign of an inner invisible state. The marriage (outward sign) is visible; what happens to the couple in marriage (inner state) is not empirically observable. Both Protestant and Roman Catholic dogmas accept marriage as sacramental in this sense though it is not as commonly referred to as a sacrament by American Protestants as it is by European Protestants and Roman Catholics. The conviction that marriage is sacramental is based on New Testament accounts of marriage—primarily such passages as Ephesians 5—and hence is Christian rather than Judaic in origin.

Not only is the institution of marriage a creation of God and the couple joined together by God, but the relationship between the marriage partners is of a permanent nature in the Judaic-Christian marriage model. First of all, because it is a unity, and the parts that make up the union cannot become separable again: "What God hath joined together let not man put asunder." And, secondly, because an ethical element, a vow of fidelity, enters into the relationship as the marriage partners exchange vows: "Keeping thee only unto him (her) until death doth you part." It is the responsibility of couple members to live up to this covenant of fidelity, and it is within their power to do so, but only with the help of God. The church does not regard man as perfect and does not believe that it is easy for him to keep the covenant. Nor does it believe that he always enters marriage in good faith, or that he in all cases takes vows seriously. The church "never considered a perfect man. They sought to enroll the average man in a social system which could reach some great civilized world unity." [2] The church teaches that it is only through the spirit of God working to regenerate and strengthen man that he remains faithful. In the Roman

[2] Carle C. Zimmerman and Lucius F. Cervantes, *Marriage and the Family,* Chicago: Henry Regnery Co., 1956, p. 63.

THE NATURE OF MAN AND MARRIAGE

Catholic Church marriage is sacramental in a dual sense: it is an outward sign of an inner union, but it is also sacramental in that it signifies and effectively causes grace in the souls of the believers. "This mutual inward molding of husband and wife, this determined effort to perfect each other is supernatural in character and only accomplished by graces of the sacrament." [3]

Specifically what are the purposes or functions of marriage in the Judaic-Christian marriage model?

Basically, the reasons for or functions of marriage are two in number. As stated in the *Catechism of the Council of Trent* when explaining "the reasons because of which man and woman ought to be joined in marriage,"

> The first is precisely the companionship sought by the natural instinct of different sex, and brought about in the hope of mutual aid, so that each may help the other to bear more easily the troubles of life, and to support the weakness of old age. The second is the desire for children.[4]

And in the words of Pius XI in his encyclical on *Christian Marriage:*

> This mutual inward moulding of husband and wife, this determined effort to perfect each other, can in a very real sense, as the Roman Catechism teaches, be said to be the chief reason and purpose of matrimony, provided matrimony be looked at not in the restricted sense as instituted for the proper conception and education of the child, but more widely as the blending of life as a whole and the mutual interchange and sharing thereof.[5]

However, in the subsequent pronouncements of Pius XII the procreative and educative functions are again emphasized as the primary functions of marriage. Speaking to the

[3] John R. Cavanaugh, *Fundamental Marriage Counselling: A Catholic Viewpoint,* Milwaukee: The Bruce Publishing Co., 1957, p. 512.
[4] *Catechism of the Council of Trent,* as quoted in John L. Thomas, *The American Catholic Family,* p. 71. Copyright 1956 by Prentice-Hall, Inc., Englewood Cliffs, N.J. Reprinted by permission of the publisher.
[5] Pius XI, *Christian Marriage (Casti Connubi),* 5th ed., New York: The American Press, 1943, p. 8, as quoted in *ibid.,* p. 71.

Italian Catholic Union of Midwives, in October 1951, he said in part:

> According to these theories [theories concerning "values of the human person" and the need of respecting them], your self-dedication for the good of the life still hidden in the womb of the mother and its happy birth would have no more than a secondary importance. . . .
> The truth is that matrimony as a natural institution, by virtue of the will of the Creator, does not have as its primary, intimate end the personal improvement of the couples concerned but the procreation and the education of new life. The other ends, though also connected with nature, are not in the same rank as the first, still less are they superior to it. They are subordinate to it.[6]

And so it has come about that procreation and education of children come to be the primary functions of marriage in the Roman Catholic version of the Judaic-Christian marriage model and the unitive function has come to be associated more with the Protestant version of the Judaic-Christian marriage model.

Protestant statements, such as the following, are in accord with statements from Roman Catholic sources quoted above.

> The essence of marriage is in the unity formed by the life partners—"they twain shall be one." According to this higher mathematics, in marriage, one plus one equals one. Of course, Jesus recognized also the procreative function of marriage, but He does not emphasize this aspect as much as does the Old Testament. The primary objective is the merging of two persons into one harmonious and creative unit of body and soul.[7]

A third function of marriage is recognized in the Judaic-Christian model, namely marriage as an outlet for sexual expression, or as commonly stated, a "remedy against sin."

[6] As quoted in Cavanaugh, *op. cit.*, pp. 159–160.
[7] T. A. Kantonen, *The Family Under God*, The Board of Social Missions of the United Lutheran Church, New York (Lithographed), p. 11.

The historic Christian church was greatly impressed with the power of the sex drive as a potential force for evil and was slow to accept sex as one of "God's good gifts to man." Hence, this third function of marriage is negatively stated as a function of marriage designed to avoid evil, rather than as positively contributing to the enjoyment of marriage for the marriage partners.

These, then, are the essential elements of the Judaic-Christian marriage model: It is an institution created by God for man's good and His glory. When two persons marry they become one—"one flesh"—a mysterious union understood only in the mind of God. This union, once established, is permanent and not to be set aside by man. The purposes of marriage are unity, procreation and education of children, and an outlet for sexual desire.

But to be fully understood, the Judaic-Christian marriage model marriage must be viewed in the light of the total Christian way of life. The Christian faith proclaims that God is love, and that His love is freely bestowed on man without consideration for man's merit. It is God's will that men shall live together in a community of love. Hence in the Christian view of life there can be no true community of men unless love is at the center as the dominant norm of human action. "You shall love the Lord your God with all your heart, and with all your soul, and with all your mind. This is the great and first commandment. And a second is like it, You shall love your neighbor as yourself" (Matthew 22:37–38). Marriage is potentially the most perfect example of this community of love, as husband and wife share their love for each other, for in the Judaic-Christian model marriage is a personal and sexual union of one man and one woman in a continuing relationship of mutual love and service based on fidelity.

Historically, the Judaic-Christian marriage model did much to bring dignity and order into sex life as it was practiced in the Western world. This is seen in the effect it had on the *Corpus Juris* as Christian principles were translated into revisions of the law.[8]

The basic Christian reforms were five in number. First, only heterosexual relations in marriage were made publicly allowable. All other forms of sex acts were classified as objectionable, nonhuman (mammalian, bestial, sinful, criminal), and as punishable. Second, this classification of "other forms" of sex as "objectionable" was applied to every social class, without regard to rank, economic condition, or occupation. The purposes of this were stated positively as an attempt to create the legal basis of a good and universal family system.

Third, some activities were made punishable by physical means such as castigation, imprisonment, and banishment. These extreme punishments were directed more at the persons whose activities for gain led to the promotion of commercialized sex. Penalties were increased all along the line so as to make this occupation undesirable as a business and escapable for those caught in its network.

Fourth, and fundamental, contracts involving nonfamily sex activities as repayment for support or gifts were made illegal. Prior to that time contracts and business agreements involving sex constituted a low occupation but were legally enforceable. Now they were illegal, not enforceable, and the inciting party was an accessory to a crime.

Fifth and finally, these acts were not taken alone but as a part of a wider movement to make the family the defined public way of life and status. Negative movements against extrafamily sex were taken as part of a positive movement to promote universal familism.

This legal system incorporating basic Christian reforms was not questioned for several centuries and from that time forward the practices were a part of all Western tradition

[8] This section is adapted from Carle C. Zimmerman and Lucius F. Cervantes, *Marriage and the Family*, pp. 61–63. Copyright 1956 by Henry Regnery Company.

and were yielded to modern public law by canon law. Since this happened scarcely a century ago in England, for instance, we can see where we derive these ideas today. The impact of the Judaic-Christian marriage model on American family law and family norms is pervasive and continuing.

But the historic Judaic-Christian marriage model was a demanding model in that under it marriage was permanent and indissoluble, and many eschewed embracing it as their marriage model for this reason. Besides, the Judaic-Christian marriage model took on trappings from time to time that made it even more unpopular—trappings that were almost certain to cause alternative secular marriage models to emerge as threats to the Christian model in Europe and America. Some of the things that made the Christian model not only unpopular but also unnatural must be enumerated.

During the early days of the Christian church and during the Middle Ages, sex was disparaged and the only occasion for sex outlet came to be times when sexual intercourse was engaged in in marriage with the conscious purpose of procreation foremost in the intentions of the marriage mates. Any other sexual outlet within or outside of marriage was regarded as immoral or illegal.

In the hierarchy of life patterns that were acceptable to the church, marriage suffered because of this growing tendency to regard every kind and degree of self-denial as meritorious. Martyrdom was the supreme example, then came fasting, almsgiving, and celibacy. Not all Christians—and certainly not the non-Christians—were prepared to adopt the ascetic life which in marriage was interpreted to mean that if the married couple were to be good Christians they should practice sexual continence even while living together in the married state.

As a part of this wave of extreme popularity of asceticism within the church there were mass withdrawals from community life. The primary object was not to escape from sex but from the "world" with all the pleasures entailed in worldly living, including sex.

But prolonged, unnatural denial of sex expression had a way of making sex an obsession. St. Jerome's experience with the hermit life is instructive.

> Sackcloth disfigured my unshapely limbs, and my skin from long neglect had become as black as an Ethiopian's. Tears and groans were my daily portion. Yet, though in my fear of hell I had consigned myself to this prison where my only companions were scorpions and wild beasts, I often found myself amid bevies of girls. My face was pale, and my frame chilled with fasting; yet my mind was inflamed with desire. Helpless I cast myself at the feet of Jesus.[9]

The only effective therapeutic for Jerome proved to be filling his mind with a rigorous intellectual discipline through the study of Hebrew.

This is what we mean by the trappings of the Judaic-Christian marriage model. Marriage had come to be associated with other elements of the "good life," as it was seen in the Middle Ages, and although a "normal" and "natural" marriage was not disparaged, no apologies were made for declaring it to be definitely a "second-best" way of life.

Thirdly, the Christian way of life had well-developed values regarding the after-life—the joys of heaven and the horrors of hell—and a well-developed hierarchy of social authority, but it had a poorly developed psychology; in fact, it had almost no positive appreciation of the drives, needs, dispositions, interests, and desires of the individual person as a real entity.

> . . . the rulers of the church took no account of the feelings of the partners. If one member wearied of a political match and sought satisfaction beyond the marriage bond the church employed every device to enforce fidelity. When, for example, Lothair I deserted his wife in favor of his concubine, the church insisted that he return. He

[9] As quoted in Roland H. Bainton, *What Christianity Says About Sex, Love, and Marriage*, New York: Association Press, 1957, pp. 30–31.

therefore made life so miserable for his wife that she was ready to resort to extreme expedients to be rid of him. But the church ruled that she must endure martyrdom rather than suffer him to live with his concubine.

In other instances unions were dissolved with similar unconcern for feelings. The church had an elaborate set of impediments to marriage which were enforced with no regard to personal attachments or aversions. Consanguinity, affinity, and spiritual relationships constituted bars to marriage.

Robert the Pious, for example, had been living happily for some years with his wife Bertha when it was discovered that he was related to her physically as fourth cousin and spiritually as godfather to her child by a previous marriage. Protracted excommunication at length constrained them to separate.[10]

With such limited appreciation of the individual and such blatant disregard for personal feelings and desires, it is not surprising to find that the Judaic-Christian model at no point elaborated on the romantic or feeling aspects of the love relationship between two persons. There was room for some conception of romance in the unitive, companionable function of marriage, but it was not developed.

There are a number of reasons why no provision was made for the romantic feelings of the marriage partners, but chief among them was the fact that the Judaic-Christian marriage model in its emergence predated the development of a science of personality; secondly, the romantic side of the love relationship is not developed in New Testament accounts of marriage; and, thirdly, the great synthesizer of medieval thought, Thomas Aquinas, did not incorporate the insights of the emerging romantic thought of his day.

Readily available to the theologian, however, were the accounts of love in earlier literature, and especially those of the Old Testament, but these were not incorporated either. Instead Thomas Aquinas took his marriage model almost

[10] *Ibid.*, pp. 49–51.

directly from the much earlier formulation of St. Augustine (354–430 A.D.).

Summary

It is important that couples planning to marry consider seriously the marriage models available to them. This is particularly true in America where several marriage models are held in high regard. The model which a couple chooses to follow will play an important part in the structure and in the functions of the marriage the couple establishes.

There are three recognizable marriage models in American culture: the Judaic-Christian, the romantic, and the rationalistic. The oldest of these is the Judaic-Christian.

In the Judaic-Christian marriage model (1) marriage is an institution ordained by God for man's good and His glory; (2) the two persons marrying become one; (3) the union is a permanent one established primarily for companionship and for the procreation and rearing of children; and (4) the marriage partners are commanded to love and be faithful to each other.

The romantic and rationalistic marriage models are described and analyzed in the following chapter.

QUESTIONS AND PROJECTS

1. What is meant by the term marriage model? What is its relationship to values?
2. List the major elements in the Judaic-Christian marriage model.
3. What similarities are there between the Jewish, Protestant, and the Roman Catholic forms of the Judaic-Christian model? What are the major differences?

4. What was the effect of the Judaic-Christian model on family law in the Roman Empire?
5. From the point of view of the American ideal, what were some of the limitations of the historic Judaic-Christian marriage model?

SUGGESTED READINGS

See chapter 4, Models for Marriage II, pp. 64–65.

4   *Models for Marriage II*

i

The first of the marriage models to emerge in the West as a significant alternative to the Judaic-Christian marriage model was the romantic model. It emerged in part as a reaction to the medieval Christian marriage model which was devoid of any element of romance. It must be made clear at the outset, however, that the romantic marriage model was never as consciously a model as the Judaic-Christian model was. In fact, it is only in retrospect, in looking back over the course of history and picking up various emerging themes, that one can view the romantic marriage model as a systematic set of marriage norms. Its protagonists and practitioners were not organized, and it had no synthesizer of the stature of a Thomas Aquinas.

In arriving at the model that has had such an impact

on marriage and the family in America, we pick up the emerging themes from a number of sources.[1]

In the twelfth century in southern France three new developments became simultaneously apparent: the rise of the Cathari with their utter repudiation of marriage in favor of asceticism; the courts of love with their cult of adultery; and the erotic mysticism of St. Bernard and the enormous vogue of the Virgin Mary. The interrelations of these three are difficult to assess.

The Cathari regarded life in the flesh as an imprisonment and propagation as sinful. Sex was to be completely eschewed. They would not even eat anything connected with the processes of sex: no eggs, cheese, butter, or milk. Luckily they did not know that fish and vegetables have sex.

Coincidentally, and in the very same region, arose the practice of courtly love. The historical specialists are agreed that the ideal of courtly love was something altogether new. This is not to say that people had never before fallen in love; there was the passion of Paris for Helen, the languishing of Dido, and Ovid's *Art of Love*. But love in these instances was considered an enslaving passion, if not an occasion for levity. Courtly love on the contrary was portrayed as ennobling, because the beloved was regarded as superior to the lover and conveyed to him something of her own worth. For the first time we have not only a cult of love but also the idealization of women. This love which ennobles had to be freely bestowed and the quality of unconstraint was best exhibited if the beloved was superior to the lover. On his part there was required a humility which never took success for granted, a constant yearning and striving after love. Courtly love called for continual courtship and courtesy.

The three conditions of this love are exhibited in trouba-

---

[1] The following seven paragraphs are adapted from Roland H. Bainton, *What Christianity Says About Sex, Love, and Marriage*, New York: Association Press, 1957, pp. 56–63.

dour songs. The first is that love ennobles. "Love is not a sin," sang one of the troubadours, "Rather it is a power that makes the evil good and by it the good becomes better." Second, the beloved must be superior to the lover. "The lady of whom you hear me sing is fairer than I can say; fresh complectioned, beautiful to look upon, without blemish. Yes, and she is not rouged, nor can anyone say evil of her, so pure and noble is she." The lover is her inferior and her vassal. "Lady, I am and shall be yours, ready for your service. I am your sworn and pledged vassal." In the third place, love must be a quest ever uncertain. "So fearful am I in regard to her, the fair one, that I deliver myself to her, imploring her mercy." Jealousy is "the mother and nurse of love," in the sense of solicitude, anxiety, and vehemence of desire.

This love was held to be impossible in marriage, because in marriage love is taken for granted, not freely given. In marriage woman is not the superior but the equal if not indeed the inferior of man. In marriage there is no exhilarating quest, no furtive fulfillment. The conditions of courtly love are best realized if the lover addresses himself to a married woman on whom he has less than a claim and whom he cannot enjoy without stealth and adventure. Hence, courtly love became the cult of adultery.

As the romantic model began to emerge, the real-life conflict of virginity, marriage, and courtly love became apparent as in the case of Abélard and Héloïse. He was a distinguished teacher who won the love of a young and brilliant girl. They had a child out of wedlock. Abélard, who had violated the hospitality of her uncle, offered to make amends by marriage. Héloïse was the one to object. Her scale of values reveals the conflicting currents of the age. In the first rank she placed virginity. Abélard had already taken lower orders in the church looking toward ordination and celibacy. He had fallen from this high ideal but should return rather than continue in sin. But if not, she would rather be his mistress than his wife. The reason was partly economic. As a teacher he could not support a wife and family and continue his career, because universities in those days were not endowed to support married professors. But the most serious consideration was that marriage was a yoke of bondage for the wife and a device for uniting properties. "I want not yours but you. I invoke God as a witness that if Augustus should offer to make me his empress I would rather be your mistress." They did marry, presumably to satisfy Abélard's debt of honor, but the scale of values remained: virginity first, courtly love second, and marriage third.

The new element introduced by the emerging romantic model lay not so much in the behavior it provoked as in the frank repudiation of the churchly view in favor of an idealization of passion elevated to a level of worship. Though the origins of this new model are somewhat uncertain, the consensus of scholars is that romantic love was something new.

Romantic love was not associated with marriage in its origins and the time when it became a part of a marriage model cannot be determined with precision; it was not incorporated into the medieval Christian model as we have seen. There are some interpreters who feel that a line is to be drawn between the north and the south of Europe and that whereas in French courts of love romance meant adultery, in Germany and England it was never dissociated from marriage. This generalization is too sweeping, but one can say that sometimes romantic love in the north found fulfillment in marriage. The fruition was neither adultery nor death, but wedded union. Hence, the "wedding" of romantic love and marriage together in a romantic marriage model was well under way before the model was transplanted to America.

In becoming "wed" to marriage it was necessary, of course, that romantic or courtly love lose some of its excesses. In the eyes of the romantic "ordinary" love was a poor substitute for passionate love, and marriage was a concession to ordinary love; hence a second-best status. In "true" or passionate love, the feelings and actions of the person in love could not be contained by canons of good and evil. It was essential that the love spirit be permitted to soar and to find its mate wherever it would. The person who loved could not be held responsible for his actions once he was gripped by passionate love. It was a destiny that should not and could not be effectively opposed. Protagonists of this love saw marriage as a strait jacket, and the church in turn viewed the protagonists of romantic love as heretics.

Romantic love lost some of these excesses—some of its asocial, antisocial, and anticlerical attributes—and came to be regarded as a proper prelude to marriage; but it did not lose all of these tendencies by any means.

It is still characterized by individual freedom and social irresponsibility in the choice of a partner, even to the extent of not recognizing the prior rights of another to the object of the romantic's love. For instance, it is permissible to break up someone else's marriage if love dictates it. Furthermore, love is honored, the beloved is idealized if not idolized, and dating and love-making are quixotic, bold, and daring adventures.

Norms of the romantic marriage model prescribed monogamous love but not the indissolubility of marriage. The net influence in America was to channel marital discontent into a pattern of divorce and remarriage or "serial polygamy."

The romantic marriage model has not had the serious philosophic attention paid to it that theologians gave to the Judaic-Christian model. The formulations of the romantic model have rather been those of the troubadour, the poet, and the writer of popular love songs rather than those of the serious philosopher. Nevertheless, as the model emerged and as it developed in America it came to be associated with some intellectually respectable naturalistic views on the nature of man and society; in fact, a major reason for the hostility of the church to romantic love has been its thoroughly secular-humanistic nature.

In referring to the romantic marriage model as humanistic it is necessary to explain what we mean by the term humanistic since its meanings have been so varied over the years. The term came into vogue in the sixteenth century but it was not until the eighteenth century, long regarded as the Age of Reason, that it connoted a conflict between the scientific study of man and theology. This naturalistic approach to man and society is seen in the writings of Rousseau, for instance. Rousseau saw man, not God, as the measure of all things. He regarded all social institutions as human creations devised by the powerful to enslave the rest of mankind. These institutions had a restraining influence that retarded the development of man. Marriage was no exception. If left to himself man would develop freely and naturally, as other animals, into the sort of creature nature intended him to become.

These ideas fortified from other sources out of eighteenth- and nineteenth-century secular humanism persisted and sustained the major non-Christian marriage model operative in America—the romantic model.

At the heart of the difference between the Judaic-Christian and the romantic models are radically different views on the nature of man and the nature and source of authority. In Christianity man is, as a result of his "fall," sinful and unwilling and unable to choose the good. Only with the help of God through a process of "rebirth" and growth in "sanctification" can he make progress on the road to perfection, a perfection that he does not fully attain during his finite life. God, the authority, has created various institutions—the family, the state, etc.—to retain the basic order of society in a sinful world. On the other hand, in the humanistic romantic model man is perfectible and is held back largely by ignorance and the trappings of society, such as the social institutions. These social institutions are man's creations and can be used, modified, or destroyed at the will of man.

Some further contrasts between the Christian and the romantic model may help make clear the rather loosely structured and ill-defined romantic marriage model.

Is marriage real or nominal, tentative or permanent? The Judaic-Christian marriage model calls for vows of fidelity, and marriage is real—not lacking in essence or substance—rather than nominal in that a mysterious union results. In the romantic model the individual person is real, marriage is nominal, and, hence, has no permanence in its own right. But man, though real, is not free; he is the slave of love. If gripped by passionate love such a slave of love may "fall in love" with his "soul mate" and if this is true the union will be a permanent one. But it is not within the control of the lovers; they cannot predict whether their love for each other will flourish or die, even if they marry in the conviction or the hope that it will not die. Note that the notion that man is a slave of love is inconsistent with a view of man as rational and has its roots in romantic love, not in humanism.

What are the functions of marriage? In the Christian model the functions are unitive, procreative and educative, and as an outlet for sexual desire. In the romantic model the function is to contribute to the mutual happiness of two inviolable individuals—inviolable so far as other persons are concerned for they are accountable only to love. The partners part if love dies; the pragmatic test of whether or not love is still alive is happiness. If their happiness approaches ecstasy, love is alive. If they are unhappy and disenchanted with each other, love is dead, and it is time to part.

In describing and analyzing the romantic marriage model

we have criticized it at several points. Something should be said about the values of perfectibility and inviolability of man in the model. Whether or not marriage is man's or God's institution is not a matter that can be empirically demonstrated, and either view must be accepted on faith. Many today, however, regard the perfectibility of man as too idealistic. Two world wars, a depression, increasing crime rates, international tension have had their effects on man's conceptions of man. Theologian Reinhold Niebuhr has said that man's destiny is to "seek after an impossible victory and to adjust himself to an inevitable defeat," and journalist Walter Lippmann denounces the humanist argument that "the New Man will be born out of his emancipation from authority." And so in regard to love and marriage also, we have come to be suspicious of the implied pristine purity of motives of persons as they fall in and out of love.

But it would appear to me that the romantic model is more vulnerable on the point of the inviolability of man than on the perfectibility of man. It can be and it has been demonstrated that man is not and cannot be inviolable. Man is highly dependent on other human beings and institutions during the entire period of his emergence. He would not be human without this socialization process. Secondly, it is not possible to have a society with two or more inviolable individuals in it. Eventually they meet and clash, and there is no solution to this clash of inviolable individuals with limitless needs and desires except a war of all against all. It is for such reasons that democracy as a model for control in society comes to the fore as a best compromise in a society that emphasizes the freedom and essential inviolability of all men—the American ideal.

The romantic marriage model is basically a socially irresponsible model; this is in large measure responsible for the emergence of the third model in America, the rationalistic marriage model.

The Rationalistic Marriage Model [2]

For many responsible, intelligent people neither faith nor feeling had provided a satisfactory model for marriage. Feeling—the romantic marriage model—provided unsure ground for building a structure as important to individuals and to society as was the family. Persons appeared to rush into marriage even in the face of their own misgivings and often against the more mature judgment of others. Many romantic marriages quickly lost the "glow" and ended in demoralization, disorganization, or outright separation and divorce.

For those who felt that the appeal in a marriage model for modern man had to be to reason rather than to feeling, the Judaic-Christian marriage model did not suffice either, even though it was cast on the side of maintaining stable marriages and condemning separation and divorce.

How were we to retain stability in American marriage without returning to what appeared to many as a rigid, dogmatic Judaic-Christian marriage model and one which, in its historic form, seemed to have little regard for "this" life and almost complete disregard for the feelings, desires, and wishes of the individual?

For some, hope for a better marriage model lay in the new and promising field of social science—particularly in family sociology. The development of social science in America was stimulated by American optimism for solving social problems. One of the major social problems in the family field had been and still was the problem of instability of the family, as dramatically demonstrated in the rising divorce rate. An important factor contributing to marital instability,

[2] The following is partially adapted from William L. Kolb, "Sociologically Established Family Norms and Democratic Values," *Social Forces*, Vol. 26, May 1948, pp. 451–456.

as the family sociologists saw it, was social irresponsibility perpetuated through the popular romantic marriage model.

American sociology of the family since its inception had been organized around the value of assuring stability in the modern family. The focus of attention in all probability reflected values held by the sociologists themselves as well as by responsible adults both in and outside of the Judaic-Christian tradition.

Family sociologists, true to their commitment to the scientific method of reaching conclusions only after careful and controlled observations of factual data, began the search for the secret of the stable marriage—the cornerstone of the stable family. But this was not enough. American family sociologists, true to the American ideal with its emphasis on individual rights, sought to find not only the prototype of the stable marriage but the stable marriage in which marriage partners found happiness and satisfaction as well as stability. That is, family sociologists were looking not for the social pressures or fears that kept couples from separating but for the cohesive factors within the marriage relationship that kept the couple willingly and happily in a permanent marriage. Among these pioneering efforts in family research the work of Ernest Burgess and Leonard Cottrell and Lewis Terman must be noted.

Basically, the sociologist's research design was a simple one. Using carefully prepared questionnaires and interview schedules, they gathered data from a reasonably large number of married couples. Comparisons were then made between data on couples who defined their marriages as happy or adjusted (or were so rated by acquaintances) and data on couples who rated low on happiness or adjustment.

What was the actual content of marriages receiving favorable happiness ratings? First of all, they were happy; that is, the spouses themselves felt that they were happy. Secondly, they were in basic agreement on fundamental decisions that were made within their families. The married pairs agreed on leisure-time preferences and engaged in outside interests together. There was mutual affection and confidence. Couples were satisfied with their marriages and felt secure in them. Marriages were permanent and conformed to the social expectations of the community. These were some of the specific values which emerged in the analysis of what constituted a successful marriage when happy or adjusted and unhappy or less well-adjusted couples were compared.

These factors fall into two general categories: first, a category of factors which reflect a high degree of acceptance of some system of social norms. Secondly, the social norms accepted appear to be those most characteristic of the American middle class. That is, happy couples came from homes whose parents were happy. The married partners had similar family background. They had better than average amount of education and lived in places other than the underprivileged areas. The data seemed to point to the conclusion that the person best fitted for marriage was a highly socialized person, that is, one characterized by traits of stability, conventionality, and conformity. The data also seemed to suggest that for a permanent and successful marriage one should marry someone who has traits similar to his own traits and who has a similar family and general socio-cultural background.

Family researchers pointed out that these results were tentative, that the couples used as subjects in the research were mostly urban and middle-class persons, and that the results might therefore be expected to emerge somewhat as they did. They further pointed out that the correlations between these factors and happiness in marriage were not high and that they left much to be desired insofar as predictive value was concerned. It was pointed out that perhaps as many as 75 per cent of the factors that made for successful marriages had not been uncovered in these pioneering studies. Researchers also stressed that, in keeping with good scientific procedure, the findings would first have to be verified with findings utilizing larger samples of people from the upper class and lower class as well as from the middle class.

But in a nation and an age in which anything that smacked of scientific findings was held in esteem, the cautions of researchers were neither understood nor heeded. The popular press featured the results and continues to do so. Worst of all, many sociologists themselves failed to use the desired caution and presented the findings of the pioneering studies as a new marriage model based on reason substantiated by factual data. In their attempt to avoid the emotional excesses of romanticism and the dogmatic rigidity of the Judaic-Christian model, and at the same time as scientists to avoid dealing with human values, they advocated a marriage model based upon implicit values and norms on which they had not reflected.

What was it that happy families were happy about? To what were they adjusted? Is adjustment a sufficient goal of individual life or of marriage in a democratic society with its visionary American ideal? These were and are questions being raised concerning this new marriage model by Nelson N. Foote, Reuben Hill, Willam L. Kolb, as well as others within and outside the discipline of sociology.

If the model for successful marriage was the "happy" middle-class family of the 1920's and the 1930's, it could mean a number of things. Had these families achieved the measure of success commensurate with an ideal or model form? On the basis of various types of evidence two different images of that family emerge. One image is that of a family characterized by absence of conflict, the prevalence of habits of accommodation, affection between the spouses, social conservatism and conformity, the unending struggle for success, and evidences that the struggle has not been without its material rewards—owned homes, appliances, television, new automobiles.

The other image of the middle-class family contains the above characteristics as easily observable phenomena but emphasizes the structure of this family as the breeding ground of neurosis and conflict. It pictures the role of the middle-class wife as empty, stultifying, and confused; the role of the husband as that of an individual subjected to all the pressures of the struggle for success; and the role of the child as determined by the conflicting attitudes of his parents toward one another and toward himself. This was the middle-class family of social psychiatry and the realistic branch of literature.

The first image portrays the family in its full glory of high social prestige, surrounded by its gadgets and grimly determined in its pursuit of status, economic success, and happiness. The second delineates the essential emptiness, the narrowness of cultural focus, and the frustrations of such happiness. These latter portrayals were not the rantings of "madmen" or "kill-joys"; they resulted from neo-Freudian observations based on clinical evidence, sociological evidence from studies of personality and role conflict, and the formulations of novelists of the realistic school.

To the extent that the latter picture of the family of the 1920's and 1930's was correct, even the characteristics and behavior patterns of the happiest would not suffice as a model for others to follow. It is obvious that such a family structure, regardless of the degree of adjustment, stability, and reported happiness, could not contribute greatly to the self-development of the family members. Personality growth or development cannot mean the extreme concentration upon status and the economic struggle, for this would seem to restrict rather than to expand the interests of the individual. Adjustment, stability, and happiness would have to be rejected as the goals of marriage insofar as they were based upon an integration of family activity around such limited goals.

Even in the broader sense—that is, without regard to their possible meaning in the American family of the 1920's and the 1930's—adjustment, stability, and happiness are not adequate goals for marriage in a society where the largest measure of personality development and individual freedom of expression are ideal limits held out to individuals. If the end or ultimate goal of life were dedication to the establishment of stable society—stable families, stable government, stable economic order—adjustment and stability would be adequate goals. But if families, as well as the state and the economic order, are to be judged by the way in which they contribute to the pursuits of human freedom and personality development, then the goal of stable families adjusted to a stable social order is too limited and must be transcended.

To meet our immediate purposes we might summarize some of the essential elements of the nascent marriage model that emerged from the pioneering researches of family sociologists in the 1920's and 1930's. The following have been highlighted in the popular press as well as in some of the marriage manuals and marriage textbooks. (1) Marriage is for mature persons—stable, adjusted, conventional, and conforming. (2) One should rationally "select" his mate against the background of traits shown to be associated with successful marriage. Selection should precede or accompany love and is initially more important than love: "It is all right to fall in love, but be careful where you fall." (3) One should select a mate only after extensive dating and intensive courtship to insure making a wise choice. Do not fear to break a dating relationship even if you are engaged, for a broken engagement is better than an unhappy or broken marriage. (4) Marry someone with whom you will be compatible, that is, someone with family and general socio-cultural background like yourself, similar personality, similar interests, and perhaps similar physical features. Like should marry like. This is not too difficult for there are many like you. Your concern is to find one of them. (5) If you choose wisely your marriage should last—not because of pressures from the outside but because you can both expect to find happiness through marriage. The personal rewards can be expected to outweigh the restrictions and compromises which even a good marriage entails.

In earlier paragraphs we criticized the rationalistic marriage model because of the inadequacy of its goals when judged in the light of the American ideal. This is not to suggest that the rationalistic marriage model and the research upon which it was based have not contributed significantly to an understanding of how marriage and the family can contribute to a good life. The same can be said for the Judaic-Christian model and the romantic model.

TABLE 1 *Marriage Models in American Culture*

Aspect of Marriage	Judaic-Christian	Romantic	Rationalistic
Origin of marriage	God	Man	Man
Structure of marriage	Monogamous	Monogamous	Monogamous
Essential basis of marriage	Mates freely chosen through personal confrontation	Impelled by love	Mates freely chosen with aid of rational mate-selection processes and techniques
Reality of marriage	Two become "one flesh," act of God: oneness	Two become one through union of love spirits or souls: oneness	Two remain two: togetherness
Functions of marriage	Unitive, companionship, procreation, outlet for sex desire	Ecstasy	Mutual happiness, mutual adjustment, companionship
Permanence of marriage	Indissoluble	Dissoluble if love dies	Goal is stability but marriage dissoluble

Summary

Two marriage models emerged to challenge the supremacy of the Judaic-Christian marriage model in Western culture. The first of these was the romantic model which first appeared as an extramarital model in the twelfth century. The romantic marriage model has had a strong impact on American marriage in spite of its lack of systematic rationale and its basic social irresponsibility.

According to the romantic model, two persons are drawn together by their feeling of love for each other; they are faithful to each other as long as their mutual love feeling lasts; and they are under some obligation to separate if their love for each other dies. Matters of procreation and the rearing of children fall outside the scope of this model.

The emergence of the rationalistic marriage model is in part indicative of a reaction to the dogmatism of the Judaic-Christian marriage model, on the one hand, and to the irrationality and irresponsibility of the romantic marriage model on the other. Numbered among the protagonists of the rationalistic marriage model are many social scientists and, in particular, family sociologists.

The rationalistic marriage model makes its appeal through reason, whereas faith in God is essential to an acceptance of the Judaic-Christian model, and feeling is at the heart of the romantic model. Rational mate "selection" rather than the irrational process of "falling in love" is the appropriate basis for marriage in the rationalistic model. Mates are selected by a conscious process of matching personal and social traits of the persons concerned. These traits have been empirically demonstrated by social and psychological research to be associated with happy and adjusted marriage. The goal of the rationalistic model is stable marriages based not on fidelity but on the mutual happiness and satisfaction which comes in a life together for two perfectly matched married persons. Perfect matching is still an ideal rather than a reality even in the minds of the most enthusiastic protagonists of the model however.

Values and norms of all three marriage models become involved in marriage models within the general framework of the American ideal—dignity, freedom, equality, and potentiality for personal development. These models are apparent in the following chapters as we examine facets of marriage and the family in light of the American ideal illuminated by empirical findings of the social sciences.

QUESTIONS AND PROJECTS

1. List the major elements in the romantic marriage model.
2. Why did the early Christian church regard romantic love as heretical?
3. What does it mean when we speak of man as inviolable and perfectible?
4. What did the family sociologists find objectionable in the Judaic-Christian marriage model? In the romantic marriage model?
5. How does the rationalistic marriage model attempt to insure both stable marriage and personal freedom?
6. List the major elements in the rationalistic marriage model.
7. On what points would you criticize the rationalistic marriage model?
8. As a model for your own marriage, would you choose one of the three major marriage models? If not, what elements would you take from each?

SUGGESTED READINGS

Bailey, Derrick S., *The Mystery of Love and Marriage*, New York: Harper & Brothers, 1952.

Bainton, Roland H., *What Christianity Says About Sex, Love, and Marriage*, New York: Association Press, 1957.

Becker, Howard, and Reuben Hill, *Family Marriage and Parenthood*, Boston: D. C. Heath & Company, 1948, Chapter 4.

Bowman, Henry, *et al.*, "Teaching Ethical Values Through the Marriage Course: A Debate," *Marriage and Family Living*, Vol. XIX, November 1957, pp. 325–339.

Calhoun, Arthur W., *A Social History of the American Family*, New York: Barnes & Noble, Inc., 1945.

Casserley, J. V. Langmead, *Morals and Man in the Social Sciences*, London: Longmans, Green & Co., 1951.

Cole, William G., *Sex in Christianity and Psychoanalysis*, New York: Oxford University Press, Inc., 1955.

Ditzion, Sidney, *Marriage, Morals and Sex in America,* New York: Bookman Associates, Inc., 1953.

Feldman, Gene, and Max Gartenberg (eds.), *The Beat Generation and the Angry Young Men,* New York: Citadel Press, 1958, Introduction, pp. 9–18.

Foote, Nelson N., and Leonard S. Cottrell, Jr., *Identity and Interpersonal Competence,* Chicago: University of Chicago Press, 1955.

Kantonen, T. A., *The Family Under God,* New York: The Board of Social Missions of the United Lutheran Church in America, pp. 1–30.

Kessler, John J., "A Broader Base for 'Humanism,'" *The Humanist,* Vol. XVI, September–October 1956, pp. 231–233.

Kolb, William L., "The Changing Prominence of Values in Modern Sociological Theory," in Howard Becker and Alvin Boskoff (eds.), *Modern Sociological Theory,* New York: The Dryden Press, Inc., 1957, pp. 93–132.

———, "The Impingement of Moral Values on Sociology," *Social Problems,* Vol. 2, October 1954, pp. 66–70.

———, "Marriage Education, and the Romantic Complex: A Critique," *Social Forces,* Vol. 29, October 1950, pp. 65–72.

———, "A Social-Psychological Conception of Human Freedom," *Ethics,* Vol. LXIII, April 1953, pp. 180–189.

———, "Sociologically Established Family Norms and Democratic Values," *Social Forces,* Vol. 26, May 1948, pp. 451–456.

Mihanovich, Clement S., Gerald J. Schnepp, and John L. Thomas, *A Guide to Catholic Marriage,* Milwaukee: The Bruce Publishing Co., 1955.

Thomas, John L., *The American Catholic Family,* Englewood Cliffs, N. J.: Prentice-Hall, Inc., 1956, Part II.

Waller, Willard and Reuben Hill, *The Family,* New York: The Dryden Press, 1951, Chapter 17.

Zimmerman, Carle C., *Family and Civilization,* New York: Harper & Brothers, 1947.

Dating:

the American mate-selection system

5 Random Dating: Dating for Fun

All societies have some plan whereby single persons can become married. There are a variety of ways in which this is done. In some societies professional matchmakers are employed by the family to find a spouse for an eligible son or daughter. In other societies a close relative—father or uncle —makes the selection of a spouse for the young person. In still others, a young man may make his own choice of a bride by asking the girl's or her parents' permission.

The American system for choosing a marriage partner is new and unique. No other society uses the system in the way in which it is used in America. Dating is the name given to our system by its inventors. According to Ernest Burgess and Paul Wallin, "Dating is an invention by the mass action of young people in the second decade of the twentieth century."

In analyzing dating we will use the terminology of the participants and refrain as much as possible from using the older term courtship. The term courtship is commonly used by the scholar but not by young people themselves. Historically, the two terms—dating and courtship—are not synonymous as will be pointed out shortly.

Nowhere else in the world are young people allowed as much freedom in choosing a marriage partner as they are in America. The only person one *must* consult in making a choice is the person being chosen. On this we insist. In keeping with our belief in the freedom and equality of all men, we grant to each person, man and woman, the right personally to choose a marriage partner. Neither sex is the privileged sex in this regard.

Each young person is expected to choose his marriage partner through the process of dating. He finds out if a person is "right" for him through intimate association with persons of the other sex by dating the "eligibles" one at a time over a period of days, weeks, months, or years. He may find the right one on the first try—even the first date. On the other hand, he may find the right one only after dating literally hundreds of eligibles. Some never find the right one.

Dating is not carried on solely for the purpose of finding a mate, however. It has a dual purpose. Burgess and Wallin's definition of dating, for instance, specifically excludes matrimonial commitment as an objective of dating. "Dating is a social engagement of a man and a woman which is for enjoyment of each other's company and involves no matrimonial commitment." In other words, the individual who asks for a date does not make a commitment to marry the person he dates. In fact, he does not even make a commitment to date her again, or she to date him. When a boy asks a girl for a date it is understood that the request is only for a particular occasion, and each is free to decide whether or not he desires more dates.

Hence, dating as practiced today is radically different from courting, the practice that preceded it in history.

By long practice courtship is a social term involving obligation, a kind of chain process which, once initiated, one is under social pressure to carry through to completion in marriage. In Colonial times when a boy asked for permission to call on a man's daughter, he in effect asked for permission to marry her if she would consent. Much more recently a first call by a man on a young woman was a public indication of interest in marriage, and repeated calling was the near equivalent of announcement of an engagement and forthcoming marriage. From its initiation to its end courtship is a public avowal of intent to marry. Back of that avowal, there has long been in America social pressure upon the individual to carry out his commitment.

In contrast, dating is a relationship expressing freedom, lack of commitment or public obligation for any sort of future action. In truth, up to the time of announcement of engagement dating participants have a minimum of accepted responsibility to continue the relationship. Continuation is largely a matter between the two concerned. That is to say, the rise of the term dating is a reflection of the freedom of the young to associate in pairs without others—parents or the community—assuming or insisting that merely because they are dating they have further responsibilities to each other or to the community. Such freedom is what distinguishes dating from courtship.[1]

Because of its dual function some dating does involve commitment to marry, whereas other dating involves only the intention of having a good time. Some dates do not involve commitment to marry (random dates). Some dates involve a latent commitment on the part of one: "If he asks me to marry him I will." Some dates involve a private or semiprivate commitment to marry on the part of both

[1] Samuel H. Lowrie, "Dating Theories and Student Responses," *American Sociological Review*, Vol. 16, June 1951, p. 337.

partners (pinned or engaged-to-be-engaged). Some dates are between persons who have made a formal commitment to marry (engagement). Some dates are between persons already married to each other. In other words, persons who have no intention of marrying each other, persons who have intentions of marrying each other, and persons already married to each other date in America.

In this chapter we will discuss only that type of dating which precedes marriage and, more particularly, that which precedes the serious quest for a marriage partner.

Random Dating

We use the term random dating to label dates that involve no commitment to continue the relationship beyond the particular date. In this type of dating a number of eligibles, as defined by the actor, would serve equally or almost equally well for the purposes of the date. Witness the fellow at the phone trying to decide whom he should call first. He is a casual dater. To him what he wants to do is more important than the person with whom he does it. Perhaps some of his pals have said, "We are going to a movie; why don't you get a date and come along?" He answers, "O.K., who should I ask?" We call such dating random because the situation—going to a movie with someone of the other sex—is more important than the specific person with whom he goes. Random dating may appear to be rather crass, as though people are interchangeable and any one of many will do, and in a way dating is random in this sense. Actually, this is usually not the case, for no two persons will fill the role of one's date in the same way, and the dater usually has at least some slight preference for one over against the others.

Some scholars in discussing this type of dating refer to it as casual rather than random. Random dating is casual in the sense that neither dater is deeply involved emotionally with the other. In fact, if a young person is going to enjoy random dating, it is important that he have enough self-control to avoid becoming overly involved emotionally with persons who have no attachment for him.

First Dates: Group Dating

For some young people first dates grow almost imperceptibly out of group activities. For others, getting the first date is a traumatic and memorable occasion.

An increase in school parties, dances, and other school and community functions in junior high school introduces the young adolescent into a type of group life where association with the other sex is for him almost inevitable, if not desirable. Recent research has indicated that such school, church, or community activities initiate the adolescent not only into heterosexual group activities on a basis of equality, but they also serve to introduce him to paired association with the other sex. The adolescent's peers prod him if he seems uninterested and support him if his sagging resolve prevents him from going through with his plans to begin to date.

Group dating is fairly common among young adolescents; in a survey of 120 middle-class parents, 84 per cent reported that their adolescents had passed through a stage which could best be described as group dating.[2] Occasionally there are public expressions of concern that parents and the school encourage or force young people into this phase of life before they are ready for it and before they would choose it

[2] E. E. LeMasters, *Modern Courtship and Marriage*, New York, The Macmillan Co., 1957, p. 96.

for themselves. This is especially true in regard to the more formal aspects of dating, such as parties and dances. As one coed reflected,

> How well I remember the awkwardness of our 7th and 8th grade school dances and then again the fun we had on sleigh-rides and parties with games and food. Casual get-togethers for that age group can't be emphasized enough.[3]

Group dating may begin when the child is eleven or twelve years of age, mainly under the supervision of parents or some other adult group. Individually paired dating, however, does not normally start at such a tender age. Hollingshead reports on Elmtown as follows:

> The more adventurous youngsters begin to date when they are 12 years of age—at picnics and family group get-togethers—and the parents are usually present. A definite dating pattern becomes clear during the fourteenth year; 20 per cent of the girls and 15 per cent of the boys report that they had their first dates when they were 13. A much larger number begins to date in the fifteenth year, and by the end of it approximately 93 per cent of both sexes are dating with some regularity. Among the sixteen-year-olds, dating is the accepted procedure, and the boy or girl who does not date is left out of mixed social affairs. Our data make it clear that between the beginning of the fourteenth and the end of the sixteenth years the associational pattern of these adolescents changes from almost exclusive interaction with members of their own sex to a mixed associational pattern similar to that found in adult life. In this period, certain activities, such as girls' "hag parties" and hunting and baseball among the boys, are organized on a single sex basis; and others, such as dances and parties, are almost exclusively mixed.
> Forty-three per cent of the boys and 58 per cent of the girls report that they experienced the thrill of their "first date" before they entered high school. Dating before entry into high school is not related significantly to age, town or country residence, or class. On the contrary, it is as-

---

[3] All cases cited are from the author's files unless otherwise indicated. Cases are used throughout to illustrate, not to prove, a point.

sociated with clique membership. Some cliques have a much higher ratio of dates than others. . . .[4]

Some of the pairing off by adolescents may appear to an observer to be more conflicting than cooperative in nature! "Roughhouse love play" is characteristic of adolescent love affairs. Various roughhouse acts are carried on in public, making possible more intimate contact between the sexes than would otherwise be publicly allowed.

A customary pattern is for a boy or girl to take something —a comb or pencil—belonging to one of the other sex whom he likes and refuse to give it back. The resulting love play over the coveted object is permitted in public because of the aspects of conflict involved in it; to the casual observer the couple may appear to be involved in a good-natured fight. Other boys and girls may tease each other too, but the resulting conflict does not take on the thinly disguised aspects of love-making present in the simulated conflict of those who like each other.

Another phase of this roughhouse pattern, as well as some of the other trauma of first dates, is seen in the following dating histories.

It happens to all girls, I guess. From jeans to party dresses, from climbing trees and playing left field with the neighborhood boys to dances, and from bubble gum and yo-yos to movies and sodas with a *boy!*

It was in the beginning of eighth grade that I sort of casually noticed that boys were sort of . . . well . . . cute. . . . To my embarrassment, I found I had "crushes" on certain boys and when they'd look at me or say "Hi" to me I'd almost wished they hadn't because I was miserably flustered. Of course I chummed around with a few girls and we began going to the football and basketball games and also the dances afterward. It was always just all the kids. Everyone mingled and no one was really paired off. Just a big group. At these dances I found out that if I started to dance with one of my girl friends, pretty soon

[4] Reprinted with permission from August B. Hollingshead, *Elmtown's Youth.* Copyright 1949, John Wiley & Sons, Inc., pp. 224–225.

a boy would cut in and although I was horrified at the thought I decided I could stand it. It seemed to me that the boys didn't exactly converse with me, or any of the other girls for that matter, but that they would insult me and get a "charge" out of it. So I'd insult them right back. This and the other forms of "goofing off" (pranks, jokes, etc.) kind of broke the nervous tension. After the dances I'd walk home with my girl friends—*slowly!*

I advanced to only one boy walking me home. At first this was all there was to it. Merely a nice, uneasy, walk home. But then there came a night when this boy walked me home and asked for a date besides. I was thrilled and very pleased with myself. I was petrified too, because I kept getting visions of neither one of us saying anything, and I didn't know how to act on a date.

Another girl writes:

To associate with a group where boys were present presented no real problem for I felt perfectly at ease with them. Whether it was in the class-room or at a social function, I mingled freely with the fellows as well as the girls. But it was the thought of spending an entire evening with a member of the opposite sex that suddenly made me conscious of how clumsy my feet seemed to be and how cold and clammy my hands were. Although I was interested in making friends with the fellows, it was always more or less a "brother-sister" relationship. As soon as I felt the relationship was becoming more than this, and that perhaps I might be asked for a date, I immediately stopped being friendly and held myself somewhat aloof.

The day arrived, however, when my coolness seemed to have no effect and I found myself faced with the problem of accepting or declining a date from my first suitor. After much urging and coaxing from a girl friend, I consented to go. Although the fellow had always been a friend of mine, I suddenly felt a total stranger to him, not knowing what to say or do. I worried for fear my friends might see me and the word get around that I had begun dating. I was certain I could never face the situation again.

By the end of my sophomore year, I began realizing that boys could be fun on a date, too, and the more dates

I accepted, the more adequate I began feeling in this thing called dating.

For first dates to be rather uncomfortable affairs is a fairly universal experience. Crist reports in his study of 120 high school students that about one-half said the first date was not an entirely enjoyable event and the source of anxiety, fears, frustrations, or worry for many. First daters are apt to be shy, fear that they will do the wrong thing, will not know what to say, and are apt to be over-cautious in any show of intimacy.[5]

But despite the discomforts, young people begin the process of dating for a variety of reasons. As part of their socialization they acquire the notion that there is nothing more thrilling this side of heaven than being in love and marrying, especially being in love. The young person realizes that if this state of bliss is ever to come to pass for him he must get started in the dating game. Random dating, even with all its trauma, is the way to begin, for in random dating one is not obligated to continue the relationship if it does not measure up to one's expectations.

Crist found that dating in the early stages was engaged in primarily because the group expected it, not because of any particular interest in the girl or boy or in dating as such. Also the desire to go steady or with a particular person was often created because of group pressure or for social approval.

Random Going Steady

We have been talking about group dating and paired random dating. There is, however, a progression in random

[5] John R. Crist, "High School Dating As a Behavior System," *Marriage and Family Living*, Vol. XV, February 1953, pp. 23–28.

dating, or a next step, that is very popular among students, particularly in high school. The participants refer to it as "going steady." [6] Since the involvement is still casual in nature we refer to this dating for purposes of description and analysis as random going steady to distinguish it from the going steady that precedes engagement among serious daters.

Group expectation plays a part in random going steady as it does in random dating. Some reasons given by the young people themselves for going steady include the following: peer group recognition and acceptance, many important social activities are date affairs, one must date to rate, going steady is a means of providing date security or participation insurance, discomfort involved in being a participant in the fiercely competitive business of random dating.

Despite these group pressures from one's peers, "liking the person" must not be ruled out in any list of reasons why young people go steady. It is obviously an important factor, as the following dating histories make clear. We also see in these dating histories that random going steady is not always viewed as an unmixed blessing, even by the persons involved in it.

George asked me to go with him and only him. He knew I dated others, although I didn't date anyone as often as him. I asked him to let me think it over. The first thing I thought of was wearing his ring. I liked the idea. I also pictured myself showing it off to my girl friends. Going steady at my high school was very popular and it seemed to me that it made a girl just a little more popular. Another thing was the fact that I would never have to worry about getting a date for certain functions. Last, but not least, I did like George, and I enjoyed his company more than the other boys I dated.

The only bad point about it was the fact that I would only date George and no one else. The good outweighed

---

[6] This term is widely used among high-school students, but not beyond high-school age. There is no generally accepted term for steady dating in use among college students. "Going steady" is used here to indicate a stage somewhat less formalized than the "pinned" or "engaged to be engaged" stage.

the bad, so I accepted. It would be too good to pass up. Just think of all the kids noticing George's ring on my finger. I told George I would go with him and things went smoothly. He insisted on seeing me every night besides every day at school.

I lost contact with my girl friends after school and was no longer included in their adventures as I used to be. As for other boys, well, they practically ignored me. George saw to that. He was a little on the jealous side and got mad when I'd walk to class or talk to another boy. This lasted for four months and then I felt myself feeling resentful and left-out, and bored. I also took this feeling out on George by snapping at him, being downright rude to him and embarrassing him in front of his friends. I also started to break dates with him. I accepted another boy's invitation to go for a ride. George found out about it the next day and asked for his ring back which more than anything else made me feel relieved.

In analyzing my dating career I realize that it became too serious and involved at too early an age. I found that I matured or learned to adjust in general, but I also discovered that I came upon serious problems which I was too young and immature to handle objectively. Much tension, worry, and heartbreak could have been avoided had this relationship of "going steady" not been established.

Even when random going steady proves to be an unpleasant experience young daters are often at a loss to know how to end the affair. Dating is regarded as a private and personal affair in our society and has been more or less ignored in the pattern of proper behavior taught to young people by parents and others. In fact, a young person is apt to feel at a loss not only in the proper procedures for breaking with a "steady," but, more basically, he may feel inadequately trained in proper procedure for making dates and in the etiquette of proper dating behavior.

Just before the school year was over I quit dating the girl at home completely. I never was much for feeding a girl a line or talking over my associations with her, and this breaking was no exception. After having gone with the girl for seven months I did not know how to go about telling her we were all through so I merely took her in after our last date, not mentioning a thing and then never took her out again. She never knew what was wrong and I never took the time to explain things. I have kicked myself many times since then for being so foolish but I guess a person must live and learn.

Summary

Random dating as a system of interpersonal relations is "something new under the sun," an invention of young Americans in the second half of the twentieth century. It is a source of companionship, fun, and prestige for young people and is not essentially marriage-oriented.

Random dating commonly begins with a group-dating phase in late childhood or early adolescence. The young dater may then proceed through various stages of random dating—first paired dates, random paired dating, random dating with a favorite date, and random going steady. Not every person goes through each of these stages, although some persons go through the last three stages over and over again. Still others never do random date but become serious daters with their very first dating experience.

QUESTIONS AND PROJECTS

1. List the differences between dating and courtship as systems for choosing a mate.
2. Why is the early dating period referred to as random dating?
3. What are the functions of random dating?
4. How did random dating in your home town or school compare with random dating as described in this chapter?

SUGGESTED READINGS

Barclay, Dorothy, "When Boy (Age 12) Meets Girl," *New York Times Magazine*, January 23, 1955, p. 39.

Breed, Warren, "Sex, Class and Socialization in Dating," *Marriage and Family Living*, Vol. XVIII, May 1956, pp. 137–144.

Burgess, Ernest W., and Paul Wallin, *Engagement and Marriage*, Chicago: J. B. Lippincott Co., 1953, Chapters 3, 4.

Byerly, Carl L., "Developing Standards of Behavior for the Early Teens," *The Bulletin of the National Association of Secondary-School Principals*, Vol. 32, 1948, pp. 69–74.

Crist, John R., "High School Dating As a Behavior System," *Marriage and Family Living*, Vol. XV, February 1953, pp. 23–28.

Herman, Robert D., "The 'Going Steady' Complex: A Re-Examination," *Marriage and Family Living*, Vol. XVII, February 1955, pp. 36–40.

Hollingshead, August B., *Elmtown's Youth*, New York: John Wiley & Sons, Inc., 1949, Chapter 9.

Landis, Judson T., and Kenneth C. Kidd, "Attitudes and Policies Concerning Marriage Among High School Students," *Marriage and Family Living*, Vol. XVIII, May 1956, pp. 128–136.

LeMasters, E. E., *Modern Courtship and Marriage*, New York: The Macmillan Co., 1957, Part Two.

Lowrie, Samuel H., "Dating Theories and Student Responses," *American Sociological Review*, Vol. 16, June 1951, pp. 334–340.

———, "Factors Involved in the Frequency of Dating," *Marriage and Family Living*, Vol. XVIII, February 1956, pp. 46–51.

———, "Sex Differences and Age of Initial Dating," *Social Forces*, Vol. 30, May 1952, pp. 456–461.

McGinley, Phyllis, "The Fearful Aspect of Too-Early Dating," *Good Housekeeping*, April 1956, pp. 60–61, 287, 288.

6 *Serious Dating:*
In Search of a Beloved

ii

The immediate reasons for dating in adolescence may be fun, a chance to go places, prestige with one's peers. These are social-enjoyment reasons. But in this book we are primarily concerned with the broader, long-range functions of dating— personality development, choosing a mate, marriage, and family living. Does random dating have anything to contribute to these long-range goals?

This question must be answered affirmatively. Random dating at its best can serve ends beyond the immediate one of having a good time. These other useful functions of random dating include the following:

1. Every society must have some rites of entry and rites of

passage to allow young adults the opportunity of passing from singleness to marriedness. Our culture does not provide a precise pattern that is to be followed; it rather allows great latitude of action to the individual. In the face of this great amount of freedom to act, random dating provides a way for the inexperienced individual to gain experience dating the opposite sex without having to make binding commitments. If his experience convinces him that he has not acted wisely in his choice of a dating partner, he need not date the person again.

2. Random dating has a broad socializing effect. It is the young person's introduction to sex-differentiated adult society, a type of society he will participate in for the rest of his life.

3. On the other hand, random dating helps wean the young person, emotionally, from his parents and home of orientation—a weaning process that will need to be carried far before the young person is ready to stand on his own feet and establish a family of procreation of his own.

4. Random dating introduces the young person to members of the other sex as companions and gives insight into the subculture influencing the thought and action of members of the other sex.

5. Random dating helps one get to know a particular person of the other sex. If both parties to a date conduct themselves in a responsible and respectful way, a new friendship has been made or an old friendship has been deepened.

6. Experience with other persons is one of the basic ways in which one's own personality develops and is enriched. If one is at all sensitive to others, the reflexive effect of another person's evaluation and reaction will change and can help develop one's personality.

7. Experience with others helps develop skills in human relations. Many young people attest to their need for skills in communication and interaction with the other sex and their almost total feeling of inadequacy in this area. Cases

of tongue-tiedness, shyness, and general feeling of inadequacy in the presence of the other sex are ubiquitous.

8. Random dating gives prestige. During the adolescent period in life when rapid change is the rule rather than the exception, the young person needs to feel anchored in persons and activities that enhance his prestige with himself and with others. If used wisely dating adds to the reputation and prestige of a boy or girl. The person who dates to the

"Marjorie—it's the shy one."
Reprinted from *Love and Hisses* by Brant House.
Copyright 1956, Ace Books, Inc.

neglect of schoolwork, family, and other types of community and group activity or the person who becomes over-involved emotionally and physically in a casual affair is not using random dating wisely.

9. Random dating fills an important dalliance function. To a greater extent than ever before, young people of school age feel that they need education or training beyond high school before beginning an occupational career. This often means some delay in becoming serious about marriage.

Random dating can fill a desire for association with the other sex until one feels ready to think seriously about marriage.

10. Random dating gives the person his "fill" of dating for fun and prepares him to move on to the satisfactions of "settled" married life.

Guiding the Young Dater

If random dating is to measure up to all that it can be, young daters must have the discipline of adult guidance and supervision. As a keen observer of young people once pointed out in my presence, the teen-age girl who says, "I've got to go in now, my dopey parents won't let me stay out any later!" may really be bragging rather than complaining. Many young persons in reflecting on early dating experience have indicated real appreciation for the parent who helped set limits and make decisions.

The parent need not feel inadequate to counsel his adolescent child since he has been through the process of random dating—or some emerging version of it—himself. He can, if he takes his adolescent's dating seriously (as he should), offer much help to a person just launching out in this bewildering, interesting, and exciting phase of life.

Besides parents, community associations such as churches and schools can help. Some communities are working out youth codes in school or through cooperative effort on the part of teachers, parents, and students. This is a step in the right direction provided too much faith is not placed in "rules" as the answer to problems of youth.

For example, the following letter was widely distributed among residents of one community:

Dear Parents and Friends of Bronxville Young People:

Here is our revision of the "Out of School Behavior Code" which was unanimously accepted by the young people of grades 7 through 12 last spring.

Since the Student Committee had an important voice in the revisions, parents can assume that this is their Code —our Code.

For the first time, the "General Laws Which Pertain to Our Young People" are listed in this booklet. This has been done to keep parents and young people informed as to our responsibilities as citizens of Bronxville.

Our mailing list includes all parents of Bronxville School, parents of teen-agers away at school, our church leaders and our Village merchants. This is being done in the sincere hope that we, as a community, will work together in a unified harmony to keep Bronxville a happy family community.

Sincerely,

BEHAVIOR PROJECTS COMMITTEE

Accompanying the letter was a copy of the pamphlet prepared by the Bronxville Parents and Teachers Association entitled "Bronxville Families Agree . . . !" Inside the reader was informed that the P.T.A. had established a community council and organized a voluntary group to take steps in a program for out-of-school behavior of young people. The council defined its purposes as follows:

1. To enlist the interest of families in out-of-school behavior of young people.
2. To build a favorable attitude in the community with respect to young people and their out-of-school concerns.
3. To discover if families in the Village could find points of agreement that could be clearly defined and written into a Behavior Code for young people and their parents.

4. To discover the extent of interest of Bronxville families in making this a more friendly, safe, attractive and interesting community.

The out-of-school behavior code contains the following points:

We As a Family Agree . . .
1. that family plans should be so organized that all members can be reached in case of emergency or change in plans.
2. that parents should be at home and available at all times when young people entertain.
3. to limit the number of guests to a group that can be accommodated easily in the home and to confine the party to a prescribed area in the home.
4. not to admit "crashers" unless it is a "casual type" party and there has been no guest list established. Any "unwanted crashers" should be politely but firmly asked to leave. If he or she refuses to comply, the host's parents should be asked to handle the situation.
5. to see to it that parties in our homes terminate at the appointed time and that invited guests be informed before the party when the party is expected to end.
6. that the host or hostess and the parents have a right to expect proper behavior at all times, that lighting be according to the wishes of the host's parents, and that their home be respected; disrespectful or unruly guests should be reprimanded.
7. that the suggested hours for the ending of social activities be:

		Grade		
7th	8th	9th	10th	11th
Informals at school or elsewhere				
9:30	10:00	10:30	11:30	12:00
Home Parties				
9:30–10	10–10:30	10:30–11	11:30–12	12–12:30
Nondating				
9:30–10	10–10:30	10:30–11	11:30–12	12–12:30

General dating:

It is suggested that the hours above be followed; but because there are so many exceptions to this category, it is felt that the parents of the girl should talk to the boy and agree on a time for the couple to be home, taking into consideration the time the social event ends.

—*The above hours refer to parties given in a home and to those to which young people may be invited.*

8. that there will be no parties held after other parties on the same evening unless parents are advised beforehand and the party complies with the rules outlined in No. 7, and that parents and young people will not plan parties that will compete with school affairs.

9. that a definite interval of time between the end of the social engagement and the arrival at home should be agreed upon by parents and young people; 7th and 8th Grade girls should be called for by an adult.

10. that the girl and her parents should agree on a definite time to return home and that the boy should be informed of this. Consideration should be given to the time required to escort the girl home and the extra time needed for the boy's arrival home.

11. that, as much as is possible, parents and young people should have a general understanding as to where and with whom time will be spent.

12. that, before the boy or girl leaves for a party, there should be clear understanding as to how they will travel to and from the party.

13. that no one should assume that he has the right, even in his own home, to allow alcoholic beverages to be served to other people's children under eighteen.

14. that young people should treat adults with respect and should in return be treated in like manner. This applies to all areas in our village—on the streets, in the stores and in the theatre.

It is recognized that there will be special circumstances in which certain rules of this Code cannot be rigidly followed. However, we feel that these principles should act as a guide to be followed except in those unusual situations agreed upon in advance by the individual families.

Serious Dating Is a Frame of Mind

Functionally, dating is of two types, random and serious. In random dating the emphasis is on social activity, recrea-

"Try to look at the bright side. You had excellent food, a good rest, and two weeks of glorious weather."

Drawing by Hoff, copr. © 1957 The New Yorker Magazine, Inc.

tion, and fun. In serious dating the function is primarily processual in nature. The dater hopes that dating will be the channel leading to love and marriage.

The serious type of dating might be called the questing type, for it is part of the eternal quest of youth. Young people, beginning at different levels in their teens, join the ranks of the universal company in search of the "right one." [1]

Serious dating as compared to random dating involves a different frame of mind on the part of the dater. It may be one or a combination of many things that "changes the mind" of the more or less carefree, casual random dater into a serious "quester"—satiations with the thrills of random dating; falling in love; the end of a course of study; the acquisition of a new job; a substantial raise in pay; the imminent prospect of a new and uncertain way of life, such as military service; the desire for deep and lasting companionship; the desire for a home and children.

The time at which a person becomes a serious dater varies with the personal characteristics of the person and the circumstances in which he finds himself. For one person the psychological status of serious dater may begin almost with the beginning of dating itself; it is possible to be "marriage-minded" even on one's first date. A second person might fall suddenly and unexpectedly in love, though this is not likely for a psychologically healthy person. For a third person the change of mind may come gradually and almost imperceptibly. Lastly, there is the person who makes a calculated and deliberate decision to find someone to marry. A very few never do become serious daters and for this, among other reasons, remain single.

Since the serious dater is at first a serious dater only in his intentions—he has not yet found and won his beloved— his reasons for dating may appear to the casual observer to be the same as those of the random dater. He appears to be dating for the purpose of having a good time, for he masks his more serious intentions at this stage of his dating. Both the serious dater and the casual dater use the same medium—dating—to accomplish different purposes. Both

[1] By permission from *Marriage and the Family* by Ray E. Baber. Copyright 1953. McGraw-Hill Book Company, Inc., p. 117.

may attend the same activity—a movie or a dance—with no apparent difference in motives. The serious dater masks his intentions for he is not in a position to know the inclinations of the person he is dating. In a mixed date—where one dater is serious and the other casual—the one more emotionally involved has the most at stake. He carries the responsibility of trying to convince his date, a free and independent person like himself, to invest more of himself in the relationship. Hence, the serious dater proceeds with caution, pretending to date only for fun but at the same time attempting to make an impression on the one he is dating.

Serious Dating a Social Reality

We have been discussing the serious dater; a serious date, on the other hand, is a date involving two serious daters. Such a date may include some social activity planned for enjoyment, but the serious daters are less interested in the date as a social activity and more interested in discovering the personality, outlook on life, beliefs, values, interests, hopes, and dreams of each other. For this reason serious daters spend less time and energy group dating, double-dating, and attending social activities and more time walking and talking and exploring the personalities of each other.

Life was carefree and happy for me. Sometimes it meant walking home together in the evenings from a coke date, attending school activities or parties, going to the movie together, or participating in the other countless activities with which students are involved. Perhaps, however, our happiest hours were spent simply chatting over a bowl of popcorn in the livingroom.

After several months of dating I discovered how much this fellow really meant to me. Our dating became more than just having a good time. It became a relationship of deep respect, trust, and love for one another. I began finding that all my ideas and thoughts included him, too. Our values, standards, and goals in life seemed to vary little.

Months went by and we began discussing our relationship in terms of a permanent one. We agreed, however, to complete our education before establishing a home together as neither of us felt we were quite ready to do so now.

Although our education has now put miles between us, our relationship has remained strong and secure. The time seems long between the vacations when we can be together, and we are eagerly anticipating the day when we will no longer be apart. We find that our relationship is still continuing to grow whether together or apart.

Serious dating, in contrast to random dating, is not an end in itself but a means to an end; simply stated, it is a way of getting from where I am now—single—to where I want to be—in love and married.

Ideally, serious dating includes the following steps or stages:

1. The person with privately held, marriage-minded motives dates one or a number of eligibles.

2. One of the eligibles whom he is dating becomes for him a favorite date.

3. If the feeling is mutual and grows they may drift into or consciously decide to go steady.

4. The next step—perhaps the most significant of all—comes when they feel quite certain of their love for each other—"psychological engagement"—and their desire to marry. In recognition of this fact some symbol or symbols may be exchanged. The couple is now widely referred to as pinned or engaged-to-be-engaged.

5. In due course, and at some appropriate moment, the couple engaged-to-be-engaged become formally engaged. Frequently this involves the presenting of a diamond ring to the fiancée by the affianced and the announcement of the event by the girl's parents.

These steps in serious dating are an emerging pattern in

our culture, and couples do not necessarily feel under obligation to follow them. The way in which any one couple proceeds from singleness to marriage may vary at a number of points from this "ideal" pattern. The pattern appears to be more generally followed by college-educated and middle-class young persons than among others in American society. Actually, variations in dating practice range all the way from the highly formal pattern of the coming-out party of the debutante—signifying her eligibility for marriage—to the other extreme of very young people who drift into marriage, often against the desires of one or both parents, and in the face of parental objection.

Summary

Though the immediate functions of random dating are companionship and a good time, random dating serves some long-range goals as well. It serves to introduce the emerging adult to the new world of relations with the other sex as companions and social equals; it helps wean him from primary emotional dependence on his parents; it is a source of enriching experiences through association with a larger number of acquaintances of both sexes; and it may help him formulate a more realistic mental image of his ideal mate.

Generally speaking, the young dater who began dating because of group pressure or for the sake of a good time begins to harbor serious thoughts of love and marriage in the later teens or early twenties. It is at this time that he becomes a serious dater and dates with motives beyond the immediate one of a good time. He hopes to find a favorite date with whom he can go steady, fall in love, and eventually marry. The process which began in the group dating of the early teens eventually leads for most persons, after some detours and a few false starts, to marriage. This signalizes the end of the quest and the beginning of a new and quite different phase of life.

But before we proceed to discuss marriage we must consider some important details of the serious-dating phase of life which have been overlooked in our panoramic view of the process as a whole. Some unanswered questions beg for attention: What is love? How does one know when one is in love enough to marry? How intimate should dating couples become? Does engagement serve any real purpose in our day? Should engagements ever be broken?

We turn to these questions in the following chapters.

QUESTIONS AND PROJECTS

1. Why has the Roman Catholic Church objected to random dating among adolescents?
2. Can random dating serve any useful purpose other than providing a good time?
3. What can the school, the church, and the community do to help make random dating an acceptable pattern of activity?
4. What characterizes the frame of mind of the random dater?
5. What characterizes the frame of mind of the serious dater?
6. What is a serious date? What functions does it serve other than providing a good time for the daters?

SUGGESTED READINGS

Burgess, Ernest W., and Paul Wallin, *Engagement and Marriage*, Chicago: J. B. Lippincott Co., 1953, Chapters 3–5.
Landis, Judson T. and Mary G., *Building a Successful Marriage*, New York: Prentice-Hall, Inc., 1958, Chapters 4, 5.
Landis, Paul H., *Making the Most of Marriage*, New York: Appleton-Century-Crofts, Inc., 1955, Chapter 8.
LeMasters, E. E., *Modern Courtship and Marriage*, New York: The Macmillan Co., 1957, Chapters VI, VII.
Leslie, Gerald R., and Arthur H. Richardson, "Family Versus Campus Influences in Relation to Mate Selection," *Social Problems*, Vol. 4, October 1956, pp. 117–121.
Lowrie, Samuel H., "Dating Theories and Student Responses," *American Sociological Review*, Vol. 16, June 1951, pp. 334–340.

————, "Factors Involved in the Frequency of Dating," *Marriage and Family Living*, Vol. XVIII, February 1956, pp. 46–51.

————, "Sex Differences and Age of Initial Dating," *Social Forces*, Vol. 30, May 1952, pp. 456–461.

7 The Meaning of Love

'Tis not her birth, her friends, nor yet her treasure,
Nor do I covet her for sensual pleasure,
Nor for that old morality
Do I love her, 'cause she loves me.
Sure he that loves his lady 'cause she's fair,
Delights his eye, so loves himself, not her.
Something there is moves me to love, and I
Do know I love, but know not how, nor why.[1]

In this chapter we deal with the meaning of love as a relationship between persons of the opposite sex. Description and analysis of love affairs based on empirical evidence is the subject of Chapter 9.

Individuals in America marry because they are in love.

[1] Alexander Brome, "Why I Love Her."

This is the justification for marriage. It is not considered right, proper, or even decent for two people to marry if they are not in love. There may be marriages of convenience, marriages for economic reasons, or marriages to link two influential families, but if the marriage is devoid of love the couple is looked upon with pity.

Burgess and Wallin asked engaged couples, "Do you think that a person should ever marry one whom he does not love?" Roughly 80 per cent of both men and women respondents said that he should not, and less than 15 per cent said that he should. The belief in love as the essential basis for marriage seems firmly established, at least among the educated, middle-class population.

TABLE 2 *Percentages of 998 Engaged Men and Women Saying Persons Should or Should Not Marry When Not in Love*

Marry When Not in Love	Per Cent	
	Men	Women
Yes	12.3	15.4
No	81.9	79.5
?	5.8	5.1
Total	100.0	100.0

SOURCE: From *Engagement and Marriage* by Ernest W. Burgess and Paul Wallin, p. 394. Copyright 1953 by J. B. Lippincott Company.

Burgess and Wallin expressed some surprise that about one in five of the men and women did not say that love is essential to marriage. Some of the conditions under which respondents felt persons might commit themselves to marriage even though not in love were older age with less favorable competitive position in the marriage market; pressure from family and friends, or their own desire to get married and settle down; a sense of duty or honor or anticipation of social disapproval if they break a relationship; rejection by the person one regards as his "one and only." The point to be made, however, is that the vast majority of respondents regarded love as the essential basis for marriage.

But love is not only the avowed reason for marrying in America, it is also the only basis for marriage completely consistent with belief in the dignity, freedom, and equality of man—the American ideal. If we take seriously our belief in freedom and if we regard the sexes as equal, then the only basis for marriage is mutual desire for each other and mutual regard for the personality of each other.

If I am a free man, the choice of a mate with whom I am to live in an intimate relationship throughout my adult life can only be made by me, on the basis of personal reasons for choice, acting in cooperation with a person of the other sex making his choice on the basis of personal reasons.

Between two free persons commitment to marry has to be based on intimate personal confrontation and attraction. Negotiations through a third party—a close relative or a professional matchmaker—will not suffice. Dating is, then, one of the best, if not *the* best, means for finding one's beloved in a society of free people.

Belief in love as the essential basis of marriage is consistent with the ultimate value we place on the freedom and equality of man. It is also consistent with our belief in man's capacity for personal growth and development.

In America, we believe that man is a creature capable of growth—given a proper community of love in which to grow. We regard a community of love made up of a husband and wife as the most ideal community in which this growth can take place. Not that it is the only community of love possible; there are parent-child, teacher-pupil, artist-critic relationships as well in which love provides the situation for personality development. "Many a person can look back upon an incident in his school career when a sensitive teacher recognized at the critical moment an emerging talent and thereby permanently exalted his conception of himself and his capabilities. These are the moments of love in its sublime power to move." [2]

The Problem of Definition

When used in reference to a person of the other sex the word "love" can carry the connotation of puppy love, sexual love, companionship love, romantic love, or Platonic love. The same word has to stand duty in expressing one's reaction to strawberries, dogs, one's mother, as well as one's sweetheart.

Since we have made the bold assertion that love is the only basis for marriage consistent with the American ideal, we are under serious obligation to make as explicit a definition of love as is possible. The difficulty cannot be met simply by framing a definition of love, however, for a definition, unless it become unduly long and involved, cannot convey the breadth and depth of the meaning of love. Presentation of several contemporary definitions of love, an analysis of the elements in a love relationship, and discussion (in Chapter 8) of empirical data from an intensive study of several hundred love affairs will suffice.

Love is to be experienced, not to be defined. Hence, any attempt to describe and analyze it objectively is in one sense doomed to failure. But the problem is not unique to love. The same difficulty is experienced in attempts to define and analyze religious experience, things of beauty, and traumatic experiences.

It may well be that when it comes to communicating about love the social scientist should retire in favor of the poet, since his discipline is freer for expression and com-

[2] Nelson N. Foote, "Love," *Psychiatry: Journal for the Study of Interpersonal Processes,* Vol. 16, August 1953, p. 248.

munication of subjective feelings and states than is the scientific posture. In any event the reader is well advised to consult the works of the artists as well as those of the social analyst if he is interested in increasing his knowledge and insights about love.

Nothing is easy! Pity then
The poet more than other men:
And, since his aim is ecstasy,
And, since none work so hard as he,
Forgive the poet poesy!

He has the same dull eyes: his ears
Are dull-attuned: his hopes and fears
Are those same ravening dogs that bay
The moon, and bury bones in clay!

Yea, wonder is that he hath done,
For all that is beneath the sun
By magic he transfigures to
A better sound, a finer view:
And—loveliest of all that's true!
He tells that you come to the spring,
And that the spring returns to you.[3]

Love Defined

Devotion to the ideals of dignity, freedom, equality, and capacity for growth in man is apparent in several contemporary definitions of love.

Love is the passionate and abiding desire on the part of two or more people to produce together conditions under which each can be and spontaneously express his real self; to produce together an intellectual soil and an emo-

[3] By permission from James Stephens, *Collected Poems*, p. 272. Copyright 1954 by the Macmillan Co.

tional climate in which each can flourish, far superior to what either could achieve alone.[4]

The love of a person implies, not the possession of that person but the affirmation of that person. It means granting him, gladly, the full right of his unique humanhood. One does not truly love a person and yet seek to enslave him—by law or by bonds of dependence and possessiveness. Whenever we experience genuine love, we are moved by this transforming experience toward a capacity for good will.[5]

Love on Trial?

In analyzing the love relationship in the remainder of this chapter and in succeeding chapters, we will attempt to live up to the demands of many of the beliefs about love inherent in the romantic model. We would not want to be guilty of suggesting anything in our analysis that would in any way dissuade youth from the use of love as the basis of mate selection consistent with the American ideal.

We do not point with any degree of satisfaction to the fact that the growth of companionship in social relations of the sexes has led to a decline of the role of romantic love. This can only be viewed approvingly if the decline is in the *excesses* of romantic love and infatuation, not in love itself, for any lessening of the emphasis on love as the essential basis of mate selection will seriously hamper the realization of the American ideal in the very area (marriage) where it is held in highest esteem and perhaps has its greatest possibility of fulfillment. Any of the following are also threats to the

[4] F. Alexander Magoun, *Love and Marriage*, New York: Harper & Brothers, 1948, p. 4.
[5] H. A. Overstreet, *The Mature Mind*, New York: W. W. Norton & Company, Inc., 1949, p. 103.

American ideal as it applies to mate selection and marriage:

1. Stress on the sameness of the sexes; the contention that men and women are essentially the same and interchangeable in the roles they play in marriage and in society.

2. Implications that individuals are not unique and that a dozen or more persons of the other sex would do as well as a marriage partner for one seeking a mate.

3. Approval of personal happiness, or personal adjustment, as the sufficient cause for marrying and for remaining married, with the suggestion that one rationally "selects" a mate with traits and characteristics that will assure happiness or adjustment. These threats to love as the basis for marriage are implicit in the rationalistic marriage model.

Love as the basis for marriage has been attacked by serious students of the family, particularly some proponents of the rationalistic marriage model. Love must prove itself a worthy basis for marrying; otherwise it is still in danger of being replaced as an ideal by some rational method of mate "selection."

On Being Someone

One of the disconcerting things about love as the basis for marriage is that love can only be experienced by relatively mature persons. The hard facts are these: to love someone you must first be someone; to love someone you must first love yourself.

The convictions supporting the American ideal take an exalted view of the capacity of man to be someone; but in the reality of everyday life one not uncommonly meets individuals who are immature. They are almost completely lacking in self-respect; they are without commitment to past or future, rudderless, other-directed. Such persons cannot be accused of self-love, even in the baser sense of egocentricism or selfishness, for one cannot be said to be self-centered about a self that does not exist. One must be someone to be selfish; one must be someone to be egocentric. To love oneself one must first be a mature person. Until one has attained some degree of maturity one can relate to others only as one who receives; there is nothing to give to a relationship of equals such as American democratic marriage demands.

Self-Love

One must be someone to love someone, but, also, to love someone one must first love one's self.

> Selfish and self-love . . . are opposites. . . . The selfish person does not love himself too much but too little, in fact he hates himself. . . . He is necessarily unhappy and anxiously concerned to snatch from life the satisfactions which he blocks himself from attaining.[6]

To love yourself and yet be able to love others or, better still, to love yourself so that you can love others requires that you accept yourself as a person worthy of respect, that you recognize your talents and capacities as well as your faults and limitations. It requires further that you resolve the anxiety inherent in self-awareness and that you have a plan for maximizing your abilities and living with and minimizing your limitations.

This is an exacting set of demands and would sound as though only perfect persons are capable of love. But there are no perfect persons, and certainly it has been demonstrated over and over again that persons who are something less than perfect are able to enter love relationships. So we say there must be a measure of self-acceptance and self-

[6] Erich Fromm, *Man for Himself*, New York: Rinehart & Company, Inc., 1947, pp. 130–131.

respect before one person can confront another as an equal and enter a relationship based on love between equals.

How large a measure of self-acceptance and self-respect is necessary in order to love others as equals we cannot say. We do know that it is also possible to be too self-sufficient so that one does not feel a need for the companionship of others.

The astute student of human nature and writer of short stories, Guy de Maupassant, gives an excellent picture of the too-stable person as lover in his short story, "Moonlight." In the following selection it is the wife who is speaking about her emotionally stable husband:

> You know my husband, and you know how fond of him I am; but he is mature and sensible, and cannot even comprehend the tender vibrations of a woman's heart. He is always, always the same, always good, always smiling, always kind, always perfect. Oh! how I sometimes have wished that he would embrace me with those slow, sweet kisses which make two beings intermingle, which are like mute confidences! How I wished that he was self-abandoned and even weak, so that he should have need of me, of my caresses, of my tears!
>
> This all seems very silly; but we women are made like that. How can we help it? . . .
>
> During the month when we were traveling together, my husband, with his calm indifference, paralyzed my enthusiasm, extinguished my poetic ardor. When we were descending the mountain paths at sunrise, when as the four horses galloped along with the diligence, we saw, in the transparent mountain haze, valleys, woods, streams, and villages, I clasped my hands with delight, and said to him: "What a beautiful scene, darling! Kiss me now!" He only answered, with a smile of chilling kindliness, "There is no reason why we should kiss each other because you like the landscape."
>
> And his words froze me to the heart. It seems to me that when people love each other, they ought to feel more moved by love than ever in the presence of beautiful scenes.
>
> Indeed, he prevented the effervescent poetry that

bubbled up within me from gushing out. How can I express it? I was almost like a boiler, filled with steam, and hermetically sealed.[7]

It is possible to be too self-sufficient and not to feel the need for intimate companionship oneself or to sense the need of it in one's beloved, just as it is possible to be too self-effacing. The optimum standard of self-sufficiency falls somewhere between the extremes of complete dependence and complete self-sufficiency.

The Love of Another

Much of what we have said about attitudes toward oneself—self-love—applies also to attitudes toward others. To love another person in a society where men are free, it is essential that one accept others as persons worthy of respect and as persons who accept and respect themselves. The importance of these attitudes toward oneself and toward others cannot be overemphasized if we are to understand the meaning of love as the basis of marriage.

Love at First Sight

The American way of seeking and finding one's beloved is through the dating process, through which, in a relatively intimate way, one has the opportunity of confronting eligible persons of the other sex. In seeking a date in serious dating, it is on the basis of some conscious or unconscious evaluating of eligible persons that a boy decides whom he will ask for a

[7] *The Great Short Stories of Guy de Maupassant*, New York: Pocket Books, Inc., pp. 196–197.

date—or a girl decides whom she will accept as a date. This "sizing up" of the other person might actually be love at first sight. For it is possible that the first time two people meet, one or both will be impressed by the way in which the other corresponds to an image he holds of a type of person that appeals to him. A person having the features, the bearing, the tastes in grooming and dress, the voice, the smile, the character that he admires can become for him an object of love on first meeting. In other words, he finds the other desirable. Should he on the strength of this first love say, "I love you, will you marry me?" he would be grossly over-estimating the importance of the "desire" aspect of love. But this is not necessarily to say that he was merely infatuated with the other person, but rather that he did not know enough about her as a person to know the potential extent and depth of his love for her.

Most persons we meet do not fulfill our image of an ideal mate in such a striking way. But even so, our choice of persons to date is not random in the sense that anyone would do as well; it is selective on the only basis on which we can be selective until we get to know the person better, namely, on the basis of the traits that first meet the eye. If, through dating, the two persons find each other even more desirable than at first meeting, the relationship may progress beyond this first superficial attachment.

Love Is Personal Desire

Love can be analyzed in terms of three types of relations between lovers. In the first place, it is common for a person in dating another to find the other desirable—desirable to look at, to hold, to caress, to possess. This desire to have and to hold another person for the personal enjoyment and satisfaction one experiences is a part of love. It is sometimes referred to as selfish love because it is *my* desire and *my* satisfaction that is involved. In a sense, I want to use the other person to satisfy my needs and wishes.

In large part love-as-desire refers to desire that is physical in nature, and specifically sexual in nature. But the desirability of another person by no means rests alone in that person's desirability as an object that can provide sexual satisfaction. As Bailey makes clear,

> . . . the fundamental, essential element is desire—a will-to-possess seeking satisfaction, either on the sensual or on the supersensual plane, in the attainment and enjoyment of its object. This desire is determined entirely by appreciation of a value residing in its object, and with attainment or possession it is fulfilled and ceases.
>
> There is no need to minimize or deprecate the "selfish" element, the *eros*, in love. If love has any meaning at all, the beloved must be allowed an objective value by reason of which she is sought, and possession of her is desired. . . . *Eros* therefore is always an indication of the beloved's value, though it is not always the true measure of that value.[8]

When viewed apart from other elements in a love relationship, love-as-desire may appear to be more akin to lust than to love, and in a sense this is correct, for it is only when love-as-desire (*eros*) is combined with other aspects of love that it becomes a love consistent with the American ideal.

Desire in the form of lust is out of keeping in a society of equals. In such a society it may be right to use things selfishly; it is never right to use other people in this way.

Desire is a normal, natural part of love of one person for another. But it is not enough; only in combination does it become love-enough-to-marry-on. We proceed to these other aspects of the love relationship.

[8] Derrick S. Bailey, *The Mystery of Love and Marriage*, New York: Harper & Brothers, 1952, p. 25.

Love Is Friendship and Companionship

An essential aspect of a love relationship is friendship or companionship (*filia*). *Eros* is the desire of one to experience another; *filia*, on the other hand, is characterized by mutual desire to be together and do things together.

The things which two persons forming a "community of love" may share are almost limitless. Some of their variety, as well as their importance to a love relationship, are pointed out in the paragraphs which follow.

Common interests may not directly evoke love, but they do provide a setting favorable to its expression, maintenance, and growth. Interest and participation in the same activities are signs of like-mindedness on the part of the partners, and cultivating these interests together involves the kind of companionship and teamwork that can strengthen a friendship or love relationship. Studies of the activities of engaged couples indicate that both the number and kind of common interests in which the couple participate together make for congeniality and unity.

Not all activities have the same effect on the relationship, however. Outdoor sports and other out-of-home activities which partners may enjoy engaging in together may contribute little to pair unity, whereas joint artistic, intellectual, and religious activities have more meaning for the relationship. Activities traditionally associated with marriage and the home, such as the desire to establish and maintain a home, the desire for quiet home life, bearing and rearing children, and religious activity, strengthen the husband-wife bond.

With increased educational opportunities for women, more job or career opportunities outside the home, greater freedom of association between the sexes, and overlapping sex roles, the opportunities for intellectual and social interstimulation and response are greatly enhanced for married partners. "An educated man values intellectual companionship in a wife more than beauty or proficiency in the household arts." [9]

It is not with just any desirable person of the other sex one chooses to mate, but with one with whom one finds an affinity, a certain compatibility and a community of interests. Lovers in this sense of the word are "pals," companions, who enjoy being together and doing things together.

Love Is a Vision and a Desire to Serve

Love is more than *my* desire and it is more than *our* companionship. It is in its third aspect that love gives fullest expression to the American ideal of dignity and capacity for growth inherent in each individual.

Before I say that I love a person it is necessary that I see and appreciate him (her) in all his uniqueness as a human being—that I see him as all that he sees himself to be and more. I must not only see him and accept him as he is, I must see him as all that he can become with proper stimulation in a love relationship, or community of love.

It is the romantic moment when I see my beloved as he (she) is and catch a vision of all that he can become—a "vision of perfection." Not that he is perfect, but as I perceive him I empathize so completely with him. I understand and appreciate all the qualities that are his, all the things that he does, all that he is capable of becoming.

There can be no love without the experience of meeting in personal relation, and that is impossible if my beloved is merely an object of my love. Each of the lovers must become a person to the other in all his freedom, dignity, and

[9] Ernest W. Burgess and Harvey S. Locke, *The Family: From Institution to Companionship*, New York: American Book Company, 1945, p. 325.

uniqueness. This is the kind of vision which calls forth a willingness and eagerness to love and serve one's beloved as one loves and serves himself. Each must know, understand, and appreciate the other not only as someone to be experienced and enjoyed—a love object—but as someone to be honored, respected, and served so that each feels that he contributes to the support and to the growth toward perfection of the other.

Ideally, it is only persons with such a vision of each other who should commit themselves to a life together. It is an important point; love-as-vision is not a romantic illusion in the glow of which the couple members hope to live out their lives together passively. Rather the vision calls for a commitment to remain together and serve each other, that is, a commitment to love, with no termination date for the love relationship.

> How do I love thee? Let me count the ways.
> I love thee to the depth and breadth and height
> My soul can reach, when feeling out of sight
> For the ends of Being and ideal Grace.
> I love thee to the level of every day's
> Most quiet need, by sun and candle-light.
> I love thee freely, as men strive for right;
> I love thee purely, as they turn from praise.
> I love thee with the passion put to use
> In my old griefs, and with my childhood's faith.
> I love thee with a love I seemed to lose
> With my lost saints—I love thee with the breath,
> Smiles, tears, of all my life! and, if God choose,
> I shall but love thee better after death.[10]

The great error in romantic love is not the encounter—the vision—as two lovers meet each other and find deep communion, but a tendency to over-idealize each other and an inability or unwillingness to accept each other's humanness and frailty. It is also a failure of attitude and will, a

[10] Elizabeth Barrett Browning, *Sonnets from the Portuguese.*

failure to make—when each feels sure of his love—a commitment to be faithful to each other. When each has seen a vision of the other, the exchange of vows of fidelity is a natural step in the relationship, growing out of a desire to be together and serve each other forever.

It is this serving of the beloved without regard to personal reward that is sometimes referred to as *agape*. It is the leaven that keeps selfish sexual desire, for instance, from lapsing into anarchy. *Agape* does not take the place of *eros* but it does come to pervade and mellow all aspects of the love relationship. In a relationship of trust and respect lovers feel free to confide and to act. Through conversation, sexual intercourse, and every medium of communication and interaction available to them, the two serve each other in love. Each, confident of the other's good will, is able not only to give to his beloved, but also to receive from his beloved what is offered in return.

Love is a combination of feeling for another, devotion to another, and commitment to be faithful [11] to another. It is known not by the number of times that each says "I love you," but it is known by its fruits. Each *is* faithful and each does show personal growth—these are the fruits of love.

To see love in its full import, we might contrast it with the romantic illusion of love as a powerful, though extremely fickle, feeling of one for another which can never be captured or brought under subservience to the will of the lover. This kind of love does not lead to confidence and trust in the love of one's beloved but constant doubt and fear that the feeling of one for the other may die or that one's love feeling may attach itself to another love object. In this kind

---

[11] Love-as-faithfulness is at the very heart of the love spoken of in the Judaic-Christian marriage model. Jesus Christ did not command his followers to *be in love*; this command no one—even God—could make of another unless the creature was a puppet of the Creator. But Jesus commanded *to love*. "Love thy neighbor as thyself" does not mean that one is commanded to be in love with his neighbor. One may find even his closest neighbor—namely, his beloved—both unlovely and unlovable at times. He is commanded to love even when he does not feel like it.

of love "the signs of love are demanded, disbelieved, and demanded again. The oftener they are required, the oftener they are simulated; the more often they are distrusted, the more often further reassurance is demanded—until it is a wonder that any sound currency for conducting valid exchange remains in use at all." [12]

Love Is Tragic

Lest we create the illusion of a perfect love relationship between two finite and imperfect persons, we must caution that a love relationship has tragic aspects, too. In love the identities of the two are not swallowed up in one. Two wills to power continue to exist and assert themselves, often at the expense of the relationship between them, and even to the destruction of one or both of them. There is always some degree of tension between what the lovers want for each other and for their life together and what each wants for himself.

Secondly, the lovers do not live in isolation. There are demands upon their time and energy from their children, for children are commonly a part of the creative expression of married love; there are also demands of the community and the larger society. All of these demands interrupt the privacy of lovers and require that their attention be directed elsewhere.

Thirdly, there are the human frailties of both to contend with—the tragedy of betrayal and the tragedy of failure. Even marriages of well-intentioned persons sometimes end in failure.

Lastly, as human beings, the lovers are aware of the temporal quality of themselves and their love, for even the

[12] Foote, *op. cit.*, pp. 250–251.

best of human relationships have a beginning and an ending.

The mature person learns to live always with the possibility of tragedy, but does not let it dominate his life. So two lovers, once they are sure of their love and have made vows of fidelity to each other, prepare for a succession of new and exciting experiences together in engagement, marriage, and parenthood.

> Love is patient and kind; love is not jealous or boastful; it is not arrogant or rude. Love does not insist on its own way; it is not irritable or resentful; it does not rejoice at wrong, but rejoices in the right. Love bears all things, believes all things, hopes all things, endures all things.[13]

Summary

As analyzed in this chapter, there are ideally four necessary aspects to a relationship between lovers. First, each individual must be a self-respecting individual. Each must love himself. Secondly, each must find the other a desirable object to experience and enjoy both sensually and supersensually. Third, the couple must feel a oneness and a desire to be together and to share experiences—many experiences but not all experiences. Fourth, each must see the other as a being of great worth, per se—worthy of one's service and worthy of every opportunity for growth and development as a person. This is love in keeping with the exalted demands of the American ideal.

QUESTIONS AND PROJECTS

1. Why is love called the only basis of marriage consistent with the American ideal?

[13] I Corinthians 13:4–7.

2. Why is the immature or poorly adjusted person apt to fall in love more suddenly and at an earlier age than the more mature person?
3. Distinguish between *eros, filia,* and *agape.*
4. What is the difference between loving and being in love?
5. Love is usually associated with happiness. Under what conditions is it appropriate to speak of love as tragedy?

SUGGESTED READINGS

Bailey, Derrick S., *The Mystery of Love and Marriage,* New York: Harper & Brothers, 1952, Part I.

Bertocci, Peter A., *The Human Venture in Sex, Love, and Marriage,* New York: Association Press, 1951.

Biegel, Hugo G., "Romantic Love," *American Sociological Review,* Vol. 16, June 1951, pp. 326–334.

Burgess, Ernest W., and Harvey J. Locke, *The Family: From Institution to Companionship,* New York: American Book Company, 1945, Chapter 12.

———, and Paul Wallin, *Engagement and Marriage,* Chicago: J. B. Lippincott Co., 1953, Chapter 7.

Foote, Nelson N., "Love," *Psychiatry: Journal for the Study of Interpersonal Processes,* Vol. 16, August 1953, pp. 245–251.

Forell, George W., *Faith Active in Love,* New York: The American Press, 1954.

Knight, Thomas S., "In Defense of Romance," *Marriage and Family Living,* XXI, May 1959, pp. 107–110.

Magoun, F. Alexander, *Love and Marriage,* New York: Harper & Brothers, 1948.

Martinson, Floyd M., "Ego Deficiency As a Factor in Marriage," *American Sociological Review,* Vol. 20, April 1955, pp. 161–164.

Martinson, Floyd M., "Ego Deficiency As a Factor in Marriage —A Male Sample," *Marriage and Family Living,* XXI, February 1959, pp. 48–52.

Rougemont, Denis de, *Love in the Western World,* New York: Pantheon Books, 1956.

Wood, Leland F., *Harmony in Marriage,* New York: Round Table Press, 1955.

8 The Beloved

When he (she) comes into view, what will my beloved be like?

Most young persons hope at some time to fall in love and marry. In anticipation of this exciting stage in life, one is inclined to speculate as to what the beloved will be like and to set up a conscious or unconscious image of him (her).

It is no longer generally held that two persons are fated for each other or, even in religious circles, that God has a specific mate picked out for the "believer." Nevertheless, when one encounters his beloved she will be a specific person, unique and unlike anyone else. Though one could perhaps work out a satisfying marriage relationship with a number of eligibles, the person with whom one falls in love is not merely one of a type but a specific, unique person with whom one establishes a unique married life, not like the life with any other potential mate. This we must make very clear, for one of the modern-day contentions is the notion that any one of a dozen to a hundred eligible persons might do as well as one's mate; but each individual is unique and a marriage made up of two unique persons is unique. If we believe in the dignity and individuality of each person, we must not—in our enthusiasm to get rid of the notion that two persons are fated for each other—substitute an equally objectionable concept, the concept of sameness or inter-changeability of persons as potential mates. Values inherent in the rationalistic marriage model easily lend themselves to such an interpretation.

In the American mate-selection system with individual free choice of a mate, theoretically there might appear to be limitless possibilities for choice, and any prediction of the type of person that might catch one's fancy would seem to be the sheerest kind of guesswork. But, in reality, people are not so fickle in their choices. As we pointed out in the first chapter there is an organization and direction to the choices we make. This is true even of so-called "choices of the heart." A young person grows up in a particular society with its values and behavior patterns. More specifically, he grows up in a subculture and within a particular family that makes the values of the society specific for him. Out of this and out of his own unique experiences he fashions mental images (consciously and unconsciously) about the kinds of people he likes and enjoys being with. So it cannot be said that a person begins serious dating without "specifications" concerning his future beloved.

What will one's beloved be like? What specifications does a serious dater carry with him as he seeks a beloved? Will the beloved meet these specifications in whole or in part? Such questions cannot be answered with finality, but some tentative answers can be given based on studies of the experiences of others.

The Image of the Ideal Mate

The term ideal mate suggests that a person has a mental image of the idealized characteristics of the person, or the type of person, he wishes to marry and that this image influences his search for a beloved. For the adolescent with his "crushes," this ideal mate is apt to be some imaginary or inaccessible person—an adult, a movie star, or other "popular" person. It may be a person known for his physique, beauty of face and form, courage, daring, charm, or poise.

As the adolescent begins to date with some regularity and begins to think more seriously of life with one of the other sex, the romantic image begins to show signs of realism. He becomes conscious of the importance others attach to character, social status, racial and religious background, economic status, educational achievement, etc., and incorporates them into his image.

An adolescent is apt to have an overriding interest in persons with "pleasing personalities who like to do things" during random dating days, but the traits of character and social standing approved by his parents and other adults take on ever increasing importance.

The adolescent growing into adulthood may not be consciously aware that he has a mental image of an ideal mate. He may be more or less aware, however, of the persons or categories of persons whom he would not consider as potential marriage partners. In fact, a chief function of the image of the ideal mate is negative. It eliminates many persons with whom one may be in proximity from consideration as potential marriage partners.

How influential is one's image? Strauss asked a group of engaged and married couples to comment on the question: "How important do you feel the 'ideal' was in picking your fiancé(e)?" Only 19 per cent of the men and 26 per cent of the women reported that the image of the ideal mate was unimportant. Two-thirds of the men and about the same proportion of the women believed it was important or at least of some importance.[1]

Parental Image

There has been much speculation regarding the extent to which the image of the ideal mate is a parental image, that is, that a person falls in love with someone possessing personality characteristics of the parent of the other sex. The interviews with engaged couples reported by Burgess and Wallin reveal some interesting differences in the effect of parental image upon choice of beloved.

One explanation seemed applicable to most of the cases. A person tended to fall in love with someone who resembled the parent with whom he had closest affectional relations as a child. If the child had had an unsatisfactory relationship with one parent—typically of the other sex—he was often attracted to an engagement partner with directly opposite traits from those of the offending parent. These latter cases —cases of negative parental image—were much less common than the first type, however.

The Desire for Intimate Association

The desire for satisfactions gained from intimate association is another factor that family researchers have singled

[1] Anselm Strauss, "The Influence of Parent-Image Upon Marital Choice," *American Sociological Review,* Vol. 11, 1946, pp. 544–559.

out as having an important influence on who marries whom. Among the satisfactions which one hopes to receive in intimate associations with others are "love and affection, confidence, sympathy, understanding, dependence, encouragement, intimate appreciation, and emotional security."

Normally the family of procreation stimulates and satisfies these desires during childhood and adolescence. But as the young person becomes emancipated from his parents and siblings in the parental home, he also becomes emancipated from the type of intimacy that characterizes associations in the parental home. In our society one gains complete social approval only if he receives the largest measure of this intimacy from his beloved rather than from his parents and siblings.

Some persons are dependent on a mate for a wide range of satisfactions, other couples report only a few, and a few claim to be emotionally independent and self-sufficient. Some couples report that both desire the same types of satisfactions, whereas in other cases only one partner reports the desire for a particular satisfaction which is met in intimate association with the other. In a small minority of cases, however, engaged persons did report that all of their major desires for satisfaction were met through intimate association with their affianced.

This is further substantiated by Strauss. Only 18 per cent of the men and women reported that all their major personality needs were satisfied in the relationship with their fiancé(e)s or spouses. An additional 12 per cent of the men and 24 per cent of the women stated that at least four-fifths, but not all, of their needs were fulfilled. On the other hand, 29 per cent of the men and 18 per cent of the women reported that less than two-fifths of their needs were being satisfied in their relation.

In answer to the question posed at the beginning of the chapter, "What will my beloved be like?" We have said so far that she will likely be someone who at least in part corresponds to one's image of the ideal mate and who at least in part satisfies the personality needs that can be met only in intimate association with other persons.

Homogamy in Physical Traits

In regard to physical traits, it is not uncommon to hear statements to the effect that opposites attract and even that marriages of opposites are somehow more interesting, exciting, or ideal than marriages of persons who are alike. The

"I don't know what you see in an old millionaire like me."
Reproduced courtesy of Chon Day.

DATING: THE AMERICAN MATE-SELECTION SYSTEM

reader may have heard it said that tall men tend to marry short women, blonds tend to pick brunettes, or that "fair-skinned" and "olive-skinned" persons are attracted to each other.

Perhaps these statements are made because in instances where couple members are "opposites" the disparity in physical traits is more noticeable to the observer, whereas couple members who are more nearly alike are not noticed. Be that as it may, the empirical evidence, on the basis of over 150 studies, points to the fact that like tends to fall in love with like. Not many of the studies have dealt specifically with physical traits, but what evidence there is by and large supports the contention that persons of similar stature (height and weight) tend to marry each other, blonds tend to marry blondes, "good-looking" people tend to marry "good-looking" people, and persons in good (or poor) health tend to marry each other. Though most of the correlations are of a low order, they are generally in the direction of homogamous mating on these physical characteristics.

Homogamy in Social Characteristics

It is in regard to social characteristics that the principle of homogamy has been most strikingly demonstrated. In the study of engaged couples by Burgess and Wallin, 47 of 51 social traits showed statistically significant differences in the direction of homogamous choices (Table 3). "This comparison is expressed in terms of the ratio of the actual resemblance to expected similarity. The way this ratio is calculated may be concretely illustrated. Everyone knows, for example, that a high proportion of engagements and marriages are of couples of the same as compared with those of different faiths. Usually Catholics mate with Catholics, Jews with

TABLE 3 *Similarity of Members of Engaged Couples on Social Characteristics*

Religious Affiliation and Behavior	Ratio of Actual to Expected Similarity [a]
Religious affiliation	2.14
Church attendance	1.69
Sunday school attendance	1.42
Church membership	1.43

Family Backgrounds	
Place lived in childhood (large city, village, etc.)	1.49
Nativity of parents (native-born, foreign-born)	1.48
Education	1.37
Present income of parents	1.34
Social status of parents (upper class, middle class, etc.)	1.28
Living at present (with parents, relatives, friends, etc.)	1.25

Courtship Behavior	
Age began keeping company	1.55
Persons gone with steady besides fiancé(e)	1.27
Discussed engagement (with no one, one, two, three persons)	1.25
Previously engaged	1.10

Conceptions of Marriage	
Should fiancé(e) work after marriage	1.64
Number of children desired	1.42
Attitude toward having children	1.31
When spouse ceases to be in love (divorce, separate, continue together)	1.28
Object to fiancé(e) having dates during engagement	1.26
Head of family (husband, wife, neither)	1.25
Prefer apartment to house	1.19
Romantic marriages more successful	1.19
Negative factors in conception of marriage (none, one or more)	1.18
Wife keep own name after marriage	1.19
Divorce justifiable if no unfaithfulness	1.15
Present sex knowledge adequate for marriage	1.15
Ever marry if not in love	1.09
Divorce justifiable	1.06
Object to fiancé(e)'s going out with opposite sex	1.06

	Ratio of Actual to Expected Similarity [a]
Conceptions of Marriage	
Positive factors in conceptions of marriage	1.07
First sex information (wholesome, partly wholesome, unwholesome)	1.08
Social Participation	
Drinking habits	1.81
Smoking habits	1.38
Prefer play or dance	1.31
Leisure-time preferences (stay at home, or go most of time, etc.)	1.29
Object if fiancé(e) smokes	1.12
Friends of opposite sex (none, one to seven, etc.)	1.10
Organizations regularly attended	1.09
Offices in organizations belong to now	1.09
Offices in organizations belonged to in past	1.08
Friends of same sex	1.07
Considered indifferent to the opposite sex	1.06
Family Relationships	
Attitude toward father at present	1.11
Attitude to siblings	1.15
Attitude toward father when a child	1.09
Rating of parents' marriage	1.14
Sex of siblings	1.11

SOURCE: Adapted with permission from *Engagement and Marriage* by Ernest W. Burgess and Paul Wallin, pp. 206–207, Table 14. Copyright 1953 by J. B. Lippincott Company.

[a] It is important to note that of the 51 social traits of engaged couples investigated, only 4 failed to show a statistically significant preponderance in favor of homogamous unions over those that would have occurred in matching by chance. In Tables 3 and 4 the possibilities that the difference between the actual and the expected percentages of similarities of couples could have occurred by chance are less than one out of a hundred.

Jews, and Protestants with Protestants. But there are also many unions of those with mixed faiths. It is, therefore, interesting to figure the ratio of the actual marrying of 'like with like' faith to that which occur by pure chance. If the 1000 men and the 1000 women in the Burgess-Wallin study had been mated by chance, 37.1 per cent would be of the same religious affiliation. Instead of this theoretical expectation, actually those with the same religious affiliation (both Catholic, Jewish, Protestant, and none) are 79.4 per cent of the couples. The ratio of the actual to the similarity expected by chance is then 79.4 per cent divided by 37.1 per cent, or 2.14. By obtaining this ratio it can be definitely stated that engaged couples of this particular study resemble each other in religious affiliation more than twice as often as the theoretical outcome calculated on the basis of mating by pure chance." [2]

The data in Table 3 give impressive evidence of the extent to which the 1000 engaged couples were more alike than chance on social characteristics. They were most alike in religious affiliation and behavior and next most alike in family backgrounds and in dating behavior. They were least alike in social participation and family relationships, but even here they were significantly more alike than chance on all the items listed. The evidence from this and other studies seems quite convincing: homogamy in social characteristics is an important factor in limiting and influencing the type of person with whom one is most likely to fall in love.

Personality Characteristics: Homogamous or Complementary?

Of the 42 personality traits studied by Burgess and Wallin, only 14 showed a greater than chance expectation for homogamous union of engaged couples. Besides this, the actual similarities on personality characteristics are not as

[2] Ernest W. Burgess and Paul Wallin, *Engagement and Marriage*, Chicago: J. B. Lippincott Co., 1953, p. 205.

marked (Table 4) as they are for social characteristics. However, there is a fairly strong tendency for persons with neurotic symptoms to be engaged to others like themselves and

TABLE 4 *Similarity of Members of Engaged Couples in Personality Characteristics As Indicated by Replies to Thurstone's Neurotic Inventory*

Personality Item	Ratio of Actual to Expected Similarity [b]
Neurotic Score	1.13
Do you daydream frequently? [a]	1.17
Are you frequently burdened by a sense of remorse?	1.10
Are you sometimes the leader at social affairs?	1.11
Does some particular useless thought keep coming into your mind to bother you?	1.05
Do you usually feel that you are well-dressed and make a good appearance?	1.04
Are you touchy on various subjects?	1.14
Do you feel that you must do a thing over several times before you leave it?	1.10
Are your feelings easily hurt?	1.13
Do you often experience periods of loneliness?	1.10
Do ideas often run through your head so you cannot sleep?	1.09
Do your interests change quickly?	1.07
Do you often feel just miserable?	1.06
When you were in school did you hesitate to volunteer in a class recitation?	1.04
Do you get stage fright?	1.10

SOURCE: *From Engagement and Marriage* by Ernest W. Burgess and Paul Wallin, p. 208, Table 16. Copyright 1953 by J. B. Lippincott Company.

[a] All questions could be answered "yes," "no," or "?."
[b] The probability that the differences in this table between the actual and expected percentages of similar responses are chance differences is .01 or less.

for nonneurotics to become engaged to nonneurotics (Neurotic Score 1.13).

The fact that studies by and large show low over-all correlations between couple members on personality characteristics deserves further consideration. Robert Winch in particular has given attention to this problem and has suggested an alternative theory to explain the selective principle at work regarding personality characteristics of couples. According to Winch, there are strong theoretical reasons for believing that within the field of eligibles, people tend to mate with those whose need patterns generally complement their own, rather than with those whose need patterns are similar to their own. In other words, we fall in love with those who complete us by satisfying our feelings of ego deficiency.

To accept the theory of complementary personality needs is not to deny the theory of homogamous selection on some personality characteristics. Nor does the theory of complementary needs imply that complementariness is an overriding factor in falling in love, setting aside other considerations. One's beloved will likely come out of a family and social group characterized by racial, religious, nationality, and socioeconomic traits which one respects—the source of the eligibles.

It is difficult to separate and define the various traits of human personality for purposes of testing complementariness, and it may be too soon to ascertain the extent to which complementariness is a factor in falling in love. However, there is sufficient empirical evidence to date to warrant serious consideration of complementariness as one of a complex of factors limiting and influencing the direction in which one's inclinations lead him in his search for a marriage partner.

The Influence of One's Associates

In addition to the image of an ideal mate, one's desire for satisfactions derived from intimate association, and homogamy and complementariness, the influence of one's associates during the dating stage of life is a factor to consider in choosing the object of one's affection.

Sussman has shown in an interview study involving 195 parent-child relationships that in 166 cases parents sought to influence their children to select mates of similar background by providing for their children a proper dating milieu and by using persuasion and threats to withdraw economic support should they marry outside the social class. In 145 of 166 cases the children appeared to comply with their parents' hopes.[3]

There are also peer groups or cliques in the school or community that have a profound influence on dating choices of young people. A recent study suggests that the influence of one's peers at the time when one is dating seriously may be strong enough to set aside the promptings of the homogamy-oriented norms of the parents. The study involved the degree of homogamous choice of mate in 88 marriages of Purdue University students. Leslie and Richardson found "no homogamous tendency whatsoever" among the couples who met and married while on campus.

> Since there appear to be no other major differences between the met-at-home and the met-at-college, this suggests, though it doesn't prove conclusively, that the direct environmental pressures operating on the two groups account for the differences in their marital pattern. The campus situation, by encouraging the association of persons of diverse backgrounds and through its formal democratic norms, appears to favor heterogamous pairings, while pairings initiated off the campus and in the vicinity of the parental home show some tendency toward homogamy. In this instance, at least, direct group pressures operating at the time of marriage seem to be at least as influential as homogamy-oriented norms that may have been internalized at earlier ages.[4]

[3] Marvin B. Sussman, "Parental Participation in Mate Selection," *Social Forces*, Vol. 32, 1954, pp. 76–81.
[4] George R. Leslie and Arthur H. Richardson, "Family Versus Campus Influences in Relation to Mate Selection," *Social Problems*, Vol. 4, October 1956, p. 121.

Propinquity

In the last analysis, of course, one's beloved will have to be a person from among those one has met and had a chance to get to know quite intimately. This means that one must meet eligibles and be sufficiently attractive to them to be received as a date or be asked for a date. In a mate-selection system where young persons pick their own mates, proximity becomes a crucial factor in the choice. "Who will she be?" can, from this point of view, be answered simply—"She will be someone whom you know or will get to know in the future."

Even in large cities with mobile populations, persons who marry commonly lived in the same residential area at the time they met, went to the same school, worked at the same or related occupations, attended the same church, or frequented the same recreational establishments. If one's beloved lives in the same community and attends the same church, it is likely that the two have more in common than just happening to be in the same place at the same time. If one's beloved lives in one's community she may very well be of the same race, of the same ethnic group, and of the same religion. For, historically, it is a principle of American community settlement that "birds of a feather flock together," and it is quite understandable that one commonly falls in love with a member of the "flock," for there is a more ready acceptance of persons like oneself and greater prospects for common agreement on values and norms.

Timing

Last but not least, one's beloved must come along at the right time, as well as in the right place. Levy and Munroe have suggested that *when* may actually be more important than *whom*. Meeting an eligible person when one feels that he is ready for serious dating may be the decisive factor in his falling in love with one person rather than with another. As one young man described his situation, timing was an important element.

Our present relationship has led us to planning for the future. My status with the draft board is quite uncertain and I will probably be going into the service soon after I graduate. We have talked it over and it is quite a problem on what to do. She does not want to go out with anyone else while I am gone and things being as serious as they are it would not work out if either of us actually did start to date while we are apart. I am not ready to get married yet. There are too many things I want to do before settling down. Our status being what it is and her feelings being what they are I find it impossible to level with her completely. I do not intend to become engaged before going into the service. I think this will be a good time to test our feelings towards each other and will give me a chance to get a few things out of my system. It will probably result in my not being completely honest with her but if it does not change my feelings towards her and only gives me a chance to let off steam it will probably result in more happiness for both of us. If things do change, this is the best time for it to happen.

Summary

No two persons are alike and the person with whom one falls in love will be a unique person, not quite like any other person that one has ever met. Yet, having said this, it is possible even in advance of meeting to forecast with some degree of accuracy what some of the characteristics of one's beloved are apt to be. First, many persons carry an image of the kind of person they would like to marry and this may influence the choice of a mate, at least by eliminating some from consideration. Secondly, some persons of the other sex satisfy one's personality needs for affection, sympathy, and understanding better than others do, and it is likely that one will marry a person who gives such satisfaction. Thirdly, one's beloved is apt to be more like than unlike oneself in health and physical characteristics. Fourthly, one's beloved will more than likely come from a family background with similar behavior patterns and values to one's own. The likes and dislikes of one's parents and peers may also influence the choice of persons to date and marry; and, finally, one's beloved will, of course, be a person whom one has met and gotten to know at a time when one is "in the mood" and ready for love.

In this chapter we have discussed some empirically demonstrated factors that play a part in the directing of love focus on one person rather than on someone else. We have not said, however, that these are the factors which should be operative, nor have we said that in any particular case any one or more of these factors will determine who falls in love with whom. What we have said is that, generally speaking, these are factors that limit and influence the direction of one's love focus.

In large part the actor—lover—may not be conscious of the extent to which these factors limit and influence his love behavior, but it has been empirically demonstrated, as reported in this chapter, that these are factors which tend to play a part whether the individual consciously brings them into play or not. To have some knowledge of them may help the reader to know and appreciate what is happening in his own life when the time comes and help him to appreciate not less but more the exciting process of falling in love.

1. How does the image of the ideal mate change as the emerging adult grows in social awareness and experience with the opposite sex?
2. What personality needs are satisfied in whole or in part through association with loved ones?
3. Does like marry like? Physically? Socially?
4. To what aspects of mate selection does the theory of complementary needs apply?
5. Does the dater listen to his parents or to his peers in choosing friends or a mate? Discuss.
6. Is it possible to predict within broad limits the attributes of one's beloved? In what sense is it correct to say that he (she) will be a unique person?

SUGGESTED READINGS

Benson, Purnell, "The Interests of Happily Married Couples," *Marriage and Family Living*, Vol. XIV, November 1952, pp. 276–280.

Bertocci, Peter A., *The Human Venture in Sex, Love, and Marriage*, New York: Association Press, 1951.

Black, Algernon D., "If I Marry Outside My Religion," *Public Affairs Pamphlet*, No. 204, Public Affairs Committee, Inc., 1954, pp. 1–28.

Burgess, Ernest W., and Paul Wallin, *Engagement and Marriage*, Chicago: J. B. Lippincott Co., 1953, Chapters 6, 7.

Foote, Nelson N., "Matching of Husband and Wife in Phases of Development," Reprint No. 7, Family Study Center, University of Chicago. Reprinted from *Transactions of the Third World Congress of Sociology*, Vol. IV.

Himes, Joseph S., "A Value Profile in Mate Selection Among Negroes," *Marriage and Family Living*, Vol. XVI, August 1954, pp. 244–247.

Keeley, Benjamin J., "Value Convergence and Marital Relations," *Marriage and Family Living*, Vol. XVII, November 1955, pp. 342–345.

Kirkpatrick, Clifford, *The Family: As Process and Institution*, New York: The Ronald Press Company, 1955, Chapter 13.

Landis, Judson T., "The Challenge of Marriage and Family Life Education," *Marriage and Family Living*, Vol. XIX, August 1957, pp. 247–252.

Landis, Paul H., *Making the Most of Marriage*, New York: Appleton-Century-Crofts, Inc., 1955, Chapters 8–14.

Leslie, Gerald R., and Arthur H. Richardson, "Family Versus Campus Influences in Relation to Mate Selection," *Social Problems*, Vol. 4, October 1956, pp. 117–121.

Roth, Julius, and Robert F. Peck, "Social Class and Social Mobility Factors Related to Marital Adjustment," *American Sociological Review*, Vol. 16, August 1951, pp. 478–487.

Strauss, Anselm, "Personality Needs and Marital Choice," *Social Forces*, Vol. 25, March 1947, pp. 332–335.

Sussman, Marvin B., "Parental Participation in Mate Selection," *Social Forces*, Vol. 32, 1954, pp. 76–81.

Winch, Robert F., *Mate-Selection; A Study of Complementary Needs*, New York: Harper & Brothers, 1958.

9 The Romance or Love Affair

In the chapters on dating and love we described and analyzed some of the general aspects of love affairs in American society. Though in prose and poetry the literature of the Western world is filled with accounts of specific love affairs, there has been, until recently, little systematically compiled empirical evidence on the nature of such affairs.

With the publication of findings based on studies of 1200 engagements, we for the first time have fairly extensive empirical data.[1] The experiences of 226 of these couples, as related to interviewers, are useful in describing and analyzing

[1] One thousand engagements in the Burgess-Wallin Study (Ernest W. Burgess and Paul Wallin, *Engagement and Marriage*, Chicago: J. B. Lippincott Co., 1953) and 200 engagements in the Landis Study (Judson T. and Mary G. Landis, *Building a Successful Marriage*, Englewood Cliffs, N.J.: Prentice-Hall, Inc., 1958). The statistics and quotations in this chapter are from these two studies.

some of the "realism" in "romance." The following discussion relates to actual rather than ideal patterns of developing love relationships.

The Burgess-Wallin Sample

The greater portion of the discussion to follow centers around findings from interviews with the 226 couples, and the reader will need to be informed of some of the characteristics of the sample population of which the 226 interviewed couples are a part. The sample is a selected sample rather than a representative random sample of all classes of engaged couples; hence, the reader is cautioned about making sweeping generalizations based on the findings of the study.

If the sample did not represent all classes of young couples, what classes were represented?

The sample couples were predominantly lower middle-class and upper middle-class persons of native-born parents of the white race. The fathers of the young persons were engaged predominantly in business and the professions.

The sample couples were literate and fairly well educated. More than a third of their parents were college-educated, and 78 per cent of the young men and 65 per cent of the young women had education beyond the high school level. The illiterate were eliminated, for participants had to be capable of filling out a self-report questionnaire in order to be a part of the sample.

Regarding religious affiliation, 50 per cent of the men and women listed their affiliation as Protestant, 18 per cent Jewish, and about 14 per cent Catholic. Viewed against the over-all religious composition of American society, the sample would have to be classified as essentially non-Catholic, particularly Protestant.

Regarding place of residence, the couples were urban rather than rural in background—in fact, many of them lived in metropolitan Chicago.

The importance of the fact that all couples were engaged at the time of the study cannot be minimized. By including only engaged couples in the sample, the impulsive "runaway, overnight" type of marriage was excluded from consideration. The couples in the study had relatively long acquaintances with each other; on the average they had known each other 45.0 months, had been keeping company 31.5 months, and had been engaged 13.2 months. In other words, they are representative of couples with fairly stable relationships.

The sample was self-selected in the sense that the couples were free to cooperate or not to cooperate as they chose. In this way they are volunteers, and the natural question is— who chose to participate? Beyond what we have already reported, it is known that those who participated were younger than those who did not participate. Secondly, they were more likely to be rated radical or liberal in their social and political ideas, rather than conservative or reactionary. Thirdly, the participators and nonparticipators differed in that greater marital success had been predicted for the participating couples.

It is impossible to measure with existing data the extent to which the pattern of events surrounding falling in love has changed in the last two decades, but we are quite certain that it has changed. For this reason it is important to note that the data on engagements in the Burgess-Wallin study were gathered in 1937–1939—twenty years ago.

In summary, data are presented on the development of love and romance among a sample of white, native American, middle-class, well-educated, predominantly Protestant, urban, engaged young persons who twenty years ago agreed to participate in a large-scale questionnaire and interview study of engagement. It is against this background that the data must be evaluated.

Romances Prior to the "Real Thing"

The love affair that leads to marriage is not the first serious affair in which the majority of young people have been involved. Though a considerable proportion, ranging from 20 to 30 per cent, had not kept company with anyone before the association resulting in engagement and marriage, the great majority had one or more associations of exclusive or preferential pairing before the relationship that ended in engagement or marriage. In many cases, engaged persons reported that prior affairs had been taken seriously; some reported that they had been in love in a prior affair and that marriage had been discussed. In fact—contrary to the dalliance theory—one out of two of the relationships preceding the "final" affair achieved sufficient intensity for the participants to think that they had been in love before. Both men and women reported so.

First Meeting

The folklore of our society contains some interesting and exciting notions about the first meeting of lovers—one's mate will suddenly appear, one or both will sense that they were "meant" for each other, they will love each other at "first sight," etc. These, and others, have been a part of the romantic marriage model. But is this the way it really happens? Burgess and Wallin asked the engaged couples, "When you first became interested in your fiancé(e), were you strangers, acquaintances, or friends?"

Almost half of the men and a third of the women indicated that they were interested in their engagement partners on initial encounter. This does not necessarily imply that they experienced love at first sight; it does suggest that one or both were sufficiently interested on first meeting to want to meet again. An additional 20 per cent of the men and 29 per cent of the women thought of themselves as friends of their engagement partners before romance began.

Physical Attraction

It has been said that the initial attraction of two people of the opposite sex for each other is physical in nature. The Chicago subjects were asked, "How soon after you became interested in your fiancé(e) did you first feel a strong physical attraction to him (her)?" Insofar as persons could recall when they first experienced a strong physical attraction, their reports indicated that characteristically the initial interest of couple members in one another did not have a marked physical attraction connected with it. At least, they had no awareness of it.

In the majority of cases, however, physical attraction followed rather quickly, being felt by a majority in less than six months. About a third of the men and women could not recall a strong physical attraction until six months or longer after they were first interested in their engagement partners.

Once physical attraction was experienced, it was generally regarded by both men and women as increasing in strength as the relationship progressed. In response to the question, "Has there been any change in the intensity of the physical attraction?" about 7 out of 10 men and women said it had increased considerably.

Of the 96 men and 69 women who did say they were

interested in their fiancé(e) from the start of their acquaintance, only 17 per cent of the men and 14.5 per cent of the women said that it was immediate or that it occurred within one or two days. Burgess and Wallin conclude that "the percentages at least suggest that when persons are interested from the start in those to whom they later become engaged they do not think of their initial interest as having a marked physical or sexual element."

Telescoped, Extended, and Average Romances

Does Cupid strike suddenly or does one's love grow slowly and imperceptibly? As a result of their interviews, Burgess and Wallin designate three patterns of romance with respect to the rapidity with which persons "travel the distance" from first date to informal engagement. They refer to these three patterns as telescoped, extended, and average courtships.

The telescoped romance is one in which dating, going steady, falling in love, and becoming engaged are compressed into a very short span. The couple's mutual emotional involvement is direct and rapid. The extreme would be love at first sight followed more or less immediately by an understanding as to marriage. It was the impression of the researchers that a "not inconsiderable minority" of couples progress from first meeting to informal engagement in a few months, or even a few weeks.

There are several explanations as to how this rapid development of love and commitment to marriage might come to pass. (1) The person might meet someone who fits his clearly defined ideal image. (2) A person one meets might have characteristics similar to a person previously loved. (3)

One might be lonely because of a lack of meaningful relationships. (4) A person might have an impulsive temperament and labile emotions and be easily moved by a show of love and affection. (5) External conditions such as prosperity or war have their effects, also. These telescoped romances are widely regarded as unwise and vulnerable. Some empirical evidence supporting this contention is presented in the chapter on engagements.

Extended romances are those in which a considerable interval of time elapses between the time the couple members begin to date and the time they become engaged. They are the romances in which the partners are relatively slow in reaching the stage of feeling they are sufficiently in love to get married.

Burgess and Wallin offer several possible explanations why there is extended involvement prior to marriage—a high degree of self-sufficiency; deliberate, reserved, and highly controlled emotional reactions on the part of some persons; fear of sexual intimacy; the experience of having been jilted; a strong career drive on the part of the female.

The average romance, the one characterizing the majority of couples, was neither of the telescoped nor of the extended variety. It lacked "the catapult-like" movement of the former and the drawn-out character of the latter. Couples who fell in love and decided they wished to marry tended to achieve this stage with "moderate rapidity"—from about six months to a year after they first began to date. Landis' study of 200 engagements at the University of California in 1957 also showed "moderate rapidity" in the development of love affairs. Couples reported an average of four and one-half months of casual dating with each other, and eight months of dating steadily before they had an "understanding."

Falling in Love

"To what extent are you in love with your fiancé(e)?" There is in the American concept of romantic love something of the notion of fate, finality, and the complete helplessness of the person once he is caught within the clutches of the love feeling. In order to test the extent to which this "violent and emotional attachment" or "head over heels" love feeling is a reality, Burgess and Wallin asked the question posed above. The responses persons made and the percentages of men and women who made them are shown in Table 5.

TABLE 5 *Percentages of 226 Men and Women Reporting Specified Love for Engagement Partner*

Extent of Love	Men	Women
Head over heels	23.5	24.8
Very much so	70.4	68.1
Somewhat or mildly	6.2	7.1
Total	100.1	100.0

SOURCE: From *Engagement and Marriage* by Ernest W. Burgess and Paul Wallin, p. 170. Copyright 1953 by J. B. Lippincott Company.

The respondents indicated a "highly unsympathetic" attitude toward the stereotyped notion of romantic love. They stated very positively that the stereotype did not apply to them. Some checked "head over heels" to indicate that their love was as great as could be, but they did not mean by it the stereotyped conception. In Landis' study roughly two-thirds of both men and women reported that "it was a gradual falling in love for both." Only 3 per cent reported that both fell in love at first sight.

The data lend themselves to the interpretation that love most commonly develops gradually and almost imperceptibly. This is not to say that there is not a sense of exhilaration and excitement attendant on awareness of being in love. But, according to the Burgess-Wallin couples, these feelings were not usually of the violent, extravagant, and quixotic nature commonly associated with the love of the adolescent or the love of the immature or emotionally starved adult. It is the latter kind of love that is commonly referred to as romantic love.

Reasons Given for Being in Love (or Evidences of Love)

Will I know when I am in love? How will I know? These are questions that plague young people, for the entire decision to marry or not to marry in our society hinges on whether or not the partners are in love.

In the light of this dilemma it may be of comfort to know that persons in the Burgess-Wallin sample reported little difficulty in knowing when they fell in love. Most persons specified the exact day, week, or month. Others reported that they fell in love so gradually that they could not say with any exactness just when it occurred. Only a small minority stated that they did not know whether or not they were in love.[2]

As to reasons why they were in love, some persons admitted that they did not know what it was that brought about their love feeling. But these persons were in the

---

[2] It is interesting to note that in the latter case interviewers reported that they were reasonably sure the persons in question were not in love.

minority; the majority attributed their being in love to three or four of the various factors which are associated with persons falling in love, such as fulfillment of personality needs, fulfillment of the ideal image, mutuality and compatibility of interests and aspirations, physical attraction, and reciprocity of love.

Of these factors, fulfillment of needs was mentioned perhaps more than any other single factor. Unless their attention was turned to it, many persons apparently did not realize that as a result of varied influences they had gradually developed an image of a member of the other sex—ideal image—in which they invested positive emotional feelings.

"Common interests and aspirations" were mentioned as reasons for love by a majority of the engaged couples, while "being loved" was less frequently mentioned as a basis for being in love than any other circumstance. Burgess and Wallin observe that though in and of itself being loved is not a cause of loving someone, it is still a powerful force in perpetuating love after it has developed.

A commonly held assumption that extreme idealization of the beloved is associated with being in love was not supported by the evidence.

Doubts and the Love Affair

The saying that only two things are certain—death and taxes—leaves out reference to love as one of the certainties in life, and many engaged couples would disagree that love does not belong among the certainties of life.

The question, "Have you felt any hesitation at all about marrying your fiancé(e)?" was asked of the 226 interviewees. About one out of two women and four out of ten men reported that at one time or another they had not been sure of their choice of a mate.

The doubts of some men or women as to whether they had found suitable marriage partners were reflected in the fact that one out of four engaged couples stated that relations had at one time been temporarily broken off. Many young people were willing to act on the assumption that greater marital happiness might await them with another person.

Summary

Serious love affairs among two samples of well-educated, middle-class young people were characterized by the fact that they had been preceded by earlier serious love affairs; initial attraction was not basically physical in nature; the average affair developed with moderate rapidity; the partners knew when they were in love and could give some reasons as to why; their love was not of the fanciful, impractical and quixotic romantic variety; and most had been hesitant about marrying the fiancé(e) at some time during the romance.

QUESTIONS AND PROJECTS

1. To what extent are the basic assumptions of the romantic marriage model borne out in the love histories?
2. To what extent do the love affairs in question resemble or differ from love affairs described in current "romance" magazines?
3. To what extent are *eros*, *filia*, and *agape* evident in the reasons given for being in love?

SUGGESTED READINGS

Becker, Howard, and Reuben Hill, *Family Marriage and Parenthood*, Boston: D. C. Heath & Company, 1955, Chapters 7, 8.

Burgess, Ernest W., and Paul Wallin, *Engagement and Marriage*, Chicago: J. B. Lippincott Co., 1953, Chapters 2–7.

Landis, Judson T. and Mary G., *Building a Successful Marriage*, 3rd ed., Englewood Cliffs, N. J.: Prentice-Hall, Inc., 1958, Chapter 13.

Rougemont, Denis de, *Love in the Western World*, New York: Pantheon Books, 1956.

Wylie, William P., *The Pattern of Love*, New York: Longmans, Green & Co., Inc., 1958.

IO   Romance and Reason I

Is there any way in which two people can be sure that they are "right" for each other and that their love relationship will be a rewarding one?

On the admission of young people, by the popularity of discussions on dating, and from the popularity of preparation-for-marriage courses, it is evident that young people take the finding of a loved one seriously and are willing and eager to listen to those who can offer constructive suggestions based on experience and empirical evidence.

Some young people who read this book will have gained the impression from one or a number of popular sources that social scientists in their studies of factors related to marriage success and happiness are now in a position to "test" two persons and predict the success of their marriage. Nothing could be farther from the truth.

Reuben Hill, using sixteen of the so-called predictive factors in a study of family adjustment to the crisis of war, found that only one—wife's childhood happiness score—was reliably important in predicting adjustment early in marriage and adjustment to the crisis of war separation. And Kirkpatrick concluded after reviewing the so-called prediction studies that "Couples should not be counseled in terms of present prognostication scores unless they are able to take the evidence with full awareness of their limitation, especially in the middle of the score range. If marriage is recognized as still a gamble, it is proper to peek at the cards dimly lighted by present scientific knowledge." [1]

This is not to say that studies of factors related to marriage success are of no value. In fact, they are of great value to experts in the field of the family and marriage counseling. In the hands of skilled counselors, the data collected through the use of a marriage-prediction schedule can be of inestimable value in discovering—in a systematic way—the trouble spots in a budding love relationship or in a marriage, with a saving of interviewing time and expense.

For a satisfying and lasting marriage it is a good idea to turn the cold light of reason on the romance before vows of fidelity are exchanged. By suggesting the use of romance plus reason we are not abandoning love as the essential basis for marriage consistent with the American ideal. However, a feeling of close attachment to another person is not necessarily love, and being in love does not necessarily mean that two persons should marry each other. This is not to deny the superior quality of love as the basis for marriage, but love does not always "conquer all." There may be impediments to marriage for two people even though their love seems strong enough to overcome any and all obstacles and demands placed upon them.

[1] Clifford Kirkpatrick, *The Family: As Process and Institution.* Copyright 1955. The Ronald Press Company, pp. 364–365.

In the following pages we raise some basic questions for consideration by the still-single individual as well as by dating couples. Under each question some insight into the considerations involved is presented. Where there are specific empirical findings supporting a point, they are incorporated into the discussion. Most of the empirical evidence comes from the marriage prediction studies.

Self-examination is a wholesome activity if it is of a constructive type leading to realistic appraisal of one's self—one's strengths, weaknesses, values, and motives. The following questions are intended for such self-examination. If the reader comes out with the feeling that he does not measure up very well, it is a normal reaction. If he finds that he measures up completely, he is probably not being honest with himself!

The following discussion is organized in terms of two major questions and a number of subquestions. The two major questions are: first, how well does each partner know himself, his personality type, his motives for marriage, and his preparation for marriage? Secondly, how well does each know and love the other?

Do You Know Yourself and Your Motives for Marriage? Are You Ready for Marriage?

1. *What are your motives for wanting to continue or intensify your present romance?* Ideally, in our society persons marry because they are in love and desire companionship with another free and respected person. But there are motives for marriage other than love and companionship—motives of which even the actor may not be aware. Perhaps no one has entirely pure, wholesome, and unselfish motives for anything he does, but one should be aware of motives that might later sour a relationship.

It is not uncommon to desire love and marriage as a way of getting out of an unpleasant situation or relationship—one is not doing well in school, not getting along with parents, "can't stand" the boss. Or a person may have been jilted in a previous romance and marry on the rebound. Any of these would constitute motives for wanting to make a change, but, in and of themselves, they cannot be considered worthy motives for marrying. It is better to face an unpleasant situation from which one is trying to escape and resolve it in some other way rather than through escape into marriage—though under the circumstances marriage may look like an exciting escape.

Of prime importance in my family was a chronic marital problem which served to distort attitudes and prevent family unity. A number of conditions were present from the beginning which made my parents' marriage a difficult one, and added to this were other problems which became aggravated over the years and which established patterns of bickering, disrespect, and intolerance. As a result of all this tension, I developed some interesting attitudes toward marriage. Possibly the most important was the failure to evaluate marriage for what it actually is, i.e., to idealize the concept of a perfect marriage in which members of the family were all gloriously happy. This was a goal which I believed to be attainable by individual sacrifice for the good of a marriage. Marriage appeared more and more desirable to me as my home situation grew intolerable.

Like escape, pity is an unworthy motive for marriage. In a misguided sense of honor a young person might continue a romance because he knows of no way out without hurting the other person. Insofar as it is genuine, this is a noble sentiment. But in the long run it is more honorable to break a loveless relationship than to make commitments of fidelity to a person one does not love.

Lastly, one's motives for continuing and intensifying a relationship may be the lowest of all motives when judged by the American ideal; namely, for selfish exploitation of the partner. The girl who "strings a boy along" only because he has a car and plies her with entertainment and gifts or the boy who gives his girl a "line" about loving her in order that he may obtain sexual privileges has chosen the lowest of motives. In a society where each person is considered worthy of respect, using another person becomes an unpardonable sin.

2. *Are you expecting too much from your future spouse and your marriage?* If you think that your present monotonous life is going to be a "bed of roses" after you marry, or that your marriage is going to provide all of your satisfactions, you are expecting too much. This is more of a problem for the woman than for the man because she commonly gives up her job and business and some of her social contacts when she marries. The busy, unmarried woman who is tired of her work and outside activities and can hardly wait until she is married to "get away from it all" may find that her marriage cannot satisfy all her desires in the way she thought it could. She may become disillusioned, bored, and easily hurt and blameful of her busy, and hence inattentive, husband.

On the other hand, the husband who says "I am the one who really needs sympathy but my wife is the one who expects it" presents the other side of the coin—a husband with inordinate expectations. As pointed out in an earlier chapter, the majority of individuals have to strike a compromise by securing the satisfactions of some of their desires through intimate association with a mate but not all of them.

Don't put all your eggs in one basket. Expect to get less, but expect to get some of your satisfactions from outside the home even after marriage.

3. *Do you know and accept yourself? Do you plan to retain your identity after marriage?* It is possible to have too good an opinion of oneself. On the other hand, it is possible to be too self-effacing. Somewhere between these two extremes a person must find himself, for it is absolutely essential in our democratic system of love and marriage—love between equals—that

each accept himself according to some fairly honest and correct interpretation of himself. If one does not accept and honor himself and plans instead to lose himself in the life of his beloved after marriage, he commits a kind of suicide. He no longer exists; he allows himself to be swallowed up in another. A marriage in which two become one in this way—the one absorbed in the other—cannot be a creative relationship growing out of the tensions of two real persons living and working together. In a democratic type of love relationship each of the principals remains a self-respecting and respected self.

But not all persons are easy to live with—for themselves or for others. This realization is part of the maturity involved in accepting oneself. There is a real possibility, for instance, that the personality needs or desires of one or both parties to a marriage may be inordinate and not capable of satisfaction by even the most ideal mate. Since persons fall in love partly because of desire for the satisfactions to be obtained in intimate association, it is not unreasonable to expect that the person with the greatest desire for such satisfactions will be more inclined to marry, other things being equal, than the person with less desire for intimate association. There is limited empirical evidence in support of this contention; young persons who are apparently less self-sufficient and more self-centered are drawn into marriage at younger ages than persons more self-sufficient and out-going in their interests. Recent studies of both young women and young men show that "other things being equal (sex, age, intelligence, position in the family, nationality, father's occupation, community and amount of education), persons who marry demonstrate greater feelings of ego deficiency than do persons who remain single." [2] On the average, the girl who was less well adjusted to herself and to her social environment married, whereas her counterpart with better emotional and social adjustments re-

[2] Floyd M. Martinson, "Ego Deficiency As a Factor in Marriage," *American Sociological Review*, Vol. 20, April 1955, p. 163.

mained single for a longer period of time. Also, the boy who was less well adjusted emotionally married shortly after graduating from high school, whereas the better-adjusted boy—who did better work in high school with the same intellectual capacity—commonly postponed marriage and continued in school beyond the high school level.[3] As suggested by de Rougemont, "When body and mind are normally vigorous the chances of love at first sight must be very slender," but when the body or mind are not, the desire to lean on someone else becomes inordinately strong.

The point that one's adjustment to self and to society cannot be overlooked in assessing one's prospects for good adjustment in marriage has been made by Terman.

> . . . we believe that a large proportion of incompatible marriages are so because of a predisposition to unhappiness in one or both of the spouses. Whether by nature or by nurture, there are persons so lacking in the qualities making for compatibility that they would be incapable of finding happiness in any marriage. There are others, less extreme, who could find it only under the most favorable circumstances; and still others whose dispositions and outlooks upon life would preserve them from acute unhappiness, however unfortunately they were mated.[4]

Burgess and Wallin have summarized in tabular form the personality items correlated with marital adjustment in two studies by Terman and associates as well as in their own study. Besides the 1000 engaged couples of the Burgess-Wallin study, 792 California married couples and 567 gifted married couples are represented in the table. Included in the table are personality items in which the differences in responses of both (or either partner) were large enough to be regarded as significant.

[3] Martinson, Floyd M., "Ego Deficiency as a Factor in Marriage—A Male Sample," *Marriage and Family Living*, XXI, February 1959, pp. 48–52.
[4] By permission from *Psychological Factors in Marital Happiness*, by Lewis M. Terman, p. 110. Copyright 1938. McGraw-Hill Book Company, Inc.

TABLE 6 *Personality Items Which Have a Marked Correlation with Marital or Engagement Success Scores*

Personality Item	Nonneurotic Response
Emotionally Stable or Unstable	
Are you often in a state of excitement?	No
Do your feelings alternate between happiness and sadness without apparent reason? [a]	No
Is it harder for you to be serene and cheerful than it is for most people? [a]	No
Do you often feel just miserable? [a]	No
Are you frequently burdened by a sense of remorse or regret? [b]	No
Do you worry too long over humiliating experiences?	No
Do you lose your temper easily? [a]	No
Are you touchy on various subjects? [b]	No
Do you frequently feel grouchy? [b]	No
Does some particular useless thought keep coming into your mind to bother you? [a]	No
Do you consider yourself a rather nervous person?	No
Do you worry over possible misfortunes? [a]	No
Do you have spells of dizziness?	No
Does your mind often wander so badly that you lose track of what you are doing?	No
Do ideas often run through your head so you cannot sleep?	No
Is it easy for you to make up your mind and act on your decision?	Yes
Do you have ups and downs in mood without apparent cause?	No
Considerate or Critical of Others	
Are you considered to be critical of other people?	No
Do you always try carefully to avoid saying anything that might hurt anyone's feelings?	Yes
Do you often disregard feelings of others when accomplishing an end important to you?	No
Yielding or Dominating?	
Do you try to get your own way even if you have to fight for it? [a]	No
In your relations with the opposite sex do you tend to be dominant and have your own way? [a]	No
Do many people think you have an extra good opinion of yourself?	No

Personality Item	Nonneurotic Response
Self-Confident or Lacking Self-Confidence	
Do you lack self-confidence? [b]	No (for men)
If you come late to a meeting would you rather stand than take a front seat?	No (for men)
Do you usually feel that you are well dressed and make a good appearance? [b]	Yes
Emotionally Dependent or Self-Sufficient	
Do you prefer to be alone in times of emotional stress?	No
Do you usually avoid asking advice?	No
Do you want someone to be with you when you receive bad news?	Yes
Do you prefer making hurried decisions alone?	No
Can you stand criticism without feeling hurt?	Yes
Companionable or Isolated	
Do you experience periods of loneliness? [b]	No
Do you often feel lonesome even when you are with other people? [b]	No
Are you troubled with shyness?	No
Do you daydream frequently? [b]	No

SOURCE: From *Engagement and Marriage* by Ernest W. Burgess and Paul Wallin, Table 76, pp. 527–528. Copyright 1953 by J. B. Lippincott Company.

[a] Critical ratio of 3 or higher for differences between high and low responses (two studies).
[b] Critical ratio of 3 or higher for differences between high and low responses (three studies).

Personality items which differentiate between successful and unsuccessful husbands and wives—on the basis of empirical research—are the following:

HAPPILY MARRIED	UNHAPPILY MARRIED
Emotionally stable	Emotionally unstable
Considerate of others	Critical of others
Yielding	Dominating
Companionable	Isolated
Self-confident	Lacking self-confidence
Emotionally dependent	Emotionally self-sufficient

The point is this—neurotic personality traits tend to be associated with unhappy rather than happy marriages.

This is not to say, however, that personality traits are static and unchanging. In fact, it is one of the cardinal principles of the new integrated science of social psychology that new situations and experiences can result in changes in the actions of persons, at any age in life. It is reasonable to assume that life in a community of love—such as a marriage based on love can provide—might result in changes for the better in the personalities of husband or wife, or both.

Burgess and Wallin studied Thurstone personality items to ascertain the extent to which responses of 390 men and 390 women remained stable from the time they answered the personality question during engagement to a time three or four years later when they were married. Fourteen, or about

TABLE 7 *Extent of Stability of Responses of 390 Men and 390 Women from Period of Engagement to Three or Four Years After Marriage*

Personality Item	Correlation [a] T	
(Nonneurotic reply in parentheses)	Men	Women
Makes friends easily (yes)	.60	.47
Troubled with shyness (no)	.50	.44
Nervous (no)	.48	.46
Feelings easily hurt (no)	.45	.45
Ideas run through head so cannot sleep (no)	.45	.42
Lacks self-confidence (no)	.43	(.38)
Frequently in state of excitement (no)	.42	.60
Worry over humiliating experience (no)	.40	.45
Get discouraged easily (no)	.40	(.36)
Ups and downs in mood (no)	.40	(.36)
Feel self-conscious (no)	(.36)	.46
Feelings of inferiority (no)	(.37)	.42
Useless thought bothers you (no)	(.30)	.42
Easy to make up mind (yes)	(.38)	.40

[a] The coefficients of association in parentheses denote those lower than .40.

one-third, of the scores on Thurstone personality items remained stable [5] over this period of time. In Table 7 they are arranged in rank order of stability for men.

Nine personality items showed low correlations—or a marked difference—between the responses given by the subjects before and after marriage. Burgess and Wallin suggest that the lowest nine items (correlations of .34 or under) for each sex may be regarded as those most likely to be affected by changes in events and in social relationships, including those resulting from marriage.

In Table 8 the personality items are arranged in rank order of changeability for men.

The responses to none of the personality items were con-

TABLE 8 *Extent of Instability of Responses of 390 Men and 390 Women from Period of Engagement to Three or Four Years After Marriage*

Personality Item	Correlations [a] T	
(*Nonneurotic reply in parentheses*)	Men	Women
Experience periods of loneliness (no)	.26	.22
Even-tempered and happy in outlook on life (yes)	.28	.29
Bothered by useless thought (no)	.30	(.42)
Usually in good spirits (yes)	.30	.18
Can stand criticism without feeling hurt (yes)	.30	(.36)
Self-confident about ability (yes)	.31	(.37)
Frequently burdened by a sense of remorse (no)	.31	.33
Worry over possible misfortunes (no)	.33	.30
Take responsibility for introducing people at a party (yes)	.34	(.35)
Feel well dressed (yes)	(.37)	.29
Interests change quickly (no)	(.38)	.29
Feel just miserable (no)	(.39)	.33
Mind wanders badly (no)	(.39)	.25

[a] The coefficients of association in parentheses denote those higher than .34.

[5] Items with a T coefficient of .40 are regarded by Burgess and Wallin as the more stable items.

stant from the earlier date to the later date, but some responses were more stable than others. The nine most unstable items might be tentatively regarded as the ones most affected by the situations and experiences of marriage whether the marriage was a success or a failure.

In conclusion, a democratic marriage of equals holds greatest promise when it involves two persons who are reasonably stable and well adjusted; but, in reality, a marriage is likely to involve two persons who are something less than perfect. Even for the less than perfect, personality growth within the community of love is possible.

4. *Are your revealing yourself to your beloved?* The idea of putting the best foot forward is, generally speaking, a good one, for all have unpleasant personality traits which are just as well held in check. But, in a relationship that is going to be as intimate as marriage, one must be careful not to mask unfavorable aspects of personality which may come to light later and cause difficulty in the day-to-day living of the couple. In the hectic round of activities that is American dating, it is possible for lovers never to get around to the important business of evaluating each other as real persons. To know that you "dance divinely" may seem terribly important to your date during dating days, but the fact that you frequently lose your temper will be more important to know in the long haul. If, when your personality is revealed to your beloved, she cannot accept you as you are, it is well that idealization and lack of acceptance of you as you are be discovered before further commitments are made.[6]

By all means put your best foot forward. Serious dating is not a time for dragging all the personal and family skeletons from the closet. But your future spouse has a right to see you as you are. Intensive dating over a period of time usually takes care of this problem, whereas a telescoped or whirlwind ro-

---

[6] Landis found that engaged persons told the fiancé(e) about "personality faults" in 100 per cent of the cases. They were less likely to tell the fiancé(e) of intimate experiences with others they had dated.

mance can concentrate on some pretty superficial aspects of personality.

5. *Are you old enough to marry?* There is a considerable body of empirical evidence (although not entirely consistent) supporting the view that marriage in the late twenties has a better chance of succeeding than a marriage between teenagers or persons in their very early twenties. But what is in-

"It would never work out, Ralph. We haven't got enough in common."
Drawing by Robt. Day, copr. © 1957 The New Yorker Magazine, Inc.

volved in being old enough to marry is not only chronological age but maturity, of which chronological age is only a rough index.

It can be argued that one does not have the right to ask another to marry him unless he has—or has reasonable prospects for—a plan for meeting the economic needs of himself, his spouse, and any children that might be born to them. It is not unreasonable to expect that the major breadwinner have a position with some semblance of a future or be making reasonable progress in a course of study leading to that end.

A person who has much formal education still ahead of him may not be free to expect another to accept him as a marriage mate. The same is true for the person who is heavily in debt. Such a person when asking for the hand of another must fully appreciate what he is asking the other person to accept in the way of responsibilities and sacrifices. In the following case, for instance, the young couple married before the husband began his college career. At the time the wife is writing, she has helped him through college, but he still has two years of graduate school ahead of him.

I have been a full-time working wife for so many years now that I don't know if I will be able to make a satisfactory adjustment to the role of homemaker and mother. Presently my job competes with our marriage and the energy that my husband and I should be expending on our marriage is used performing the household chores that would normally be my responsibility. Prolonged postponement of discussion of minor grievances builds up into major problems at times. Relaxation, such as it might be, often becomes a time for recovering from exhaustion rather than a healthy, active participation in recreation together or with friends.

The early years of married life with all of the necessary expenditures, as well as my husband's attempt to meet college expenses, causes a tight money budget. Such a budget often keeps the amount of spending to an embarrassing minimum. For me, it means not being able to purchase any frivolous things, and for my husband it means not being able to buy the morning coffee for his friends.

Being a little venturesome by marrying early and working together at the many problems involved may actually prove to be a rewarding experience to a young couple. We are only suggesting that the couple be realistic as well as romantic about the early years of marriage. If the young husband asks his wife to share heavy responsibilities, beyond the adjustment normal to a marriage, the new and tender relationship between them may not be able to carry the added load. The trials of married life may be more burdensome than postponing the marriage date until they are ready for the responsibilities.

It isn't only the economic or vocational age of the prospective husband that needs to be considered. The prospective bride also needs to think along these lines. If she has wanted the experience of a job and pay check of her own and the carefree and relatively affluent life of a career girl, it is well that she get some of this experience before she marries. She needs enough vocational career experience so that her views on the life of a working girl are realistic. Besides this, she needs training and experience in a vocation that she can fall back upon for support if the marriage should require her financial support, or if something should happen to impair her husband's economic capacity, forcing her to become the main breadwinner for the family.

In summary, whether one is old enough to marry can be answered in part in terms of the economic or vocational age, particularly of the prospective husband, but also of the wife prospective.

Are you old enough to marry—what is your emotional age? Emotional ages refers to the degree of emotional maturity of a person. By emotional maturity we mean readiness to give up basic dependence on parents for emotional support and the attainment of a degree of emotional poise as a self-confident and self-respecting person with a capacity to enter intimate love relationships not primarily as a dependent but as an equal.

Undue attachment to parents and parental home is an important indicator of a lack of freedom to give oneself to another in marriage. A normal progression of emancipation means that during infancy and childhood the child is dependent upon his parents, during the teens he comes to rely more and more on himself, and in marriage he is free to give himself to another. It is difficult for any person to appreciate how dependent on his parents and his parental home he is until situations arise in which he must of necessity make a choice between his spouse whom he loves and his parents whom he also loves—as when a business promotion for the husband requires a move for the young couple to a location far distant from the parental home of one or both partners. It is in such situations that the strength of loyalties and attachments shows up.

It is important before marriage that a person force himself to a realistic appraisal of the extent of his dependence on his parents. This in no way implies that a repudiation of parents is in order. Parent and child should remain deeply attached and the best of friends, but there is no question about it, "when the chips are down," one's loyalty is first to his spouse and second to his parents. It cannot be any other way if the married partners are to achieve the unity that can result from strong attachment to each other.

Emotional maturity also involves readiness to accept children and their dependence and demands. Not that the couple will necessarily plan for a baby soon after marriage, but there should be some serious examination before marriage of attitudes toward children and readiness to accept them. The acceptance of the intimacies of sexual intercourse and all of its consequences—including babies—is an important part of emotional maturity basic to the satisfactions that marriage can give.

There is another kind of age perhaps most basic of all and in part the basis of emotional maturity. This is referred to as moral age or moral maturity. The morally grown-up person has a built-in system or internalized set of regulators, guides, and goals for action. To the extent that one is other-directed —either directed by parents or peers—one is not a person. One is not ready for marriage if he has not faced up to the problems of a basic value orientation by which he orders his life. Only one with such an orientation is prepared as a full-fledged partner to enter into relations with others as equals.

This is the kind of self-examination that each partner should make of himself as a prospective spouse. In the right kind of love relationship the two can be of immeasurable help to each other in their examination. Each can be an audience responding as the other acts, helping that actor—by sympathetic but critical responses—to make the most realistic appraisal of himself not only as he is but also of his potentialities. Such actor-audience dramas can be enacted in a relationship characterized by love, trust, and respect if they involve two self-respecting and other-respecting individuals.

Do You Know and Love Each Other?

1. *Do you know him (her)?* Extensive and intimate dating allows persons to get to know each other better than was true under the old American system of premarital relations known as courtship. Hence, couple members are less likely to idealize and idolize each other than under a system with minimal opportunities for persons to get to know each other well as persons before marriage. Today, as Burgess and Wallin found, overidealization of the loved one is not common. This is all to the good.

But even with the intimacy possible within the American dating system, it is not an easy matter to get to know a person to whom one is greatly attracted. And perhaps it is not possible until vows of loyalty and fidelity have been exchanged, for we fear to confide unless we completely trust the other and his motives.

As we pointed out in the chapter on the meaning of love, one should get to know his beloved as no one else knows her, not only in the nature of her personality, but also in what she hopes to be and do with her life in the future—a vision of what she can become in an accepting and stimulating community of love. One does not know his beloved if he knows her only as she is, for, in a sense, she will not be this way even until tomorrow. To know her is to have become aware of the value orientations to which she is loyal and by which she governs and directs her thoughts and actions. To know her in this way one must be receptive, be willing to observe and listen, be sensitive to her expressions and to her wishes. Otherwise there is always a danger that one is dating a figment of one's own imagination, an extension of one's ego, a wishful projection rather than a real person.

In summary, to know a person involves a measure of understanding of the personality of the other, plus a knowledge of the value orientations which are likely to guide his life in the future. For only by knowing his values can knowledge be gained as to the direction of his life. If he has no clear-cut values it is impossible to predict the direction of his growth or development.

This is what it means to know another person, but knowledge is not love. Love is more than knowledge; hence the next question.

2. *Do you love him (her)?* Knowing is basic to loving, for loving a person one does not know is tantamount to being in love with an illusion. Under this condition, getting to know the personality behind the illusion is certain to be a revealing experience—and a gamble—as he turns out to be the same, or more, or less to one's liking than was the illusion. So love is not knowledge, but it is based on knowledge.

To love a person of the other sex whom one knows means to accept that person, desire that person, and be willing and eager to serve that person. It also involves a promise to be faithful, for love involves wanting one's beloved to have a chance to grow and develop to the full stature of the vision one has of him. It involves letting him have a life of his own —a career or careers in the broadest sense of the word. It involves a willingness and a desire that one's beloved may have satisfactions independent of one's own and even in spite of one's self. For the husband, it may mean baby-sitting at a sacrifice of his own convenience and activity so that his wife may regularly participate in activities in the community that are strictly her own—women's club, volunteer work, part-time employment, or whatever she may desire. For the wife, it may mean off-schedule meals, lonely hours, changes in plans, as her husband meets the demands and opportunities of his career and she fits her life to his.

Summary

No one would deny to lovers the thrills of a romantic love affair. Nevertheless, since the love affair also constitutes a period of preparation for marriage it is well to turn the cold light of reason on the partners and on their romance before they exchange vows of love and fidelity. This involves each getting to know oneself and one's motives for continuing or intensifying the relationship, as well as one's expectations regarding married life.

In a democratic marriage of equals it is important not only that each know himself but also that each accept himself. In the process of self-examination each must determine his marriageable age in terms of vocational, emotional, and moral maturity.

During dating days each must get to know the other, for love is not possible without knowledge of the object of one's love.

QUESTIONS AND PROJECTS

1. What motives for marrying do you regard as consistent with the American ideal?
2. Elaborate on de Rougemont's statement, "When body and mind are normally vigorous the chances of love at first sight must be very slender."
3. What is the difference between emotional maturity and moral maturity? How is each related to marriage?

4. What is the difference between knowledge of and love of another person? What is the relationship between knowledge and love in this regard?
5. Is there any relationship between personal adjustment and marital adjustment? Discuss.

SUGGESTED READINGS

See Chapter 11, Romance and Reason II, p. 181.

I I   *Romance and Reason II*

The mate-selection process must not be oversimplified through the use of a check list of factors taken from the marriage prediction studies. We caution against the tendency to believe that if one's beloved checks out on a long list of homogamous traits, he is one of that dozen or hundred persons who would likely be a satisfactory mate. This procedure involves a potential threat to replace love with a so-called rational method of mate selection.

Be that as it may, family sociologists have made an important contribution to intelligent mate selection by demonstrating that differences between couple members can make married life a more difficult proposition than it needs to be. These differences may not appear to be threats to love and marriage during dating days, but it is well to consider them before marriage vows are exchanged. We turn to a consideration of some of these differences.

What Is the Nature of Your Differences?

1. *Race.* It is not a biological factor that creates potential problems when two persons of different races marry but cultural or social factors. In other words, it is the way in which our society defines race and the meaning we attach to it that creates the problem. In many societies—with different interpretations of race—interracial marriages occur with little trauma for the individual or for the society. Not so in America; about half of the states have laws making interracial marriages illegal and over the whole of the nation social participation is pretty much within rather than across racial lines. The interracial married couple finds itself without a circle of associates in social groups of either race. And the children born of an interracial marriage may be ostracized by both the majority and the minority racial groups. Even today there are few communities in America which can accept interracial married couples with complete equanimity.

Interracial marriages are possible (in about half of the states), but lovers must decide whether their love for each other can stand up under the social pressures and rebuffs that are likely to ensue in our consciously multi-racial society. Though evidence is limited, the empirical data strongly support the contention that racially homogamous couples have an easier time of it than do racially mixed couples.

2. *Religion.* Since most dating in America is carried on in a setting of recreation, play, and a good time, it is possible for a couple to move along the glorious romantic road toward marriage without considering the deeper and more pervasive meanings of life. Couples come face to face with beliefs in

times of crisis, but in a country that has enjoyed as much peace and prosperity as America has, and with a youth-serving culture, it is possible for people to grow to maturity with relatively little crisis or suffering. Hence, couples may have to make a conscious effort to formulate their beliefs and to examine the similarities and differences in them, for it is almost certain that if no crisis during dating has brought beliefs to the fore, crises surrounding getting married and raising a family will—difficulty over money, birth control, concern and intervention of well-meaning relatives and friends, illness in the family, etc. It is at times when they feel inadequate and when they and others doubt the wisdom and rightness of their actions that young couples are forced to consider the beliefs and values governing their actions.

In America with three major religious groups—Jewish, Protestant, and Roman Catholic, and some variations on the major themes—there is a very real possibility that a person will meet and fall in love with someone with markedly different beliefs and value orientation from his own. If the differences are no greater than the differences between most church bodies within Protestantism, the couple should be able to overcome them without serious difficulty. This is not to suggest that the doctrinal and cultural differences between their churches may not be very real to the couple and deserving of careful appraisal and resolution.

There is literature available pointing out the differences between major religious beliefs in the Western world, and couples considering an interfaith marriage might get help from such sources, or from practitioners within the different faiths. But there is no substitute for discussion between the couple members themselves in terms of what *they* believe and how *their* differences can be resolved or accommodated, for they are the ones who must live with the decisions made.[1]

If the interfaith romance involves a Jew and a Roman

[1] James A. Pike, *If You Marry Outside Your Faith*, New York: Harper & Brothers, 1954.

Catholic or a Roman Catholic and a Protestant the differences cannot, in most cases, be resolved without much effort and not a small amount of "heartache." The seriousness of the problem will vary with the strength of convictions and strength of attachment to religious orientations on the part of each. If both take religion lightly and have only a nominal association with the church, no conflict may at first arise. But the couple cannot be so sure that the near relatives—who seemed so distant during the dating period—will not take a very active and concerned part. And for the couple, religion may begin to loom large when children are born to the marriage or when other crises arise.

During our breakup, Tom and I had both done a lot of thinking about our religion, and this time when the subject was brought up, we decided to take instruction in each other's beliefs, and to discuss them in an intelligent way. Each Thursday night we would meet after our instruction class and discuss what we had learned that evening. The similarities were not discussed as heavily as the differences.

Much against our inner convictions and the embarrassment of attending a radically different church, Tom did attend church with me and I with him. We felt that our instructions would be to no avail unless we could see them put into practice at a church service. I can honestly say that through this experience Tom and I each took a new look at his own church and began to understand it in a different but beneficial way.

We did become engaged. However, our engagement was short-lived and proved to be a bitter experience. At first our relationship together was beautiful. It was thrilling to look at furniture and homes, discuss family size, type of wedding, and so forth. But soon pressures began to pour in upon us. It all started when my cousin spoke to the pastor about us. I honestly don't understand why she stepped in now after staying out of the affair previously, but the pastor called me into his office, and we had a long serious talk about the complications that could arise after marriage even if one or the other "turned." I was hurt and angry with Lois.

Then our parents, who prior to this time knew very little about the entire affair, became involved. I had been brought up in a very strict home, and feared what my parents would say. However, Tom and I decided that I should go home and tell them the entire story. Instead I wrote them a letter, and the news came as quite a shock to them. They were concerned over the religious difference, and I knew that if I ever "turned" I would hurt them deeply.

While Tom had not met my parents, I had met his. They had been very wonderful to me and did not openly show or express their feelings, but I could sense that they wished I were Catholic. I know from various sources that considerable pressure was put on Tom at home for going with a Lutheran.

After much correspondence with my parents I told them I would break up with Tom but if we reunited for a third time we would get married despite all obstacles. My mother felt that this separation would give us a chance to think more clearly. Consequently, I took the initial step in breaking the engagement, and anyone who has gone through this bitter experience will know it almost crushes a person. Tom telephoned every night for nearly three months after, and though I was tempted to, I did not talk to him. Finally he stopped calling and I have neither seen nor heard from him since.

It took about a year before I could feel at ease on a date, and I still find myself comparing other fellows with Tom. I honestly wonder if I will ever marry and if I do, if my marriage will be as happy as I think it would have been with Tom. Yes, I think our marriage would have worked, but as I look back, the odds were pretty much against us.

If the marriage involves persons from the major branches of Christianity—a Roman Catholic and a Protestant—though both accept Jesus Christ as Lord and Savior, differences in doctrine and ritual are apt to create real stumbling blocks for the young couple. One of the important aspects of the problem in such a contemplated marriage centers in the antenuptial agreement. The Roman Catholic Church attempts to shield its members from the hazards and problems of inter-faith marriage by insisting upon pledges by both the Catholic and the non-Catholic parties prior to marriage. These pledges are contained in the antenuptial agreement. The section to be signed by both parties commonly contains the following pledges:

I agree

1. To contract marriage indissoluble except by death, according to the rules, regulations, and discipline of the Roman Catholic Church, and in no other way.

2. To have all children of either sex, born to said marriage, baptized only in the Roman Catholic Church, educated only in the Roman Catholic faith, according to the teachings of the Roman Catholic Church, in a Roman Catholic school wherever possible.

3. That the Roman Catholic party and all the said children born of said marriage may at all times without hindrance of any kind freely practice and exercise the Roman Catholic religion; and in the event of death they shall be buried in a Roman Catholic cemetery and in no other.

The section to be signed only by the Roman Catholic party contains the following pledges:

I solemnly promise:

1. That no other marriage ceremony than that per-formed by a Roman Catholic priest will take place.

2. That I shall practice my Roman Catholic religion faithfully, and that I shall do all in my power, especially by example, prayer, and the frequentation of the Sacra-ments, to bring about the conversion of my non-Catholic partner.

3. That I shall lead a married life in conformity with the teaching of the Roman Catholic Church regarding birth control, realizing fully the attitude of the Roman Catholic Church in this regard.

A couple contemplating a Roman Catholic–non-Cath-olic marriage will want to consider seriously the implications of the pledges to be signed, for once they are signed—if signed in good faith—free and open inquiry into the various facets of religion with freedom to act is at an end for the couple, and presumably for their children as well. Many couples sign the antenuptial agreement and subsequently break it or ignore it. It would seem more honorable to consider the implications of the pledges in advance of any signing and take whatever action seems best to the couple.

In case of marriage between a Jew and a Christian there are pervasive doctrinal differences to be considered as well as cultural and social differences. Jews, particularly Orthodox Jews, have maintained a remarkably complete subculture centering around religion and the home with a wealth of ritual that is foreign to the experience of the Christian. It is not only a matter of difference in religious beliefs that is involved in such a marriage but some deep-seated differences in the total way of life.

Empirical studies of marital adjustment generally support the view that similarity in religious faith is conducive to adjustment. By and large the studies have lacked sophistication in regard to religion, however, and the findings can be accepted on only the most tentative basis. This lack of sophistication in the study of the religious factor in marriage adjustment is due to at least two causes. First, religion is an extremely difficult factor to assess empirically, and secondly, empirical social science—since Max Weber and until very recently—has made only sporadic attempts to consider it as an important institution and a source of ultimate values.

3. *Age*. Age differences between partners create few problems in marriage in our society since, generally speaking, the age differential between partners is not great. Age difference can create problems if the partners represent different generations—the June-December marriage, for instance. Such marriages require adjustment of differences in physical stamina and sexual desire, differences in values between two genera-

tions, differences in desired social activities, and the real possibility of a long life alone for the younger member of the marriage.

A number of empirical studies have included data on age differences; the results are not consistent, though similarity in age seems to be favorable to good martial adjustment, other things being equal.

For couple unity it is not so important that the backgrounds out of which the two persons come be similar; what is important is what kinds of persons have emerged out of the backgrounds. The partners, in testing and measuring their love for each other, must not place the stress on the type of family or social and religious background out of which each has come but on the nature of the personality, the character, the values, and aspirations for living that each has acquired out of his particular background. Difference in background is meaningless except as it conditions the present life of a person. Differences have been resolved if out of these differences two persons have emerged with similar approaches to problems of life and a mutual feeling for a set of beliefs and values that will govern their life together. If we accept the premium value placed on *the man* in America rather than on his family, socioeconomic class, etc., then each person must be judged on his merits, not on the milieu out of which he has emerged.

This emphasis on the individual at the expense of the setting out of which he comes does not mean the lover will not view his beloved with regard to the extent to which social variables have affected her personality. For the idea of a completely self-made man is an illusion—each person bears the marks of the life he has lived, and one can know his beloved better as she is now by knowing the social milieu out of which she came.

In summary, it is not a past homogamy that is important to success in marriage but a present homogamy—a unity of will and purpose that has grown out of similar, or different backgrounds.

What Is the Nature of and the Prospects for the Unity a Couple Seeks in Marriage?

So far in our discussion of the application of reason to romance we have seen lovers largely in terms of each looking at himself and each looking at the other, not as two persons contemplating the prospect of life together. This, of course, is a basic and central concern, and we turn to it now.

We do young lovers an injustice if we give the impression that it is easy to achieve unity in marriage—that it is easy to live always with at least one other person in mind. It is not. The tendency to selfishness and self-centeredness is universal. Love cannot be extolled enough as the finest basis of a relationship between two people, but love has its tragic side as indicated in the discussion of the meaning of love. There is truth in the statement of William Graham Sumner that marriage is an experiment in "antagonistic cooperation," for the unity that two people seek in marriage is a unity out of diversity. It is in a certain measure an attempt to place one will in the place where two wills operated before. Not that the will of one of them, the husband for instance, will replace the will of the two, but that each acts from here on always with the wishes of at least one other person—one's spouse—in mind. Each of the lovers as a respected and self-respecting person will continue to have a life and career of his own after marriage, but the careers have to be made to dovetail, not to clash.

The career problem as one couple saw it and resolved it is the theme of the following quotation from an engagement history.

The next big problem that came up in our lives was the problem of what I would do for my life's work. I had already to some extent decided that I wanted to become a minister. June knew this and accepted it with some reservations. When the time came that I must declare myself, I had decided that the Lord had called me and that I was to become a minister. We sat and talked over all the phases of this work. We talked about leaving the state and her family—it is going to be harder for her to leave her family than it is for me to leave mine—and other phases of the work. Right from the start I told June that she would be the second thing in my life. I was first of all a man of God's and secondly her man, and that she would be playing the role of second all of her married life. If I did not love June very much then, my love grew for her tenfold that night. She told me that she accepted that fact heartily. She said that she would gladly follow me any place that I went. She felt that her job was to please me and to work with me to raise a family and care for that family and everything else was secondary to this. This was a high experience in our engagement and I shall always remember this as one of the highlights of our engagement.

Besides the interlocking careers, each successful marriage contains a large area of common will and purpose which tends to take the place of or supersede the separate wills and purposes. If this is not so, the marriage lacks unity.

In assaying their rightness for each other, couples must not look primarily to past experiences of each but ahead to a unity to be achieved now and in the future. How do we adapt to each other now, and how do we adapt to the present situation, and how adaptable are we to future changes? These are important questions for the unity the couple seeks now and in the future.

Do we have the will to succeed? Are we interested in home and family? This adaptability to present and future, though given little attention in the researches of social scientists to date, would appear to be crucial for marriage adjustment.

Whether or not the couple will be motivated in the direction of making a success of marriage may be evident in part in the types of interests each has and the extent to which the interests are held in common. Studies have shown that commonness of interests is correlated with adjustment in marriage, but, as Benson has demonstrated in an analysis of interests for 580 of Burgess and Wallin's couples, some refinement of the common interest theory is in order.

It appears that whether mutuality of interest is favorably associated with adjustment depends upon whether the interest is familistic or not. In other words, the type of interest determines whether mutuality is favorable to marriage success or not. The relationship between the number of mutual interests and marital adjustment and the relationship between this number and the feeling of partners that their interests are mutual were both found to be much smaller relationships than had generally been believed to be the case.

The following are the mutual interests classified by Benson as familistic and favorably related to marital adjustment; it is followed by a list of interests classified as individualistic.

Familistic Interests

Home interest score higher than median.
Home of one's own as a reason for marriage.
Quiet home life as one's wish in life.
Children interest score higher than median.
Children as a reason for marriage.
Religious interest score higher than median.

Individualistic Interests

Commercial entertainment interest score higher than median.
Sports participation higher than median.
Mobility interest score higher than median.
Travel as one's wish in life.
Good time or happiness as one's wish in life.
Make money as one's wish in life or comfort and ease as a reason for marriage.
Fame or status as one's wish in life or career as a reason for marriage.

Not all of the differences were statistically significant, but "in the aggregate the pattern seems beyond statistical doubt." In other words, it was the mutual interests in home, children, and religion that were related to successful marital adjustment rather than mutual interest in commercial recreation, sports, travel, making money, and other evidences of personal success. Rather than ask "Do we have the same interests?"

"Don't be silly, Edna. What in heaven's name would I be doing in anything casual?"
Reproduced courtesy of Stan Hunt.

Benson suggests that marriage partners might more appropriately ask, "Do we both have familistic interests?"

Adapting to spouse and to marriage involves loving one's spouse, having a will to succeed, and having interests in home, family, and religion. But also involved are personal capacity to adapt and knowledge of techniques of adaptation. Some persons apparently lack flexibility and are not as able to adapt to other persons because of a rigidity in personality; and persons with the capacity to adapt may lack knowledge of techniques of adapting. One may understand people and know what to do to get along with them but be unable to adapt to them because of some inability to put the understanding and knowledge into action. The extent to which it is possible depends on flexibility of personality. Lack of flexibility is

"Golly, Muriel! I never dreamed I'd ever meet anyone as crazy about the 'National Geographic' as I am."

Drawing by Richard Decker, copr. © 1958 The New Yorker Magazine, Inc.

manifested in rigid and stereotyped responses in interaction with other persons. "Persons who are tactful, diplomatic, or popular with a great variety of people probably have great flexibility of personality. Persons whose environment and experience have been highly homogeneous, standardized, and stable are probably low in flexibility." [2]

[2] Ernest W. Burgess and Paul Wallin, *Engagement and Marriage*, J. B. Lippincott Co., 1953, pp. 626–627.

Can Adaptability Be Increased?

If it is so important to be able to adapt, a logical question is "Can adaptability be increased?" In general we can answer by saying that, as stated in the Preface, it is one of the basic assumptions of the author that personality growth and development can take place under appropriate conditions and with adequate stimulation in the form of rewards and punishment. Secondly, the entire book is intended to suggest the types of experiences—direct and vicarious—which will help the reader prepare for the adaptations necessary to successful marriage.

To answer the question more specifically, however, it must be admitted that knowledge of the nature of adaptability, the extent to which adaptation is a worthy goal, and how it might be maximized is limited at the present time and in need of systematic theoretical and empirical investigation.

From knowledge of the socialization of the child and other insights out of social psychology, it seems safe to assume that the ability to understand and evaluate the feelings and desires of other persons can in part be acquired and enhanced. On the other hand, this capacity to empathize is inborn and hence modifiable only within limits. Some of the data presented in Chapter 2 might lead one to believe that the capacity and the motivation to empathize is somewhat greater in women than in men.

To the extent that the empathizing quality can be learned or developed, it is important that the person place himself in situations where breadth and intimacy of association with people will be maximized. This involves drawing acquaintances from a broader base plus getting to know them so well that it is possible to understand and appreciate the standpoint from which they view life. There are still some communities in the United States where such heterogeneity of acquaintance is not possible, but such communities are rapidly diminishing in number.

As a substitute for direct personal experience, the person desiring to increase his ability to empathize might study personality in a systematic way and read autobiography, biography, and other literature intended to reveal the inner life of man. Functional marriage courses are designed precisely to meet a part of this need.

The increase in the ability to empathize falls within the limits of one's capacity to do so and one's willingness to do so. The person without the capacity to adapt to situations and persons is referred to as rigid. The person who can adjust is referred to as flexible. Flexibility is in part a matter of inborn capacity and in part a matter of conviction and desire to understand others and to relate to them.

But capacity to adapt and willingness to adapt are not enough; a person must also have a command of the appropriate responses. This capacity to respond is also in part a matter of flexibility. But, within that capacity, knowing the appropriate responses and having some practice in them are important. In part this command of appropriate responses is nothing more than an awareness of social etiquette. Many a person is "tongue-tied" in the face of the person in need of understanding and sympathy. He is tongue-tied because he lacks command of the appropriate acts and expressions for his concern.

Insofar as the ability to adapt relates to marriage, some of the appropriate attitudes and appropriate responses are discussed in the chapters on oneness, togetherness, and self-realization in marriage—particularly taking the audience role or the supportive role when the spouse takes the creative or expressive role.

Summary

In marriage it is not so important that the backgrounds of the partners be similar as that the present actions and future plans of the partners be compatible and that they possess the willingness and the capacity to adapt to each other and to changing conditions. If we accept the American ideal, we accept the belief that the qualities of the individual outweigh considerations of race, religion, socioeconomic class, or family background. Nevertheless, differences in backgrounds may have so differentially influenced the values and actions of the prospective marriage partners that they are unable—though in love—to overcome the effects of the differences. Hence, the cold light of reason should be focused on differences before marriage.

Adaptability to persons and situations is an important trait in marital adjustment, and there are indications that, if one is willing, he might increase his faculty for adapting to persons and situations. This capacity for personal growth is a part of the faith in man inherent in the American ideal. The empirical proof of it is still fragmentary.

QUESTIONS AND PROJECTS

1. Do you agree with the way Tom and his girl friend resolved the problems of their interfaith love affair? If not, how should they have resolved them?
2. Is difference in social backgrounds important in mate selection? If so, in what way?
3. In what ways is matching of social backgrounds inconsistent with values inherent in the American ideal?
4. What does the paradoxical expression "antagonistic cooperation" mean when applied to marriage?
5. Is commonness of interests related to success in marriage? If so, in what way?

6. What can a young person do, if anything, to increase his ability to adapt to other persons?

SUGGESTED READINGS

Benson, Purnell, "The Common Interests Myth in Marriage," *Social Problems*, Vol. 3, July 1955, pp. 27–34.
————, "The Interests of Happily Married Couples," *Marriage and Family Living*, Vol. XIV, November 1952, pp. 276–280.
Bertocci, Peter A., *The Human Venture in Sex, Love, and Marriage*, New York: Association Press, 1951.
Black, Algernon D., "If I Marry Outside My Religion," *Public Affairs Pamphlet*, No. 204, Public Affairs Committee, Inc., 1954, pp. 1–28.
Burgess, Ernest W., and Leonard S. Cottrell, Jr., *Predicting Success or Failure in Marriage*, New York: Prentice-Hall, Inc., 1939.
————, and Paul Wallin, *Engagement and Marriage*, Chicago: J. B. Lippincott Co., 1953.
Foote, Nelson N., "Matching of Husband and Wife in Phases of Development," Reprint No. 7, Family Study Center, University of Chicago. Reprinted from Transactions of the Third World Congress of Sociology, Vol. IV.
Keeley, Benjamin J., "Value Convergence and Marital Relations," *Marriage and Family Living*, Vol. XVII, November 1955, pp. 342–345.
Kirkpatrick, Clifford, *The Family: As Process and Institution*, New York: The Ronald Press Company, 1955, Chapters 4, 13, 15.
Locke, Harvey J., *Predicting Adjustment in Marriage*, New York: Henry Holt & Co., Inc., 1951.
Pike, James A., *If You Marry Outside Your Faith*, New York: Harper & Brothers, 1954.
Roth, Julius, and Robert F. Peck, "Social Class and Social Mobility Factors Related to Marital Adjustment," *American Sociological Review*, Vol. 16, August 1951, pp. 478–487.
Strauss, Anselm, "Personality Needs and Marital Choice," *Social Forces*, Vol. 25, March 1947, pp. 332–335.

12 *The Meaning of Engagement*

Dating, the American system for getting from singleness to the married state, is a fairly new social invention and one that even now is showing signs of change. Many persons no doubt regard engagement, on the other hand, as an old, clearly defined, changeless part of the system. But this is not so as we discover when we survey the engagement practices of Americans today.

It is true that engagement, or betrothal, is a very old practice in human culture—how old we do not know. It is practiced in some of the so-called primitive societies and goes back in at least one of the traditions out of which American culture developed—the Judaic-Christian—to very early times. Betrothal plays an important part in accounts of marriage in the Old Testament, for instance the familiar account in the

Book of Genesis of Jacob fulfilling the conditions of engagement (betrothal) by working for his future father-in-law, Laban (Genesis 29).

Regarding American society today, however, engagement is not universally practiced, is not clearly defined as to its form or meaning, and is not clearly defined as to its functions.

On the surface it might appear that engagement is more clearly defined than other stages in the dating process because of its more clear-cut symbols—particularly the diamond ring which seems clearly to distinguish the nonengaged from the engaged. But we are forced to agree with Kuhn that:

> . . . the engagement situation in our society is one which is left almost completely undefined by its symbols. The symbols are commonly the wearing of a ring or fraternity pin, the announcement of engagement at a party and in the newspaper, exclusive courtship over a long period of time, the words "I love you. Will you marry me?" and so on. The significance or meaning of engagement, however, is not at all standardized or universal.[1]

The evidence suggests that the practice of engagement, though hoary with age, must take its place alongside random dating and serious dating as an emergent, rather than as a universal, established subsystem in the American mate-selection system.

In the pages to follow we look more specifically at the facts—that engagement is not a universal practice in American society, that the forms vary, and that the meaning and functions vary. It is important for the dating couple to consider these things, for it cannot be taken for granted that lovers' views on engagement will be compatible, since society allows so much latitude in these matters. Even within relatively homogeneous groups of college students, the author has noted marked differences between men and women concerning the extent of commitment implied in engagement.

---

[1] Howard Becker and Reuben Hill, *Family Marriage and Parenthood*, Boston: D. C. Heath & Company, p. 276.

Engagement Is Not Universally Practiced in America

Of 2000 couples who brought their marriage problems to the chancery court of the Chicago Archdiocese between 1942 and 1948, 36 per cent had not had a formal engagement with some external signs in the form of a ring or an announcement to friends and relatives.[2] Similarly, in a study of 374 unhappy married couples, 140, or 37 per cent, had not experienced an engagement period before marriage.[3]

It is also known that couples in the lower classes and persons who experience a second or third marriage commonly dispense with the formal engagement. We should not conclude, however, that engagement is not popular or very much in vogue at the present time. The custom of engagement, though far from universal in American society, is widely practiced in the middle and upper classes, and particularly among persons marrying for the first time.

The Form That Engagement Takes Is Not Universal

Engagements may take a variety of forms ranging from informal to very formal and from private to public. Hollingshead's description of engagement among Class IV and V couples in Elmtown is a good example of the informal and private type of engagement.

[2] John L. Thomas, *The American Catholic Family*, Englewood Cliffs, N. J.: Prentice-Hall, Inc., 1956, p. 194.
[3] Paul Popenoe and Donna Neptune, "Acquaintance and Betrothal," *Social Forces*, Vol. 16, 1938, pp. 552–555.

When a boy asks a girl to marry him and the girl agrees, the couple normally keep it secret if their parents object to their courtship; if the parents do not object, the couple sometimes tell their families and friends, but not usually, as the courtship pattern decrees this to be a private matter. None of the engagements in the married group, so far as we have been able to determine, has been announced publicly by parties, showers, or a "piece" in *The Bugle*.

After a couple become "engaged," they go out together three, four, and five nights a week. If the boy has a car, they usually go for a ride and park in one of the half-dozen popular petting spots—the Buggy Wash, the Three Pines, near the Boy Scout Camp, in the park, near the graveyard. Heavy petting followed by sexual relations often occurs in the parked car, except in the very coldest weather. Some couples use contraceptives, but most trust to nature. In the natural course of events, a very high percentage of the girls become pregnant.[4]

On the other hand, in "high society" engagements tend to be formal—with announcement by the prospective bride's family and social occasions in honor of the prospective bride and in some cases the prospective groom. They are also public in the sense that the announcement of the engagement is reported for the whole world to know through the medium of a mass-circulation newspaper.

A somewhat different type of formal and public engagement is that associated with marriages after the Judaic-Christian model. It has been the practice to announce a couple's intentions to marry by "publishing the banns," that is, by giving notice three times in the parish church of each of the espoused. When and where practiced, publishing the banns has the effect of causing couples who are church members to have formal and public engagements of at least several weeks' duration prior to marriage. The purpose of the banns is to discourage, if not to prevent, hasty and un-

4 Reprinted with permission from August B. Hollingshead, *Elmtown's Youth*, p. 428. Copyright 1949, John Wiley & Sons, Inc.

wise marriages on the part of adherents of the faith.

Between the extremes of the informal and the formal, and the secretive and the public, there are all shades of variation in the form that engagement has taken and now takes in American society. For example, the traditional stereotype of the man more or less unexpectedly dropping to his knees and stammering out his intentions to the girl he wanted to marry may have been characteristic of American courtship as a mate-selection system, but the proposal in our informal and intimate dating system of today often comes about after frequent and extended discussions of marriage by the couple and as no surprise to either of them. Landis found that of 200 engagements almost a third reported that there never was a formal proposal and acceptance. They "just understood" that they were engaged. Even in the cases where the man made a definite proposal (about 70 per cent of the cases), most of the girls said the proposal came as no surprise.

The setting of the proposal may vary greatly from the old stereotype (Table 9). About one-fourth of the proposals

TABLE 9 *How Men Propose*

	Number	Per Cent
At her home	272	23
Riding or driving	293	25
Vacation, resort, train, or ship	150	13
By letter, telegram, or telephone	63	5
Private party, dinner, or dance	123	10
Street, park, restaurant, or other public place	242	20
Miscellaneous	38	4
Total	1181	100

Source: Adapted with permission from Paul Popenoe, *Modern Marriage*, p. 267. Copyright 1940 by The Macmillan Co.

took place at the girl's home (how many of them were of the stereotyped on-bended-knee variety we do not know), another one-fourth while the couple were "riding or driving," and the remainder took place in a variety of private and public settings.

That the form of the engagement is variable in American society can also be seen in the answers of over 500 single and married students when asked to indicate how much time elapsed between first date and engagement (Table 10). The

TABLE 10 *Average Length of Time Elapsed from the First Date to Engagement*

	Number	Percentage
1–2 weeks	11	2.0
3–4 weeks	15	3.0
1–2 months	50	9.0
3–4 months	70	13.0
5–8 months	105	19.0
9–11 months	39	7.0
1–2 years	142	26.0
3 years up	114	21.0
Total	546	100.0

SOURCE: Judson T. and Mary G. Landis, *Building a Successful Marriage*, 2nd Ed., p. 178. Copyright, 1948, 1953, by Prentice-Hall, Inc., Englewood Cliffs, N.J. Reprinted by permission of the publisher.

answers demonstrate the fact that there is no standard amount of time set down in the norms governing engagement procedure in our society. In roughly one-fourth (27 per cent) of the cases less than five months elapsed from first date to engagement, and in another one-fourth (26 per cent) five months to a year elapsed. One to two years elapsed in another one-fourth (26 per cent) of the cases, and 21 per cent reported a time lapse of upwards of three years.

The Meaning of Engagement Is Not Universal

There are basically two meanings of engagement vying for acceptance at the present time in America, engagement as commitment (stemming from the Judaic-Christian marriage model) and engagement as a testing period (stemming from the rationalistic marriage model) or, in other words, permanent engagement and tentative engagement.

The first, and older, meaning holds that engagement symbolizes a commitment on the part of each partner to marry within a reasonable time after the proposal has been made and accepted and to be faithful to vows of fidelity from that time on. This is the meaning of engagement consistent with the proposal "Will you marry me?" and the affirmative response "I will." What the one, traditionally the man, "proposes" is marriage. The other affirms or rejects the proposal with an affirmative or negative response.

The second meaning of engagement—engagement as a testing period or tentative engagement—conceives of engagement as the last stage in the increasingly intimate relationship between two unmarried persons. We do not, to my knowledge, have any stereotyped language symbolizing this rite of passage as we do in the proposal of the first type of engagement. The proper exchange of vows—that is, proper in the sense of being consistent with this meaning of engagement—might well be "I love you, let's become engaged, and if it works out, let's get married," with the response (if affirmative) "I love you, too. Yes, let's become engaged."

The exchange of expressions consistent with tentative engagement is not unlike the exchange of expressions between two persons who make a decision to "go steady," in fact, tentative engagement might correctly be viewed as a decision to "go steadier." There is one very important difference, however. Implied if not stated in "Let's become engaged" is an implied or stated commitment to marry if the engagement period works out as it is hoped it will.

In permanent engagement the engagement stage of dating begins with exchange of intentions to marry between two persons who feel that they are "one" or married psychologically and want within the near future to become socially and legally married. In tentative engagement, the couple members are fond of each other and are perhaps in love with each other but want a period of intimate dating in which to test out their compatibility and their desire to marry each other. The purpose of tentative engagement is to facilitate the testing of personalities in order to see how well suited they are to each other. The rite of passage through which engagement is entered is not then by way of a proposal to marry but a proposal to test out their "suitedness" for each other.

The Functions of Engagement Are Not Regulated by Institutionalized Norms in American Society

That the functions of engagement are not regulated by formal norms in American society further attests to the fact of an emerging free-enterprise system of dating and mate selection. Couple members are free within some pretty broad limits to work out their love relationships as they please. But with two meanings of engagement vying for acceptance, it is not possible to have one set of functions for engagement.

We will in the following chapter spell out in some detail some functions of engagement that seem to be consistent with our over-all discussion of the mate-selection process. But first it will be necessary to explore further the two views of engagement.

The Supporting Groups

It might be instructive to young people contemplating marriage to know which point of view regarding the nature and meaning of engagement each of them holds and why the views are held.

By and large it is the upper class, and to a lesser extent the middle class, that has accepted the idea of formal engagements and it is the lower class who dispenses entirely with engagement or regards it as a private affair. The acceptance or rejection of engagement—as well as the form it should take—is, therefore, primarily a class-differentiated alternative in our society and is an emergent without any real significance so far as the American ideal is concerned.

In regard to meaning, however, the groups holding to engagement as commitment to marry or engagement as a testing period do not divide primarily along class lines. The division finds the church and the state as chief defenders of permanent commitment and a nonorganized group of scholars, including a number of social scientists, particularly family sociologists, most explicitly defining and defending tentative engagement.

The Judaic-Christian position is grounded in the Scriptures—both Old and New Testament. There are no specific norms either in the Old or the New Testament concerning the rites through which marriage must be entered. Nevertheless, just as the legal ceremony is binding in Western society, so engagement (betrothal) was for Biblical marriage the thing which bound a man and a woman together.

It was the promise of marriage that was the important

commitment. The actual exchange of marriage vows, though not without its significance, was somewhat in the nature of an anticlimax, a formality. In Biblical marriages some time elapsed between the engagement and the time when the marriage was consummated by first sexual intercourse; this time was a time of preparation for marriage and family life, not a testing period. In other words, engagement—"kiddushin"—was an act by which the woman was consecrated to her husband, set apart for him exclusively, though some preparations were in order before he took her to himself and they lived together as man and wife.

Against this background the church took its stand on engagement as at least morally binding—if not legally binding—on the couple. This belief can be found in the writings of theologians of the Christian church; it is clearly apparent in the teachings and practices of the Lutheran Church, for instance.

The Lutheran theologian, C. F. W. Walther, in the first book on pastoral theology for the church body of which he was a member, makes it very clear that rightful engagement was tantamount to a consummated marriage. He states that mutual consent is the efficient cause of marriage; hence marriage has taken place as soon as the consent has been given. As evidence he cites Scriptural passages which speak of the betrothed persons as husband and wife (Genesis 29:21; Matthew 1:18–20) or passages wherein sexual relations with an engaged woman are punished in the same manner as sex relations with another man's wife (Deuteronomy 22:22–29; Hosea 4:13).

The church not only said that engagement was tantamount to marriage, but there is evidence that it acted out of consideration for this view of engagement as well. Indiscretions between the unmarried—such as sexual intercourse— were not as harshly treated if the couple members were engaged to each other as if they were not engaged.

In the minutes of various congregations mention is made of young people who had had sexual intercourse before marriage but during the time of engagement. The usual procedure was to state that in such cases the sin of adultery had not been committed, but the couple had given offense, and, therefore, the matter should be brought before the congregation and the repentance of the couple announced from the pulpit. Great emphasis was placed upon ascertaining whether or not the couple sinned before or after engagement. For example, one conference gave the opinion: "If they had relations before engagement, then their act is fornication, if after, then she has broken the confidence entrusted to her, anticipated the marital bed, and given offense to the world. This must be told her." [5]

It was not uncommon to dismiss from Lutheran seminaries ministerial candidates who had broken an engagement, since this for all intents and purposes was tantamount to divorce. Neither this practice nor the procedure described above are commonly practiced by Lutheran groups today, however.

Roman Catholic canon law does not take the position that engagement is tantamount to marriage, though it does treat engagement as a serious undertaking. To quote from a Roman Catholic source, "A formal engagement is one which is made in writing and signed by both parties in the presence of the bishop or pastor, or in lieu of such a witness, in the presence of two other witnesses. It imposes a serious obligation, and should be broken for grave reasons only." [6]

The views of some of the other Protestant churches have not been as clearly spelled out as has the position of some Lutherans and Roman Catholics and seem to fall somewhere between the view of engagement as commitment and engagement as a testing period.

[5] *Research Project in Marriage and Family Living* (Mimeographed), Part II, p. 59.
[6] John R. Cavanaugh, *Fundamental Marriage Counseling: A Catholic Viewpoint*, Milwaukee: The Bruce Publishing Co., 1957, p. 141.

The State

The force, other than the church, which has supported engagement as commitment has been the state. The state takes its stand not primarily on religious grounds but rather as a result of its concern with order and justice. As late as 1948 John S. Bradway could write, in attempting to convey what the concept engagement means to the lawyer, "In law an engagement to marry is a contract comparable to commercial contracts, such as the purchase of an automobile, a labor-management contract, a partnership agreement." He also stated that "the conventional family may be said to have a beginning at the time a man and a woman become engaged to marry." He added, however, that there is considerable difference of opinion as to whether the law should allow breach of promise suits.

The unpopularity of breach of promise action among offended lovers today is generally known. It is significant to note that though Burgess and Wallin's 1000 couples had had extensive experience with broken engagements, in relating their reactions to broken engagements the resort to breach of promise suits was not mentioned as a possible recourse.

As a part of this general trend, a number of states have passed laws abolishing the breach of promise action. Hence a major legal support for the view of engagement as commitment has been withdrawn. This fact, plus the unpopularity of the breach of promise suit as a recourse in case of broken engagement, means that, for all practical purposes, persons who break engagements today need hardly consider the possible legal consequences.

Whether the official support of the churches that have defended engagement as commitment will also be withdrawn is problematical. A large part of American Protestantism is quite similar in its views to that of the supporters of engagement as a testing period. Modifications in the official position of the major supporting Lutheran body are not unlikely. Also, there is nothing essentially inconsistent between this view and the Roman Catholic position in that both hold that for sufficient cause an engagement may be broken.

With legal and religious support for the view of engagement as permanent withdrawn, other things being equal, there would seem to be a strong possibility that engagement as a testing period will become more firmly established. This is especially true since its major proponents and advocates, the family sociologists, have a receptive audience of young people through the medium of courses in the family and marriage preparation.

The belief that engagement is a morally binding commitment is not dead, however, and will perhaps not die. This interpretation of the responsibility involved in engagement as spoken of in the Scriptures continues to have adherents. In a recent study of 219 Lutheran Church-Missouri Synod pastors, 69 per cent answered affirmatively the question "Do you believe that a valid engagement is just as morally binding as marriage?" and 55 per cent of 599 of the religiously active laity also answered in the affirmative.

More important in keeping engagement as commitment alive, perhaps, is the fact that young people will—because of the very nature of love—continue to propose marriage and regard the proposal as a sign of devotion and commitment to fidelity. Thirdly, there is strongly implicit in engagement as a testing period the idea that engagement is a commitment to marry if the testing period proves to be satisfactory. Because of moral or religious convictions, because of the nature of love, and because many tentative engagements eventually become firm commitments to marry, the engagement as commitment is likely to remain—particularly in an age that is as marriage-minded as the present one.

The Rationale of Tentative Engagement

The most concise, definitive, and persuasive arguments for engagement as a testing period come from social science experts on the family. In general they commend the practice of engagement as a good one not on the basis of its prevalence but rather because they think it "makes sense." Hence the practice per se is regarded as worth while, and the argument in favor is as follows. There are many engagements which should be broken, and a high rate of broken engagements is preferable to a high rate of desertion or divorce. For this reason, couples should enter engagement in the full realization that the engagement might be broken. If couples recognize this, the break, if it comes, will be less traumatic than it would be if they were not anticipating the possibility of its occurring.

This is a concise statement both of engagement as a testing period and its justification—namely, many engagements are premature and ill advised and they should be entered as tentative arrangements because they might not stand the test of intimate association. Secondly, it is better to have poor matches broken during engagement than through desertion or divorce after the couple is married.

Summary

Though the engagement custom is an ancient one and long established in Western culture, it is nevertheless not a universally practiced prelude to marriage in America. Furthermore, precise and generally accepted norms and ritual governing the form which engagement takes are not present in American culture. Engagement may take a variety of forms, ranging from informal to very formal, from private to public.

To add to the confusion, there are two definitions of the nature and meaning of engagement vying for acceptance. Tentative engagement—engagement as a testing period—is receiving the greater amount of popular support, though permanent engagement—engagement as commitment—is not dead in American culture.

QUESTIONS AND PROJECTS

1. How does the engagement experience differ among lower-class, middle-class, and upper-class couples?
2. What does "publishing the banns" mean? Why are they published?
3. Which meaning of engagement—permanent or tentative—seems to make the most sense from your point of view? Build as strong a case for it as you can.
4. Engagement as commitment has been under serious attack in the past several decades. Will it survive or will it be replaced by tentative engagement? Defend your answer.

SUGGESTED READINGS

See Chapter 13, The Functions of Engagement, page 214.

13 *The Functions of Engagement*

Anyone who accepts the American free-enterprise system of mate selection can hardly quarrel with arguments emphasizing the necessity of shopping around and of keeping love relationships tentative until the couple members feel reasonably sure of their love for each other and their desire to marry. And, though breaking serious relationships is somewhat traumatic, if they are to be broken there is less at stake if this fact is discovered in the intimate association before rather than after marriage.

It is questionable if one could find a serious defender for the view that there should not be a tentative period before mate selection is final—the logic and the empirical evidence are overwhelming. All the evidence of the last chapters argues for keeping the relationship on a tentative basis until the couple members feel quite sure in their knowledge, acceptance, and love of each other.

Hence, the crucial question is not whether commitments between couple members should be tentative, but rather when, if ever, the tentative period should end.

In engagement as commitment the tentative nature of the relationship ends with the proposal and its acceptance. Engagement as a testing period implies that the tentative nature of the relationship should not end before the exchange of marriage vows; anything up to this point should be regarded as tentative.

But by no means all students of the family accept the moment of the proposal and its acceptance or even the moment when marriage vows are exchanged as the time at which the tentativeness of a relationship should end. Some defenders of the American ideal have argued that the tentative nature of the relationship should extend to the time of the birth of the first child. That is, the couple should regard their marriage as a testing period but only until the birth of a child, for by that time something very tangible has been done that cannot be undone. They hurt not only themselves by a break but also the life of an innocent third party.

More common today than the person who consciously keeps his love relationship on a tentative rather than a permanent basis until the birth of the first child, however, is the person who commits himself permanently not to another person but to love (romantic marriage model).

The person who commits himself to another person says in effect "I will remain faithful to you come what may—riches or poverty, sickness or health." The person who commits himself to love says in effect "I will remain faithful to you come what may so long as I love you." The commitment (albeit unconsciously) is to love, not to another person.

The interesting thing about this kind of commitment is that since love has elements of belief, reason, and will, as well as elements of feeling, it is possible that a person could conceivably fall out of love when he wanted to (because of the elements of belief, reason, and will), though he may not recognize the reason for his action. The person who believes that his commitment must be to love rather than to a person, or a person who believes that he is at the mercy of love, is likely to be an unstable marriage partner. For, rather than attempting to discipline and "socialize" his love and make it responsible, he takes a permissive attitude and is willing to go where he thinks his love leads him. When his secretary proves to be more appealing to him than his wife, he can interpret it to mean that he is no longer in love with his wife and that the honorable thing to do is to leave her.

Burgess and Wallin found empirical evidence of this belief about love. They asked engaged couples in their sample, "Do you think that when married people cease to be in love they should divorce, separate, or continue living together?" According to answers given about 80 per cent of the engaged couples were approaching marriage with a conviction that persons should either divorce (60 per cent) or separate (20 per cent) when they were no longer in love. Something less than 20 per cent of the men and women were in favor of husband and wife continuing to live together if they ceased to be in love.[1] This would appear to indicate a loyalty to love over against loyalty to a person (one's spouse) or to marriage. It would be unfair to interpret this as an irresponsible attitude, for, granted the validity of this romantic conception of love, the person could well be said to be acting in a responsible way—responsible to his beliefs about the nature of love and his relationship to it.

The following case from Floyd Dell's book, *Love in*

[1] Ernest W. Burgess and Paul Wallin, *Engagement and Marriage*, Chicago: J. B. Lippincott Co., 1953, pp. 394–395.

Greenwich Village, shows clearly some of the implications of loyalty to love rather than loyalty to another person:

> We met each other at the Liberal Club and became good friends. We were very fond of talk. We talked over everything in the wide world. We neglected food and sleep, in the passionate enthusiasm of discussion. We held the same views on literature and art, we agreed in hating capitalism and war. And, incidentally, of course, we agreed in disbelieving in marriage. We considered it a stupid relic of the barbaric past, a ridiculous and tyrannical convention. We were altogether enchanted with each other's enlightened opinions.
>
> One evening, as Rosemary and I talked, there came in the midst of our intellectual discussion, a pause—a moment in which we gazed at each other in one of those silences that can end only in a kiss. And a moment later we knew—what anybody else, no doubt, could have told us all along—we were in love.
>
> The occasion seemed to demand a pledge of some kind. And so, instead of promising, in the old-fashioned way, to be true to each other, we promised, in a more modern fashion, that each would be true to himself. "And," said Rosemary, "when the time comes, and one of us falls in love with somebody else, we won't lie about it. We will tell each other and part. Freely, and without regrets or recriminations!"
>
> It was true that our relationship would be condemned by nasty-minded people. However, we knew scarcely any nasty-minded people. Our friends were all modern young people like ourselves, many of whom secretly or openly had dispensed with ceremony in their love arrangements. And we had no anxious relatives to come snooping around, asking to see our wedding certificate. Moreover, being poor, we were obscure; no one in New York would care how we lived. We could be lovers openly and fearlessly. Nevertheless, we both felt very adventurous and a little frightened when we went out to look for a place to live.[2]

[2] From *Love in Greenwich Village* by Floyd Dell, pp. 240–243. Copyright 1926. George H. Doran Co. Reprinted by permission of Doubleday & Co., Inc.

The most extreme view of the tentativeness of love relationships is that lasting commitments should never be made either to another person or to the love of another person. One might hold this view either out of conviction or because of extreme self-centeredness. The person holding this view does not make commitments without reservation to people, and he does not make commitments to love. If he makes commitments, he makes them only to himself.

The so-called "beat man" holds such a view of love out of convictions. Since he rejects the past in his rebellion against organized authority, and since his view of the future is one devoid of hope, even sex becomes just another "kick." His involvements with the other sex are momentary or, at best, temporary.

Some pertinent empirical evidence relating to this idea of "permanent tentativeness" of all relationships can be found in the responses of engaged persons in the Burgess-Wallin study. Couples interviewed were asked to indicate under which, if any, of a series of given conditions they would permit themselves extramarital relations. Forty-eight per cent of the 225 men who answered the question and 72.9 per cent of the 225 women said that "under no conditions" would they permit themselves extramarital relations (Table 11). On the other hand, 118 (52 per cent) of the men and 61 (27 per cent) of the women indicated circumstances which they believed would justify their having extramarital relations.

On an average each man who felt that he would permit himself extramarital relations indicated two conditions under which he might do so. The average woman who stated that she would permit herself extramarital relations indicated roughly 1.5 conditions under which she would do so. Having extramarital relations is widely regarded as prima facie evidence of unfaithfulness. Insofar as it is true, such persons would have to be said to be entering marriage with only tentative commitments. They would in effect be saying,

TABLE 11   *Percentage of 118 Men and 61 Women Who Would Permit Themselves Extramarital Relationships Under Indicated Conditions*

Condition	Men [a]	Women [a]
General dissatisfaction with spouse	20.3	16.4
Spouse's illness (temporary)	1.7	0
Spouse's illness (chronic)	22.9	9.8
Unfaithfulness of spouse (once)	15.3	6.6
Unfaithfulness of spouse (repeated)	44.1	49.2
Strong attraction to another person	17.8	23.0
Wish for variety	2.5	3.3
Wanting to arouse spouse's jealousy	0.8	1.6
Spouse's frequent absence	14.4	6.6
Frigidity of wife	51.7	—
Unsatisfactory sexual response from husband	—	24.6
Wife's pregnancy	3.4	—

SOURCE: From *Engagement and Marriage* by Ernest W. Burgess and Paul Wallin, Table 58, p. 401. Copyright 1953 by J. B. Lippincott Company.

[a] The percentages total more than 100 because some of the men and women checked more than one category.

"If I am happy and satisfied I will be faithful to my spouse, but if I should become dissatisfied with him (her), or if he should become ill, or if I should become interested in another person, or if I should not find my spouse sexually satisfying, or if my spouse were unfaithful to me, I would not feel obligated to be faithful." The engagement vows would have to be regarded as tentative and conditional, holding only so long as the respondent was happy and satisfied with his spouse and with his marriage.

In conclusion, the question of the tentativeness or permanence of engagement must be fitted into a much broader context, namely, the tentativeness or permanence of any love relationships either during engagement or during marriage. The meaning of a commitment to a loved one is a crucial matter for couples to discuss. The value they place on the vital matter of faithfulness to each other will become apparent and will be very important to their life together during marriage. They are well advised to face the matter of commitment and faithfulness realistically before vows are exchanged.

A person should not assume that his beloved interprets the symbols of various stages in the dating process in the same way that he does. Studies on at least three college and university campuses have demonstrated a marked difference between the sexes in the meaning which each attaches to pinning and engagement. The data in Table 12 show that

TABLE 12   *The Meaning of Pinning and Engagement As Seen in the Responses of Over 1200 Students on Three College and University Campuses*

	Men Per Cent		Women Per Cent	
The Meaning of Pinning and Engagement	Yes	No	Yes	No
If a girl wears a boy's frat pin it means:				
They are going steady	31		12 [a]	
They are engaged to be engaged	63		80 [a]	
They are engaged	27	47	44	28 [b]
	11	76	44	39 [c]
Wearing his frat pin is as binding as wearing his engagement ring	11	84	31	64 [c]
Couple members should consider engagement as binding as marriage	30	60	63	31 [c]

SOURCE: Partially adapted from Judson T. and Mary G. Landis, *Building a Successful Marriage*, 2nd Ed., p. 182. Copyright, 1948, 1953, by Prentice-Hall, Inc., Englewood Cliffs, N.J. Reprinted by permission of the publisher.

[a] 450 University of California students.
[b] Over 700 Michigan State College students.
[c] 113 Gustavus Adolphus College students.

on every item women respondents tended to regard pinning and engagement commitments as more binding than did men. These data point up the importance of couple members knowing each other's interpretation of the meaning of not only pinning and engagement but, more important, the meaning of marriage vows.

There is a striking difference, for instance, in responses to the statement "Couple members should consider engagement as binding as marriage." Thirty per cent of the men students answered "Yes" to this item, and 63 per cent of the girls answered in the affirmative. Surely this is a subject for serious discussion by prospective marriage mates.

Engagement and the American Ideal

Perhaps a word about the relationship between tentativeness versus commitment in the light of the American ideal (dignity, freedom, and equality of all men) is in order. If we accept man as more worthy of respect than any other inanimate or animate object on earth, then commitment to love rather than commitment to a beloved becomes heresy, for it places loyalty to feeling above loyalty to another person.

In the same way, to make commitments to be faithful only to one's self and to keep all relationships with others on a tenuous and tentative basis is heretical when viewed against our belief in the freedom and equality of all men. Under such a belief system it is never right to use other persons as objects for one's own gratification and then to discard them. To sever one's relationship with a person who has given of himself on one's behalf (assuming that he has) is to exploit that person without taking responsibility for the consequences. To marry a woman, to possess her, and enjoy the gifts of love she has to give, and then to abrogate one's responsibility to her and to the consequences of that love is a luxury that is not consistent with democratic values. If lovers part by mutual consent, the conditions are somewhat altered, but still it is a moot question whether or not their responsibility for each other ends.

Random and Serious Dating As Testing Period

Even those who think that the tentative nature of a love relationship should at some time end—either in a broken relationship or in a permanent relationship—agree that it should not become permanent too soon. The couple should feel reasonably sure of their love and should have carefully weighed the possibilities of love eventuating in marriage. With our emergent system of dating this testing period can now come before engagement rather than afterwards.

It may well be that persons who advocate the tentative nature of engagement have not taken full cognizance of the possibilities of our rapidly emerging dating system. In an earlier day when courting rather than dating was the practice there was really only one stage before marriage when couple members could get to know each other intimately—that was betrothal or engagement. The couple, though they may have been fond of each other, were not regarded as a couple and did not have the freedom of association of a couple until after engagement, if at all. A boy who showed any interest in an eligible girl was expected to indicate his intentions to marry her very early in the relationship or to turn his attentions elsewhere. Under such a system of mate selection there is good reason to believe that the two did not know each other as persons before they became engaged. They may have known of each other, they may have known each other's families, they may even have been passing acquaintances in the community before they were engaged, but they did not test (according to modern standards) whether or not they were suited to each other. Against this background there was good reason for social scientists and others to urge the couple to use engagement as a testing period before vows of fidelity were exchanged.

But this is no longer the situation. Couples may rush into engagement and marriage without adequate preparation for lasting commitments to each other; they may, but they need not. Here is one of the most important differences between the courtship system of mate selection and the dating system of mate selection.

The American system of dating, as it is emerging, allows for testing at several stages prior to formal engagement. In fact, we now have not one stage before marriage (engagement) but a possibility of five stages! There is random dating for finding out in general about the opposite sex as companions; there is random going steady for finding out what it is like to associate in dating exclusively with one person of the other sex; there is serious random dating in which the person who is serious about getting married can, without commitment but with some degree of privacy and intimacy through paired, unchaperoned dating, size up other persons as possible mates; there is serious going steady in which one or both are well aware that some possible testing for future marriage is taking place. Last of all there is pinning or engaged-to-be-engaged for testing and trial with very few persons involved in the secret.

When they feel sure of their love for each other and the possibilities of its eventuating in marriage, they can become formally engaged, with all the fanfair, symbols, parties, announcements that they, their parents, and their friends feel are appropriate to the occasion. The anxiety and frustrations of the testing period are at an end, and the couple can enjoy their exalted status—"Everyone loves a lover"—in the fullest possible way.

Against these possibilities inherent in our emerging system

of dating, engagement need no longer be a testing period. What then becomes of the functions of engagement in our emerging dating system?

With such ample opportunity in our mate-selection system for love to develop and testing and trial to take place before formal engagement, the engagement becomes that period between the time of announcement of intention to marry and the date of marriage itself. It becomes a period of preparation for marriage in the area of specific decisions that must be made or should be made in regard to the wedding, the honeymoon, and other practical problems of life together.

Engagement now emerges not as the uneasy and uncertain testing and trial period. Instead it assumes some of the aura of romance with which engagement as commitment is blessed. The girl can plan for the wedding without reservation regarding her own intentions or the intentions of her fiancé; she can bask in all the glory and honor shown the girl who is soon to be married. The aura of romance surrounding engagement returns and can be fully and confidently enjoyed; the testing has taken place and both are confident that they have passed the test! This is a view of engagement quite out of keeping with the view revealed in the following engagement history of a young man.

If I were to advise other people on their engagements, looking at mine, I would have to say that this is entirely different from going with a girl on a casual to semi-serious basis. When you become engaged, the time has arrived when you no longer put on a front. Many times you are not going to like what is presented to you. You are going to wonder sometimes if this was the right thing to do. I would say that if you can weather the storms and come through them still wanting to have the girl near you, or the boy as the case may be, and still feel that something is missing when the other party is not near you, then you have chosen wisely.

If we regard engagement as commitment it is clear from this young man's testimony that the couple had become engaged too soon. No one would consciously make a commitment to marry a person who was "putting on a front." This would be engagement to an illusion rather than engagement to a real person. Clearly this couple needed to regard their engagement as a testing period even though it had already been formalized with the presentation of a diamond. Such superficial acquaintance is not a necessary condition of engagement under our present informal and intimate dating system; the time to "no longer put on a front" is during the serious going-steady or pinned stage of the relationship, not the engagement.

What is the purpose of formal engagement? Practically speaking, formal engagement is a time of preparation for the wedding, the honeymoon, and the experiences of life as a newly married couple. We can mention only a few of these specific preparations.

Regarding the wedding, there are matters such as the nature of the wedding, the date of the wedding, the place of the wedding, the officiants, the attendants, the guest list, the reception, gifts for the attendants, announcements, music, etc. Regarding the honeymoon, there are plans involving the nature of the honeymoon, the place, the length of the honeymoon, reservations for accommodations, transportation, etc. These are specifics in connection with the wedding and honeymoon themselves. There are others not so directly involved in these two events. We turn to a brief consideration of some of these.

The couple will have discussed before they became engaged the attitudes of each toward the bride's holding a job after marriage. Now, if they are agreed that she shall work, it usually means work in a new location for her, and she may want to look into job possibilities in "his" town. Also, housing is difficult in many places, and the couple may want to do some preliminary house-hunting during the formal engagement period.

They will have discussed attitudes toward children, too—perhaps also the number they would like—and their attitudes toward control of family size. If they are agreed in principle on some form of control, there is the matter of getting expert and specific instruction in the use of control techniques.

If both have been in reasonably good health, the matter of health will have entered their thinking very little during dating days, but before marriage each may want a physical examination, and the bride-to-be may want to know specifically if there are reasons why she should not bear babies or if there are conditions that might require medical treatment. The time of this premarital examination might be the time for instruction in conception-control techniques and methods.

The following engagement history gives a picture of some of the premarital decisions in an engagement that is not a testing and trial period but one involving wedding and family plans on the part of two people who definitely plan to marry.

What a difference that little diamond made in our lives! Now we had something specific which we could both plan and work together for. First of all, we were going to wait until I graduated to get married, but that was two years away so we tried to find a way in which we could move the date up a little.

When we finally decided on the day for the wedding we really started to make plans for the future. First of all we went to see our pastor and had the church reserved. Then we looked further into the possibilities of working in the college town. With her five years of secretarial experience her chances of finding a job were very good. The next step in the process was looking for a place for us to live. The first thing I did was to reserve a place in the housing unit at school in case we couldn't find any suitable places in town.

As the time for the wedding drew near, Nancy went

to a baby doctor and had a check-up to be sure that everything was functioning properly. While she was there she also checked into the methods of birth control. As I would still have another year of school left after our marriage, we wouldn't be able to have any children until after graduation. The doctor recommended that she use a diaphragm which she then purchased.

The following case is also instructive for it illustrates that even though the testing period is behind them, there are still problems which couples recognize but cannot necessarily resolve prior to marriage—as well as problems which they may not previously have recognized as problems.

We are not anticipating a marriage totally devoid of problems. We would prefer to postpone our children until the latter part of John's last year in graduate school, but we must be prepared to accept and be enthusiastic about a pregnancy before that time if it does occur. This would make it much harder financially, but it is by no means a catastrophic possibility.

I am from a two-child family, and John has two brothers and a sister. John would like to have four children, and I prefer two. Rather than make a decision at this time, we have decided to wait until the question is more nearly at hand, because we realize that our only contacts with family living are as children, and that evidently we want to copy our parents' examples.

Our difficulties about money promise to be most persistent, especially in view of the fact that we will not have a large income. Both John and I are keeping expense accounts in order to give us some idea of how much money we are spending now, so that we can set up some type of budget for next year.

We must realize that many problems which we anticipate now will never materialize, and that many will come up which we never dreamed would happen.

A couple cannot anticipate and resolve all of the problems of the early years of marriage during the engagement period, but the more recognized and resolved in advance, the better.

How Long Should the Engagement Be?

How long should an engagement be? Long enough to get the things done that must be done during engagement. But this, though true, is not very helpful, and the question is worth more serious consideration.

One must consider not only the engagement but also the length and intensity of the acquaintance before engagement. By and large, empirical studies have shown that the longer periods of acquaintance are correlated with marriages that last. But length of acquaintance is only one consideration; depth and intimacy of acquaintance are the real issues. Some couples, if they are serious daters, get to the "business at hand" of getting to know each other very quickly; others do not. Since we do our serious dating in a setting of recreation and good times, it is possible to date for a long time without ever getting to the serious business of really considering each other and the relationship.

In the American dating system, the engagement can be a rather short period once the partners have made up their minds about each other and their prospects for marriage. It may be difficult to lay all the plans in less than two or three months, particularly if the bride-to-be is going to school or holding down a full-time job. On the other hand, the engagement should likely not run much over a year unless the lovers must spend much time apart, for the desire to be one and to live together becomes more and more intense for the couple in love and if the wedding is postponed too long the engagement period may become one of anxiety and frustration rather than one of pleasant anticipation.[3]

A rule of thumb might be a long enough acquaintance so

[3] The problem of intimacy in long engagements is discussed in a later chapter.

that the couple feel confident of their love and the possibilities of its eventuating in marriage plus a long enough engagement to have the fun of doing the preparations for marriage in a way that will make it a satisfying and pleasant experience and memory. Some couples may accomplish all of this in less than a year's time, but it is unlikely that most can do so.

Should Engagement Ever Be Broken?

An engagement—engagement as commitment to marry—cannot be made with the proviso, tacit or explicit, that if it doesn't work out it can be broken. With such a proviso, engagement becomes just an extension of the testing period. For couples who feel sure of their love, vows to love and to be faithful to each other can be made at the time of engagement as well as in the wedding ceremony; hence both couple members can proceed with preparations on the assumption that the engagement will not be broken.

This is not to say that engagements should never be broken; such a view would be unrealistic. If something comes to light or develops during the engagement which makes a successful marriage seem impossible, the engagement should, of course, be broken. There is no particular heroism involved in two persons' entering a marriage that has the earmarks of failure before it is begun. But to have to break the engagement after genuine commitments of love, devotion, and fidelity have been exchanged should come as a shock and disappointment to the pair. The blow will fall particularly on the partner who feels that the relationship need not have ended; and it will be difficult for both to the extent that each had come to know, to appreciate, and to desire the other. According to their own admission persons do recover from broken love affairs, but any love affair involving unique persons is a unique experience and as such will not be duplicated even if one or both subsequently fall in love again.

Couples who have been in love and must part will want to part with as much grace, kindness, and consideration for the feelings of each other as is possible. There will be heartache, but a broken engagement is perhaps less serious than a broken marriage; and sometimes one might even come to view a broken love affair as a valuable, though unpleasant, experience.

In one respect I feel pangs of conscience about this affair, but from another aspect the experience is priceless. It's a maturity in its own right allowing an insight to human nature which can't be duplicated.

Summary

Commitments made in a budding love relationship should be kept tentative until love has developed and the couple feel reasonably sure that they know, accept, and love each other enough to make lasting commitments. Only with lasting commitments of devotion and fidelity can a free individual worthy of respect and the right to personality growth—the American ideal—be expected to enter a relationship where he gives freely of himself in a community of love with another person.

QUESTIONS AND PROJECTS

1. According to the romantic marriage model, when should the tentative period of a love relationship end? Elaborate.
2. What decisions should a couple make concerning their relationship before they become engaged?
3. Is it possible that one's fiancé(e) might hold a meaning of engagement different from one's own?

4. How many testing stages are there prior to the engagement period in contemporary dating?
5. What activities characterize the engagement period in permanent engagement?
6. What are some of the circumstances under which it would be justifiable to break a permanent engagement?

SUGGESTED READINGS

Becker, Howard, and Reuben Hill, *Family Marriage and Parenthood*, Boston: D. C. Heath & Company, 1955, Chapter 9.

Burgess, Ernest W., and Paul Wallin, *Engagement and Marriage*, Chicago: J. B. Lippincott Co., 1953, Chapters 8–10.

Kanin, Eugene J., and David H. Howard, "Postmarital Consequences of Premarital Sex Adjustment," *American Sociological Review*, Vol. 23, October 1958, pp. 556–562.

Kirkpatrick, Clifford, and Theodore Caplow, "Courtship in a Group of Minnesota Students," *American Journal of Sociology*, Vol. 51, 1945, pp. 114–125.

Monahan, Thomas P., "Does Age at Marriage Matter in Divorce?" *Social Forces*, Vols. 31–32, October 1953, pp. 81–87.

Popenoe, Paul, and Donna Neptune, "Acquaintance and Betrothal," *Social Forces*, Vol. 16, 1938, pp. 552–555.

Thomas, John L., *The American Catholic Family*, Englewood Cliffs, N. J.: Prentice-Hall, Inc., 1956, Chapter 7.

$I4$ Intimacy in Dating

▮▮

In other chapters we have discussed the progression in psychological and social intimacy between couple members in dating. There is a concomitant progression in physical involvement as attachment between two persons increases. Because of the concern over sex as a part of dating behavior in America, we have chosen to single this subject out for special consideration.

One gets the impression that in word, and perhaps in deed, sexual intimacy is a major American preoccupation. Why is this so?

Surely ambivalence in values and norms and ambivalence between normative patterns and the behavior patterns of daters is in large part responsible for the concern. The following are some of the ambivalent and contradictory norms and practices in dating in America:

1. American culture has a history of prudishness regarding the human body, its exposure, and its functions, particularly sex functions.

2. Concomitantly, there is a history of rigid norms of sexual morality—stemming from the historic Judaic-Christian marriage model—condemning any and all sexual outlet prior to marriage and outside of marriage—masturbation, premarital intercourse, extramarital intercourse, and a variety of perversions. Historically these rigid norms have applied more to the actions of women than of men—our so-called "double standard" of morality.

3. On the other hand, there are romantic norms which are permissive—stating that any activity is permissible for those who are in love; this is our heritage from the romantic marriage model.

4. Consistent with some of the rationalistic norms is a belief that sex experimentation and testing before marriage are important as preparation for successful marriage.

5. Through random dating we permit unchaperoned, private, paired dating among adolescents at a time when, for the boy, the sex drive is nearing its high point of development.

6. There are norms emphasizing the pleasure in sexual activity and the prestige that sex conquests bring among peers, particularly in the male subculture, again reflecting the double standard.

With a rigid public morality in the area of sex and a more lenient sexual morality among daters, and with unchaperoned, private, paired dating among adolescents, there is little wonder that responsible groups in American society show concern over the sex behavior of daters.

Incidence of Intimacy in Dating

In the light of this ambivalence, what is the nature and extent of intimacy in American dating?

Actually, we do not know. Since dating is a private affair, and with the public code of morality as rigid as it is, physical intimacy in dating becomes a private and secretive matter. Not only do young people not confide in their elders in these matters, but, if the involvement is of an intimate type, they may not reveal it to anyone, not even their friends in the peer group. For this reason, plus the fact that so much dating is of the paired rather than the group variety, daters are not sources of reliable information on the dating activities of their peer group because they really do not know.

Having said this, we must add that young people have been quite willing to discuss their own intimate activity in dating if they can be assured anonymity or at least that they will not be exposed or censured. Hence it is possible to say some things about involvement prior to marriage.

First, we will discuss intimacy in dating in a general way and then speak more specifically about intimacy at different stages of the dating cycle.

Limited physical contact, involving holding hands, some hugging, and kissing, is common in American dating, and, if it does not become a preoccupation of the daters, it seems to be taken in stride by them as well as by the parent generation. "A little lovin'" is regarded as one of the thrills of dating in our society. It does not imply commitments on the part of the daters to each other nor emotional attachment between them.

However, in our intimate dating system, limited intimacy, commonly referred to as necking, frequently develops for the couple, wittingly or unwittingly, into more extensive fondling and caressing by one or both of the daters. This practice is referred to as petting. The effect of petting is to stimulate erotic arousal. Necking may also stimulate erotic arousal in the more easily stimulated, but petting will quite generally do so, except in the least easily aroused where the reaction may be one of disgust rather than stimulation.

That petting frequently leads to extreme erotic arousal is evidenced in the fact that in Kinsey's samples 39 per cent of the females reported having petted to orgasm by age twenty-five, and 31 per cent of the male subjects so reported.[1] That heavy petting is apparently on the increase in our society is seen in the fact that 15 per cent of the girls born before 1900 had petted to orgasm between the ages of twelve and twenty-five, whereas 43 per cent of the girls born between 1920 and 1929 so reported.

The most advanced stage of physical involvement, coitus, is severely frowned upon by society when indulged in by the unmarried, particularly the nonengaged. Nevertheless, as reported by Kinsey, the majority of persons who marry have experienced sexual intercourse prior to marriage. For the women in his study, 50 per cent had had intercourse prior to marriage, and for the men, 98 per cent of those with 0–8 years of schooling, 85 per cent of those with 9–12 years of schooling, and 68 per cent of those with 13-plus years of schooling had had sexual intercourse prior to marriage.

Men commonly experience intercourse with other partners than the affianced; this is not so true of women. Empirical data from studies of dating activity show clearly that the largest group of females having had sexual intercourse prior to marriage are those who had coitus only with the fiancé. This group includes 45 to 70 per cent of all nonvirginal women.[2] Of Burgess and Wallin's engaged couples

---

[1] Alfred C. Kinsey, Wardell B. Pomeroy, Clyde E. Martin, and Paul Gebhard, *Sexual Behavior in the Human Female*, Philadelphia: W. B. Saunders Co., 1953, p. 267.
[2] Ira L. Reiss, "The Treatment of Pre-Marital Coitus in 'Marriage and the Family' Texts," *Social Problems*, Vol. 4, April 1957, p. 334.

approximately 45 per cent had premarital coitus,[3] and only a small minority of these had intercourse no more than once. Findings of more recent research involving a sample of 190 wives of Midwestern university students are in agreement. Of 177 respondents, 43.5 per cent reported premarital coital experience. Approximately two out of three engaged couples who had sexual relations reported having them occasionally or frequently.

The dramatic change, or revolution, in the premarital sexual behavior of Americans in the last forty years is characterized by the marked increase in petting and coitus among social equals, especially among engaged couples. This has meant a decrease in the activities of males with prostitutes and an increase in the premarital petting and coital experience of other girls and women.[4]

Even with the increase in intimacy between social equals, heavy petting and sexual intercourse are not the chief sources of orgasm for young people today. Masturbation remains the largest single means of achieving an orgasm, providing 66 per cent of total orgasm for men and 65 per cent of total orgasm for women in the sixteen-twenty age group, according to Kinsey.

As pointed out in the chapter on men and women, there has been a tendency not to emphasize the differences between the sexes but to emphasize or overemphasize the similarities. This has meant, among other things, that the marked differences in the sex drive of the sexes has been partly overlooked in the literature until the researches of Kinsey and associates. The differences are important to an understanding of activity in dating and marriage.

Though Kinsey found that there is more variation in

[3] Eugene J. Kanin and David H. Howard, "Postmarital Consequences of Premarital Sex Adjustment," *American Sociological Review*, Vol. 23, October 1958, p. 557.
[4] Winston Ehrmann, "Some Knowns and Unknowns in Research into Human Sex Behavior," *Marriage and Family Living*, Vol. XIX, February 1957, p. 19.

sexual desire between members of the same sex, and for both sexes, than has been commonly assumed, the empirical evidence showing man to be the sex aggressor in relations between the sexes is quite conclusively demonstrated.

There are both biological and social reasons for the sexual aggressiveness of the man in our society. It is one of the most important findings of the Kinsey studies that in the case of the boy sexual maturity in terms of sexual activity is reached in the middle or later teens, whereas for the girl greatest satisfaction from sexual activity does not occur until much later. The number of women reaching orgasm from any source after marriage increased steadily to age thirty-six to forty, perhaps reflecting the more permissive setting that marriage provides. Nearly 100 per cent of the men in the Kinsey sample experienced orgasm in coitus in marriage, whereas 9 per cent of the married women never experienced orgasm from any source.

Kinsey further points out that men and women are different in readiness of sexual response. Men are easily aroused sexually not only through contact with the other sex but also through other stimuli such as suggestive pictures and suggestive stories. Men are also more preoccupied with sex than are women.

This preoccupation is due in part to the physiological and psychological sexual readiness of the man, but it is also due to the fact that sex plays a major part in social interaction between men in American society. They look at and talk about women in terms of sex, they joke about sex, they carry about and show each other suggestive literature and objects, they participate in sexual activity with prostitutes, pick-ups, girl friends, and married women.

This greater preoccupation of men with sex is recognized and partially allowed for in our "double standard" of sex morality. The double standard has never been a shared ultimate value of our society, but it is a very old "sub rosa" norm of American society. It is a sub rosa norm because it is contrary to some of our most cherished values, particularly the American ideal of dignity, freedom, and equality of all men and of both sexes. A statement of the meaning of this covert norm for premarital relations has recently been formulated:

> Premarital sexual intercourse is wrong for all women; women that indulge are therefore bad women. Premarital sexual intercourse is excusable (if not right) for all men and thus men that indulge are not thereby bad men.[5]

"We find the defendant . . . 36–24–36!"
Reproduced courtesy of John W. Frost.

Persons who accept the double standard of premarital sexual activity accept the view that complete sexual abstinence is not to be expected of the man before marriage; hence there must be a supply of women who break the double standard in order that men might uphold it! The double standard is implemented as follows:

> The supply of women available for premarital sexual intercourse will be composed of bad women who have already demonstrated their badness by previous sexual in-

[5] Ira L. Reiss, "The Double Standard in Premarital Sexual Intercourse: A Neglected Concept," *Social Forces*, Vol. 34, March 1956, p. 225.

dulgences or whose character, personality, class level, race, etc., is such that they could be considered inferior, different or bad. One should not entice a good girl (good in character, personality, class, race, etc.) into breaking the double standard for that would be leading her astray.[6]

The difference in sex norms of the two sexes is reflected in the responses of high school and college students to direct questioning. As shown in Table 13, high school girls were

TABLE 13 *Responses by 298 High School Seniors to Questions on Sex Norms*

		Boys N 121 Per Cent	Girls N 177 Per Cent	"Gap" Per Cent
I really have to like a person before I'll neck with him (or her)	Agree	47	92	45
	Disagree	43	2	41
	Uncertain	10	6	—
I kiss a person good night only if I like him (or her) very much	Agree	51	88	37
	Disagree	40	5	40
	Uncertain	9	7	
If a person will neck on the first date, I won't have much use for them	Agree	34	67	33
	Disagree	55	19	36
	Uncertain	11	14	
It's OK for steady couples to pet	Agree	58	18	40
	Disagree	25	61	36
	Uncertain	17	21	
Going all the way might hurt my chances for later happiness in marriage	Agree	51	93	42
	Disagree	37	2	35
	Uncertain	12	5	
It is difficult to keep from petting, when you realize you might be four years in college or working, and even longer before you get married	Agree	65	28	37
	Disagree	25	60	35
	Uncertain	10	12	—
Most boys I know will go "as far as they can"	Agree	69	12	57
	Disagree	26	81	55
	Uncertain	5	7	

SOURCE: Adapted with permission from Warren Breed, "Sex, Class and Socialization in Dating," *Marriage and Family Living*, Vol. XVIII, May 1956, Table II, p. 139.

[6] *Ibid.*

quite definitely of the opinion that they should not become involved in any intimacies even at the "milder" level of necking unless they definitely liked the boy. Ninety-two per cent of the girls agreed that this should be the standard. On the other hand, only 47 per cent of the boys agreed that they would neck with a girl only if they "really" liked her. This supports an observation made by Eckert, "For women, there are generally three steps: (1) friendship, (2) respect and love, and (3) sexual intercourse." That is, women do not become involved, or do not desire to become involved, physically, until after there has been psychological acceptance of the man. Men, on the other hand, not uncommonly desire physical involvement, even of the most intimate type, without any thought given to the desirability of the girl as a friend or companion. The visit of a man to a prostitute or his date with a "pick-up" precisely for the purpose of having sexual intercourse with her is evidence of the fact that, setting aside moral scruples or accepting the double standard, men will voluntarily engage in the activity in the third step without going through the first and the second.

The variable effect of the double standard on the sexes may in part account for the fact that whereas only one-half of the boys agreed that "going all the way might hurt" their chances for later happiness in marriage, 93 per cent of the girls felt that it might do so.

The pressure of the double standard as brought to bear by one's peers is shown in Hollingshead's analysis of sexual activity among the out-of-school adolescents in Elmtown.

A withdrawee boy who had not "laid a girl" by the time he was old enough to leave school claimed that he had to protect himself from being called a "sissy," or "a pansy," by his clique mates. A boy who is known or believed to be a virgin is not respected by his peers. A boy is condemned severely, however, if he does not have enough knowledge of contraceptives and prophylactics to keep from getting "in trouble." . . .

The class IV and class V boys place a high value on

"making a girl." Thus, a boy achieves status in his own eyes when he "makes a girl" the first time he takes her out. If a girl is known as "an easy mark" and a boy does not seduce her with relative ease, he believes that there is something wrong with either himself or his "technique." This egocentric pride in their sex prowess motivates many boys deliberately to "fool with" girls they know they can have in the course of an evening.[7]

Anyone who is not convinced that men, particularly in the social classes Hollingshead is writing about, commonly dispense with the steps of friendship and love and respect has but to read Hollingshead's chapter on sex and marriage in its entirety.

But we would not give the impression that the double standard of sexual morality is prevalent only among high school students or out-of-school adolescents. Studies of college students have also shown differences in responses between men and women on sex norms (Table 14), though the differences have not been as pronounced as those found for the high school population. The greater permissiveness of the girl when love and respect has developed is shown in the percentages of those approving of "mild necking or petting" in the engagement period. Ninety-one per cent of the boys approved of this activity and 84 per cent of the girls approved—a difference of only 7 per cent between the sexes. In other words, the dating stage with the highest level of love and respect shows the girl to be permissive regarding involvement, supporting the observation by Eckert.

The "gap" between percentages in the responses of boys and girls in high school is larger than that between college men and women. This may be a real or only an apparent difference. It may be due in part to the difference in questions and the difference in the way they were posed, it may be due to a local situation in the city where the high school students lived, it may be due to the fact that colleges are selective

[7] Reprinted with permission from August B. Hollingshead, *Elmtown's Youth*, copyright 1949, John Wiley & Sons, Inc., p. 421.

TABLE 14 *Responses by College Students to Questions on Sex Norms from Selected Studies*

Question	Boys Agree Per Cent	Girls Agree Per Cent	"Gap" Per Cent
"All right to kiss on first date" [a]	35	17	18
Approve "mild necking or petting [b] for pre-engagement period" [c]	54	15	39
". . . for engagement period"	91	84	7
Approve "heavy necking or petting for pre-engagement period" [b]	7	0	7
". . . for engagement period"	30	12	18
"Girl must neck to be popular" [d]	44	15	29
"Girl must pet to be popular" [d]	21	4	17
Approve sex relations: for both [e]	19	4	15
for neither	57	70	13
for men only	9	19	10
between engaged only	15	7	8

SOURCE: Adapted with permission from Warren Breed, "Sex, Class and Socialization in Dating," *Marriage and Family Living*, Vol. XVIII, Table 1, p. 138, and Judson T. and Mary G. Landis, *Building a Successful Marriage*, 2nd Ed., p. 178. Copyright, 1948, 1953, by Prentice-Hall, Inc., Englewood Cliffs, N. J. Reprinted by permission of the publisher.

[a] Harold T. Christensen, *Marriage Analysis*, New York: The Ronald Press Company, 1950, p. 226. Sample: 1385 unmarried Mormon students at Brigham Young University, 1946–1947.
[b] *Ibid.* Sample: 234 students at University of Wisconsin, 1939.
[c] "Necking" usually refers to kissing and light caressing "above the neck." "Petting" includes more intimate contact with the erogenous zones, short of sexual intercourse, which is "going all the way" in the folk phrase.
[d] William M. Smith, Jr., "Rating and Dating: A Re-study," *Marriage and Family Living*, Vol. XIV, November 1952, pp. 312–317. Sample: 602 students at X College, 1950.
[e] Judson T. and Mary G. Landis, 1953, *op. cit.*, p. 134. Sample: 1600 students in 11 colleges in 1952.

in their choice of students whereas the high schools are much less selective, or it may actually represent a real difference in that college students have learned democratic norms of governing dating activity and have more generally accepted them. Comparative study of high school and college students would be necessary before one could ascertain the extent and the meaning of the differences in responses. Be that as it may, the important fact so far as our present discussion is concerned is that differences in responses between the sexes reflect a double standard at both educational levels and in all of the studies.

The differences in attitudes and activities of the sexes can be seen also in the greater aggressiveness in initiating intimacy in dating on the part of the boy—positive controls—and the limits set on intimacy by the girl—negative controls. If the girl is a "good" girl, the boy is inclined to move with caution in suggesting or initiating intimacy or to refrain entirely. If she has a reputation of being a "bad" girl, or if she comes from a group that the boy does not respect, he may proceed on the assumption that he will take all that is allowed even to the point of sexual intercourse if the girl is willing.

That "one should not entice a good girl" is strongly supported by both the responses of the boys and the girls as shown on Table 15. Only one boy in eleven stated that the boy should proceed in initiating physical intimacies if the girl objects and he thinks that she means it. On the other hand, 43 per cent of the boys agreed that the boy should not

TABLE 15   *Responses Regarding Patterns of Positive and Negative Control of Physical Intimacy in Dating Among High School Students*

		Boys N 121 Per Cent	Girls N 177 Per Cent
If the girl says "no" and the boy does not think she means it, he should stop	Agree	41	61
	Disagree	43	17
	Uncertain	16	22
If the girl says "no" and the boy thinks she means it, he should stop	Agree	89	96
	Disagree	9	3
	Uncertain	2	1

SOURCE: Adapted with permission from Warren Breed, "Sex, Class and Socialization in Dating," *Marriage and Family Living*, Vol. XVIII, May 1956, p. 141.

stop if he thinks that the girl is not sincere in her protestations. In other words, the girl is expected to set the limits—negative controls—for physical intimacy in dating, but she may set them at a level where she thinks she should set them rather than where she necessarily wants them set. It is then regarded as a part of the boy's privilege—or responsibility—to test the sincerity of her protestations.

Studies among college students show similar patterns of the boy providing the positive and the girl the negative controls regarding amount of love-making (Table 16). Though

TABLE 16   *Patterns of Positive and Negative Control of Physical Intimacy in the Dating of College Students*

| | Campus A [a] | | Campus B [b] | |
| | Reported by | | Reported by | |
	Boys N 576 Per Cent	Girls N 265 Per Cent	Boys N 21 Per Cent	Girls N 39 Per Cent
Dates on which behavior initiated by:				
Boy	75	79	65	66
Girl	25	21	35	34
Dates on which behavior went no farther because: No opportunity	23	13	13	15
Girl would not	30	30	23	30
Boy would not	5	2	4	5
Neither tried	43	55	60	50

SOURCE: Winston Ehrmann, "Student Cooperation in a Study of Dating Behavior," *Marriage and Family Living*, Vol. XIV, November 1952, p. 323.

[a] A southeastern university.
[b] A Midwestern college.

the boys initiated more of the intimacy as reported by both boys and girls, it is interesting to note the large percentage of cases in which "behavior went no farther" because "neither tried" (between 43 and 60 per cent). This is likely due in part to the respect tendered by a boy to a girl in his own social class. This is in accord with the norms of the double standard. But as Ehrmann points out—on the basis of interviews with a number of his respondents—"neither tried" was also primarily negative control by the girl, though the attitudes about it were different. "This type of control usually represented an equilibrium point that was acceptable to both parties. The male did not try to go beyond it because he knew that the girl would not go farther or because he felt that he ought not to try to go farther in consideration for her moral attitudes." Hence, though double-standard norms sanctioning sexual aggressiveness are prevalent in the sub-culture of the man, chivalry apparently is not dead!

TABLE 17 *Date Relationship and Erotic Intimacy Level at Which Offensiveness Occurred Among High School Senior Girls, by Episode*

	Necking and Petting Above the Waist		Petting Below the Waist		Attempted Intercourse and Attempted Intercourse with Violence		Total	
	N	%	N	%	N	%	N	%
First date	146	30	14	16	12	14	172	26
Occasional date	148	31	24	27	23	26	195	30
Regular date, "pinned," and engaged [a]	186	39	52	58	52	60	290	44

SOURCE: Adapted from Eugene J. Kanin, "Male Aggression in Dating-Courtship Relations," *American Journal of Sociology*, Vol. LXIII, September 1957, p. 200. Copyright 1957 by the University of Chicago.
[a] The only four episodes reported under the engaged category are to be found in the attempted intercourse and attempted intercourse with violence cell.

Sexual aggressiveness of the man often causes offense to the girl as pointed out in recent questionnaire studies of aggression in the dating experience of high school and college girls. Of 262 college freshmen (reporting on dating experience during their senior year in high school and the following summer), 62 per cent reported episodes that were offensive to them, and of 291 college girls reporting, 56 per cent reported themselves offended at least once during the school year at some level of erotic intimacy. The nature of the date relationship and the nature of the offensive activity are presented in Tables 17 and 18.

Summary

American ambivalence about sex expression helps to make of it a major preoccupation of our culture. We have never quite accepted sex as natural and potentially wholesome— one of "God's good gifts to man." On the other hand, we cannot and do not want to eschew the enjoyment of it.

Our recent invention in human relations—random dating for the very young—has only heightened our concern over sex and sex expression. For we know that random dating is structured in such a way that intimacy is possible and highly probable. Sublimated sex expression—necking and petting— is widely practiced. And direct sex expression—coitus—is not uncommon to American dating.

In accordance with natural tendencies and the permissions and proscriptions of the double standard of morality, the man is the aggressor in initiating intimacy in dating. That there is a considerable gap between the sex norms of men and women has been empirically demonstrated, as has the fact that the aggressive conduct of men is often offensive to women.

QUESTIONS AND PROJECTS

1. Defend or attack the statement, "The concern of the parent generation over dating intimacy among adolescents is largely groundless."
2. How do you account for the apparent increase in petting and coitus among social equals in recent decades?

3. Is there any biological basis for the aggressive activity of the man in pursuing intimate involvement?
4. Are there any social or cultural reasons for his aggressive behavior? Elaborate.

SUGGESTED READINGS

See Chapter 15, Lovers' Dilemma, pp. 243–244.

$I5$ Lovers' Dilemma

Intimacy in Random Dating

There has been relatively little study of the nature and extent of love-making in random dating, and what there is shows contradictory results.

Several students of dating, basing their observations on responses of college students, agree that physical intimacy is not particularly prevalent or involved in the random stage of dating. LeMasters observes that the necking and petting problem in American dating is not located primarily in the random stage of dating but that it occurs in later stages: going steady, pinning, and engagement.

Burgess and Wallin reached a similar conclusion in their earlier study. In summarizing their observations of the code

TABLE 18 *Date Relationship and Erotic Intimacy Level at Which Offensiveness Occurred Among College Girls, by Episode*

	Necking and Petting Above the Waist		Petting Below the Waist		Attempted Intercourse and Attempted Intercourse with Violence		Total	
	N	%	N	%	N	%	N	%
Ride home, first date, occasional date	411	55	60	31	25	30	496	49
Regular or steady date	295	39	104	55	43	52	442	43
Pinned, engaged	42	6	27	14	15	18	84	8

SOURCE: Adapted from Clifford Kirkpatrick and Eugene Kanin, "Male Sex Aggression on a University Campus," *American Sociological Review*, Vol. 22, February 1957, Table 2, p. 55.

as it operates among college students, they state that "The goodnight kiss is reserved for the second or third date; necking for keeping company (in the sense of repeated dating) and going steady (being pinned); petting for engagement; and sexual intercourse for marriage."

On the other hand, recent studies of sex aggression (Tables 15 and 16) show that half (49 per cent) of the offensive behavior reported by the college girls (Table 16) took place in a relationship that would have to be classified as random dating—"ride home," "first date," and "occasional date"—and that 31 per cent of the cases of "petting below the waist" and 30 per cent of the "attempted intercourse and attempted intercourse with violence" took place on the random date. There is an association between offensiveness at a mild level of erotic intimacy with a non-involved pairing and offensiveness at a serious level with "pinned" or engagement relationships, however.

In random dating there is so little at stake in the relationship between the daters—that is, they are not usually greatly involved either psychologically or socially—that breaking the relationship is an easy out if the actions of one or the other are offensive. This is evidenced in the responses to the question "What did you do?" as a reaction to offensive behavior. Of the college girls 34 per cent indicated that they practiced "selective avoidance" of the offending party.

"Oh, she's in good hands! That nice, fine
boy from such a respectable family!"
Reproduced courtesy of Ted Key.

Intimacy in Random Going Steady

Aggression at the more advanced levels—petting and attempted intercourse—occurs in the more stable dating relationships of high school daters (Table 16). Only 27 per cent reported attempted petting below the waist on the "occasional date," whereas 58 per cent of the "regular date, pinned and engaged" group so reported.

Additional evidence that random going steady among

high school students may be associated with more advanced levels of love-making is seen in the statements of high school students. These comments from boys, for example:

> I'd never lay a hand on a girl I respect. That is, maybe, until we started going steady and really liked each other.

> I'd never force a girl. I take a girl out just to have a good time. I like to go dancing. Of course it's different if you're going steady.[1]

And these from two high school girls:

> I have to know the boy and like him very much before I'll kiss him good night. I have been going steady for a while so I kiss him.

> When we started going steady, I talked to other girls who were going steady. They convinced me that everyone going steady petted. . . .[2]

The following case corroborates further the contention that even in random dating the more stable phase—going steady—is accompanied by more intensive love-making.

> Every boy I went steady with was different—a complete different type. But still I always had one problem with every one of them, namely love-making. Just how much and how far could it go? Except for Tom, most of the boys and I agreed on the answer. It just went as far as necking.

Crist discusses the problem of intimacy in reporting on his study of high school dating. He points out that steady dating has some advantages in that it relieves many students of emotional and psychological problems involved in getting dates in our free-enterprise, hence competitive dating system. On the other hand, however, he found that many persons who were going steady faced emotional and psychological problems growing out of the going-steady relationship. They

---

[1] Warren Breed, "Sex, Class and Socialization in Dating," *Marriage and Family Living*, Vol. XVIII, May 1956, p. 140.
[2] *Ibid.*

had difficulty making adjustments to the expectations and intimate associations involved.

Two people determine to go with each other and no one else. They decide to be together as much as possible—not only when there is a date affair in the school or community but at other times as well. This time together, with resulting boredom plus feelings of belonging to each other, often leads to increased love-making. In fact, the norms governing random going steady call for intensified love-making, especially the norms for the boy.

As we pointed out earlier in this chapter, it is one of the more important findings of the Kinsey studies that the man develops to a high point of sex readiness and performance by the teens, whereas the woman may not reach this point until her mid-twenties or later. Hence there may be a biologically inherent reason for the difference in sex interest in adolescents. If so, it is further enhanced by the double standard with its greater permissiveness for the boy than for the girl.

These are facts that must be made apparent to adolescents as they begin dating. Girls especially should be aware that the average boy is more easily aroused sexually than is the average girl. This knowledge they are entitled to have as they permit or initiate necking and petting activity in dating. It is customary to accuse boys of exploiting girls for sexual advantage (and not without cause), but for the girl to encourage erotic arousal of her date without intending to provide sexual satisfaction for him is also a type of exploitation.

Love-Making Among Lovers

Premarital dating activity may be carried on in "body-centered and unaffectionate" relationships—prostitution and rape are the most extreme types—or it may be carried on in "person-centered and affectionate" relationships as when a couple deeply in love is involved. For the couple in love—love of the type defined in the chapter on love—intimacy before marriage is apt to have strong person-centered and affectionate elements and constitute love-making in the best meaning of the word. For it is natural and normal that two persons who like each other very much or who are in love should become more involved with each other and constantly desire each other more, physically, psychologically, and socially. Love-as-desire is an important part of real love.

But herein lies a problem. In a society such as ours with its strong prohibitions against sexual involvement outside of marriage, and its permissive attitudes toward unchaperoned, intimate, paired dating, even couples who desire to conform to the mores of society find it difficult to equate their growing desire to possess each other with the standard of limited involvement outside of marriage. Couples discover that yielding in part to desire and progressing in their involvement from necking to light petting does not solve the problem. Light petting only increases erotic arousal and tends to lead to heavy petting. The sex urge per se can be completely satisfied only through coitus or some other means of achieving orgasm. For a couple in love, there is not only the strong sex urge of the man. The woman in love is also permissively inclined toward growing involvement and may become sexually aroused. And, even if not aroused herself, she has a growing desire to please the one she loves in any way that she can.

For couples who have permitted themselves much love-making and still have strong convictions against sexual intercourse before marriage, the experience of the young couple related below is not atypical.

Our parents trust us alone and have trusted us alone for about the entire length of time that we have been going together. This presents a very dire problem to us. Now when we are alone it is very difficult to refrain from having sexual intercourse. I was endowed with a very strong sex drive and Ruth, needless to say, has these same drives, only not quite as strong as I do. The time has come many times when I have had to leave because I could not trust myself to refrain from intercourse. The past few months this has been a very real problem to us because heavy petting has become regular practice when we are alone in her home after her folks retire for the night. Many times we have come close to losing all control and completing the act in intercourse. It is a very real problem to us and we are struggling with it. We hope just to last until I graduate and we are married in June. I can see no solution save that we get married.

Some couples avoid the problem by not allowing themselves such a degree of intimacy. But for the couple that has permitted its love-making to go from stage to stage, it is very difficult to reverse the practices as the young couple above experienced. A couple in love having reached an advanced state of love-making rarely returns to a less involved state. If lovers advance in their involvement to the point of coitus, this tends to become the established pattern of intimacy for the remainder of the engagement period.

Solving the Problem

Some would say that no couple should become so involved. Others would say that when caught in the predicament of the couple whose case is related above, the best thing is to go all the way and give free expression to love.

As Burgess and Wallin point out, 50 per cent of the engaged couples in their sample took this way out, the remaining one-half did not. But to point out that people in America are not consistent in their solutions does not help the couple struggling with the problem.

For a person not yet heavily involved in a love relationship, it would seem to be the better part of wisdom to decide to engage in intimacies only after being reasonably sure of the love of the other person and the possibilities of marriage. If such a rule were followed the couple would become involved in intimate caressing no sooner than the formal engagement period or the period when they were engaged-to-be-engaged, and would postpone coitus until married. A decision to proceed in this way is consistent with the American ideal—to treat uncommitted persons of the other sex as possessing dignity and as worthy of respect. A man who does not respect his date may feign love in order to receive sexual favors. Or he may insist that his girl friend prove her love for him by submitting to intimate love-making. But, as we have pointed out several times before, in a society where each individual is regarded as worthy of freedom and respect, it is never right to exploit another person for selfish advantage, particularly if one does not intend to accept the consequences of one's actions—psychological, physiological, and social. The most dramatic illustration of the consequences of intimacy without shared responsibility is, of course, the case of the ubiquitous unwed mother.

Even with the democratic values inherent in the American ideal, and perhaps in part because of it, each person is very much alone in the decisions he makes in his dating relationships and is largely dependent on his own good judgment and the respect and good intentions of his dating partner.[3] Society, in the form of public opinion, law, and the punitive power of the state, is in no position to be definitive in its standards of sexual morality, nor can it in all respects protect the rights of individuals—particularly not in intimate, unchaperoned, small-group interaction as in

[3] Kirkpatrick and Kanin, and Kanin, found a paucity of reliance upon parents and the formal agencies of control on the part of high school and college girls who had been the victims of offensive erotic activity on the part of dating partners. However, warnings from parents seemed to pay dividends in that the girls who had been warned appeared to rely more on parents in times of difficulty.

dating. Rather it is necessary to have rules that are general in nature which can be applied to all without much attention to the nature of the relationship between the daters. It is in this light that the norm of not-too-intimate love-making before marriage is applied. The society—through the state—cannot look into the "hearts" of the lovers to see if their expressions are a sign of true love for each other or mere exploitation.

Reiss suggests, however, that we do have an increasingly popular permissive standard of intimacy for those in love. Actually the difference in attitude toward relations between those in a stable relationship and those not so involved is very old. As we have previously pointed out, it was not uncommon in Biblical times to treat with greater charity the involvements of those who were engaged, and this has been true even in some church bodies in America. But the conditions under which intimacy was permitted were different then than they are now. The earlier form of the Judaic-Christian marriage model permitted intimacy only for unmarried couples who had exchanged vows of fidelity. In a society where love relationships are apt to be regarded as testing periods, the lovers do not experience the same sense of security and support of the society.

There is empirical evidence showing that increasingly more engaged couples are having intimate sex relations, but the growing emphasis on engagement as a testing period rather than on engagement as commitment means that engagement, too, holds little assurance that the relationship will eventuate in marriage. Hence there is a basic inconsistency. Society takes a permissive attitude toward sex relations between engaged couples and at the same time withdraws its support—both legal and religious—from engagement as a permanent commitment. Perhaps no society in the history of man has coupled so much freedom of action for lovers with such limited acceptance of the consequences of their actions.

Hence, we repeat, the young dater is left largely to his own good judgment and reliance on the good judgment, good intentions, and willingness to accept the consequences of love-making on the part of his dating partner.

For the couple desiring to conform to the older standard of sex morality, there are fewer risks physiologically, psychologically, and socially in moving the wedding date ahead than there are in physically consummating their relationship before they are married.

It is perhaps most important of all, however, that they discuss and agree on their decision regarding the time at which to allow complete freedom of expression in their relations with each other, and that they agree in accepting and sharing the consequences of their decision.

Empirical data does not shed much light on the problem as correlations between premarital chastity and success or happiness in marriage are far from conclusive in favoring involvement or chastity. Part of the reason for the inconclusive nature of the findings may be the lack of refinement in the studies. More fruitful have been the systematic interviews, such as those which Kirkendall has carried on with college-level men. Some of his "tentative insights" are helpful.

An intercourse relationship which is accompanied by feelings of unity and acceptance appears to rest upon certain definite considerations. These considerations are a capacity for full and free communication between the partners, an ability to handle such unhoped for consequences as pregnancy, discovery, and parental disapproval, a genuine concern for each other's welfare, and upon the couple's paramount concern with the quality of their relationship, rather than sex itself. I have come across a number of intercourse relationships, all involving engaged couples, in which the partners have felt that while they were having intercourse their sense of intimacy and feeling of trust, confidence, and understanding also increased. This has resulted, I believe, from the presence of the factors indicated in the [second] sentence of this paragraph.[4]

On the other hand, Kirkendall observes that most intimate love-making is not so reasoned nor the couple so well agreed in the responsibility that they will share regarding the consequences of their action. He concludes:

> In my judgment, practically all of the premarital coitus in the pre-engagement period, and an undetermined portion of intercourse in the engagement period, occurs under conditions which both then and eventually, result in more suspicion, distrust, and less ability to set up good relationships. Couples who are relatively immature, who are unready to bear the responsibility of a permanent marriage relationship, who are over-eager for the sexual experience, who are unable to communicate with each other in a really trusting and confidential way will find it practically impossible in our culture to set up a sexual relationship which contributes to increased trust, confidence, and good will toward each other and toward people in general.[5]

Summary

There are conflicting norms governing intimacy between daters in the American dating system. Some of them, particularly the double standard, are out of harmony with the American ideal.

Generally speaking the man is more aggressive and more permissive regarding love-making at all levels of random and serious dating. This is in part related to his physiological and psychological nature and in part to the support he receives from the permissive male subculture.

[4] Lester A. Kirkendall, "Premarital Sex Relations: The Problem and Its Implications." Reprinted by permission from the April, 1956 issue of *Pastoral Psychology*. Copyright 1956 by Pastoral Psychology Press, Great Neck, N. Y.
[5] *Ibid.*

Love-making becomes more intimate as the emotional involvement of the lovers increases. The woman is particularly concerned to keep the love-making consistent with the degree of emotional involvement.

The dilemma between chastity and complete physical intimacy as a norm is particularly difficult for couples who are much in love but not yet married. From the point of view of the American ideal, their decision must be democratically arrived at, and they must be willing to share mutually the physiological, psychological, and social consequences of their actions. Neither of the responsible marriage models—the Judaic-Christian or the rationalistic—grants special privileges to either sex in the love-making prior to or outside of marriage. Any support for special privilege must be found in the culturally illicit double standard of morality or in the nebulous norms of the romantic model.

QUESTIONS AND PROJECTS

1. Is there a difference in the nature and the extent of intimacy in random going steady as compared to random dating?
2. Are there any qualitative differences between the love-making of lovers and the love-making of random daters? If so, what are the differences?
3. As you see it, what is the nature of public reaction to intimate love-making of lovers in America?
4. What potential psychological and social problems threaten lovers who practice extensive intimacy prior to marriage?
5. What problems face young lovers who consider moving ahead the date of marriage in an attempt to accommodate their desire for more intimate involvement?
6. What pattern of intimacy prior to marriage do you feel to be consistent with values inherent in the American ideal? In the three marriage models?

SUGGESTED READINGS

Blood, Robert O., Jr., "Romance and Premarital Intercourse—Incompatibles?" *Marriage and Family Living*, Vol. XIV, May 1952, pp. 105–108.

Breed, Warren, "Sex, Class and Socialization in Dating," *Marriage and Family Living*, Vol. XVIII, May 1956, pp. 137–144.

Burgess, Ernest W., and Paul Wallin, *Engagement and Marriage*, Chicago: J. B. Lippincott Co., 1953, Chapters 11, 12.

Christensen, Harold T., "Studies in Child Spacing: I—Premarital Pregnancy As Measured by the Spacing of the First Birth from Marriage," *American Sociological Review*, Vol. 18, February 1953, pp. 53–59.

Crist, John R., "High School Dating As a Behavior System," *Marriage and Family Living*, Vol. XV, February 1953, pp. 23–28.

Ehrmann, Winston, "Some Knowns and Unknowns in Research into Human Sex Behavior," *Marriage and Family Living*, Vol. XIX, February 1957, pp. 16–22.

———, "Student Cooperation in a Study of Dating Behavior," *Marriage and Family Living*, Vol. XIV, November 1952, pp. 322–326.

Hamblin, Robert L., and Robert O. Blood, Jr., "Pre-Marital Experience and the Wife's Sexual Adjustment," *Social Problems*, Vol. 4, October 1956, pp. 122–130.

Hartel, Frank J., *et al.*, *Sexual Behavior: How Shall We Define and Motivate What Is Acceptable?* Proceedings of a Panel Discussion, 37th Annual Meeting and Social Hygiene Day Regional Conference of the American Social Hygiene Association, New York, February 1, 1950.

Kanin, Eugene J., "Male Aggression in Dating-Courtship Relations," *American Journal of Sociology*, Vol. LXIII, September 1957, pp. 197–204.

Karpf, Maurice J., "The Effects of Prostitution on Marital Sex Adjustment," *Marriage and Family Living*, Vol. XV, February 1953, pp. 65–71.

Kinsey, Alfred C., Wardell B. Pomeroy, Clyde E. Martin, and Paul H. Gebhard, *Sexual Behavior in the Human Female*, Philadelphia: W. B. Saunders Co., 1953.

———, Wardell B. Pomeroy, and Clyde E. Martin, *Sexual Behavior in the Human Male*, Philadelphia: W. B. Saunders Co., 1948.

Kirkendall, Lester A., "Premarital Sex Relations, the Problem and Its Implications," *Pastoral Psychology*, Vol. 7, April 1956, pp. 46–53.

Kirkpatrick, Clifford, and Eugene Kanin, "Male Sex Aggression on a University Campus," *American Sociological Review*, Vol. 22, February 1957, pp. 52–58.

———, Sheldon Stryker, and Philip Buell, "An Experimental Study of Attitudes Toward Male Sex Behavior with Reference to Kinsey Findings," *American Sociological Review,* Vol. 17, October 1952, pp. 580–587.

Landis, Judson T., and Kenneth C. Kidd, "Attitudes and Policies Concerning Marriage Among High School Students," *Marriage and Family Living,* Vol. XVIII, May 1956, pp. 128–136.

Reiss, Ira L., "The Double Standard in Premarital Sexual Intercourse: A Neglected Concept," *Social Forces,* Vol. 34, March 1956, pp. 224–230.

———, "The Treatment of Pre-Marital Coitus in 'Marriage and the Family' Texts," *Social Problems,* Vol. 4, April 1957, pp. 334–338.

Robertson, Priscilla, "On a Scientific Standard of Personal Ethics," *The Humanist,* Vol. XVI, September–October 1956, pp. 217–223.

Stokes, Walter R., and David M. Mace, "Premarital Sexual Behavior," *Marriage and Family Living,* Vol. XV, August 1953, pp. 234–249.

Vincent, Clark E., "The Unwed Mother and Sampling Bias," *American Sociological Review,* Vol. 19, October 1954, pp. 562–567.

Marriage

16 *The Wedding and the Honeymoon*

⦁⦁⦁

Much of the specific and detailed planning in the engagement period is involved with two significant events, wedding and honeymoon. This involves deciding upon the date convenient for both partners and for others intimately concerned in the wedding and deciding on the type of wedding—formal or informal, religious or civil. It involves deciding on the setting—the bride's home, the judge's chambers, or the church. It involves communicating with those directly concerned in the wedding ritual itself—officiant, attendants, musicians, caterers, as well as the guests.

The couple has freedom insofar as these matters are concerned, but let us consider first some matters regarding their proposed marriage which they are not free to choose.

The Role of the State in Marriage

Couples are "on their own" during dating and engagement. They make their own decisions with little outside interference. It is not so with marriage. Once the couple arrives at the point in their relationship when they would like to marry and live together, society, in the form of the state, steps in with pertinent questions about them and about their relationship. If the state is not satisfied with their answers to the questions, they cannot marry, for the state is powerful at this stage in the couple's relationship. The state will want to know the ages of the couple members. In 28 states it will want to know the race of each partner. It will want to know if they are of sound mind and, in some cases, of sound body. It will want to know of any prior marriage commitments by either of them to any other person. It will want to know of their relationship to each other—are they close blood relatives, for instance. It will want to know if either is being forced or coerced into marriage.

Why does society, the state, which has granted the couple such freedom during dating days, become so concerned with this next step—marriage?

The answer is that the state is an agency of the citizens for guarding the welfare of all citizens. It is responsible for seeing that things are done decently and in order, that agreements are kept, that persons and property are protected. Since marriage involves all of these, society insists that the marriage involve adults free to act on their own behalf and actually acting on their own behalf, that proper records be made, and that witnesses representing society be present to vouch for the event.

Hence, for the first time in their developing relationship, the lovers are confronted by an organized social entity possessing more power than they have to make decisions pertinent to their relationship. This may at first thought seem to be inconsistent with the American ideal, but it is not. As pointed out in the first chapter, the only creature with rights equal to one's own rights is another human being. There must be an agency to see that the rights of all are kept within some kind of balance. This is why the state steps in at vital points where commitments binding people are made.

The Nature of the Wedding

If the couple members are basically secular in their orientation to life and follow the romantic or the rationalistic marriage model, they may decide to be married by an official of the state, such as a justice of the peace or judge, with a marriage service consisting of a minimum of ritual beyond the exchange of vows. Such a ceremony is normally conducted in the place of business of the officiant. In the case of a justice of the peace, it might take place in his home or office or in the case of a judge, in his chambers. However, church weddings with pastors officiating are customary in America, and the couple, even though not closely affiliated with any church, might contract with a church and its pastor for the performance of this service. Churches and pastors vary in their policy regarding their willingness to offer this service to persons "outside the fold." It is not done by Roman Catholic clergy nor can the Roman Catholic sanctuary be used in this way.

If the couple accepts a basically Christian marriage model, they will have a clergyman as officiant and the ceremony will be performed either in the church or in a private home if the participants are Protestant or in a church if both are Roman Catholic.

In other words, in America a legal marriage ceremony has an officiant representing the state, but this officiant can be either an official of the state or a clergyman; and the form that the ceremony takes is of no particular concern to the state so long as the questions asked by the state have been satisfactorily answered.

Just how informal the ceremony can be and still be legal is seen in the following account of a wedding as related by Hollingshead.

Late one chilly, wet winter afternoon, a class V country girl arrived in the prosecuting attorney's office, mildly hysterical and grim in her determination to see justice done. Her ankle-high men's shoes were soaked from walking over seven miles of country roads, and her legs were covered with mud and coal dust. That morning she had told her mother she was pregnant, and a family quarrel ensued among the girl, mother, and grandmother. When the father came home for lunch, he was told of the girl's condition. Another quarrel developed, this time between the father and the girl, with the grandmother and the mother doing what they could to keep the father from "horsewhipping" the girl. In his rage, the father told her to marry the boy before sunset. "When I come home, if you aren't married, I'll kill you both." The girl also reported that the father took his shot gun and a box of shells out of his truck and drove off to work. The girl's mother said, "You better go marry him; you know your father." The girl requested the prosecuting attorney to find the boy and make him marry her "right now." The attorney sent a sheriff's deputy and had the boy brought to the courthouse. The prospective groom drove a truck, which he parked in front of the courthouse while he came in with the deputy. The girl sat silent and wooden-faced in the attorney's office as the boy was brought in and confronted with her statement. He admitted he had been "with her a few times." The attorney asked, "Do you know what this means?"

"Sure, I'll marry her, but I won't live with her. The kid isn't mine."

"When do you intend to marry Martha?"

"Now's as good a time as any. I gotta deliver that load yet tonight; so let's get goin'."

The attorney turned to Martha and asked, "Do you want to get married now?"

"Yeh, the sooner the better; the old man means business."

At this, the little party walked out of the prosecutor's office and down the broad marble stairs to the county clerk's office where the groom-to-be bought a marriage license. The party solemnly went to the judge's office, where the judge read the marriage service. After he had pronounced them man and wife, he signed the marriage certificate. The young couple stood quietly looking at one another while this took place. The judge rose and carefully rolled the marriage certificate into a scroll. As he flipped a rubber band around its center, he said, "Young lady, you are a married woman now."

The girl grinned, and the boy said, "Is that all?"

The judge said, "I guess so."

To the prosecutor, "Can I go now? I wanna get that load off before dark." As he was told that he could leave, the boy turned, put his grimy cap on, and bolted for the door. In a few seconds the truck started and pulled away from the curb.

The girl said, in a voice with a slight tremble in it, "Thanks, I better get started home." She then turned, walked out the back door, across the courthouse yard, and down the back street toward the bridge over the Indian River.[1]

That American marriage norms are not very specific as to the form marriage must take becomes abundantly evident when one realizes that the wedding described above and the formal wedding performed in a candle-lighted sanctuary with music and splendor—and using such an order of service as the one to follow—are both a part of the same society!

[1] Reprinted with permission from August B. Hollingshead, *Elmtown's Youth*, copyright 1949, John Wiley & Sons, Inc., pp. 430–432.

THE FORM OF SOLEMNIZATION
OF MATRIMONY [2]

At the day and time appointed for Solemnization of Matrimony, the Persons to be married shall come into the body of the Church, or shall be ready in some proper house, with their friends and neighbours; and there standing together, the Man on the right hand, and the Woman on the left, the Minister shall say,

DEARLY beloved, we are gathered together here in the sight of God, and in the face of this company, to join together this Man and this Woman in holy Matrimony; which is an honourable estate, instituted of God, signifying unto us the mystical union that is betwixt Christ and his Church: which holy estate Christ adorned and beautified with his presence and first miracle that he wrought in Cana of Galilee, and is commended of Saint Paul to be honourable among all men: and therefore is not by any to be entered into unadvisedly or lightly; but reverently, discreetly, advisedly, soberly, and in the fear of God. Into this holy estate these two persons present come now to be joined. If any man can show just cause, why they may not lawfully be joined together, let him now speak, or else hereafter for ever hold his peace.

And also speaking unto the Persons who are to be married, he shall say,

I REQUIRE and charge you both, as ye will answer at the dreadful day of judgment when the secrets of all hearts shall be disclosed, that if either of you know any impediment, why ye may not be lawfully joined together in Matrimony, ye do now confess it. For be ye well assured, that if any persons are joined together otherwise than as God's Word doth allow, their marriage is not lawful.

The Minister, if he shall have reason to doubt of the lawfulness of the proposed Marriage, may demand suffi-

[2] *The Book of Common Prayer* (Protestant Episcopal Church in the United States of America), New York: Oxford University Press, Inc., 1938, pp. 300–304.

cient surety for his indemnification: but if no impediment shall be alleged, or suspected, the Minister shall say to the Man,

N. WILT thou have this Woman to thy wedded wife, to live together after God's ordinance in the holy estate of Matrimony? Wilt thou love her, comfort her, honour, and keep her in sickness and in health; and, forsaking all others, keep thee only unto her, so long as ye both shall live?

The Man shall answer,

I will.

Then shall the Minister say unto the Woman,

N. WILT thou have this Man to thy wedded husband, to live together after God's ordinance in the holy estate of Matrimony? Wilt thou love him, comfort him, honour, and keep him in sickness and in health; and, forsaking all others, keep thee only unto him, so long as ye both shall live?

The Woman shall answer,

I will.

Then shall the Minister say,

Who giveth this Woman to be married to this Man?

Then shall they give their troth to each other in this manner. The Minister, receiving the Woman at her father's or friend's hands, shall cause the Man with his right hand to take the Woman by her right hand, and to say after him as followeth.

I N. take thee N. to my wedded Wife, to have and to hold from this day forward, for better for worse, for richer for poorer, in sickness and in health, to love and to cherish, till death us do part, according to God's holy ordinance; and thereto I plight thee my troth.

Then shall they loose their hands; and the Woman with her right hand taking the Man by his right hand, shall likewise say after the Minister,

I N. take thee N. to my wedded Husband, to have and to hold from this day forward, for better for worse, for richer for poorer, in sickness and in health, to love and to cherish, till death us do part, according to God's holy ordinance; and thereto I give thee my troth.

Then shall they again loose their hands; and the Man shall give unto the Woman a Ring on this wise: the Minister taking the Ring shall deliver it unto the Man, to put it upon the fourth finger of the Woman's left hand. And the Man holding the Ring there, and taught by the Minister, shall say,

WITH this Ring I thee wed: In the Name of the Father, and of the Son, and of the Holy Ghost. Amen.

And, before delivering the Ring to the Man, the Minister may say as followeth.

BLESS, O Lord, this Ring, that he who gives it and she who wears it may abide in thy peace, and continue in thy favour, unto their life's end; through Jesus Christ our Lord. Amen.

Then, the Man leaving the Ring upon the fourth finger of the Woman's left hand, the Minister shall say,

Let us pray.

Then shall the Minister and the People, still standing, say the Lord's Prayer.

OUR Father, who art in heaven, Hallowed be thy Name. Thy kingdom come. Thy will be done, On earth as it is in heaven. Give us this day our daily bread. And forgive us our trespasses, As we forgive those who trespass against us. And lead us not into temptation, But deliver us from evil. For thine is the kingdom, and the power, and the glory, for ever and ever. Amen.

Then shall the Minister add,

O ETERNAL God, Creator and Preserver of all mankind, Giver of all spiritual grace, the Author of everlasting life; Send thy blessing upon these thy servants, this man and this woman, whom we bless in thy Name; that they, living faithfully together, may surely perform and keep the vow and covenant betwixt them made (whereof this Ring given and received is a token and pledge), and may ever remain in perfect love and peace together, and live according to thy laws; through Jesus Christ our Lord. *Amen.*

*The Minister may add one or both
of the following prayers.*

O ALMIGHTY God, Creator of mankind, who only art the well-spring of life; Bestow upon these thy servants, if it be thy will, the gift and heritage of children; and grant that they may see their children brought up in thy faith and fear, to the honour and glory of thy Name; through Jesus Christ our Lord. *Amen.*

O GOD, who hast so consecrated the state of Matrimony that in it is represented the spiritual marriage and unity betwixt Christ and his Church; Look mercifully upon these thy servants, that they may love, honour, and cherish each other, and so live together in faithfulness and patience, in wisdom and true godliness, that their home may be a haven of blessing and of peace; through the same Jesus Christ our Lord, who liveth and reigneth with thee and the Holy Spirit ever, one God, world without end. *Amen.*

*Then shall the Minister join their right
hands together, and say,*

Those whom God hath joined together
let no man put asunder.

Then shall the Minister speak unto the company.

FORASMUCH as N. and N. have consented together in holy wedlock, and have witnessed the same before God and this company, and thereto have given and pledged their troth, each to the other, and have declared the same by giving and receiving a Ring, and by joining hands; I pronounce that they are Man and Wife, In the Name of the Father, and of the Son, and of the Holy Ghost. Amen.

The Man and Wife kneeling, the Minister shall add this Blessing.

GOD the Father, God the Son, God the Holy Ghost, bless, preserve, and keep you; the Lord mercifully with his favour look upon you, and fill you with all spiritual benediction and grace; that ye may so live together in this life, that in the world to come ye may have life everlasting. *Amen.*

The laws respecting Matrimony, whether by publishing the Banns in Churches, or by Licence, being different in the several States, every Minister is left to the direction of those laws, in every thing that regards the civil contract between the parties.

And when the Banns are published, it shall be in the following form: I publish the Banns of Marriage between N. of —, and N. of —. If any of you know cause, or just impediment, why these two persons should not be joined together in holy Matrimony, ye are to declare it. This is the first (second or third) time of asking.

The reader will note in the service the elements of the Judaic-Christian marriage model discussed in Chapter 3.

It is important to point out not the differences between the ceremony as performed in the judge's office and the service quoted above but the essential element common to both. The element which makes two persons husband and wife in either ceremony is the exchange of vows by the bride and groom. Neither state nor church marries the couple; they marry each other. It is their free and public (before witnesses) exchange of vows which marries them. After they have "consented together in holy wedlock" the officiant pronounces (synonyms—articulate, utter, speak) them man and wife. He does not "marry" them; he is rather a representative of the state—and in the latter case of the church—and he officially witnesses and announces what has been done by the couple.

The wedding is an event, a rite of passage, actually almost a momentary event in the long relationship of lovers. It is an important event, but it does not in and of itself create a marriage. In the eyes of society, the two are married, but the important concern is whether or not they are psychologically wed. The building of marriage is not like the wedding—a momentary event—but a lifelong process which began in the preparation before the event and continues in the honeymoon and beyond.

The Honeymoon

The honeymoon with its roots deeply grounded in romanticism is a strange and exciting interlude between single life and the wedding, on the one hand, and settling down to the daily routine of living as husband and wife, on the other. It is a practice followed by American couples today regardless of the marriage model followed—Judaic-Christian, romantic, or rationalistic. It is not so commonly practiced in the lower as in the middle and upper classes, in part, perhaps, for economic reasons.

Even though a couple may have been eagerly anticipating the wedding for some time, the wedding itself—and the honeymoon to follow—may seem awesome and almost frightening. To have lived under the scrutinizing eye of society with its condemnation of intimacy for engaged couples, and, with the wedding, to have all social barriers to intimacy removed calls for sudden adjustment to a new psychological and social status that may be traumatic even for the person most eagerly anticipating married life. The honeymoon is the setting for making this sudden change of status under the most favorable conditions.

Findings of recent empirical research suggest that the amount of trauma involved in the honeymoon can be over-

THE SATURDAY EVENING POST

"Bridal suite."
Reproduced courtesy of Ted Key.

emphasized. In a study of 190 wives of university students, only 17 per cent evaluated the sexual experiences of the first two weeks of marriage as "unsatisfying" or "very unsatisfying." In fact, only 4.5 per cent of the total group reported difficulties stemming from sexual incompatibility. A considerable degree of sexual adjustment was reported to have occurred within a short span of time in the honeymoon even for wives without previous coital experience, despite any difficulties of the wedding night.[3]

The honeymoon is a part of our romantic tradition and a good part of it. Though there have been romantic misconceptions about the honeymoon, such as that there will be no period in life before or after to compare with it,[4] it nevertheless serves a very useful function and can be all that the couple had hoped and dreamed that it would be.

The honeymoon gives the couple a chance to recuperate from the fascinating but perhaps emotionally exhausting days preceding the wedding, as well as the wedding itself. Secondly, it gives the couple time to be alone, to enjoy each other, and to get to know more about each other and what life together means before they return to their respective roles, old and new, in the community and in the home. A successful honeymoon requires some planning in advance, however.

What are the criteria of a good honeymoon? In the first place, it should be planned to be a leisurely period—not tightly scheduled with mileage to make and things to see to the point that it becomes fatiguing and nerve-wracking rather than relaxing. A certain amount of planned activity will keep the couple from becoming bored with each other. The activity should include things that are enjoyable to both partners and should be cushioned by ample leisure, allowing for relaxed meals, leisurely walks and talks, and hours of isolation for love-making par excellence.

As to the length of the honeymoon, "prolonged periods of idleness are not conducive to social gain." Perhaps most couples will find a honeymoon of a week to three weeks sufficiently long to be alone together and sufficiently long

[3] Eugene J. Kanin and David H. Howard, "Postmarital Consequences of Premarital Sex Adjustments," *American Sociological Review*, Vol. 23, October 1958, pp. 561–562.
[4] In a study involving 50 married women, 80 per cent considered it untrue that "there is no more ideal happiness in all married life than during a honeymoon." Stanley R. Brav, "Notes on Honeymoons," *Marriage and Family Living*, Vol. IX, August 1947, pp. 60, 65.

for the amount of money that they feel they can budget for it. It is better to have a honeymoon of three days, however, than a postponed trip of three weeks.

Traditionally the honeymoon is the first occasion for sexual intercourse, and this may be a part of the honeymoon most filled with anticipation and trepidation. In their intimate embraces in engagement lovers feel the desire to consummate the relationship, and now all barriers are down. Society has turned its back on the couple and given them, for the first time, complete freedom to enjoy each other. Some of the bride's fears regarding first intercourse have likely been allayed by the results of a thorough physical examination prior to marriage. The prospective groom, too, if he has any doubts about his own sexual capacity, has occasion to raise questions at the time of an examination. Despite this, first intercourse is a new experience and a sensitive one because it involves psychological as well as physiological factors.

More sophisticated couples who have been able to discuss their forthcoming sex life together may determine to postpone first intercourse until they have had some chance to recover from the excitement of the wedding and the "getaway" and restrict first-day activities to extensive love-making short of intercourse. For others, any such postponement would seem impossible or absurd.

Frequently couples do not achieve complete sexual satisfaction during the honeymoon but still regard the honeymoon as successful. Of a sample of 50 married women, 74 per cent were ready to describe their honeymoon as "a complete success," and 64 per cent would go so far as to say that "a honeymoon is the achievement of all pre-marital romantic desires," though nearly half of those replying (48 per cent) admitted that they failed to achieve complete sexual harmony during the honeymoon.[5]

Anyone acquainted with the physiological, psychological,

[5] *Ibid.*

and sociological factors contributing to satisfying sex relations will not expect complete sexual satisfaction early in the marriage. In fact, the couple that achieves complete sex satisfaction during the honeymoon should be considered the exception rather than the rule. More needs to be said by way of explanation, but this will be postponed until we discuss sex adjustment in marriage in a later chapter. The only point to make here is that full sexual satisfaction during the honeymoon is too much to expect, and secondly, as Brav has pointed out, many women find the honeymoon to be very satisfying even without complete sexual satisfaction.

In conclusion, honeymoons that have had some planning and in which the expectations are not exorbitant serve a valuable function.

Summary

Prior to the wedding the state, representing order in society, has pertinent questions to ask the couple before licensing their proposed marriage—questions regarding age, prior marital status, freedom of consent, etc. In other words, for the first time in their growing love relationship someone other than the couple is officially authorized to make decisions regarding their contemplated marriage.

The wedding itself—secular or religious—is the event that legally brings into being the husband and wife relationship which the couple desires and for which they have been making preparations. The essential element in the wedding ceremony is the free exchange of vows of the persons marrying.

Following the wedding ceremony it is customary—in the middle and upper classes at least—for the newly married couple to spend a period of a week or more of leisure on a honeymoon before settling down to homemaking, the job, and the routine of everyday living.

The honeymoon provides an ideal setting for first experiences in the intimacy granted only to married couples. Hence, the honeymoon can be a vacation for two busy young people and a time of exclusive concern with themselves and their relationship in a setting of new-found freedom.

QUESTIONS AND PROJECTS

1. How and why does the state intrude in the plans of couples prior to the wedding?
2. What is the essential element, or elements, in the wedding? Elaborate.
3. Read the Form of Solemnization of Matrimony and list as many elements of the Judaic-Christian marriage model as you find contained in the service.
4. What are the functions of the honeymoon?
5. Is a honeymoon essential to successful marriage?

SUGGESTED READINGS

Blood, Robert O., Jr., *Anticipating Your Marriage*, Glencoe: The Free Press, 1955, Chapter 8.

Brav, Stanley R., "Notes on Honeymoons," *Marriage and Family Living*, Vol. IX, August 1947, pp. 60, 65.

Duvall, Evelyn M., and Reuben Hill, *When You Marry*, New York: D. C. Heath & Company, 1953, Chapters 9, 10.

Kanin, Eugene J., and David H. Howard, "Postmarital Consequences of Premarital Sex Adjustment," *American Sociological Review*, Vol. 23, October 1958, pp. 556–562.

17   *Oneness in Marriage and the Strategy of Harmony*

▌▌▌

To think, to feel, to act as one—this highly idealistic goal is the aim of many if not all lovers as they look forward to life together as a "community of love." The glorious days of romance and the engagement and the happy and sacred event of the wedding give promise of what is to be. The prospects may seem at times almost "too good to be true."

The couple may be overidealistic at this stage in the relationship, yet this very enthusiasm, this will to succeed, is not the least of the assets the newlyweds bring to the task at hand. The task is not an easy one, as we will presently show, and achieving unity will require effort for the entire life of the couple. For as each personality changes, the nature of the paired unity will also change. Achieving unity is a never-ending process in marriage.

How is a unity, a marriage, created? What is the strategy of harmony? This is what the present chapter is about. Answering these questions is a big assignment, and with our present knowledge of the dynamics of interpersonal relations, only the fool would say that he had all the answers.

"Our first day apart! I'll be home for coffee break."

Reprinted from *Cartoon Annual No. 3.*
Copyright, Ace Books, Inc.

The Twofold Function of Marriage

In every marriage there is a twofold function—to achieve unity in love for the couple and to maintain freedom for personal growth and development for each partner. The latter is a peculiar demand of the American ideal.

The unity which the couple seeks to achieve is made

difficult because of two basic desires of each partner. The person who marries gives expression to one of the basic desires—the desire to be respected, loved, and accepted into an intimate marriage relationship and, in a sense, absorbed and swallowed up by it—to become a part of a "community of love."

On the other hand, each mature person also desires to be independent, to be recognized as a unique and free person

Reprinted from *Cartoon Annual No. 3.*
Copyright, Ace Books, Inc.

with personal prestige and not as a member of a group. One desires autonomy, independence, recognition.

The existence of tension between the desire to belong and the desire to be free is one reason why we spoke in an earlier chapter of love as a tragedy, for love entices the individual into a relationship which is always a threat to his freedom. It is a threat to his recognition and prestige as a unique individual, and this is more true for the wife than for the husband.

The love of another person provides the strongest impetus known to man for compromising some of his freedom for the satisfactions to be derived from intimate association. Yet, in practice, when the powerful attraction which draws lovers together brings them to a certain point of oneness, resistance begins to operate in one or both. This mounts until it overwhelms the force of attraction.

> This hostility admits of the simplest explanation. There is no need to posit some mysterious antipathy between the sexes. It is nothing more than the self-defense of the individual ego against the threat of incorporation into another personality. The deep urge of the human spirit for freedom and independence stands at the gate and says, even to the one most loved in all the world, "Thus far, but no further." [1]

Welding the two desires of two free individuals—the desire for freedom and the desire to enter as fully as possible into a love relationship—into a smooth functioning marriage is the goal which the newlyweds must seek to accomplish. Every marriage which lasts achieves some kind of a balance between these two forces or desires, but it is always a delicate balance.

If the married partners view marriage according to the rationalistic marriage model—that is, as a relationship for the satisfying of personal needs that "must not make demands upon the individual which interfere with his health, efficiency, happiness, or potentialities of total personality development," [2]—then there is danger that the impulse in each to maximize satisfactions without sacrifice of self will lead to a relationship characterized by self-centeredness. There is the ever-present threat that the stronger of the pair will in his self-assertion come to dominate the relationship and tip the delicate balance between reward and sacrifice in his direction. Or stated in another way, if each is oriented

[1] David R. Mace, "Personality Expression and Subordination in Marriage," *Marriage and Family Living*, Vol. XV, August 1953, pp. 205–206.
[2] Willard Waller and Reuben Hill, *The Family*, New York: The Dryden Press, Inc., 1951, p. 368.

toward using the relationship and the spouse for personal gain—to maximize what he receives and minimize what he is willing to give for the sake of the relationship and for the sake of the beloved—an equitable balance of satisfactions for both is almost impossible to achieve. This is love as desire in its purest self-centered form.

At the other extreme, however, is a marriage based on a

"I'd say that was a strike, wouldn't you, dear?"

Reprinted from *Cartoon Annual No. 3.*
Copyright, Ace Books, Inc.

goodly element of *agape* in which one or both partners tends to give himself in complete self-surrender, to lose his identity completely, and to be swallowed up in the other or in the marriage. The dangers of this type of marriage are no less great when viewed against the values of the American ideal. To the extent that one member submerges his personality, the relationship is no longer a marriage, with the advantages that marriage can give, because one of the partners to the relationship has committed "ego suicide." He has been absorbed in the personality of his mate or in the marriage and has no identity of his own. The tension between two real persons that results in growth in the marriage and growth in the personalities of each of the partners is lost.

This temptation to lose oneself does not only develop out of a misguided notion of the meaning of *agape*, however. It can also be the result of a lack of self-acceptance and self-respect so that one loses himself completely in his spouse or in the marriage. A healthy marriage can have neither completely inviolable personalities nor completely absorbed personalities.

For the sake of clarity we have chosen to deal only with the psychological aspects of unity in marriage and the prerequisites and strategy of decision-making in this chapter. Discussion of sociological unity, or "togetherness" in marriage, and personality growth in marriage are discussed in chapters to follow. In life, of course, these aspects of marriage are not separable. They are "all of a piece" and there is constant tension between them in a marriage of two mature personalities.

The Importance of the Early Years

Many of the major adjustments of a husband and wife to each other and to the status of a married couple come in the first few years of marriage. That these are the critical years is revealed in the annulment and divorce statistics. As seen in Table 19, more divorces and annulments occur within the first year of marriage (9.7 per cent) than in any other single year, and a sizable percentage of marriages (6.4 per cent) do not survive for one full year. The median duration of marriages which end in divorce or annulment is only 6.5 years. Sixty-one per cent of all divorces and annulments come within the first ten years of marriage.

TABLE 19 *Percentage Distribution of Divorces and Annulments by Duration of Marriage in Years: Total of 23 Reporting States, 1956*

Duration of Marriage [a]	Per Cent
Under 1 year	6.4
1–4 years	34.5
1 year	9.7
2 years	9.4
3 years	8.2
4 years	7.1
5–9 years	26.0
5 years	6.4
6 years	5.4
7 years	4.8
8 years	4.7
9 years	4.8
10–14 years	14.1
15–19 years	8.1
20–24 years	4.8
25–29 years	2.8
30–34 years	1.6
35–39 years	0.9
40 years and over	0.7
Total	100.0

SOURCE: U.S. Department of Health, Education, and Welfare, National Office of Vital Statistics, *Divorces and Annulments: Detailed Statistics for Reporting Areas*, Vital Statistics—Special Reports, National Summaries, Vol. 48, No. 2, March 25, 1958, p. 28.

[a] Excludes cases for which duration of marriage was not stated.

The importance of adjusting to each other early in marriage is further indicated in a study of the length of time it takes married couples to adjust and the ratings they gave to their marriages. Couples were asked to rate independently the success or failure of their marriages and the time required to adjust in each of six areas: spending the family income, relationships with in-laws, sex relations, religious life in the home, choosing and associating with friends, and social activities and recreation.

The study shows a close relationship between length of time it takes to adjust and happiness ratings of the marriages. As seen in Table 20, over half of the couples rated

TABLE 20 *Composite of Time Reported to Adjust in Six Areas in Marriage and Happiness in Marriage*

| Time Reported | Happiness in Marriage | | |
	Very Happy Per Cent	Happy Per Cent	Average Per Cent
Satisfactory from beginning	53	35	12
1–12 months	50	34	16
1–20 years	35	44	21
Never	19	35	46

SOURCE: Adapted from Judson T. and Mary G. Landis, *Building a Successful Marriage*, 2nd Ed., Figure 51, p. 262. Copyright, 1948, 1953, by Prentice-Hall, Inc., Englewood Cliffs, N. J. Reprinted by permission of the publisher.

their marriages as very happy if they had made a satisfactory adjustment from the beginning, whereas only one-fifth (19 per cent) rated their marriages as very happy if they never made a satisfactory adjustment in these areas.

Some couples rated their marriages as very happy even though there was one of the six areas in which they had not made a satisfactory adjustment. But if they failed to adjust in as many as two of the six areas, 77 per cent rated their marriages as average or unhappy; and if they failed to adjust in three or more of the six areas, all couples rated their marriages as average or unhappy. Of the 409 couples, only 11 had failed to adjust in as many as three areas; however most married couples who had failed to adjust in more than two

MARRIAGE

areas were not in the sample because they had already separated.[3]

The importance we would want to attach to this study is that there are recognizable areas—not that these six are the only ones—in which couples must make a reasonably satisfactory adjustment if they are to have a satisfactory relationship with each other, and that the relationship between them will be most satisfactory if these adjustments are made early in the marriage.

These adjustments must, of course, be made by the couple, either consciously or unconsciously; adjustments do not just happen with the passage of time.

Whenever two or more persons associate together for any length of time, there are decisions to make and problems to solve relative to their associating together. This is no less true for married lovers than it is for other persons in association. It is essential, therefore, that the married couple have some mutually accepted method or methods for solving problems and making decisions—some strategy of harmony —in their married life together.

Three patterns of decision-making among married couples have been conceptualized by Farber. These he refers to as authoritarian, mutual verbal coercion, and mutual discussion.

Before discussing these patterns of decision-making, it is well to point out that married partners are rarely, and perhaps never, equals. First of all the fact that couple members are not of the same sex is a factor of real significance. As we pointed out in Chapter 2, there is the matter of difference in physical stature and brute strength. Though resort to physical force or violence is not a generally approved pattern for making decisions in marriage in American society, any reading of the newspaper over a period of time will convince the skeptic that it is used. In many other cases, threat or coercion—either latent or manifest—is used in ways that

[3] Judson T. and Mary G. Landis, *Building a Successful Marriage*, 2nd ed., Englewood Cliffs, N. J.: Prentice-Hall, Inc., p. 262.

would not be regarded as newsworthy. There is empirical evidence of the use of force and threat of use of force in the recent studies of male aggression in dating.

But perhaps more important than physical stature and brute strength are the inherent differences in intellectual, psychological, emotional, and interest traits of the sexes. It is true that there is a great deal of overlapping in masculinity and femininity between the sexes; nevertheless differences between the sexes are not merely chance differences, and this needs to be recognized in decision-making in marriage.

> The superior physical strength of the male, the nature of the sex drama as basically flight and pursuit, the vulnerability of the female in her maternal role—these have resulted in an age-old pattern of masculine dominance and feminine submission. In the love relationship this remains, and probably always will remain, the normal pattern of interaction, corresponding to the emotional needs of husband and wife.
>
> There is also the *cultural* tradition which views the man as leader and protector, bearing the main responsibility for the home; while the woman nestles happily in the security he provides for her. The egalitarian conceptions popular today minimize this reciprocity in the husband-wife relationship. Yet there are evidences that something may thereby be lost which the normal woman needs.[4]

More will be said on this topic when we discuss the matter of family headship in the following chapter. There is one more factor to consider in our elaboration of the fact that decision-making in marriage is never between equals.

> Finally there are *personal* factors in the make-up of individuals which require variations in the response pattern in marriage. There are people who *want* to be dominated—and not all of them women! . . . The marriage of a strongly dominant and an exceptionally submissive person may be successful where unions between two

[4] Mace, *op. cit.*, pp. 205–207.

dominants or two submissives fail. . . . Successful marriages display a remarkable variety of patterns.[5]

The Authoritarian Pattern in Decision-Making

In the authoritarian pattern a decision is arrived at by one of the marriage partners independent of the other. It is then related to the spouse, and the spouse acquiesces to the decision. This is a traditional pattern for decision-making in many societies in which one partner, more commonly the husband, is recognized as the head of the family and little attention is given to the thoughts and feelings of individual members of the family. It also played an important part in the historic, Judaic-Christian marriage models. The pattern is not without its adherents in American society today.

In practice the authoritarian pattern may not be so dogmatic as it would at first appear to be. There are certain common practices employed under such a pattern that mitigate what would appear to be an inflexible and autocratic rule by the head of the family. For instance, the division of labor in the patriarchal family usually meant that though the woman had a subordinate role to play in the family at large, the domestic functions of cooking, cleaning, caring for children, etc., were clearly marked out as her realm. She did have a domain for autocratic rule of her own if she chose to make decisions in this way.

It is also possible under an autocratic system for the subordinate member of the couple to make suggestions within a posture of subservience in the hope that the dominant member will incorporate the suggestions into future decisions without feeling that his authority is threatened thereby.

The subordinate member may also make a request that a decision be made by the dominant member without tak-

[5] *Ibid.*

ing responsibility for making the decision, hence clearly recognizing the role of the family decision maker.

It may even work to the advantage of the subordinate member in influencing a decision if the subordinate member plays up the subordinate role. The weeping wife, for instance, is a classic stereotype of attempts to melt the heart of the recognized decision maker with tears. Such a technique, whether seriously or playfully used, may be flattering to the decision maker. He must be moved to sympathy by such a show of subservience for the technique to have its intended effect. We would not imply, however, that the weeping technique is only a technique, it may be a genuine and even a desired subservience that is felt on the part of the subordinate partner. Among couples who regard themselves as respected and self-respecting equals, the subservient posture only calls forth reactions of disgust.

Verbal Coercion in Decision-Making

In the verbal-coercion pattern as in the authoritarian pattern of decision-making, the decision is made by only one partner, but verbal coercion implies that the consent of the spouse must be obtained. Hence it is somewhat less autocratic than the authoritarian pattern. Discussion takes place after one partner has made a decision. This partner then tries to obtain the consent of his spouse by exerting strong persuasion. If both couple members are emotionally independent, decisions will be made through mutual verbal persuasion with each attempting to influence the decision by resort to talk. Where mutual verbal persuasion is the pattern, the decision-making process may result in intensive and extensive verbal battles. Logically, if both are rational about the matter, the discussion should end when the person with most of the valid arguments on his side has persuaded the other. But verbal battles dominated by reason are perhaps exceptions rather than the rule. If the verbal battle ends, it may be because the partners decide to compromise on a decision. They agree to disagree but not to talk about it. One yields to the greater intensity of desire or persistence of the other,

"It cost me two tantrums and a night at my mother's house."

Reprinted from *Love and Hisses* by Brant House. Copyright 1956, Ace Books, Inc.

or, out of love or for other reasons, the one "gives in" without being convinced about the rightness of the arguments of his spouse.

Mutual Discussion As a Pattern of Decision-Making

In the third major method of decision-making, decisions are arrived at only after mutual discussion. This method is most successfully employed where married partners are both somewhat emotionally dependent.

The mutual-discussion method is widely heralded in America since on the surface it appears to be the method most consistent with values in the American ideal. But students of interpersonal relations have pointed out that mutual discussion is adequate as a problem-solving technique only if both facts and feelings are employed as data in arriving at decisions. David R. Mace has stated the case very well.

Sometimes restrained discussion is advocated as a better alternative than quarreling. But the danger is that cold discussion may arrive only at an *intellectual* solution which fails to do justice to the *emotional* elements in the conflict. In my view it is best that, within reasonable limits, these *emotional* elements be expressed. Marriage partners can come to terms on a basis of reality only when they have *felt* the heat of each other's hostile feelings. A marriage should be able to include the expression of both positive and negative emotions if it is to be a really satisfying relationship.[6]

There are many other factors to be considered in making decisions and solving problems, regardless of the pattern followed, and we will discuss some of the major ones in the following pages.

Factors in Successful Decision-Making

THE WILL TO SUCCEED

Since in America marriage involves a voluntary commitment on the part of two free individuals, adjustment in marriage is possible only if the persons involved possess the desire to have the marriage succeed. There was a time in our society when much of the pressure to adjust came from outside of the marriage, and it is only in the last few decades

[6] *Ibid.*, p. 206.

that divorce, for instance, has come to be accepted by those on the outside as a necessary safety valve for "bad" marriages or as a privilege of free persons who have volunteered to enter a marriage relationship.

Even on the strength of such evidence, however, we cannot rule out the fact that external pressures help hold a marriage together, for, besides the law, one's family, friends, and members of the community by and large look with greater favor on a marriage that succeeds, and a failure is apt to be regarded as something of a reflection on the couple involved—at least in the minds of those not intimately acquainted with the situation. But, recognizing the external pressures to conform, the internal pressures are most important in a society where marriages are voluntary commitments.

What are some of the internal or personal reasons for desiring to make a successful marriage?

In a society where love is the prelude par excellence and the one acceptable essential basis for marriage, love must provide a major part of the motivation for wanting the marriage to succeed. First there is the love of the other as an object to be experienced (*eros*). Secondly, there is the motivation that comes from the satisfaction in being together and doing things together (*filia*). And, thirdly, lovers are motivated by their devotion and dedication to each other (*agape*)—the willingness to sacrifice that the other may grow and develop. In summarizing their findings on "the dynamics of marriage," Burgess and Wallin concluded that "A growing and deepening love between husband and wife appears to be the most dynamic aspect of a successful marriage."

Secondly, the desire to do what is right involves, for many Americans, an inner conviction that permanence of marriage and faithfulness to spouse is proper behavior. This conviction is central to one embracing the values in the Judaic-Christian marriage model, for instance.

TRAITS OF PERSONALITY [7]

Not all persons possess an equal capacity for empathy and flexibility; nevertheless these traits seem to be crucial in getting along with others and basic to a capacity to solve problems in marriage. We will discuss some of the more important traits of personality in this section and some character traits, insofar as the two are separable, in the section that follows.

Health. By health we mean much more than mere absence of disease. Rather it signifies the progressive maximization—within organic limits—of the ability of the organism to exercise all of its physiological functions and to achieve its maximum of sensory acuity, strength, energy, coordination, dexterity, endurance, recuperative power, and immunity. A popular synonym is "good physical condition."

Endurance of strain makes physical demands, but the capacity to bear strain is not a constant; it can be cultivated in advance of its use. A striking example is the frequent recovery from despair and breakdown of relations between persons through vacation and rest, hygiene and recreation. A benevolent spiral seems to extend from radiant health to a cheerful mien, from a cheerful mien to a friendly response, and back again to a capacity to get along with others in the stress and strain of intimate life together.

Intelligence. To be able to see relationships among events; to be able to abstract and symbolize experience and to manipulate the symbols into meaningful generalizations; to be articulate in communication; to be skillful in mobilizing the resources of environment and experience in the services of

[7] This and the following section draw heavily from two sources: Peter A. Bertocci, *The Human Venture in Sex, Love, and Marriage,* New York: Association Press, 1951, pp. 124–143, and Nelson N. Foote and Leonard S. Cottrell, Jr., *Identity and Interpersonal Competence,* Chicago: University of Chicago Press, 1955, pp. 51–57.

a variety of goals; these are the kinds of intellectual capacity so essential to successful problem-solving in marriage or in any other type of human grouping.

Empathy. People appear to differ in their ability to interpret correctly the attitudes and intentions of others and in the accuracy with which they can anticipate and predict their behavior. This type of social sensitivity rests on what is called the empathetic responses. Empathetic responses are basic to taking the role of another and hence to social interaction and the communicative processes upon which social integration rests. They are essential not only in understanding one's spouse, but also in understanding oneself. Love and the American ideal as guiding principles in husband-wife relations depend heavily on this capacity to empathize—to understand oneself and one's spouse and to be willing to act on the insights. The lack of empathic responses results in misunderstanding.

Acceptance of self: autonomy and perspective. We have touched frequently upon the importance of self-acceptance since self-acceptance is crucial to mutual discussion between equals. The aspects of autonomy are a clear conception of oneself; a stable set of internal standards or values guiding one's actions; self-direction and self-control in one's actions; confidence in one's reliance upon oneself; self-respect; and the capacity for recognizing real threats to self and of mobilizing realistic defenses when threatened. That is, autonomy is the genuine ability of self-government.

By perspective we imply a correct appraisal—not too high and not too low—of one's own importance in the lives of others and in the perspective of history. It is the kind of appraisal that should give rise not only to appreciation and gratitude but also to humility and meekness. It is the kind of appraisal that in all likelihood might eventuate in a posture of humor, for there is a close association between a sense of humor and a sense of life and one's own importance in and to it.

A sense of humor as used here is not to be confused with the ability to see the point of a joke or some comic situation, though this is not necessarily excluded, but rather humor as used here refers to the insight into the difference between what one is and what he thinks he is. It is more than knowing the difference between pretension and performance; it is an attitude one takes toward such knowledge because he sees himself in relation to the whole human enterprise.

Persons who lack a sense of humor may be unwilling to look at all the available facts concerning themselves and their efforts. In one way, a sense of humor refers to a sensitive and intricate balance between caring and not caring, between valuing and recognizing the vanity of valuing. Yet it must be emphasized that a sense of humor does not mean that one takes nothing seriously or tries to laugh everything off defensively. Rather such a perspective inspires one to live without calculating the return for every single effort.

In a marriage lacking a sense of humor, the lovers are apt to take their efforts in decision-making so seriously that every one of their motives and sacrifices is weighed as if their whole marriage depended on that effort. A correct appraisal of personal worth and significance in the world is apt to inspire gratitude for what one has and what one receives from others, humility about one's own importance, and a willingness to accept some limitation on one's own freedom, rights, and satisfactions.

Judgment. Judgment refers to the ability—which develops slowly in human beings—to estimate and evaluate the meaning and consequences for oneself and loved ones of alternative lines of conduct. It means the ability to adjudicate among values or to make correct decisions; the index of lack of judgment (bad judgment) is mistakes. These are the products of an antecedent process in which skill is the important ingredient. Obviously neither small children nor incapacitated adults can make sound decisions in the sense indicated; and it is equally obvious that among normal adults there is wide variation in this ability. Some persons acquire reputations for unusually good judgment, and some others become conspicuous for the opposite. Unity in marriage creates a situation where it should be possible to pool the resources in judgment of both marriage partners.

Creativity of mind. Creativity is commonly associated with artistic and intellectual activities, but it can also include capacity for innovations in behavior or real reconstruction of any aspect of the social environment. It involves the ability to develop fresh perspectives from which to view accepted routines in marriage and to make novel combinations of ideas and objects and so define new goals, endow old ones with fresh meaning, and invent means for their realization. In relations between husband and wife creativity is the ability to invent or improvise new roles or alternative lines of action when problems arise and to invoke such behavior in one's spouse. Among other things it seems to involve curiosity, self-confidence, something of the venturesomeness and risk-taking tendencies of the explorer, and a flexible mind with the kind of freedom characteristic of spontaneous play. In relations with his spouse the uncreative person is continually in dilemmas and impasses—"at his wit's end."

Flexibility of action. Creativity of mind and flexibility of action are closely related. One may understand his spouse and know what to do to get along with her, but he cannot adapt to her unless his understanding and knowledge can find expression in a change in his behavior. The extent to which this is possible depends on flexibility of personality. Lack of flexibility implies rigid and stereotyped responses, which beyond a given point incapacitate the individual for social life as in the case of the neurotic, psychotic, or feebleminded. Persons who are tactful, diplomatic, or well-liked by a variety of people likely possess flexibility of personality. Persons whose environment and experience have been stable and lacking in variety are probably low in flexibility as a result. They have not been exposed to a sufficient variety of situations and relationships to acquire and appreciate any considerable skill in changing roles and attitudes.

CHARACTER TRAITS

Honesty. Honesty is the willingness to convey a true impression of one's actions and motives. It is more than telling the truth. We frequently tell the truth when we hope thereby to suggest a false impression of what the real situation is. The honest lover accepts the responsibility of conveying the truth to himself and to his beloved. The problem of being honest is the problem of conveying to oneself and to one's beloved what each needs to know in order to plan and act realistically and intelligently.

It is not easy to keep honesty consistent with kindness. Honesty may well be considered a long-run kindness to all concerned provided the motive for honesty is helpfulness.

Courage. Courage is closely related to freedom of action. It is the willingness to live for a goal despite the conscious danger of pain, failure, or criticism. It means the willingness to go on working despite the limitations, the willingness to be a failure, if need be, at something worth-while.

Courage has an interesting relationship to decision-making in marriage. It is in a sense the opposite of being a cooperative and compromising person. Only individuals with some direction to life and the courage to carry through are real persons. In a marriage of equals it is in the long run easier to adjust to a person with the courage of some convictions than to the person with a constantly shifting standpoint.

Forgiveness. Forgiveness is the willingness to help those who have hurt us to feel our earnest concern for their legitimate interests and values. It is more than the willingness to overlook the evil intent and action. It is the positive willingness to help the other to feel no ill will on our part. On the contrary, the "enemy" can see that the person who has been hurt is anxious that the "enemy" suffer as little as possible from the results of his intent and action. Especially in a relationship of love, as between husband and wife, the emphasis in forgiveness is always redemptive. "Forgiving love" may even create or restore companionship between husband and wife where it no longer exists. This forgiving part of the strategy of harmony has been called the "strategy of reconciliation," for, ideally, it surrounds the offender with so much sincere and unselfish concern that a genuinely new beginning is made possible on a new and higher level. Forgiveness is one of the most personally demanding, perhaps the most demanding, of all the techniques in the strategy of harmony.

A SHARED VALUE SYSTEM AND INTERACTION OVER VALUE DIFFERENCES

One of the most important functional imperatives in the maintenance of a marriage—or of any other social system for that matter—is that the value orientations of the husband and wife be integrated in some measure.

Marital integration is based on consensus of husband and wife regarding the rank-ordering of ends or goals to be achieved in marriage. If there were complete consensus, it would mean that all values were similarly ranked by both husband and wife—values pertaining to the ends or goals to be achieved and values pertaining to how they were to be achieved (means). Such integration or oneness would be theoretically possible but highly unlikely, for, when a couple marries, two value systems are brought together in interaction with each other.

It has been found that agreement by husband and wife on basic values is directly related to marital success. There is still room, however, for variation and nonconformity, particularly among values which are considered by husband and wife to be of lesser importance. In other words, it is not the "little" complaints that destroy marital harmony.

A couple can be too slavishly loyal to a set of values. If the marriage is to be a creative relationship, there must be some room for change in values as well as in actions. In fact, it can be argued that marital interaction is creative only when it involves the values of husband and the values of wife in honest and open consideration of differences. It is no doubt true that most marriages need more honest conflict and less harmony brought about through the suppression of feelings. This is the kind of honesty we spoke of earlier in the chapter.

In a free exchange of views—tempered by love—present values may be strengthened by added evidence brought out in the discussion; they may be corrected by new insights, or they may be discarded for what appear to be more adequate and satisfying values that are more consistent with what the persons now believe. The marriage grows by such activity and the personalities of the partners develop as well.

By the growth of a marriage we mean that husband-wife interaction makes possible the development of a unique marriage culture and gives this unique marriage culture significance as it serves in turn to guide the actions of the marriage partners. Hence some degree of shared ultimate values is absolutely essential to pair unity. Without it couples reach an impasse that either becomes chronic or sets barriers beyond which integration is not possible. This agreement or consensus should be on values which the married couple regards as the basic life values, and they must have the intelligence to recognize differences in their hierarchy of important values. Persons take a stand on what they firmly believe. Married couples must be able to discern what values are worth the energy, the effort, and even the strife of taking a stand. The line is not always clear between courage of conviction and just plain foolhardiness.

For many couples, adherence to some particular religious faith in common provides the value basis for their unity, as well as providing the basis for a statement of their ultimate values. Such a basis for decision is evident in the following statement of the young husband.

> Marital adjustment was aided by a strong religious conviction. We both attended the same church, regularly entering into its various activities both before and after marriage. The church became the center of interest for both of us, and all other activities were oriented to it. When problems arose in our marriage, the religious answer was there to aid in the solution. Status and acceptance were given to our marriage by the members of the congregation and the pastor. Vows said before the Altar of God and the congregation were seriously important to us and not to be taken lightly. The vows also carried a Divine Blessing which gave the marriage a higher acceptance.

Conversely, the ubiquitous interfaith marriage is a constant reminder of the divisive power of religion in marriage. Using the common example of religious difference over values in the area of sex expression, Himes and Taylor show the primacy of values over personality flexibility in bringing harmony into marriage.

> The Protestant who believes sexual relations can serve other purposes besides procreation will not find his problem solved by understanding and accepting the orthodox position of the Catholic Church as expressed by his wife. He is going to remain frustrated or have a large family to care for—and either case might create problems too burdensome for the marriage. Flexibility of personality cannot substitute for some degree of agreement on the fundamental question of what is right and wrong. People need a basis of agreement if they are to work and play together.[8]

[8] Norman E. Himes and Donald L. Taylor, *Your Marriage*, New York: Rinehart & Company, Inc., 1955, p. 158.

AN OBJECTIVE VIEW OF VALUES AND THE DECISION-MAKING PROCESS

Time does not solve all problems. Time may remove the conditions that made a problem troublesome, but if a problem is anchored in a disagreement over important values it will continue openly to plague the marriage relationship or become a latent problem showing its ugly head in a number of seemingly unrelated areas. It may become the wedge that eventually drives the marriage partners from each other.

Even more discouraging, however, is the fact that doing something about it will not necessarily solve the problem. It may be unsolvable—as when the couple members hold different basic values and neither feels able or willing to compromise his. The time to deal with unsolvable value impasses is, of course, in the dating and, at the latest, the engagement stage of the relationship.

More common in marriage than couples with unsolvable value impasses are couples who lack adequate command of what they believe and why and hence are not in a position to make intelligent compromises in the area of values. To solve problems each spouse must have a reasonably clear picture of what he believes, why he believes it, and some ability to empathize with his spouse in any conflict over value differences.

If the ability of marriage partners to make decisions is to be improved, they must have an awareness of the decision-making processes they employ. The couple must be aware that they are making decisions and solving problems; otherwise any improvement in their decision-making ability will be on a purely trial-and-error basis. For the couple not having difficulty with decisions, it is not of great moment whether they are aware of their strategy of harmony or not. But for the couple not doing so well, it would seem that evaluating the decision-making process would be crucial.

If the couple sees eye to eye on basic values, the problem of goals of any particular decision-making session need not be approached with apprehension as a threat to either person or to the marriage, for they can rest assured that whatever the decision it will be one that falls within the agreed-upon shared values. The goal, however, is not obvious in every problem under consideration, and one of the purposes of mutual discussion is to clarify and rank specific goals in conformity with ultimate values.

If the couple agrees on the goal or end, the next step in making a decision is to reach agreement on the means to the end. This is a minor problem, relatively speaking, once the end has been agreed upon, though it may not appear to be minor at the time to the persons intellectually and emotionally involved in the problem.

To choose a relatively simple problem for purposes of illustration, the couple may agree that something should be done about the fact that the neighbor's dog barks all night and keeps them awake. The end requires little discussion if both want to get a good night's sleep. The question may rather be one of means—how to remove the source of irritation. Should they talk to the neighbor? Should they call the police? Should they reprimand the dog?

An important part of any discussion of means is apt to involve a discussion of who is to do it, or who is to do what in terms of the agreed upon solution. This is what is referred to as defining the roles. Is it a problem for the husband or the wife, or both?

In summary, in the decision-making pattern there are three basic questions once a problem is recognized:

(1) What do we want (ends)?

(2) How shall we get what we want (means)?

(3) Who shall do it (roles)?

The Sociopsychological Processes of Marriage Integration

Perhaps the most insightful analysis of sociopsychological processes in the dynamics of achieving marriage unity to date is that of Harriet Mowrer. She discusses the process of "becoming one," utilizing the sociopsychological mechanisms of identification, differentiation, emulation, idealization, enhancement, and interhabituation. The following section is adapted from her excellent discussion.[9]

At the time of marriage there is little more than an emotional tie with another person. Marriage unity is achieved through the interplay of a number of mechanisms which are in part catalytic agents in the accumulative process of unity.

The first mechanism through which unity is transmitted is identification. It consists in solidarity of thinking and feeling toward one's beloved so that what one marriage partner experiences is the reflection and counterpart of what the other experiences (empathy). This solidarity, based first upon sex attraction, becomes in time overlaid with concrete expression of likeness in behavior so that there is built up a constellation of experiences which symbolize a further conviction of oneness. If identification is not arrested early in marriage, it becomes the basic mechanism in achieving the ultimate pattern of accord. The very essence of marriage is loss of a considerable degree of individuality if the couple achieves any high degree of adjustment or unity, just as the individual loses his individuality as he becomes a member of any group. This does not mean, of course, that comparatively speaking, a high degree of marriage unity exists only

[9] As quoted in Howard Becker and Reuben Hill, *Family Marriage and Parenthood*, Boston: D. C. Heath & Company, 1948, pp. 347–354.

where there is complete loss of individuality. Ideally, a marriage will, paradoxically, contain a maximum of identification or unity coupled with a maximum of personal freedom. Achieving the balance is the dilemma of marriage.

The second mechanism, differentiation of marital roles, contributes to marital stability in producing an interdependence between husband and wife, both emotional and physical. This differentiation tends to emphasize the husband's role as the chief source of economic support and the wife's role as the partner responsible for the care and supervision of the household and the children. On the emotional side the differentiation follows the cultural pattern less closely. Here the peculiar needs of the pair play a more important part in determining the roles each will play, for in modern marriage each person plays not one or two roles but many in the drama of unity. For instance, a wife may be to her husband a mother, a child, a sister, a companion and comrade, a sweetheart, a playmate, a social butterfly, a hostess, a symbol of his economic and professional status, a nurse, a confidante, or a business associate, as well as a wife. In turn, the husband may be in addition a father, a brother, a protector, a lover, a companion, a playboy, or a teacher.

Differentiation makes for unity to the extent to which each marriage partner can with facility and finesse shift from role to role as the occasion demands and yet always play a complementary rather than a conflicting role. This is discussed in greater detail in the next chapter.

The third unifying mechanism for the achievement of marriage unity is emulation, in which one of the marriage partners, because of respect and admiration for certain traits and characteristics of the spouse, strives to reproduce them in himself. The emulated spouse, whose ego is thus flattered and gratified, reacts appreciatively. Out of this interactive appreciation further unity is developed.

Emulation occurs only in terms of traits possessed by the marriage partner, but idealization, another unifying mechanism, assigns to the spouse traits which he does not possess, at least to the degree to which they are attributed to him. When the idealized person is stimulated to acquire some semblance of the idealized traits, he becomes more in harmony with the expectations and anticipations of the other person and this results in greater unity. It is difficult to conceive of any marriage being successful without some idealization.

Somewhat allied to idealization is enhancement, in which some characteristic of one marriage partner culturally unacceptable to the other becomes channeled into a form which has social approval and enhances the status of the individual in the eyes of the spouse. In this way the elements of a pattern which previously made for cultural differentiation are recast so that they become highly satisfying to both mates and elevate the stature of the previously subranked mate both in his own eyes and in those of his partner. As a result the entire marriage becomes overcast with the light of this enhanced status. This mechanism is particularly operative in cases where there is considerable difference in cultural background and experience which might otherwise be expected to lead to marital conflict.

An illustration is provided by the man who, reared in a rural environment, prefers hunting to "social" affairs and likes to dress casually and to avoid the more formal contacts in life. When he later moves to a city he feels out of place. He is married to a woman who, although reared in a small-town environment, has attended college, traveled abroad, and developed interests quite foreign to her husband's. In the process of adjustment, the husband's hunting interests have been redefined in terms of a gentleman's interests in shooting and frequent hunting trips and rifle tournaments where he often wins prizes. These accomplishments enhance his status in the eyes of his wife, who now likes to buy him sportsman's clothing and tell of his activities, and at the same time they provide an acceptable formula of being too busy with these activities to participate in those in which his wife engages. Since the character of his hobby is such as to virtually preclude participation on the part of a woman, a culturally accepted demarcation of their leisure-time interests results. Furthermore, what in the earlier period in marriage symbolized cultural diversity and inferiority now becomes a symbol of cultural identification.

Another important part of the unity of any marriage is that which results from interhabituation. Marriage entails the living together of two persons, and living together means that a host of habitual patterns of responses are built up upon which the individuals become dependent. There are among other things the household responsibilities and functions which are more or less shared. Setting the alarm clock at night, turning it off in the morning, preparation of breakfast, retrieving the morning newspaper from the doorstep, closing the garage door, bringing in the milk from the back-door step, are but a few of the myriad of habitual acts which become established in terms of responsibility and expectancy.

But interhabituation is more than simply a matter of responsibilities and conveniences of the household. Habit patterns also become established in the social intercourse between husband and wife—patterns of expectancy and dependency in regard to when each will be in the other's company or be available for social functions and dining out.

Of even greater significance are the emotional aspects of interhabituation. This covers a wide range of reactions which give rise to interidentifying feelings and emotions: the good-night and morning kisses, the affectionate pat of assurance and understanding, the sympathetic attention to one's trials and problems no matter how small or great, the amicable chiding of one's forgetfulness, the confidential talks, the planning of the campaign to impress the boss, the little white lies to protect the other's ego; all these and more give impetus toward emotional unity.

This emotional interdependence is supplemented by a

variety of symbolic elements, some of which may be slightly irritating in some respects and yet if absent would leave a void. These elements are usually physical objects which symbolize pair interaction. Thus the way the pictures are hanging in the home, the arrangement of the furniture, the decorating scheme of the familiar walls, the pieces of bric-a-brac, the little plants stuck here and there, the smoking paraphernalia, the sight of familiar bits of the other's clothing, such as a pair of house-slippers with the familiar scuff on the heel sitting in their accustomed spot in the room or the bathrobe with the pockets bulging with Kleenex —all of these evoke pangs of feelings of solidarity, each relatively unimportant yet of considerable import in their totality.

Interhabituation also involves the development of habits of sexual experiences in which the stimuli and recurrent occasions for intercourse become stabilized. That is, frequency, amount of preliminary sex play, time setting, etc., follow a recurring pattern, peculiar to the needs of the particular couple. Some degree of timidity, insecurity, inhibition, misunderstanding, and tension characterize the period of early sexual adjustment. Once, however, sexual adjustment has achieved a smooth-running pattern, confidence, feelings of contentment and well-being, mutuality, and further identification replace these earlier disturbing and often frustrating elements.

The importance of interhabituation as a mechanism, whether physical, emotional, or sexual, is attested by the fact that even temporary separation of spouses in successful marriages is often unpleasant and disturbing because of the interference with the smooth flow of these patterns. This in large part accounts for the elevation of the emotions in the experience of reunion even though but a short time has elapsed since separation.

In this social-psychological world of similarity of ideas, thinking, feelings, and attitudes, there develops a continuity of meaning and a universe of discourse which has peculiar significance to the married couple. Even the trend of thought of the married pair often shows a high degree of identity, and emotional reactions to experience become similar in character.

Summary

"To be as one" is a goal common to newly married couples. This is natural and generally wholesome. Yet there is within each normal individual not only the desire to belong but also the desire to remain a unique and inviolable person. If each married partner is to retain and develop his unique nature while immersed in group life, oneness in marriage must not become complete oneness. The tension between two real persons must remain.

Every married couple must have some mutually acceptable method of arriving at decisions—authoritarian, mutual verbal coercion, or mutual discussion. Certain traits of personality—good health, intelligence, the ability to empathize, autonomy, perspective, judgment, creativity of mind, and flexibility of action—and certain character traits—honesty, courage, forgiveness—also contribute to marital adjustment.

In their strategy of harmony, it is important that the partners share ultimate values and be able to view with objectivity the essential and the nonessential values as they strive for compromise and agreement.

As the couple lives together in harmony, the sociopsychological process of integration—identification, differentiation, emulation, idealization, enhancement, and interhabituation—helps to create a smooth-functioning unity of thought and action.

QUESTIONS AND PROJECTS

1. In your own words, what is the twofold function of marriage consistent with the American ideal?
2. Why are the early years so important to adjustment in marriage?
3. Why do we say that a person loses some of his individuality when he joins a group, such as a marriage? Does this constitute a threat to his individuality? If so, in what way?
4. How would you describe a "hen-pecked" husband in terms of the frame of reference of this chapter?
5. In a free society, is it "right" for married couples to solve their problems by the authoritarian method?
6. Are verbal coercion and quarreling merely different names for the same phenomenon?
7. After reading the chapter, make a list of the traits of personality and character discussed. Without referring to the book write a brief explanation of each, indicating how it applies to the marriage relationship.
8. Is there a difference between flexibility of personality and flexibility in value orientation?
9. In decision-making is the primary problem one of determining ends or means? Discuss.

SUGGESTED READINGS

Becker, Howard, and Reuben Hill, *Family Marriage and Parenthood*, Boston: D. C. Heath & Company, 1948, Chapter 11.

Bertocci, Peter A., *The Human Venture in Sex, Love, and Marriage*, New York: Association Press, 1951, Chapter 4.

Burgess, Ernest W., and Paul Wallin, *Engagement and Marriage*, Chicago: J. B. Lippincott Co., 1953, Chapter 19.

Cavanaugh, John R., *Fundamental Marriage Counselling: A Catholic Viewpoint*, Milwaukee: The Bruce Publishing Co., 1957.

Farber, Bernard, "An Index of Marital Integration," *Sociometry*, Vol. 20, June 1957, pp. 117–134.

Foote, Nelson N., and Leonard S. Cottrell, Jr., *Identity and Interpersonal Competence*, Chicago: University of Chicago Press, 1955, Chapter 2.

Landis, Judson T., "Length of Time Required to Achieve Adjustment in Marriage," *American Sociological Review*, Vol. 11, December 1946, pp. 666–677.

Mace, David R., "Personality Expression and Subordination in Marriage," *Marriage and Family Living*, Vol. XV, August 1953, pp. 205–207.

Perlis, Mildred E., "The Social Functions of Marriage Wit," *Marriage and Family Living*, Vol. XVI, February 1954, pp. 49–50.

Qualben, Paul A., "The Church and Marriage Problems," *The Seminar on the Family and Christian Education*, St. Olaf College, Northfield, Minnesota, August 5–9, 1957, Vol. VIII, pp. 1–15.

Winter, Gibson, *Love and Conflict*, Garden City, New York: Doubleday & Company, Inc., 1958.

Wood, Leland F., *Harmony in Marriage*, New York: Round Table Press, 1955.

18 *Togetherness in Marriage: Complementary Roles*

⦁⦁⦁
▮▮▮

In the last chapter we spoke about the desire for and the processes by which a husband and wife become one—how they come to think, feel, and act as one. But that is only one part of marriage; there is oneness, twoness, and individuality in marriage in accord with the American ideal. In this chapter we will discuss twoness or togetherness and in the chapter to follow individuality or self-realization and marriage.

By togetherness we mean that in any functioning system —in this case marriage—there must be a division of the work to be done in connection with the maintenance and functioning of the system between the participating persons. There must also be integration of roles if the system is to be maintained and to function. Hence, in the case of marriage, the married couple must agree on where the marriage is going and on what is to be accomplished. Secondly, they must agree on who is to do what. In other words, there must be agreement on ends and agreement on means.

"Goodbye, dear, and remember—no matter how discouraging things may become at the office, you always have me to come home to."

Drawing by Whitney Darrow, Jr., copr. © 1957 The New Yorker Magazine, Inc.

There are three basic questions that must be dealt with in this chapter. What functions are performed in a marriage and in a family? Who is to carry out each function? And, thirdly, how can what each marriage partner does be coordinated into a smoothly functioning marriage? To include all of the major functions of husband and wife, we will consider both the marriage functions and the family functions of the marriage partners, though marriage and family are separate social systems. For purposes of this discussion it is permissible to refer to both systems with the hyphenated term, marriage-family system.

The Major Functions of a Marriage-Family System

As Zimmerman has pointed out, "this family social system stemming from marriage is partly inviolably private and partly (also inviolably) public." There is an inside and an outside to every marriage-family; there are inside functions of the system as a private system and there are outside functions of the system as a part of the community and the larger society. In American society, the outside functions on behalf of the marriage-family system are basically two in number.[1] Both of the outside functions must be performed by either the husband or wife, or both. No other members of the nuclear family are capable of carrying them out. Both functions are what have come to be referred to as instrumental or task functions. First of all, some member of the marriage must be outside the home doing something in the general economic-productive order of society—the occupational role. This occupational role is, of course, a part of the economic or occupational system of the society, and hence the marriage has a public function as its member spends a major part of his time out in the community doing a part of this necessary economic-productive work of the society. This role is both a part of the occupational system of the society

[1] With the exception of the infant, individual members of the family have additional outside roles in a variety of community organizations—only for the infant does the family offer a wide enough range of roles.

and a part of the marriage system, for it is the marital role which succeeds in bringing into the marriage-family system the dollars needed to support the system through the purchase of items which fulfill the needs and provide some of the luxuries of marriage-family living. When America was primarily an agricultural nation this occupational function was performed within, rather than outside, the marriage-family. Today the individual job, not the products of the cooperative activities of the family as an agricultural group, is the primary source of economic support for the family.

The second function performed outside the home is that of representative of the marriage-family in the community and in the society. The marriage-family system must carry someone's name—it is the Johnson family or the Gambino family; property must be in someone's name; if members of the family get into trouble, someone must represent the family; in major purchases that are made someone must represent the family. In other words, one of the marriage partners must act as a representative of the marriage-family in the community with authority to act for it, on the basis of his own decisions or decisions democratically arrived at in the marriage-family system.

Within the marriage-family system the basic and essential functions—the inside functions—are more numerous. These include functions surrounding sex expression and its consequences—engaging in sexual intercourse, bearing the babies, socializing the babies, etc. Secondly, it includes the functions of managing the home, coordinating the activities of the members of the family, and disciplining them when they get out of line. Thirdly, there is the very important function of social and emotional leader or sociometric star within the home—the giver of affection, the chief sympathizer and empathizer, and the one who puts oil on troubled waters when there is misunderstanding or ill will between members of the family. The function of spiritual leader is closely related to these functions, also.

Dividing the Marriage-Family Functions

Is there any rational basis for a division of labor within and outside the home, or must the division be on an arbitrary or chance basis? Yes, there is a rational basis for division of labor between husband and wife based on the fact that there are qualitative differences between the sexes, as pointed out in Chapter 2 and elsewhere in the text. The basic sex functions of the marriage are clearly and unmistakably differentiated and the psychological differences in terms of abilities, interests, and motivations between the sexes are more differentiated by sex than chance would dictate.

What do these "givens" mean in terms of differentiation of roles between the marriage partners?

Let us begin with some of the functions inside the marriage-family system. In regard to sex expression and the consequences of sexual activity, the roles are clearly delineated because of the qualitative differences between the sexes. Only the female of the species has the capacity to conceive, carry the fetus, give birth, and nurse the newborn child. Also, since the male, generally speaking, has a more highly developed sex drive and desire for sex outlet and a stronger psychological set toward sexual intercourse than the wife, it is natural that in the sex act the husband should play the aggressor role and the wife primarily the submissive role. Since sex expression as a function of the marriage is to be discussed in greater detail in a separate chapter, it will not be discussed further here. All we want to point out in this connection is that certain of the functions within the marriage-family system are so clearly sex-differentiated as to the requirements needed to fulfill the function that there can be no argument as to who will carry them out.

Who should be the outside and who should be the inside representative or leader of the marriage-family? Again the problem is somewhat settled for the married couple with children, for the woman is by the very nature of her sex function—menstruation, pregnancy, birth, nursing of the infant—immobile and confined to the home, whereas the husband is not rendered immobile or confined in the slightest degree by his sex role. These are the biological facts of the case.

Secondly, as indicated in Chapter 2, there are some psychological facts to consider in deciding who should be outside and who should be inside leader of the marriage-family system. Since men are, by and large, more aggressive, extroverted, and interested in abstract and mechanical things and have more brute strength, it is reasonable that, relatively speaking, they should be "out facing the world," solving the philosophical and technological problems of the society and, in the process, bringing home the pay check. By the same token it is reasonable that the wife who is somewhat confined by her sex role and inclined toward greater interest in personal things and more sensitive to culture and beauty should be in the home caring for the child, ministering to the needs of her husband, and creating a family cultural and educational oasis for each member of the family. Hence, the leadership inside the family comes to rest with the wife, and the leadership of the marriage-family system in the community comes to rest with the husband.

Who should be chiefly responsible for the educative function—socializing the children, helping them to gain the basic skills in thought and action that will make it possible for them to live with others? Who shall bring out the unique personality inherent in each child? Once again, it is the wife who most logically performs this function of educating and drawing out the potentialities of the children in the early years. By and large she would appear to have sensitivity to others and their needs which is so important in the early impressive and formative years of the child's life. And, once again, she is the one who is accessible in the home for answering questions and teaching in other ways. In a sense, the home becomes a classroom during all the hours that the children are awake.

The husband, on the other hand, is away for long hours, and his role in socializing and drawing out the personality of the child has to be mainly supportive of the efforts of his wife. He acts as her assistant during the hours that he is at home. As the children grow, the special gifts of the husband are employed in teaching them and helping them to think in broad terms, introducing them to the outside world through sports, travel, and other things. During this phase the wife assists her husband.

A division of labor develops rather naturally around the power-and-authority function of the marriage-family system. Who should be boss of the family? The answer is not so simple as the traditional statement that the husband should be the boss. For in her domain—the home—the wife must have the power and the authority to speak for the couple and to discipline the members of the family. Outside the home, since the man is the primary representative in the larger community, it makes sense that he should be invested with authority to decide and act in accordance with the agreed-upon goals of the marriage-family.

When both parents are at home, who should be boss? It is not so important who has the power as it is that the couple agrees on values, procedures, and discipline and that someone acts when authority and power are needed. It is a pretty good rule for the parent who is at the scene of action to act as authority, with the other spouse always prepared to support his action. If either is to defer to the other, there is some logic in the wife deferring to the husband when he is at home, for, since he must of necessity be away much of the time, there is a real possibility that he will come to be regarded as a junior partner in marriage in the eyes of the children. By some show of deference to his authority on the part of the wife, the children may regard him as an equal of his wife, at least in the over-all job of maintaining order and discipline in the family.

Looking back over the functions and the major responsibility of each marriage partner, one is impressed that the pattern of husband outside and wife inside the home has not changed greatly in its major outlines from what it has traditionally been in America. In fact, as Parsons and Bales point out, the husband and wife roles in one sense show greater rather than less differentiation along sex lines today than they did in former times.

It is our suggestion that the recent change in the American family itself and in its relation to the rest of the society . . . is far from implying an erasure of the differentiation of sex roles; in many respects it reinforces and clarifies it. In the first place, the articulation between family and occupational system in our society focuses the instrumental responsibility for a family very sharply on its one adult male member, and prevents its diffusion through the ramifications of an extended kinship system. Secondly, the isolation of the nuclear family in a complementary way focuses the responsibility of the mother role more sharply on the one adult woman, to a relatively high degree cutting her off from the help of adult sisters and other kinswomen; furthermore, the fact of the absence of the husband-father from the home premises so much of the time means that she has to take the primary responsibility for the children. This responsibility is partly mitigated by reduction in the number of children and by aids to household management, but by no means to the point of emancipating the mother from it.[2]

The major difference between marriage then and now is not that division of labor has ceased to be along sex lines

[2] Talcott Parsons and Robert F. Bales, *Family, Socialization and Interaction Process*, Glencoe: The Free Press, 1955, pp. 23–24.

as husband and wife divide up the tasks of the marriage-family, but rather that many couples are taking the American ideal seriously and are applying it to their marriage and family.

The acceptance of marriage as a companionable relationship between equals has evidenced itself in an upsurge of cooperation and sharing of work within the home. It is not uncommon for the husband to be adept at taking over some of the roles traditionally reserved almost exclusively to the wife, and to take over without any threat to his manly ego. In a study of women college graduates, 49 per cent reported that the husband helped with the dishes, 49 per cent reported that he helped with other household chores, and 66 per cent reported that he helped with the children.

In outdoor cookery it is often the husband who takes over almost completely. He does not reluctantly don the apron but may even have his own equipment—an apron, chef's cap, and an assortment of utensils and recipes that add to rather than detract from his prestige.

There are two kinds of husbands according to Elder. She reports that most developmental husbands (70 per cent) say that the husband should help regularly with the housework, while only 20 per cent of the traditional husbands feel that the husband should regularly help. Nearly half of the traditional husbands said that "housework is woman's work." [3]

The intermingling of roles extends the areas of understanding between husband and wife and increases the opportunities for companionship, as well as fulfilling the very practical need of providing a substitute to take over in an emergency when the wife-mother needs relief from the routine of home and children.

Regarding the outside functions of the marriage-family system, the acceptance of the American ideal has meant that

[3] Rachel Ann Elder, "Traditional and Developmental Conceptions of Fatherhood," *Marriage and Family Living*, Vol. XI, Summer 1949, p. 100.

the wife commonly assumes a part of the occupational or income-producing role and that she also represents the family in the community and society at large. No one would argue that the husband should not have an occupational role, but on the question of whether the wife and mother should have an occupational role, it is not difficult to get an argument in most any group.

Statistics show that more and more wives have occupational roles with a steady increase from 1940 to 1950 and from 1950 to 1955,[4] reaching a high of 11.8 million working wives in April of 1955—an increase of some 600,000 over the previous year.[5]

Findings of a recent study by Sanford M. Dornbusch and David M. Heer suggest the interpretation that women are coming more and more to accept work outside the home as a normal and desirable pattern for them.

That the wife's working outside the home results in poor adjustment of husband and wife in marriage is not supported by empirical evidence; in fact, her working, if she wishes to, may actually contribute to good adjustment in marriage.

It would appear that there is no clear-cut evidence for a dogmatic negative or affirmative answer to the question, Should the wife-mother have an income-producing job outside of the home? In accordance with the American ideal, it would be consistent to allow women as complete freedom to enter the occupational field as we allow to men.

However, to say that the wife's out-of-home role does not necessarily contribute to the disorganization of the marriage or of the family is not the same thing as saying that it does not make any difference to the marriage-family whether she works outside the home or not. If a woman chooses marriage as one of her careers, part of her time and energy will be given to the role of wife to her husband; and if the

[4] Glick, Paul C., *American Families*, New York: John Wiley & Sons, Inc., 1957, pp. 90–91.
[5] "More Working Wives Than Ever," *Marriage and Family Living*, Vol. XVIII, February 1956, p. 29.

couple has children, the wife must almost of necessity make homemaking a major career at least until the children are launched from the home. If the wife-mother—who is the sociometric star of the home—is to have another major role it will mean that the homemaking career must be shared with someone else, housekeeper or husband, and the number of children and the spacing of children will have to be carefully coordinated with the wife's occupational role.

If competing or overlapping roles of husband and wife results in conflict or antagonism, empirical evidence would suggest that it is not necessarily because both are playing the same roles but perhaps because there is lack of agreement between them as to whether or not it is right for each to play these roles, or disagreement over who is to have major responsibility for each role. Many husbands are unprepared emotionally to accept the wife as an occupational equal, or even to accept the wife in a supportive, part-time, occupational role. The traditional husband in particular is apt to be unaccepting of a working wife and whether or not we will have more husbands accepting or promoting outside work for wives is a moot question. A recent study shows quite a disparity between the coming generation of husbands and wives. Of 416 adolescent boys, 78 per cent gave an unqualified negative answer when asked if they expected that their future wives would have jobs; however, of 485 girls in the same school, 56 per cent said without qualification that they expected to work at some job outside the home after marriage, and only 24 per cent said they expected not to work at all outside the home after marriage.[6]

But it isn't always difference of opinion over the wife's role outside the home that causes the difficulty when there is lack of agreement over marital roles. It can be differences of opinion over the husband's role inside the home that is

[6] Raymond Payne, "Adolescents' Attitudes Toward the Working Wife," *Marriage and Family Living*, Vol. XVIII, November 1956, pp. 345–346.

the problem, as the following case of sexual inversion shows so dramatically.

Mr. Baker's attitudes and interests are those his wife would normally possess. He likes to cook and his wife resents his considering himself superior in this respect. Each is jealous of the other when one receives compliments for a new dessert. Both clash over one another's activity in beautifying the home. Mrs. Baker feels that she is the one to arrange the flowers for the table when dinner guests are expected, but her husband insists that he should do it because he has more artistic ability. Each complains of the other's emphasis upon personal appearance. He resents her attractiveness and strongly disapproves of the amount of time she spends on make-up. He really wishes to do the same things and thus projects his guilt-feelings upon her. When she is ill for a day, he suggests that he carry out her plan to launder some of her clothing; here he reinstates the earlier inverted role in which he washed his baby sisters' clothing. He resents the fact that she does not "play up to him," give him presents occasionally, and defer to his wishes more often; and she says that he never sees himself as the giver of attention and affection in any situation.[7]

Expressive and Supportive Roles in Marriage

The role-sharing that we have been speaking about has another side to it, namely role-sharing with the avowed purpose of giving both physical and particularly emotional support to one's spouse in order that he might be sustained in roles that are regarded not as shared but as differentiated by husband and wife. In this regard there are an infinite number of roles that each marriage partner can take to sus-

[7] From a chapter by Harriet R. Mowrer in Howard Becker and Reuben Hill, *Family Marriage and Parenthood*, Boston: D. C. Heath & Company, 1948, p. 349.

tain his spouse, provided he is willing to help, capable of empathizing, and flexible enough to carry through. There are times when one person needs to be sustained and supported in his role and the other person can afford to play a subordinate and supportive role. For instance, when the husband comes home from work and announces "I got an

THE SATURDAY EVENING POST

"Look, I'll make a deal with you. You don't tell me about your day—I won't tell you about mine."

Reproduced courtesy of Stan Hunt.

unexpected promotion today, let's celebrate," this is clearly a situation in which the husband's role should be dominant and expressive and the wife should sustain him in his enthusiasm by taking a complementary, supportive role. The sensitive and responsive wife will recognize immediately what this event means and will take her cue from his enthusiasm and suggestion and will respond somewhat as follows, "That's wonderful! I'm so happy! Yes, let's celebrate! What shall we do?" The husband has, perhaps unconsciously, said, "Tonight, I want you to take the role of my companion on a date," and she has responded in a way that meets his need by sustaining him in his enthusiasm.

On the other hand, on another day the husband may come home from a routine day at work and find that his wife is in a state where she is "fit to be tied." The phone has been ringing all day, the cake she was baking for the women's club meeting fell, and baby has been "perfectly horrible" all day. This is clearly a situation in which the wife has every right to be expressive and the husband to play the supportive role.

If the husband has any capacity and motivation to empathize—men are apt to be more lacking in these traits than are women—he will realize that she is asking to be sustained as she almost breaks under the strain of her sometimes thankless roles of homemaker and mother. The adaptable husband can melt her frustration and restore her perspective in a hurry by taking a social-emotional role more commonly associated with women's work. He can show her tenderness, suggest that she get out of the house for a short time while he tends the baby and finishes "putting the evening meal together." After a walk around the block, a cup of coffee with a neighbor lady, a shopping trip, or a new hat, she is apt to return with composure, grateful for a husband who sustains her in her major roles when the going gets "rough."

Assuming the sustaining role is one tangible way of expressing what it means to live in a love relationship where each feels free to express his satisfactions as well as his frustrations, secure in the knowledge that he will be accepted and understood by his spouse and that his spouse is prepared and willing to take the supportive role when the occasion calls for it. The man who has a wife at home who treats him in this way can be expected to show the effect of it in his role as outside representative of the marriage-family; and the wife who knows that she is loved and has experienced the understanding and support of her husband can approach her task as mother with the confidence and the resolve that her children, too, shall know what it is like to experience sustaining love.

In a mature marriage there will be a continuous exchange of roles between one partner and the other as the occasion requires. Like two skilled dancers, the experienced married couple can undertake with the ease and confidence born of long experience the execution of complex movements in which, despite their constantly changing roles, they present an articulated pattern of graceful harmony.[8]

Summary

In every marriage there are tasks to be performed within the home and tasks to be performed outside the home on behalf of the marriage-family system. For a marriage to function smoothly the major inside and outside tasks must be divided between husband and wife in some acceptable way.

There are some obvious—and some not so obvious—biological, psychological, social, and historical reasons why the husband plays a major part in performing the outside tasks and the wife a major part in performing the inside tasks.

In regard to power and authority, each in his own area of responsibility must have a measure of authority and the power to enforce it if his leadership is to be effective. Agreement on marriage and family goals, agreement on the means of achieving them, and support of each other's roles reduce the need for a "boss" per se.

Though the major marriage and family roles are sex-differentiated in much the same way that they were fifty to a

[8] David R. Mace, "Personal Expression and Subordination in Marriage," *Marriage and Family Living,* Vol. XV, August 1953, pp. 206–207.

hundred years ago, there is more overlapping of sex roles today. Notable are the large numbers of married women gainfully employed outside the home and the growing number of developmental husbands sharing in the tasks of the home. There is need for sensitivity and responsive taking of roles—expressive and supportive—in the social and emotional interaction of husband and wife.

QUESTIONS AND PROJECTS

1. How does the term *role* as used by the sociologist differ from the term as used in the theatre?
2. What part do inherent biological factors play in the division of labor between husband and wife?
3. In what way is the concept of family boss inconsistent with values inherent in the American ideal?
4. Why does the breadwinning role fall on one or two members of the family today rather than on all members of the family as it commonly did in early rural America?
5. Consistent with the American ideal, what view might one take of out-of-home careers for the wife-mother?
6. In your own words, what is the meaning and importance of expressive and supportive roles in marriage?

SUGGESTED READINGS

Dornbusch, Sanford M., and David M. Heer, "The Evaluation of Work by Females, 1940–1950," *The American Journal of Sociology*, Vol. LXIII, July 1957, pp. 27–29.

Duvall, Evelyn M., *Family Development*, Chicago: J. B. Lippincott Co., 1957, Part I.

Elder, Rachel Ann, "Traditional and Developmental Conceptions of Fatherhood," *Marriage and Family Living*, Vol. XI, Summer 1949, pp. 98–100, 106.

Farber, Bernard, "An Index of Marital Integration," *Sociometry*, Vol. 20, June 1957, pp. 117–134.

Foote, Nelson N., "Love," *Psychiatry: Journal for the Study of Interpersonal Processes*, Vol. 16, August 1953, pp. 245–251.

———, "Matching of Husband and Wife in Phases of Development," Reprint No. 7, Family Study Center, University of Chicago. Reprinted from *Transactions of the Third World Congress of Sociology*, Vol. IV.

Hacker, Helen M., "The New Burdens of Masculinity," *Marriage and Family Living*, Vol. XIX, August 1957, pp. 227–233.

Jacobson, Alver H., "Conflict of Attitudes Toward the Roles of the Husband and Wife in Marriage," *American Sociological Review*, Vol. XVII, April 1952, pp. 146–150.

Kenkel, William F., and D. K. Hoffman, "Real and Conceived Roles in Family Decision Making," *Marriage and Family Living*, Vol. XVIII, November 1956, pp. 311–316.

Mace, David R., "Personality Expression and Subordination in Marriage," *Marriage and Family Living*, Vol. XV, August 1953, pp. 205–207.

Parsons, Talcott, and Robert F. Bales, *Family, Socialization and Interaction Process*, Glencoe: The Free Press, 1955, Chapters I, II, VI.

———, and Edward A. Shils (eds.), *Toward a General Theory of Action*, Cambridge: Harvard University Press, 1951, Part 2, Chapter 4.

Strodtbeck, Fred L., "Husband-Wife Interaction over Revealed Differences," *American Sociological Review*, Vol. 16, August 1951, pp. 468–473.

Thomas, John L., "The Social Web of Marriage," *Social Order*, Vol. VI, May 1956, pp. 199–204.

19 *Self-Realization and Marriage*

Ideally, every individual needs to feel that he is productive, that he is doing something which he and others regard as worth-while, that he is making headway in some particular endeavor or career. For the husband much of this need can be met through his life work, or vocation. Bureaucracy in business and government, and assembly-line production in industry are said to thwart some of a man's desire to be creative and productive, but nevertheless the satisfaction of doing a job well, receiving seniority and advancement, and supporting a wife and children can still drain off much of the husband-father's feeling of need to be doing something significant. He may supplement his career in industry or profession with roles in business and fraternal groups, youth work, and sports.

Each marriage partner invests himself in marriage. But, in accordance with the American ideal, he invests only a part of himself, for he continues to invest much of himself in his own development and a part of himself in his spouse's development. In this sense when we speak of self-realization and marriage it is correct to speak of marriage as "a pair of intercontingent careers." Career is here intended to refer to the process of orderly development of the person within the

"You know something, George? You're not happy."

Drawing by Steig, copr. © 1958 The New Yorker Magazine, Inc.

context of his relationship to others and most particularly to his spouse.

For the wife-mother the chief career possibilities center in the home. In a day when there were fewer opportunities for a woman to express herself, homemaking was apparently a sufficient career for many women, and they felt that both God and man looked with favor on it. Caring for one's husband, bearing and rearing the children, baking, sewing, cooking, preserving foods, provided many opportunities to feel productive and creative. One of the things which the move toward emancipation of women did was to rob home-making of its exalted status as a sufficient career for women. The result was that society came not to regard it as a career. Many women came to feel apologetic rather than proud of their work. The expression "I'm *just* a housewife" is commonly heard. The social significance and status of a career is important to the person occupying that status, but it is also important that the career have prestige or psychological status in the mind of the person holding the status. One person can say "I am *just* a high school teacher"; another can say "I am a teacher"; and there can be a world of difference in the psychological status revealed by each. So also one wife may say "I am *just* a housewife," and another may say "I am a wife and mother." Hence, career has an objective social status, but, more important, it must have a subjective psychological status that is reasonably exalted to make the individual feel productive, creative, and unique. In American culture the careers with prestige for both men and women have been the careers outside the home; to be a good father or a good mother rarely brings prestige beyond the circle of kinsmen and a few close acquaintances.

When we then define marriage as a pair of intercontingent careers we are saying that the orderly personality development of each marriage partner is a career in itself in the broadest sense and that it is lived out in terms of some major careers—in the more specific meaning of the word—partially dictated by and partially not dictated by the fact that each is a participant in a marriage-family system. We also imply that the way in which each carries out his career and the success with which he carries it out depend in large part on the nature of the continuing interaction between the two careerists.

A good example of the importance that is being attached to the significance of the spouse in the way a man works out his career is seen in the recognition given to the wife in the field of American business. Our use of this example is for purposes of illustration. It does not constitute approval of the practices described.

Over the last few decades, as is now so frequently observed, the corporation has been evolving a pattern of social community able to provide their members with more and more of their basic social wants. Yet, the corporation now concedes, one of the principal members of its community remains officially almost unnoticed—to wit, the Wife. For the good of the corporation, many executives believe, it is time the matter was remedied. "We control a man's environment in business and we lose it entirely when he crosses the threshold of his home," one executive says mournfully. "Management, therefore, has a challenge and an obligation to deliberately plan and create a favorable, constructive attitude on the part of the wife that will liberate her husband's total energies for the job." Others, though they might not put it quite so badly, agree that the step is logical.

Just how to do this . . . is a problem that has many a management understandably baffled. On one very basic matter, however, management is not in the slightest baffled. It knows exactly what kind of wife it wants. With a remarkable uniformity of phrasing, corporation officials all over the country sketch the ideal. In her simplest terms she is a wife who (1) is highly adaptable, (2) is highly gregarious, (3) realizes her husband belongs to the corporation.[1]

In other words, she is a woman who recognizes the occupational career of her husband as all-important and actively seeks to support him in it. We are suggesting that each marriage partner regard the development of the other as all-important and worthy of support.

[1] William H. Whyte, Jr., "The Wives of Management," *Fortune,* October 1951, p. 86.

The Nature of Husband-Wife Interaction

What is the nature of the interaction between husband and wife that advances the self-realization of each?

In the last chapter we spoke of the use of expressive and supportive postures to sustain one's spouse in his major inside or outside roles through acts of understanding, kindness, and whatever kind of support one's ability to empathize would allow. Here we will speak of the use of expressive and supportive postures and the part they play not so much in sustaining but in creatively promoting the growth of one's spouse toward fullest possible self-realization in a community of love.

What relationship of lover to loved one is most conducive to the optimal development of each? [2] A beginning toward the precise characterization of the ideal form of this relationship can be made by likening it to the relationship of artist (expressive role) and audience (supportive role). There are, of course, all kinds of artists and all kinds of audiences. But almost every artist is acutely conscious of the bearing of his audience upon his performance and development as an artist. To attain an audience that is critical but appreciative, objective but hopeful, and neither patronizing nor condemnatory nor sentimentally adulatory is the ideal his experience leads him toward. This ideal audience expects from him a performance as good or better than he has given before; it expects him to work hard for it. But it identifies with the artist and is sympathetic in an informed, under-

[2] This section is adapted from Nelson N. Foote, "Love," *Psychiatry: Journal for the Study of Interpersonal Processes*, Vol. 16, August 1953, pp. 248–251, and Nelson N. Foote, "Matching of Husband and Wife in Phases of Development," Reprint No. 7, Family Study Center, University of Chicago. Reprinted from *Transactions of the Third World Congress of Sociology*, Vol. IV, pp. 31–32.

standing way. Thus it never unrealistically demands that he exceed his powers, achieve a result he never aimed for, or be something he is not. Best of all is the audience that clearly differentiates between the artist and the work of art, judging the latter as a finished product but the former as a never fully disclosed realm of potential productivity. Such an audience is only disappointed when its favored artist does less than his best.

Everyone knows the prodigies of creativity which are occasionally unleashed when a person discovers and is discovered by the perfect critic. Such incidents are the imputed reference when a husband speaks of his wife as his "best friend and critic," although the phrase has become shopworn through sentimental usage. To be critical is thus to be neither hypercritical nor hypocritical. To achieve the delicate adjustment which is required means that criticism itself must become almost an art. Many a great artist has been intimately associated with a great critic.

The ideal audience, however, is often the artist's fellow workers with whom he tends to compare himself in measuring his own worth. It is never quite as positive a stimulus for the artist to have his creative productions praised by a teacher or master as it is to have them praised by those who are themselves his potential emulators and who know intimately what these creative productions cost the artist.

Thus the relationship most conducive to development may be further described as one of social equality and of reciprocity. It cannot be a relationship of superiority and subordination. Nor can it even be the relationship of couselor and client, contrary to some present-day currents of thought, for even the most nondirective counselor-client relationship is unequal and unilateral.

Discussion and sociability are two of the activities indispensable to carrying on the dialectic of creation and criticism from which comes personal development. By equality, however, is not meant sameness; quite the contrary. Each person is unique and ultimately incommensurable with any other.

In the best art, the artist performs at the limit of his capacities. By performing at the limit of his capacities, he continually transcends the limits of those capacities. That is, he goes beyond the point he had previously reached in the development of his capacities.

The marriage partner—as lover or "fellow artist"—is in a most strategic position to affect development of his spouse in a beneficent or a destructive way. Within the zone of changing self-conceptions—between what is completely accepted and what seems impossible—many characterizations given by another are not manifestly either true or false; it is their acceptance by the self and the premising of action upon them that makes them true. One's direction of growth as well as the rate of learning are powerfully affected by the responses of those particular persons upon whom he inescapably depends for evaluation of his actions. Depending upon the roles they play, they may convince him that he is basically a faker or a budding genius, a leader or a clown, or a multitude of other potential identities. Either way his resulting actions are likely to prove them right.

Now wives in general have had much practice in playing the roles of friendly critic and stimulating audience. When their expectations sensitively and confidently run slightly ahead of their husband's performance, they account for many prodigies in male careers. But, traditionally, husbands are hardly prepared to reciprocate and act with sympathy and understanding toward a wife whose household duties no longer seem to challenge her capacities.

The usual husband whose wife is discontented, or who has become discontented with his wife, rarely analyzes the situation in developmental or interactional terms. In counseling he may expostulate that if he only knew what she wanted, he might be able to supply it. That is, he makes the simple and misleading motivational assumption that discontent arises from unsatisfied wants and requires only their gratification to disappear—a view that can work havoc in parent-child relations as well.

There are a small number of marriages in which the wife outgrows the husband, through expanding her interests and activities while he becomes narrow, deformed, or arrested, despite her efforts to stimulate his social or intellectual growth. And there are also those happy few prototype pairs in which each is successful in facilitating the career of the other. But the commonest picture in American marriage is that in which the husband has no concept whatever of contributing by his manner of speaking and listening to the elaboration of his wife's career, particularly when she has no ostensible professional career. Although her constructive achievements with home and children may be honored, her ventures in other directions appear more often to be subject to insensitive disparagement rather than to insightful and competent facilitation.

The conception of love as the interpersonal condition optimal for self-realization or self-transcendence is a hard doctrine from which many will shrink, because it puts the claim of love to the test of the results produced; it implies a conception of marriage in which the success of the marriage is judged by the degree to which each partner contributes reciprocally to the continuous development of the other.

The Integration–Self-Realization Dilemma

In concluding this section (three chapters) on marriage it is well to point out that the concepts of marital integration—unity and togetherness—and the concept of self-realization are not compatible with each other and provide for a constant tension which seems to be inevitable and perhaps even wholesome in the marriage of two free and equal persons. One distinction that can be drawn between self-realization and marital integration is that in the former, husband and wife may each be personally adjusted in that each feels satisfied with the self-realization that he is achieving as he pursues his separate and distinct ends; whereas marital integration, on the other hand, rests on agreement on common ends and the development of complementary roles appropriate to realizing these common ends. Marital integration is more descriptive of consensus in interaction. Self-realization is not.

The extent to which self-realization contributes to or detracts from marital integration will in part depend on the specific careers chosen by each marriage partner. It is obvious, for instance, that if the wife and mother chooses the career of traveling salesman as her primary career the integration of the marriage-family system is almost certainly jeopardized. The major occupational career chosen by the husband may also affect the integration of the marriage-family system. One of the major marital-prediction studies gave considerable attention to the relationship between occupation of husband and happiness of the marriage. Some rather striking differences were noted between different occupations and marital happiness ratings. The researchers concluded that the (1) occupational groups that are mobile are less happy and (2) occupational groups over which the community exercises less control are less happy. Traveling salesmen fall in both of these categories and are ranked near the bottom on happiness rating; teachers and ministers, on the other hand, are relatively immobile and subject to extensive and intensive control and rate near the top so far as happiness of their marriages is concerned. One possible interpretation of these data is that tension develops between marital integration and types of self-realization.

Beasley makes a case for democracy as the setting best suited to resolving the integration–self-realization dilemma.

Since democracy does not promise the maximum goal fulfillment to individuals, why not forsake it for a system which at least allows open competition for satisfactions available to the group? Mother "needs" a career in order to feel herself a fulfilled individual; the children "need" her guidance and affectionate presence at home in order to feel secure; Father "needs" to be relieved of home responsibilities in order to succeed at his profession. Maximums are impossible with any system; optimums are the most that can be hoped for; and democracy is the only system that aims at concerted effort toward individual human fulfillment. Through it Mother may enjoy a measure of career satisfaction, Father's home duties may be held to the minimum commensurate with group living, and the children may be accorded the optimum security necessary for their growth and development.[3]

It is instructive to take a look at marriage-partner roles that frustrate rather than promote self-realization in marriage. The Family Study Center at the University of Chicago has noted six types of husbands and wives who habitually dominated, stifled, and embarrassed their mates. Inherent within each type is an element common to all—lack of respect (conscious or unconscious) for the mate as a person. For example, the interpreter does not respect the individuality of his spouse sufficiently to permit him to speak for himself; the romantic makes no effort to explore the richness of personality of his spouse as a real and unique person; the man-hater does not accept anyone of the other sex, including his spouse.

> The Interpreter likes to tell the group what her husband thinks about everything from friends to politics, leaving him with nothing to say. The male counterpart tells his wife: "Don't think—leave everything to me."
> The Romantic hides almost total ignorance of what her (or his) mate is really like behind a smokescreen of hand-holding, kissing, and endless declarations that "our marriage is perfect."

[3] Christine Beasley, "How Can the Family Breed Democracy," *Marriage and Family Living*, Vol. XV, August 1953, pp. 204–205.

The Squelcher has a knack for expressing devastating criticism just when the husband (or wife) is trying to make a good impression on somebody else.

The Ammunition-Collector gets the group to agree to an innocent-sounding statement; then uses it to attack a favorite activity of the husband (or wife).

The Self-Sacrificer willingly "gives up everything" for the husband (or wife)—as long as the mate feels guilty about accepting the sacrifice.

The Man-Hater (or *Woman-Hater*) singles out the mate as the main object of her (or his) contempt for the opposite sex.[4]

Summary

Each married person invests only a part of himself in marriage. He continues to give attention to his own personality development and to his career or careers. Ideally, each person needs to feel that he is "amounting to something" in his own right.

There are limits of time and limits to the amount of energy one can expend; and, theoretically at least, time and energy given to one's spouse and one's family is time and energy that cannot be expended on personal concerns. On the other hand, however, marriage can be an asset to self-realization if each spouse creatively promotes the growth of the other.

Foote has used the analogy of the artist and the audience as containing the basic elements essential to creative interaction. The ideal audience has faith in the actor and expects a good performance but empathizes and sympathizes with him and does not expect the impossible. The competent actor is aware of the respect of the audience, as well as their

[4] From John Kord Lagemann, "What Husbands and Wives Need Most," *Redbook Magazine*, January 1956, p. 82, as quoted in *Marriage and Family Living*, Vol. XVIII, February 1956, p. 64.

expectations and encouragement. He responds by performing at the limit of his capacities and even transcends the limits of those capacities by going in his performance beyond the point he has previously reached.

By and large wives are better critics (audiences) than are husbands. In Western society husbands have traditionally played the actor role. For the democratic or equalitarian marriage to become a reality, the husband must also be prepared to assume the audience or critic role.

Husband-wife adjustment is never static. This is particularly true in a marriage where each is seeking and being encouraged to seek greater self-realization. There will be tension between integration of roles as one goal of marriage and self-realization of each mate as another goal of marriage. This tension need not become critical if both husband and wife accept the paradox of marital integration and self-realization as goals of marriage.

QUESTIONS AND PROJECTS

1. What did emphasis on the emancipation of women do to the status of homemaking as a sufficient career for women?
2. What is the relationship between expressive and supportive roles and actor and audience roles?
3. Referring again to Chapter 2, do you see any reasons for woman's apparent capacity for playing the audience role?
4. What is the difference between equality and sameness when referring to marriage partners?
5. In what ways is self-realization a threat to marriage?

SUGGESTED READINGS

Beasley, Christine, "How Can the Family Breed Democracy," *Marriage and Family Living*, Vol. XV, August 1953, pp. 201–205.

Cole, William G., *Sex in Christianity and Psychoanalysis*, New York: Oxford University Press, Inc., 1955.

Duvall, Evelyn M., *Family Development*, Chicago: J. B. Lippincott Co., 1957, Parts II, III.

Farber, Bernard, "An Index of Marital Integration," *Sociometry*, Vol. 20, June 1957, pp. 117–134.

Foote, Nelson N., "Love," *Psychiatry: Journal for the Study of Interpersonal Processes*, Vol. 16, August 1953, pp. 245–251.

————, "Matching of Husband and Wife in Phases of Development," Reprint No. 7, Family Study Center, University of Chicago. Reprinted from *Transactions of the Third World Congress of Sociology*, Vol. IV.

Goode, William J., *After Divorce*, Glencoe: Free Press, 1956.

Heinecken, Martin J., "A Theology of Marriage," *The Seminar on the Family and Christian Education*, St. Olaf College, Northfield, Minnesota, August 1957, Vol. I, pp. 1–33.

Whyte, William H., Jr., "The Wife Problem," *Life*, January 7, 1952, pp. 32–48.

Williams, Robin M., Jr., *American Society*, New York: Alfred A. Knopf, Inc., 1951, Chapter 4.

20　*Sex Expression in Marriage*

In the three chapters on marriage we have discussed a number of functions of the marriage-family system performed primarily by husband and wife; one of these—sexual intercourse—is exclusively a husband-wife activity in the marriage-family system and an important one to the marriage since it can contribute (1) to unity, (2) to togetherness or companionship, and (3) to self-realization in marriage.

Sexual expression is found in any society to be associated with a number of relationships between the sexes other than marriage, but it is as a part of a relationship between two persons in love who have exchanged vows of devotion and fidelity to each other that the sex act can reach the fullness of its contribution to personal and couple satisfaction. It is with this latter, the only relationship within which intimate love-making is generally approved in our society, that we will deal in the following pages.

To those who would object that too much has already been written about sex and that we can help put sex in perspective by "playing it down," we would say that much has been written about sex, but much of what has been written is irresponsible or factually in error. Silence is not a corrective for error. Others will object that sex is natural and that a couple will discover how to carry on good sex relations without being told. Surely no "manly" man would want to admit that anyone could tell him anything about sex; nevertheless we are faced with the fact that many couples are apparently failing to achieve the gratification that can be experienced in a harmonious sexual relationship. It is a serious oversimplification to say that sex is natural. It is true that the basic capacity for sex expression is natural or inborn, but no couple should enter marriage taking refuge in the false security that they will naturally make a satisfactory sexual adjustment to each other.

Much can be learned that will contribute to satisfying sex relations in marriage, but our society has not been progressive in its training of young people for satisfying sex expression. The very subject of sex has been much-tabooed until in the last few decades, and even with a more permissive attitude today, we have not capitalized on the possibilities for careful and systematic education in sex attitudes and sex knowledge.

The man who regards himself as a hungry animal sexually and all women as eligible for conquest and the woman who regards sex as one of the burdens to put up with in marriage are hardly prepared for the joys that can come through sex expression of equals in love. Men may be handicapped in their preparation for sex expression in marriage by the sex attitudes prevalent in the male subculture and, in some cases, by their own premarital sex experiences.

In accordance with the double standard, men are not as

subject as are women to prohibitions against intercourse outside of marriage. They may find that sex relations are most easily secured from girls who are not their social equals and whom they would not be disposed to marry—prostitutes, pick-ups, or casual associates whose company is sought more or less exclusively for sexual purposes. In such situations the sexual response is divorced from love and affection and the conception of mutual sexual satisfaction. The focus of the man's attention is on the satisfaction of his own sexual desire, the person by whom it is satisfied is of secondary importance. Such experience is far from ideal as preparation for intimate love-making in a marriage of equals, such as the American ideal would specify.

The difference, then, in the attitudes with which men and women approach marriage is in part a difference in permitted and advocated experiences within the subcultures that each has experienced.

Some of the recent art-of-love literature must also share the blame for wrong attitudes toward sex expression in marriage, but in quite a different way. There was a time when sex was accepted as a man's prerogative and something to be tolerated by women. The art-of-love literature, taking its cue from the emphasis on sex sameness in the last fifty years, has pointed up the woman's equal capacity for, and equal right to, sex satisfaction. As a result, marriage partners who discover a divergence between them in sexual desire and capacity are concerned, especially informed couples who have read the art-of-love literature.

The "problem of frigidity" then arises in such marriages when the literature emphasizes a certain level of sexual desire as being normal and the desired goal. This point may be illustrated—not proven—by a recent case in which a woman described her marriage of fifteen years' duration. The marriage was accompanied by mutual interests, genuine warmth, admiration, and respect, but the wife had minimal desire for sexual intercourse. The couple reported that they did not regard this as a problem and had believed that they were "happily married." However, after reading some of the recent publications and magazine articles, this husband and wife began to worry that there was something missing in their sex life. They experimented with a variety of techniques in an effort to "warm me [the wife] up to the point where I would *desire* sexual expression as much as my husband." However, this resulted in extreme frustration for her. She indicated that she "had nothing against sex," but she just didn't feel sexually excited toward her husband regardless of how many techniques they used or how skillfully those techniques were employed.

. . . The problem of "frigidity" for such a couple may be created in a definitional sense by the tyranny of the "majority norm" and by writers positing an ideal depth of sexual desire on the part of wife and husband. Unaware of such an idealized norm, this couple might never have thought there was anything wrong with their sex relationship and the wife would not have been labeled as "frigid" by either of them.[1]

Interviews with couples in the Chicago study also yielded comments which illustrate that securing physical release or satisfaction from sex relations was primarily regarded as a "problem" for the wife, and husbands were apt to feel guilty in pressing for intercourse or to find it psychologically unsatisfactory themselves when they believed their wives were not getting the satisfaction to which they were entitled.

Actually, then, this informed generation, in its effort to achieve complete equality in sex satisfaction, may hinder rather than help sex adjustment because of the partial truths that have been disseminated through the popular literature of our day. We will return to this matter presently.

A different problem in regard to sex—more particularly the enjoyment of sex—has come from the historic Judaic-Christian marriage model and the attitudes it encouraged or at least did not discourage. As Bailey has pointed out, early

[1] Clark E. Vincent, "Social and Interpersonal Sources of Symptomatic Frigidity," *Marriage and Family Living*, Vol. XVIII, November 1956, p. 356.

Christianity left an entirely mistaken view of sexual pleasure. Since medieval times to the present, there has been a widespread sentiment that sex is evil.

That religious attitudes might even affect sexual pleasure in marriage is suggested in the findings of Kinsey. No significant differences were found in the proportion of copulations that led to orgasm for religiously devout, moderate, and inactive groups of women, except that the more devout Catholic groups did seem to have been more restrained in their first year of marriage with a distinctly higher percentage completely failing to reach orgasm and a distinctly lower percentage reaching orgasm in most of their coitus.

More recently, Christian theologians have rediscovered or come to emphasize a permissive view toward sex expression in marriage found in both the Old and the New Testament—a view more consistent with the romantic and rationalistic views that sex is natural, good, wholesome, and inevitable. As an example of this newer viewpoint, Bailey states that sex is to be regarded as one of God's good gifts to man which is to be received with thanksgiving. In fact, he goes so far as to say that ignorance, clumsiness, or want of sympathy can have devastating consequences, and that all who intend to marry have a positive duty to acquire an adequate knowledge of sexual techniques.

Differential Sex Desire

We still have not touched upon one of the fundamental reasons why sex adjustment in marriage is often a difficult and complicated problem for the young couple, namely, the difference in sex interest and sex desire on the part of the husband and the wife.

One of the disservices of the credo of equality of the

sexes and the art-of-love literature is that they for a long time discouraged careful empirical research on the differences between men and women. We are a little less naive and a little less crusading on behalf of equality today and are able to take more reasoned account of the differences between the sexes and to make allowance for them. The change from a naive definition of equality to a more sophisticated definition will be adopted only slowly, however. In the meantime, the naive definition has been widely accepted and has done some good in the liberation of women and some harm when it glossed over important differences between the sexes.

Kinsey reports that the average woman marries to establish a home, to establish a long-time affectional relationship with a spouse, and to have children whose welfare may become the prime business of her life. Although most men would admit that all of these are desirable, in the forefront of a man's motivation to marry, according to Kinsey, is anticipation of regular sex expression through coitus. Burgess and Wallin also found that the sexual relationship was placed higher in the hierarchy of marriage values by men, whereas women were more likely to say that they would not seriously miss sex if it were taken out of the marriage.

To the extent that this is true, sex adjustment can be difficult for marriage partners who do not appreciate the differences. The man who has been led to believe that any woman can have the same physiological and psychological response as can the man is apt to be disillusioned by his wife's lack of responsiveness. On the other hand, the wife who thinks of her husband as having sex interests similar to the average woman may be offended to find that he is more highly sexed.

The difference in desire for sexual intercourse in marriage is shown in Table 21 which represents answers of nearly 600 middle-class married couples who had been married for from three to five years. A larger proportion of

TABLE 21 *Number of Times Per Month Intercourse Preferred by Husbands and Wives*

Number of Times per Month	Husbands	Wives
	Per Cent	Per Cent
Four or Less	17.6	25.0
Five–Eight	35.8	38.4
Nine or More	46.5	36.7

SOURCE: Adapted with permission from *Engagement and Marriage* by Ernest W. Burgess and Paul Wallin, Chart 48, p. 663. Copyright 1953 by J. B. Lippincott Company.

the women than of the men reported a preferred frequency of less than five times a month, whereas a greater percentage of the men reported a desire for sex relations nine or more times per month.

In Terman's study of over 600 husbands and wives about one out of two husbands and wives approximated optimum frequency of coitus, that is, they were having intercourse approximating their desired frequency. Of those who were not having the desired amount, 43 per cent of the husbands and 23 per cent of the wives were characterized by marked or moderate sex hunger; roughly less than 5 per cent of the men had more sexual intercourse than desired whereas about 10 per cent of the women were moderately satiated and about 15 per cent were markedly satiated, having intercourse about twice as frequently as their reported desired amount.[2]

Additional evidence from the Kinsey studies also suggests that it is the husband rather than the wife who is chiefly responsible for the regularity of marital coitus.

Not only does the husband have desire for more frequent sexual intercourse, but he also has the experience of orgasm more regularly in intercourse. Among the men and women studied by Kinsey, about 100 per cent of the men and 70–77

[2] As reported in Ernest W. Burgess and Paul Wallin, *Engagement and Marriage*, Chicago: J. B. Lippincott Co., 1953, p. 667.

per cent of the women were on the average experiencing orgasm in sexual intercourse.[3]

The man is also psychologically more attentive to sex, and he may, therefore, be disturbed, angered, or peevish if he does not get the same kind of concentration of interest and effort on the part of his wife. She, on the other hand, because she is less aroused by psychological stimuli, is more easily distracted than her husband in the course of sexual relations. He may be continuously stimulated by seeing his wife, by engaging in erotic conversation with her, by thinking of sexual techniques, and by any number of other stimuli which keep him aroused even though intercourse is interrupted.

Perhaps two-thirds of the females find little if any arousal in such psychologic stimuli. Consequently, when the steady build-up of the female's response is interrupted by the male's cessation of movement, change of position, conversation, or temporary withdrawal from the genital union, she drops back to or toward a normal physiologic state from which she has to start again when the physical contacts are renewed. It is this, rather than any innate incapacity, which may account for the female's slower response in coitus.[4]

It is a common complaint of husbands that the wife seems uninterested or distracted, but this is likely an incorrect appraisal of the situation. What is involved is her lack of stimulation by the sort of psychological stimuli which are important to him.

Such differences between females and males have been known for centuries, and are pointed out in the classic and Oriental literature. From the most ancient to the most modern erotic art, the female has been portrayed on occasion as reading a book, eating, or engaging in other activities while she is in coitus; but no artist seems

[3] Alfred C. Kinsey, Wardell B. Pomeroy, Clyde E. Martin, and Paul H. Gebhard, *Sexual Behavior in the Human Female*, Philadelphia: W. B. Saunders Co., 1953, p. 393.
[4] *Ibid.*, p. 627.

to have portrayed males engaged in such extraneous activities while in coitus.[5]

Burgess and Wallin found that wives were apparently not greatly disturbed at being deprived of sexual satisfaction in marriage. Many women entered marriage with negative attitudes toward sexual intercourse and, though they failed to achieve complete satisfaction in this one area of relations with their husbands, they did not seem to be unhappy as a result.

It has been claimed that women's lack of interest in sex and lack of satisfaction is due almost entirely to the inhibitions that the double standard impose during her adolescence. But recent empirical findings seriously question this interpretation. A recent study shows that experience or lack of experience in premarital intercourse seems to bear no consistent causal relationship to the wife's sexual adjustment. In this same regard, Kinsey and associates found that a distinctly greater percentage of women from the higher educational groups reached orgasm. This is the educational group

TABLE 22   *Incidence of Orgasm in Coitus Among Married Women* [a]

In the first year	63 per cent of coitus resulted in orgasm
By the fifth year	71 per cent
By the tenth year	77 per cent
By the fifteenth year	81 per cent
By the twentieth year	85 per cent

SOURCE: Alfred C. Kinsey, Wardell B. Pomeroy, Clyde E. Martin, and Paul H. Gebhard, *Sexual Behavior in the Human Female*, Philadelphia: W. B. Saunders Co., 1953, p. 408.

[a] Within the first month of marriage, 49 per cent of the wives have experienced orgasm in coitus; one year after marriage, 75 per cent have experienced orgasm at some time in coitus; by the fifth year, 83 per cent; by the tenth year, 87 per cent; and by the fifteenth year, 90 per cent.

[5] *Ibid.*, p. 669.

with the lowest rate of premarital intercourse and a group
to whom the double standard applies.

Though the "inhibitions theory" is not borne out in the
research data, one should not conclude that sex experience
within a stable love relationship does not contribute to the
wife's more complete response to intimate sexual relations.
Empirical evidence shows a definite increase in incidence of
orgasm in coitus for those with longer marital experience.

From what we have said about the differences between
the sexes—no individual is merely the average of his sex—
it becomes apparent that adjustment is necessary before sex
can give anything near the optimum in satisfaction for both
husband and wife.

Sex Adjustment and Marital Happiness

There was a time, within the last few decades and in
the recent literature, when anything short of mutual orgasm
in the sex act was regarded as failure on the part of the
couple. This prevalent attitude left the wife feeling guilty
and the man feeling that he was not a man or that he had
not mastered the techniques of arousing his wife. With
greater knowledge of differences between the sexes, it is now
being more realistically suggested that the goal for both
should be satisfying sexual intercourse—that is, the adjustment should be mutual but not necessarily identical.

Orgasm must not be taken as the sole criterion of satisfaction; complete satisfaction may come from the unrestrained mutual sharing in sexual intercourse. For one, more
commonly the husband, intercourse nearly always brings
orgasm and accompanying tension release. The wife may
find her satisfaction in knowing that he has enjoyed the intimate contact and in realizing that she has contributed to

his pleasure. It may bring no physical relief for her but only a feeling of being loved and needed. As long as the couple has realistic expectations and each partner is satisfied with what he obtains from intimate love-making, sex expression can contribute to unity, companionship, and self-realization in marriage.

Sexual incompatibility is often said to be the major cause of divorce or marriage failure, but the empirical evidence is not convincing. Whether or not the sex factor is significantly determinative of success or failure in marriage is largely a matter of conjecture at present. Rather, poor sex adjustment is bound up with other emotional problems, and it is a moot question whether sex problems are not more affected by other problems than the cause of trouble.

Specific Functions of the Sex Act in Marriage

Just as the sex act may mean different things to the two partners, so it will from time to time vary in its meaning for both of them. One function intimate love-making performs is that through it man and woman come to understand the meaning of their masculinity and femininity in a significant and impressive way.

It is more than coincidence that sexual intercourse is referred to as "to know" in Biblical writings—the source of the Judaic-Christian marriage model. Sexual intercourse has also been referred to as a type of communication more adequate than speech or any other type of communication in transmitting the concern of two persons for each other's enduring happiness, as an expression of their love for each other and their desire to experience each other in the fullest possible way. Hence, it can be said that intimate love-making has a unitive function, for the act itself affirms a trust, a dependence, a oneness.

Sexual intercourse also has a specifically physiological function, namely, the procreation of children.

But for those who are quite permissive and uninhibited in their sex expression, intimate love-making often lacks the sober and solemn unitive and procreative significance and is engaged in for recreation or pleasure as play activity. Or it may be engaged in for the personally satisfying fulfillment of a hunger need (self-realization) which it provides.

Levy and Munroe have caught these different moods and functions and express it as follows:

> Study of the sex activity of relatively uninhibited happily married couples demonstrates very beautifully both the unorthodox nature of their impulses and the ease with which they are integrated into a "normal" heterosexual pattern. Sometimes the pair will be close and affectionate. Tenderness will pass into a rather solemn passion, a confirmation of their abiding love for each other. At other times their mood will be wholly frivolous. . . . Often, too, intercourse will be a routine satisfaction of a bodily need about as romantic as orange juice, toast, and coffee for breakfast. Our uninhibited happily married couple will take all of these variations and find them good.[6]

Conditions Contributing to Sexual Satisfaction in Marriage

Physical and psychological adequacy at time of intimacy. Generally speaking, early in marriage the couple will find intimate love-making more satisfying if they are not tired physically and mentally, for coitus itself makes demands on both kinds of energy. As their experience increases, however, coitus may be satisfying even when tired; it may prove

---

[6] John Levy and Ruth Munroe, *The Happy Family*, New York: Alfred A. Knopf, Inc., 1941, p. 129.

to be just the relaxing tonic needed for a tired mind or body. Early in marriage the couple will likely find that because of the newness of the activity, the lack of experience, and anxiety over possibilities of failure that it will be better if they are not fatigued.

Love and respect for each other. Love and respect for each other are continuing states which undergird and make meaningful the complete giving of oneself to another. Particularly for the woman, coitus can be quite meaningless and undesirable unless she feels she is giving herself in love to someone of whose love and respect she is sure. This is the abiding condition; but within it, either or both may be more or less happy with self and with spouse at any particular time and this will affect the quality of the satisfaction. Happiness at time of intercourse is, generally speaking, a contributing factor to success in intercourse, but, as the couple comes to know and appreciate each other's states of mind, the joy of being held, caressed, and needed by someone else can be stimulating even to a depressed spirit.

Complete privacy. Sex is a personal and private experience in our culture. A person brought up by strict rules of privacy may find it traumatic to share privacy with a loved one and will want to be completely sure of privacy from others. Some couples may even desire a measure of privacy from each other—in terms of darkness, subdued lighting, or even by being partially clothed during intercourse. It is a part of acceptance and respect of one's beloved to respect this desired privacy. By nature and by training this desire is apt to be greater on the part of the woman particularly early in marriage.

Time. It is conceivable that couples who have been married for some time might have completely successful coitus with not over ten minutes of time elapsing from the beginning of the relationship to the end, but for only the most uninhibited of the newly married would this be possible. Preparation for coitus on the part of the young man may be almost instantaneous—merely the thought of coitus with the beloved or slight tactile stimulation may place him in a state of readiness. It is the woman who may need more time to feel ready to respond wholeheartedly. As was indicated earlier, she is apt to be more easily distracted and may require privacy, intimacy, and suggestion to relax her natural and long-conditioned inhibitions against giving herself to a man.

Ideally, coitus should generally proceed out of and be the concluding act of a love scene between the two wherein there have been words of affection and love, kissing, and caressing. When the two are ready in mind and body intromission can take place as a natural and exciting next step in the love scene. The love play "from head to toe" may be heightened as feelings of love and feelings of sexual desire mount for both until with orgasm they reach a high point of the experience and each is lost in the ecstasy of the other's embrace.

Bossard and Boll have shown through the following example how psychological preparation for intercourse can play a significant part in the satisfaction received.

One rainy evening, about the second year of their marriage, Mr. and Mrs. Brett were playing cribbage. As the game went on in a desultory sort of way, the conversation between them took an intimate turn, followed also by various little intimate acts, such as playfully touching each other. Finally, as the regular bedtime hour approached, Mr. Brett suggested sex relations, to which Mrs. Brett acquiesced with more than customary willingness. In the following weeks, several more cribbage games culminated in this manner. In each of these cases, the sexual act had been very satisfactory to both husband and wife. Then followed the experience of several sex relationships without the cribbage preliminary. Soon, without any deliberate planning or formal agreement, the cribbage game came to be the regular preliminary to sex relationships. . . . Gradually, each step leading to sex relations between the Bretts has come to be ritualized around the cribbage game, ranging from the first shy references to cribbage to the final consummation. . . . They say that there are times when sex relations occur without this particular preliminary, but agree that it does not "seem so right" as when they lead up to it via the ritual route.

In somewhat disguised form, this ritual case was then read to a number of married couples, and most of them promptly agreed that some ritualizing of the sex relationship and of the steps leading up to it obtained in their particular case; that is to say, there were certain regularized "right" ways of preparing for sexual intercourse, which, when followed, made for a more satisfactory relationship than when not observed.[7]

It is generally agreed today that there are no right techniques for bringing about sex satisfaction, no right bodily positions of the partners in relation to each other, no right time of day for love-making, and no right frequency of sex experience. Each is to be determined by the couple in respect for their mutual desires and wishes. But marriage partners are, for the sake of each other and for the sake of the relationship, obligated to make sex as satisfying an experience as possible. Equipped with some knowledge of the facts of life, permissive attitudes, and love and tenderness on the part of both, intimate love-making should become a recurring satisfying communion between husband and wife.

Summary

Optimum sex expression is a learned rather than a natural accomplishment of the married couple.

In America we have been largely silent in the area of proper sex attitudes and sex knowledge, while sub rosa sex culture and the double standard of morality have provided

[7] James H. S. Bossard and Eleanor S. Boll, *Ritual in Family Living*, Philadelphia: University of Pennsylvania Press, 1950, pp. 188–189.

their share of erroneous and irresponsible sex education. The historic Judaic-Christian marriage model did little to emphasize the positive contribution of sex expression to marriage and, unfortunately, the more recent art-of-love literature has also contributed its share of false impressions.

We now recognize differences in sexual desire and sexual response between men and women and between persons of the same sex. We also recognize satisfactions in coitus apart from procreation of children and apart from the physiological experience of orgasm. It is important that each mate have some appreciation of the sexual nature of the other sex and, more particularly, some appreciation of the sexual nature of his spouse.

For married couples who accept sex as one of the "good gifts," sexual intercourse can contribute to their sense of oneness, to their companionship, and to the self-realization of each spouse.

QUESTIONS AND PROJECTS

1. To what extent is sexual behavior natural? To what extent is it learned?
2. What are the major sources of information and misinformation concerning sex and sexual activity?
3. To what extent have the different marriage models promoted or interfered with the dissemination of information about sex?
4. Why is knowledge of the other sex—and one's spouse in particular—so important to sex adjustment in marriage?
5. How can sex satisfaction contribute to oneness in marriage? To togetherness? To self-realization?

SUGGESTED READINGS

Bailey, Derrick S., *The Mystery of Love and Marriage*, New York: Harper & Brothers, 1952, Part II.
Burgess, Ernest W., and Paul Wallin, *Engagement and Marriage*, Chicago: J. B. Lippincott Co., 1953, Chapter 20.

Cavanaugh, John R., *Fundamental Marriage Counselling*: A *Catholic Viewpoint*, Milwaukee: The Bruce Publishing Co., 1957, Section II.

Foote, Nelson N., "Sex As Play," *Social Problems*, Vol. I, 1954, pp. 159–163.

Hamblin, Robert L., and Robert O. Blood, Jr., "Pre-Marital Experience and the Wife's Sexual Adjustment," *Social Problems*, Vol. 4, October 1956, pp. 122–130.

Kinsey, Alfred C., Wardell B. Pomeroy, Clyde E. Martin, and Paul H. Gebhard, *Sexual Behavior in the Human Female*, Philadelphia: W. B. Saunders Co., 1953.

———, Wardell B. Pomeroy, and Clyde E. Martin, *Sexual Behavior in the Human Male*, Philadelphia: W. B. Saunders Co., 1948.

Landis, Judson T., "The Effects of the First Pregnancy Upon the Sexual Adjustment of 212 Couples," *American Sociological Review*, Vol. 15, December 1950, pp. 766–772.

Landis, Paul H., *Making the Most of Marriage*, New York: Appleton-Century-Crofts, Inc., 1955, Chapters 21, 22.

Mihanovich, Clement S., Gerald J. Schnepp, and John L. Thomas, *A Guide to Catholic Marriage*, Milwaukee: The Bruce Publishing Co., 1955.

"Ten Years Out—A Survey of the Women of '40 at Smith and Wisconsin," *Mademoiselle*, September 15, 1950 (Mimeographed), pp. i–iii, 1–34.

Vincent, Clark E., "Social and Interpersonal Sources of Symptomatic Frigidity," *Marriage and Family Living*, Vol. XVIII, November 1956, pp. 355–360.

21 Maintaining the Marriage

With this chapter we conclude our discussion of marriage per se. Marriage and family are distinctly different social systems, serving different purposes and therefore having different functions. Much confusion has arisen because we fail to keep in view the fact that any household which contains both parents and children has two social systems operating within it at one and the same time.

The marriage system ministers exclusively to the needs of husband and wife; the family system ministers primarily to the needs of children and secondarily—but not unimportantly—to the needs of parents. These two social systems, operating under one roof with different but overlapping membership and different functions, simultaneously demand the attention of the members who operate in both, namely the husband-father and the wife-mother.

How much time and attention to devote to marriage and how much to devote to family is a real and ongoing dilemma for both husband and wife. It is a particularly troublesome dilemma if the marriage partners are not conscious of the two systems and the marked differences in the marital and parental roles.

There has been much confusion in the definitions of marriage and family and in the resulting analysis of these two social systems. Marriage is regarded by some as a prelude to family, a brief preparatory period that ends with the birth of the first child. After that husband and wife are absorbed in their father and mother roles with only minor attention to husband and wife roles.

On the other hand, some people regard marriage as a subsystem of the family. Early marriage days are then referred to as "the beginning family" or "the expectant family." After the children have left home the marriage is referred to with the uncomplimentary designation of "empty nest."

It is as correct to speak of the family as a subsystem of marriage as it is to speak of marriage as a subsystem of the family. But perhaps it is more correct to speak of both marriage and the family as social systems, closely related to each other and with some overlapping personnel, but nevertheless two distinct social systems with different functions to perform on behalf of the members and on behalf of society.

In Table 23 the two systems and their relationship to each other is shown, together with the approximate length of time in years of each stage in the cycle. The marriage cycle actually begins before marriage if we think in terms of couple and not only in terms of the married couple, and the family cycle goes beyond the launching stage if we regard the dispersed family as family. But since the "nest is empty" we have left this stage out in Table 23.

Since we tend to lose sight of the marriage in our em-

TABLE 23 *Stages in the Couple Cycle and the Family Cycle*

The Couple Cycle		The Family Cycle	
Random and serious dating couple	1.0 yr. [a]		
Engaged couple	1.0 yr.		
Newly married couple	2.0 yrs. [b]		
Married couple with		Child-bearing family	2.5 yrs. [b]
children in the home	26.5 yrs.	Child-rearing family	17.5 yrs. [b]
Older married couple	13.5 yrs.	Child-launching family	6.5 yrs. [b]
Total years	44.0 yrs. [c]		26.5 yrs.

[a] Burgess and Wallin report that the average engaged couple had gone together for six months to one year before engagement.
[b] Source of data, U. S. Census, 1950.
[c] Conditions prevailing in 1950 point to 41 years of married life before the death of one spouse or the other, more commonly the husband. Glick, Paul C., *American Families*, New York: John Wiley & Sons, Inc., 1957, p. 68.

phasis on the family, and since society appears to value parental roles more than marital roles of the couple, some attention must be given to the vital marriage system which begins before the family system and lasts for an extended period beyond the launching of the youngest child.

The young couple has, roughly speaking, four years as a couple before the birth of the first child. Part of this time is the random dating stage when they can perhaps not be thought of as a couple since they do not think of themselves as a couple and society does not recognize them as one. But with the serious dating stage, they are thought of as a couple and they regard themselves as a couple. With engagement they are a couple in a more formal sense and with the wedding they are a couple in a legal sense.

As we have pointed out earlier, the wedding is an event that "marries" the couple in the eyes of society, but marriage unity is a status to be achieved. Up to the time of the birth of the first child, acquaintances and relatives and the couple themselves generally regard themselves as a couple. But with the birth of the first child confusion sets in for the married partners, for the relatives, and for other acquaintances and associates.

Does marriage end with the first child, that is, does marriage as a social system function only until the marriage becomes a family and then end? Psychologically it may if the couple members think it does and should, and in the view of society its functions definitely pale before the family functions. Evidence of this attitude can be seen in the examples of the mother who feels guilty when she leaves the children with a competent baby-sitter and accompanies her husband on a short trip, the wagging tongues when something happens to a baby that was left with a baby-sitter while the couple were out on a date, or the couple who stopped "going out" when their first child was born.

But in essence and in function marriage is not family and need not cease to be and to function as a distinct social system even during the child-bearing and child-rearing stages.

The essential basis for marriage is the love of man and woman for each other. This love is what draws them together into a unity and into a twosome which functions to give expression to love through the enjoyment of each other as objects, the feeling of oneness, the enjoyment of companionship, and the serving of each other. The child plays no part in this relationship either with respect to its origin or to its continuing functions.

In America partners marry because they love each other, and potentially their love finds expression through their oneness and their togetherness. The child has nothing to do with this relationship at its beginning and he cannot enter it as an equal and companion because of differences in age, experience, and maturity. If the couple are to remain a marriage this relationship must always remain something to which the child is strictly extraneous. Children are not a part of its structure and not a part of its functions; they are rather conditions to the relationship.

This is not to say that the young couple will not want to become a family as well as a marriage. They may feel that it is a condition which will enrich their relationship to each other; they may want to share their great love for each other with children; they may want to perpetuate their love through the procreative act. Whatever the reason or reasons, the family is created by a different essential event than is the marriage. Psychologically, perhaps the couple becomes a family when they decide they want a baby and in their sexual relations seek to bring about a conception, or at least do nothing that might prevent it, but the birth of the child is usually regarded as the beginning of the family, for birth introduces the third member who makes a family a reality—a system both structurally and functionally.

The birth of the first child is a very significant event. In the first place it is significant because it does in fact usher in family life. It is also significant in what it does to the marriage as well. In the best of marriages the birth of the first child will be a turning point. It will disrupt most if not all routines that the young couple have established for themselves. The couple expect this and accept it. But in some households the marriage never recovers from the traumatic experience of the birth of the first child. The wife may unconsciously or consciously become a devoted mother and give her husband and her marriage second place, and even some husbands dutifully accept this as one of the inevitable burdens of parenthood.

However, today the important difference between marriage and family is becoming clearer, and many young couples consciously keep both the marriage and the family alive and interesting. One of the major techniques used is to limit the number of children so that there is time and energy available for both the roles of marriage and the roles of family.

In this connection, Paul Popenoe has written a brief but astute article called "Give the First Baby Second Place." In it he suggests that the father of the baby should be given second place for a short time when the baby is born, but that it is the mother's responsibility to see that he takes second place for as short a time as possible, the marriage being put back into first place quickly. "It is, in fact, a logical necessity. *In any marriage*, it is a misfortune, for the children as well as the parents, if the parents do not love each other more than they love the children. (Of course, it is a different kind of love.) The child will have to lead his own life, and he will be severely handicapped if he is given first place in the family. But the mother and father cannot lead their own lives—they must live with reference to each other and to their marriage. They must, therefore, put the marriage first." [1] One perhaps need not take sides as to which should take first or second place. The point we are trying to make is that both systems must retain their importance, and in time, as Popenoe points out, the marriage is the longer-lived of the two and must not be sacrificed for the shorter-lived social system.

What happens in and to the marriage after the launching of the children will reflect the place given to the marriage during the family stage. The marriage partners who have let their marriage "go" for the sake of the children will indeed find themselves with an "empty nest" with nothing to fill the void so far as their marriage is concerned. So many couples "fail to live a good third act." The married couple who keeps alive their interest in each other and in the things they can enjoy together but cannot enjoy with their children may find themselves not only without an "empty nest" feeling but may even be impatient at times to have the family phase come to an end so that they can enjoy the freedom of being just a couple again.

The nest need be anything but empty. The husband is apt to be near the peak of his earning power, and the wife may have had part-time or even full-time employment as

[1] Paul Popenoe, "Giving the First Baby Second Place," *Ladies' Home Journal* (Reprint).

the children were being launched. This period of good earning power, the shortest working hours, and the longest vacations that the breadwinner has ever enjoyed provides exciting prospects for travel, hobbies, and a variety of expenditures that the couple could never afford while there were dependent children in the home.

With reliable methods of family control, it is within the realm of possibility for a married couple to decide—in a way consistent with their values—whether they wish to add to their experiences the rewards and responsibilities of a family or whether they wish to remain only a marriage.

Choosing to have children and to become a family is the pattern almost universally followed by couples in our society. It is a natural pattern and a pattern wholeheartedly approved of in American society. Of the three marriage models only one, however—the Judaic-Christian—is a family model as well as a marriage model. All versions of the Judaic-Christian model approve of and encourage couples to have children. In fact, the Orthodox Jewish and the Roman Catholic models give first place to family functions and second place to marriage functions insofar as the two can be separated.

Summary

To choose to be a family is not to eschew the satisfactions of being a married couple. By controlling family size, by spacing the birth of babies, and by limiting the length of the child-bearing phases of family life, couples are able to maintain the marriage even during the child-bearing and child-rearing stages.

If marriage functions are carried on during the family stage of the relationship, the postfamily stage is less likely to be of the "empty nest" variety. The couple that has not let family functions replace marriage functions can look forward with eager anticipation to the older married couple stage—the stage following the launching of the last child from the parental home.

Many couples preparing to marry accept the idea of a family stage in the relationship without much thought or planning. Recent research has revealed that today's couples are apt to be more unrealistically romantic about what to expect from parenthood and family life than they are about what to expect from marriage. With this in mind the final section of the book is devoted to discussion of family planning, life within the home, and relations between the family and the larger community.

QUESTIONS AND PROJECTS

1. Describe the structure of marriage as a social system. What are its functions?
2. Why is it incorrect to speak of marriage as a subsystem of the family? Is it correct to speak of the family as a subsystem of marriage? Explain.
3. In your opinion why are parental roles more highly prized in our society than are marriage roles?
4. How can relations between husband and wife during the child-bearing period affect their relations with each other after the children have left the parental home?
5. What roles or careers might married partners pursue after the children are launched from the parental home?

SUGGESTED READINGS

Bailey, Derrick S., *The Mystery of Love and Marriage*, New York: Harper & Brothers, 1952, Part 2.
Bossard, James H. S., and Eleanor Stoker Boll, "Marital Unhappiness in the Life Cycle," *Marriage and Family Living*, Vol. XVII, February 1955, pp. 10–14.
Cavan, Ruth Shonle, *The American Family*, New York: Thomas Y. Crowell Company, 1956, Chapter 20.
Duvall, Evelyn M., *Family Development*, Chicago: J. B. Lippincott Co., 1957, Part III.

Kirkpatrick, Clifford, *The Family: As Process and Institution*, New York: The Ronald Press Company, 1955.

Koos, Earl L., *Marriage*, New York: Henry Holt & Co., Inc., 1957, Chapter 20.

Skidmore, Rex A., and Anton S. Cannon, *Building Your Marriage*, New York: Harper & Brothers, 1951, Chapter 21.

Winch, Robert F., and Robert McGinnis, *Selected Studies in Marriage and the Family*, New York: Henry Holt & Co., Inc., 1953, Chapter 18.

The Family

22 *Marriage and Family Planning*

There are a number of plaguing questions concerning sex activity: (1) Is sex expression right? What kind of sex expression is right? Between whom is sex expression acceptable? (2) What are the right or best functions of sex—procreative, unitive, recreative? In what order? (3) What is the right or optimum size of family? (4) If it is acceptable to limit the size of family, what are the right methods? What are the best methods?

Because the human sex drive is not seasonal as it is with most other creatures, and since the human female is normally fertile for a part of each menstrual cycle, couples having an average rate of sexual intercourse could reasonably expect to produce at least 15 to 20 offspring during their married life. But very few couples desire so large a family.

Herein lies one of the major adjustment problems of married couples—the right and best method of managing sex in marriage.

Recent empirical data on family size indicate that couples are exercising control over natural sex expression and its natural consequences, for the average number of children ever born in completed families is only 2.35 with the last child born when the mother is only 26 years of age.[1] This means that couples are doing one or several of the following things. They are refraining from having sexual intercourse either periodically or permanently; they are having intercourse but are interrupting the process of conception; they are having intercourse and permitting conception to take place but are destroying the fetus before birth (abortion) or the offspring after birth (infanticide).

Answers to the questions posed should be of practical value to the young couple attempting to order their sexual life in marriage.

1. Is sex expression right? Perhaps there is no question regarding sex on which there is as much agreement in our culture as on this one. The romantic regards sex expression as right since sex is natural and pleasurable and man is the measure of all things. But also the religionists, who have been most obstructive in regard to sex expression, now generally agree that sex expression is natural and proper and pleasing to both God and man as one of the good and perfect gifts of God.

There would be some disagreement as to who might enjoy sex expression, however. Some romantics would grant the privilege to all who are in love regardless of status—married or single. But only sex expression in the form of sexual intercourse between those who have exchanged their vows of devotion and fidelity is generally approved religiously and legally in our society.

2. What are the right or best methods of sex expression

[1] *Family Living*, May 1957, p. 1.

within marriage? Romantics would generally hold that any type of sex expression which gives satisfaction to husband and wife is right and proper, for they alone are involved and are the judges of their own activity. At the other extreme the Roman Catholic Church has been most insistent that proper sex expression embraces only natural, uninterrupted, penal-vaginal intercourse. Protestant groups have not been as proscriptive and have left more to the discretion of the marriage partners. A recent statement by Cole, "an activity does not become a perversion until it is used compulsively as a substitute for the standard coital pattern," would perhaps come close to stating a Protestant view, insofar as one exists.

3. *What are the right or best functions of sex expression within marriage?* Once again the answer of the romantic would be that the right or best function is the function which the couple feels will bring them the greatest happiness at the particular time. Insofar as the Judaic-Christian—more specifically the Roman Catholic—view is concerned, sex expression in marriage should never be engaged in without at least the possibility of conception taking place. Hence, it follows that only penal-vaginal intercourse is acceptable as a method of sex expression or release. The Roman Catholic Church regards the primary end of marriage to be the procreation and education of new life, not the personal improvement of marriage partners concerned. Hence it follows, in answer to the question posed above, that the right and best function of sex expression for the Roman Catholic is the procreative function with the unitive function a secondary one. The third function, recreative, is denied to the couple, for sexual intercourse for the purpose of pleasure may be venially sinful and if too passionate or unnatural it may be regarded as mortally sinful.

The Protestant formulation of the Judaic-Christian position is more permissive and can be found in recent pronouncements of several denominations. We have chosen to quote in full the statement on "Responsible Parenthood" of the Augustana Evangelical Lutheran Church since it contains a Protestant statement on the functions of sex plus Protestant views on several other questions under consideration.

RESPONSIBLE PARENTHOOD

1. Scripture teaches that children are a gracious gift from God (Gen. 33:5), "an heritage of the Lord" (Psalm 127:3), "who may bring much joy but who may also cause much heaviness of heart to their parents" (Proverbs 10:1).

2. A married couple normally expects to have children as the fruit of their marriage. This is in fulfillment of God's blessing first given in the Garden of Eden and renewed to Noah and his sons, "Be fruitful, and multiply" (Gen. 1:28; 9:1).

3. Because children are intended by God as a blessing and a reward (Psalm 127:3), every child may justly expect love, care and nurture from its parents. To be unloved or rejected by its parents is a cruel tragedy which may forever mar the child's personality and may subject the parents to the dangers of the millstone the Savior described (Matt. 18:6).

4. To enable them the more thankfully to receive God's blessing and reward, a married couple should plan and govern their sexual relations that any child born to their union will be desired both for itself and in relation to the time of its birth.

5. The means which a married pair uses to determine the number and the spacing of the births of their children are a matter for them to decide with their own consciences, on the basis of competent medical advice and in a sense of accountability to God.

6. So long as it causes no harm to those involved, either immediately or over an extended period, none of the methods for controlling the number and spacing the births of children has any special moral merit or demerit. It is the spirit in which the means is used, rather than whether it is "natural" or "artificial," which defines its "rightness" or "wrongness." "Whatever ye do, do all to

the glory of God" (1 Cor. 10:31) is a principle pertinent to the use of the God-given reproductive power.

7. Scripture recognizes that a couple may wish for a limited period to practice marital continence as a religious expression, but cautions against its prolonged practice (1 Cor. 7:5). Continence in the marriage relationship, however, when its sole purpose is the selfish avoidance of pregnancy, is equally as wrong as is the use of contraception toward this same selfish goal.

8. An unrestrained production of children without realistic regard to God-given responsibilities involved in bringing children up "in the discipline and instruction of the Lord" (Eph. 6:4) may be as sinful and as selfish an indulgence of the lusts of the flesh as is the complete avoidance of parenthood. God does not expect a couple to produce offspring at the maximum biological capacity. The power to reproduce is His blessing, not a penalty upon the sexual relationship in marriage.

9. In planning their family a married couple would wisely heed the Psalmist who pointed out the special blessings that may accrue to larger families and the rich joys from children born in one's youth (Psalm 127:4–5). They are then more likely also to experience the truth that "Grandchildren are the crown of the aged" (Prov. 17:6).

10. Having children is a venture in faith, requiring a measure of courage and confidence in God's goodness. A married couple should accept parenthood without a rigorous calculation of all the costs involved. Income and standards of living, pressures for advancement in one's work, concern over the maternity process and over the health of the mother or of the child, and the uncertainties of the times or of social conditions should not be given undue consideration in determining a couple's acceptance of parenthood responsibilities.

11. Should an unexpected pregnancy occur the Christian couple will accept the responsibility involved, prayerfully seek the blessing God offers, and be ready to accord the new child the love due him. Except as a medical measure to save the mother's life, abortion will not be resorted to by Christians, obedient to the commandment, "Thou shalt not kill."

12. A married couple desirous of children but seemingly unable to have any of their own should seek competent medical counsel. In their desire for help they will not neglect the resource of prayer to which Rachel and Hannah, among the company of noted women, turned in their barrenness. Perhaps it will come true for them as it is recorded for Rachel: "And God hearkened to her, and opened her womb. And she conceived and bore a son . . ." (Gen. 30:22–23).

13. In those cases where both husband and wife are shown to be fertile but are unable to initiate pregnancy, the artificial insemination of the wife with the husband's semen, performed under the administration of a competent medical practitioner, may be justified.

14. Because of its moral implications as well as its clouded legal, social, biological and psychological aspects, the conscientious Christian will avoid participation in the process of artificial insemination wherein the semen of a man other than the wife's husband is used. In this process the unity of "they twain" is jeopardized by an unknown person intangibly but realistically present in the child he has sired.

15. Sex relations outside of marriage, whether before an intended marriage or outside an established marriage bond, are a violation of God's will. The use of contraceptives by the unmarried can indeed reduce the risk of an illegitimate child, but this changes the character of premarital relationships just as little as the fact that one party to adultery may be sterile changes the nature of adultery.

16. The Christian couple anxious for but unable to have children of their own have other courses open to them. Perhaps they can adopt children through legitimate channels which safeguard the interests both of prospective parents and of children. Perhaps they can find constructive outlets for their interests in direct child-serving occupations or in community services for the welfare of children, thus reflecting the Master's concern for children (Mark 10:13–16).

17. Much as they may regret their inability to have children the Christian couple will come to accept this fact as God's way of directing them to some other sphere

of useful service in His kingdom. Their personal fruitfulness and the fruit of their faith can show itself in works of love and kindness to the least of His brethren. In so accepting their role and selflessly yielding themselves to God in Christian service to man, they may even find Him adding His blessing in the form of the long-desired child of their own

18. Any planning for the number and spacing of the births of their children must be practiced prayerfully in accord with the fruits of the Spirit rather than in indulgence of the lusts of the flesh, and in the full freedom of the redeemed believer who feels his stewardship responsibility to his Lord. When so practiced it can bring the conscientious Christian husband and wife a deep appreciation for God's gracious blessings, a greater joy in the responsibility which parenthood brings, and a richer satisfaction over their partnership with God in His creation of each new life entrusted to them.[2]

4. Granting procreation as one of the functions of sex in marriage, what is the right or optimum number of children for a family? We will touch on this question only briefly here since it will be more fully considered in the following chapter. Once again the answer of the romantic would be that the couple should have the number of children they desire. Some persons might not desire to have children and desire to remain a marriage rather than to become a marriage plus a family. Others would find delight in a few children and still others in a large number of children.

Followers of the Judaic-Christian model have been inclined in the past to give the easy and sweeping generalization "as many as God gives us." But in considering the matter in a realistic way for our society, both Roman Catholic and Protestant spokesmen have been inclined to agree that, with our improved medical care and the fact that we have already done a pretty good job of multiplying and filling up the earth, some control of the procreative function by the

[2] *Augustana Evangelical Lutheran Church Report of the Ninety-Fifth Synod,* June 14–20, 1954, Rock Island, Illinois: Augustana Book Concern, 1954, pp. 229–231.

couple is in order. The Protestant statement quoted above states that "an unrestrained production of children without realistic regard to God-given responsibilities . . . may be as sinful and as selfish as indulgence of the lusts of the flesh as is the complete avoidance of parenthood." Recent Roman Catholic statements also speak in terms of an ideal size of family, with four or five children as a suggested size rather than the number the couple could bear.

5. If it is permissible and good to limit family size, what is the right and best method to accomplish this? The romantic and rationalistic protagonists would regard this as a matter of personal preference and medical knowledge. That is, the marriage partners would use whatever method they found to be most advantageous, that gave the best protection against conception, and that was demonstrated to be medically safe.

Protestants who have made statements take a similar view, except that the individual is regarded as being not only responsible to himself but also to God. Point 6 under the statement quoted spells out the Protestant position quite clearly. The emphasis is not on the moral quality of the method but on the medical quality and the spirit in which the method is used.

The most proscriptive view on the use of conception control grows out of Roman Catholic dogma. The Roman Catholic position is that insofar as the use of contraception is authorized, only one method is regarded as right, namely, continence, or the refraining from sexual intercourse either for extended periods of time—even up to the length of the marriage under certain conditions—or for shorter periods of time. Continence for shorter periods is known as "rhythm" and refers to the period before, during, and after the time of ovulation in the female menstrual cycle. All other methods are regarded by the church as artificial and sinful; continence is defined as a natural method of conception control.

Some methods of control of family size are regarded as

reprehensible and wrong by all religious groups as well as by the state, namely, infanticide and abortion. In societies where human life is less sacred than it is in our society, infanticide has been a widely practiced method for controlling the size and the type of family desired, by killing the excess girl babies, the twins, the deformed, etc. But in our society it has been roundly condemned by all groups as inconsistent with the American ideal and is seldom resorted to.

Abortion—the destruction of the fetus before it is viable —is also immoral and illegal according to religious and legal standards in America, with some exception for therapeutic abortions. Though it shares many of the same prohibitions as infanticide, it is apparently quite widely used by the married and the unmarried to prevent the birth of an unwanted child.

Methods of Control

A listing of methods of control would include the following:

Methods which restrict or prevent normal penal-vaginal intercourse:
1. abstinence.
2. continence for a long period.
3. continence for a short period—rhythm.

Methods which allow intercourse but are intended to prevent the sperm cells from entering the vagina:
1. coitus interruptus.
2. coitus reservatus.
3. condom.
4. vasectomy.

Methods which permit sperm cells to enter the vagina but are intended to keep them from entering the cervix:

1. sponges and tampons.
2. stem pessaries.
3. diaphragms.
4. cervical caps.
5. spermicidal foam powder, jellies, creams.
6. suppositories.
7. douche.

Methods that permit sperm cells to enter the cervix:
1. intrauterine coils and rings.
2. abortion.
3. salpingectomy.
4. cauterization of uterine cornua.
5. irradiation of ovaries.

It is difficult to say which are the best methods of control. One might say that the best method is that which most effectively prevents conception. But this would make abstinence the best possible method. Hence, there are factors other than efficiency to be considered, though pregnancy has occurred with the use of every known control method except abstinence. This is not to say that all other methods are equally unreliable. In a study of "relatively fecund" Protestant couples in Indianapolis who always used contraceptives, contraception in general was 92 per cent effective from the point of view of reduction in uncontrolled fertility.[3]

To be regarded as an ideal method of control, a method would have to be:

1. *Morally acceptable.* For most persons in our society this would rule out infanticide, for many it would rule out abortion, and for some it would rule out all but the natural methods, abstinence and continence.

2. *Harmless.* The method should not be injurious to the

[3] Charles F. Westoff, Lee F. Herrera, and P. K. Whelpton, "XX. The Use, Effectiveness, and Acceptability of Methods of Fertility Control," in P. K. Whelpton and Clyde V. Kiser (eds.), *Social and Psychological Factors Affecting Fertility*, New York: Milbank Memorial Fund, 1954, p. 938.

THE FAMILY

health of the users. Since some methods are known to be dangerous or suspect of being potentially dangerous, the only safe way for the couple to choose a contraceptive method or methods is to choose those that are medically approved; bichloride of mercury as a douche, intrauterine stems, intrauterine rings and silk coils, and others have been seriously questioned as to harmfulness, for instance.

3. *Reliable.* It was found in the Indianapolis study of Protestant couples that, in general, the feeling that a method was reliable was without question the most important consideration in the choice of a contraceptive and that other reasons were relatively unimportant.

No clinic would guarantee any method or claim that it was completely effective even if properly used; nor is there a method that is universally applicable or simple enough for all to use effectively. Nevertheless, some methods have been demonstrated to be definitely more reliable than others. In the Indianapolis study, it was found that the three most effective methods were diaphragm and jelly, condom, and withdrawal while the least effective was the safe period, or rhythm. Next least effective were the douches. A woman using a water douche could expect four or five unplanned pregnancies within a 25 year period, while a woman using diaphragm and jelly could expect a maximum of one unplanned pregnancy.[4]

4. *Free from interference with the spontaneity of the sex act.* Many if not most of the methods of control offend on this point. Coitus interruptus, wherein the male withdraws before ejaculation, and coitus reservatus wherein ejaculation is controlled, fall in this category. Also, except for the couple who plan their love acts in such a rational and systematic way that they can always or usually predict when either or both will be receptive, the methods which must be or are usually resorted to just before intromission, or before ejaculation, or just after ejaculation—condom, sponges and tampons, dia-

[4] *Ibid.*, p. 938.

phragms, spermicidal powders, jellies, creams, suppositories, douches—would fall in this category.

Some of the contraceptive methods do not interfere with the spontaneity of the sex act in that they are more or less permanent—sterilization (vasectomy and salpingectomy), irradiation, cauterization, and some of the newer experimental methods, such as the use of hormones, hypodermic injection of sperm to produce spermatotoxins, pills to be taken orally, etc. Of these sterilization has come to be widely used. Its major limitation, other than the fact that many people object to its use, is that it renders the person permanently sterile. Attempts to reverse the operation have been successful in a relatively small percentage of cases.

5. Psychologically, sociologically, aesthetically acceptable to the couple. A goodly number of the commonly accepted methods of conception control are not aesthetically acceptable because they interfere with the spontaneity of the sex act. There are other reasons also why a particular method is not satisfactory for a particular couple. These would include unconscious drive toward pregnancy which causes carelessness in use, unacceptable because wife hesitant about touching herself, husband not willing or able to take responsibility, etc.

There are many reasons then, besides the efficiency of the method, why the rate of success with methods of control is not greater than it is.

Back, Hill, and Stycos in a study involving 888 lower-class families found that those most likely to use control methods efficiently were couples with a family-centered approach— that is, couples who placed an emphasis on planning were able to communicate with each other on the matter and had the ability to come to a joint decision on planning and the use of contraceptives.[5]

[5] Kurt W. Back, Reuben Hill, and J. Mayone Stycos, "The Dynamics of Family Planning," *Marriage and Family Living*, Vol. XVIII, August 1956, p. 195.

Effects of the Use of Control Methods

The most obvious and most intentional effect of the use of methods of control is to limit family size, to space children, and to allow for a period of marriage before the birth of the first child, should the couple desire it. Secondly, the use of a reliable method may facilitate sex adjustment by removing or reducing the possibility of a pregnancy that might otherwise lessen sexual satisfaction for couples who do not desire a baby at the particular time or already have all the children they desire.

On the other hand, one of the effects of so-called artificial methods is that some of them might lessen the satisfaction in sex because of the inconvenience involved or because the contraceptive may actually, in a mechanical way, cut down the degree of sensitivity and satisfaction.

It has been said that artificial methods are injurious to health and cause sterility. It is true that some artificial control methods are potentially injurious and should be avoided. However, there is no proof that the use of medically approved contraceptives is injurious to health or leads to sterility; rather, there is evidence that they do not reduce the fecundity of the user.

Conception Control for the Sterile

For a smaller percentage of couples, the problem is not negative control of conception, that is, how to restrict the number of pregnancies, but a matter of positive control, how to make pregnancy possible or how to increase the number of pregnancies. The percentage of sterile couples in the population probably does not exceed 10 percent of all couples.[6]

There are numerous reasons why the couple might be sterile. Some can be corrected if both husband and wife seek medical help. The fact that the male is potent is sometimes misinterpreted by the couple to mean that it cannot be the husband who is sterile. This is not true. There is no absolute connection between potency and fertility. In fact, the husband should be the first to seek medical examination, for tests of his fertility are simple to make, whereas testing of the wife is somewhat more complicated and time-consuming. Many of the conditions resulting in lessened fertility or sterility respond to treatment.

The answers are not all in. There is need for more scientific research and discovery in conception control, both positive (how to induce conception) and negative (how to prevent conception).

Summary

The rightness or wrongness of controlling sex expression continues to be a moot question in American culture because of the marked differences of view on the subject in the several marriage models and the even greater difference within the Judaic-Christian marriage model itself.

Generally speaking, some limitation on conception is permitted, if not advocated, within each of the marriage models. There is sharp disagreement on the proper methods of control, however, with the Roman Catholic model being most proscriptive. In the romantic, rationalistic, and Protestant forms of the Judaic-Christian models, satisfaction of

[6] David Loth, "Planned Parenthood," *The Annals*, Vol. 272, November 1950, pp. 95–101.

the marriage partners is one sufficient reason for having sexual intercourse. Contraceptive methods may be used to this end. In the Roman Catholic form of the Judaic-Christian model, satisfaction of the marriage partners is never a sufficient reason for sexual intercourse—nothing must be done to interfere "artificially" with the possibility of conception occurring in any instance of the sex act.

For married couples who approve of the use of conception control methods, there are a number of medically approved methods available. The approved methods vary in cost, effectiveness, etc.

Couples are well-advised to consult a qualified medical authority whether they are seeking methods of preventing the occurrence of conception or methods of facilitating conception.

QUESTIONS AND PROJECTS

1. Make a list of the prescriptions on sex expression in marriage as held by proponents of the three marriage models.
2. What is the difference between so-called natural and artificial methods of conception control?
3. What kinds of negative control of family size do adherents of all the major marriage models reject?
4. What is meant by positive conception control methods? Why has less attention been given to these than to the negative control methods?
5. Why is it correct to say that there is no one conception control method acceptable to all couples?

SUGGESTED READINGS

Back, Kurt W., Reuben Hill, and J. Mayone Stycos, "The Dynamics of Family Planning," *Marriage and Family Living,* Vol. XVIII, August 1956, pp. 195–199.

Cavanaugh, John R., *Fundamental Marriage Counselling: A Catholic Viewpoint,* Milwaukee: The Bruce Publishing Co., 1957, Section III.

Greenberg, Joseph H., "Social Variables in Acceptance or Rejection of Artificial Insemination," *American Sociological Review*, Vol. 16, 1951, pp. 86–91.

Kanin, Eugene, "Value Conflicts in Catholic Device-Contraceptive Usage," *Social Forces*, Vol. 35, March 1957, pp. 238–243.

Loth, David, "Planned Parenthood," *The Annals*, Vol. 272, November 1950, pp. 95–101.

Westoff, Charles F., Lee F. Herrera, and P. K. Whelpton, "XX. The Use, Effectiveness, and Acceptability of Methods of Fertility Control," in P. K. Whelpton and Clyde V. Kiser (eds.), *Social and Psychological Factors Affecting Fertility*, New York: Milbank Memorial Fund, 1954, pp. 885–951.

23 *Preparing for Parenthood*

In earlier times it was customary for married couples to accept children as their fate, pleasant or unpleasant, but nevertheless inevitable. If the parents were religiously oriented, they might resolve to accept all the babies "God sent them" as a part of "His will" or "His superior planning."

Today there is little question in the minds of most people as to the advisability as well as the possibility of some planning and control of conception and family size.

The contribution of planned parenthood to the stability of the family is roughly that of the architect to the stability of a house. Many beautiful, enduring buildings have been erected without the benefit of a blueprint. Many happy, healthy families have grown without thought as to the number or spacing of children. Nevertheless, home builders usually prefer both the architect and planned parenthood, for the very good reason that distressing experience can be avoided.[1]

All of the major religious groups have had something to say on the subject, and the general tone of statements on family size by both Jewish and Christian authorities recognizes the need for planning and control. There is some variation in the position of Jewish groups. The Orthodox

groups denounce all forms of contraception, but recognition is given to the fact that there are extenuating circumstances. Except for these, married couples are expected to have at least two children before they are entitled to practice even the natural methods of birth control. The Conservative and Reformed Jews are more permissive. Though they hold that absolute prevention of offspring is reprehensible, they do believe that limitation of offspring is, in some cases, desirable or at least permissible even though "artificial" methods of control are employed.

[1] David Loth, "Planned Parenthood," *The Annals*, Vol. 272, November 1950, p. 95.

There seems to be confusion in interpretations of the Roman Catholic view on family size. Some have interpreted the stand of the church to mean that the church favors unlimited procreation. A statement from A *Guide to Catholic Marriage* may help to clear up this misunderstanding.

> The Catholic Church does not hold that married couples are under the obligation (1) to bring into the world the maximum number of children, (2) to exercise no prudence and common sense, (3) to bear offspring up to the so-called physiological limit, (4) to work unthinkingly for the maximum increase in population, (5) to bring on an ever increasing bumper crop of babies. It does not condone imprudence or intemperance.[2]

John L. Thomas, has also stated the Catholic position on family planning as follows:

> It is assumed that since children are one of the great blessings of marriage and the privilege of cooperating with the Creator in the procreative act is one of the noblest in the marriage state, Catholic spouses will have the number of children they feel they can reasonably support and rear. Ultimately, the decision governing the number of children must rest on the mutual consent of the spouses.[3]

Regarding the actual number of children that might be considered a standard for Roman Catholic couples, Father Gerald Kelly has suggested the following:

> . . . if the duty to procreate is considered in the light of similar obligations toward society, as well as toward one's neighbors, it is in itself limited. It would bind each couple to make an ordinary, or an average, contribution in terms of the population needs. This would mean that every fertile couple that chooses to use their marriage

[2] Clement S. Mihanovich, Gerald J. Schnepp, and John L. Thomas, *A Guide to Catholic Marriage*, Milwaukee: The Bruce Publishing Co., 1955, p. 256.

[3] John L. Thomas, *The American Catholic Family*, pp. 72–73. Copyright 1956 by Prentice-Hall, Inc., Englewood Cliffs, N.J. Reprinted by permission of the publisher.

rights should have a family of perhaps four or five children, if they can, because that seems to be approximately the number required of each couple in order to make proper provision for the population needs.[4]

Depending upon one's interpretation of "population needs," one might arrive at a higher or lower average number of children as the standard. If one interpreted population needs to be the number of children required to replace the present generation, the average number of children per family would be considerably less than the four or five suggested by Father Kelly. Each of these statements by Catholic authors is an extension or an interpretation of Pope Pius XII's discourse to Italian midwives in 1951.

It is true that the Roman Catholic Church sanctions only the somewhat unreliable rhythm method as a conception control method, yet in a speech later in 1951 Pope Pius expressed the hope that science would succeed in providing this "licit" method with a sufficiently secure basis, hence expressing a favorable attitude toward more effective family planning.

The position of the Protestant churches, insofar as pronouncements have been made, is not far different from those of the Conservative and Reform Jews or the Roman Catholics but perhaps it is somewhat more positively stated. For a fairly complete and explicit Protestant statement the reader is referred again to the statement on "Responsible Parenthood" in the last chapter.

It can be said, in summary, that all the major religious groups at least recognize family planning as a legitimate possibility for married couples, and some religious groups go so far as to make family planning a definite responsibility of the married couple.

With the heavy responsibility of deciding on the number and spacing of children placed on the shoulders of the

[4] John R. Cavanaugh, *Fundamental Marriage Counselling: A Catholic Viewpoint*, Milwaukee: The Bruce Publishing Co., 1957, p. 282.

marriage partners themselves, what are some of the things to be considered in planning a family?

Things Decided Before Marriage

For the couple approaching marriage in a mature and realistic way, the matter of children will have entered prominently into discussions before marriage and even before engagement. Before they became engaged, they might well have discussed how each of them felt toward children and how they felt about having children of their own. Since children are an integral part of most families, any particularly unusual attitudes toward parenthood on the part of either should be brought into the open prior to engagement. Such attitudes might well become one of the conditions in deciding whether to marry or not to marry a particular person. We are thinking particularly of the wish of some persons to forego parenthood altogether. Since this is fairly uncommon, the more traditional partner has the right to react to it before engagement vows are exchanged. Burgess and Wallin found, for instance, that of 635 men and women, 2.2 per cent of the men and 1.1 per cent of the women did not desire to have any children in their marriages.[5] Of 653 husbands and wives over 10 per cent of both husbands and wives indicated that they had no great desire to have children.

Several studies show that at least a small percentage of couples use conception control methods not to limit or space but to avoid having children altogether. *Mademoiselle Magazine* in a study of 282 married women ten years after graduation from college found that 35 had had no children and that

[5] Ernest W. Burgess and Paul Wallin, *Engagement and Marriage*, Chicago: J. B. Lippincott Co., 1953, p. 705.

of these, 17 or 6 per cent of the total group reported that not having children was intentional. In view of the traditional Judaic-Christian stand, it is interesting to note that in earlier times there were many theologians who held that married couples had no positive duty to procreate.

In summary, it would seem that whether or not the couple want their marriage relationship to eventuate in family is a decision that is so crucial to the plans of one or both partners that it should be considered prior to marriage. For couples deciding to have a family some general discussion of the desired number and spacing is also appropriate to the premarital period.

Things to Decide After Marriage

How soon to have the first baby. It is customary, especially among the middle and upper classes, to postpone conception for a time after the marriage. The argument for this is that marriage partners want to have some time to enjoy the experience of marriage before taking on the experience of parenthood and family. There would appear to be some wisdom in such a decision, for adjusting to the new roles of husband and wife may be sufficient for a time without further complicating the problem by adding the roles of father and mother soon after marriage.

The satisfactions of marriage and the satisfactions of parenthood are not the same, and many young couples look forward to having a baby only after first having a period in which they can concentrate their full attention on the satisfactions of their own love relationship without the distractions, as well as the satisfactions, of a baby. After six months, a year, or two years of married life together they may eagerly plan and prepare for the advent of a baby.

Physical stamina and health of the couple members. Couple members will want to give some attention to their own physical stamina and health at the time they plan the conception of the baby. They will want to feel that they are at their physical best at the time the baby is conceived.

If quite a period of time has elapsed since the premarital physical examination, if the premarital physical examination was cursory in nature, or if either has doubts about his physical condition, a preconception physical examination is in order. Since the wife not only conceives but also carries and nourishes the fetus for nine months prior to its birth, she may regard a preconception examination as a "must."

Social and economic readiness. A decision to have a baby is usually also a decision to try to get along for an extended period of time only on the income of the major breadwinner. Not many couples enter marriage with sufficient savings to finance an addition to the family, and both spouses may want to work for a time before beginning a family.

The security of the breadwinner's job is a consideration as well as the amount he earns. Marriage partners also have to ask themselves if they are willing to forego some of the satisfactions they could buy if they did not have the baby, including some of the gadgetry of the modern home—TV, hi-fi, new automobile, etc. It may seem crass to weigh the advantages of a baby against the advantages of a new car, but in a money economy the considerations are partly of this nature, and it is good to be rational, as well as sentimental, about the prospects of a new addition to the family.

The initial costs of having a baby can be taken care of by careful planning of health insurance coverage. A policy with maternal benefits will cover the cost of confinement and birth if the policy is in force before the baby is conceived. Hence, the young couple will want to examine carefully their health insurance program prior to conception.

Adequacy of housing and community. A baby can be contained in a very small apartment if the couple and the apartment owner are willing. The inexperienced couple may feel that the apartment need not be larger for two adults and a baby than for two adults because, after all, babies are very, very small. Realistically, however, the modern baby, if he is to live in the style to which his peers are accustomed, brings with him a set of equipment that the average apartment for adults does not need and cannot normally hold.

Reproduced courtesy of Paul Peter Porges.

The bedroom will contain a bulky bassinet and shelves and drawers filled with dozens of diapers and other clothing. The bathroom will contain a bulky bathinette, a special toilet stool for His Highness, and bottles and cans of baby powder, baby oil, baby shampoo, baby soap. The livingroom will have a bulky play pen, and the kitchen cupboards will be stocked with an assortment of baby foods to suit the taste of the most discriminating gourmand.

When the baby begins to crawl and toddle there must be a reasonably safe play space of adequate size. Is an efficiency apartment adequate to receive this auspicious character, and how long can it contain him? These are pertinent questions for the couple planning an addition to the family.

Number and spacing of children. Besides questions involving the right time for the arrival of the first baby, the couple will want to give some attention to the question of how many children they want and how they want them spaced. Discussion of an over-all plan should at this stage end only in a tentative family plan, however. There are several reasons for this. First, the stark reality is that the couple may not successfully carry out the plan even with the best of intentions. They may decide to have two children and, depending on conception control methods used and the efficiency with which they are used, end up with four. Or they may decide on six children and end up with two, or none, for reasons of low fertility, sterility, etc. They may plan to have their two children spaced two years apart and end up having them ten years apart. For the present we must not overemphasize the voluntary nature of parenthood.

Secondly, couples get so little actual experience taking care of and living with babies and children until they have their own that they may like to have a "trial run" before committing themselves on family size. They may find the experience of having the first baby more rewarding than they had expected or less rewarding than they had expected. Junior may turn out to be their dream child or their Waterloo.

There are several reasons a trial run is a sensible approach for a couple planning to have a family. First, young couples in our society are apparently ill-prepared to face the realities of having babies and living with children. This has been very strikingly pointed out in a study of a small sample of married couples. Of 46 couples interviewed, 38, or 83 per cent, reported extensive or severe crisis in adjusting to the first child.[6] The reason for the crisis seemed not to rest in the fact that the marriages were not adequate to cope with a new member, that one or both parents had serious neurotic problems, or that the baby was not wanted. In fact, 35 of the 38

[6] E. E. LeMasters, "Parenthood As Crisis," *Marriage and Family Living*, Vol. XIX, November 1957, 352–355.

pregnancies in the crisis group were either planned or desired. The reason that seems to explain the crisis was rather that the parents were almost completely unprepared by training or experience to receive a baby into their home. As one mother said: "We knew where babies come from, but we didn't know *what they were like.*"

The mothers reported the following feelings or experiences in adjusting to the first child: loss of sleep (especially during the early months); chronic "tiredness" or exhaustion; extensive confinement to the home and the resulting curtailment of their social contacts; giving up the satisfactions and the income of outside employment; additional washing and ironing; guilt at not being a "better" mother; the long hours and seven day (and night) week necessary in caring for an infant; decline in their housekeeping standards; worry over their appearance (increased weight after pregnancy, et cetera).

The fathers echoed most of the above adjustments but also added a few of their own: decline in sexual response of wife; economic pressure resulting from wife's retirement plus additional expenditures necessary for child; interference with social life; worry about a second pregnancy in the near future; and a general disenchantment with the parental role.

The mothers with professional training and extensive professional work experience (eight cases) suffered "extensive" or "severe" crisis in every case.

In analyzing these cases, it was apparent that these women were really involved in two major adjustments simultaneously: (1) they were giving up an occupation which had deep significance for them; and (2) they were assuming the role of mother for the first time. . . .

In all fairness to this group of parents, it should be reported that all but a few of them eventually made what seems to be a successful adjustment to parenthood. This does not alter the fact, however, that most of them found the transition difficult.[7]

There is at least one other reason for keeping the size of family and the spacing of children a tentative plan until

[7] *Ibid.*, pp. 353–355.

some experience has been gained living with a child. Perhaps it can be explained in this way: marital adjustment and family adjustment are not the same thing. Good pair adjustment does not guarantee good family adjustment. It is only natural for two people very much in love with each other to emphasize or overemphasize the romantic aspects of having a baby born of their love relationship and hence be ill-prepared to receive the less romantic aspects of having a baby in the house. The adequate marriage can weather the crisis, as LeMasters has pointed out, and it may be stronger for having had the experience. But the weaknesses of the unsuccessful marriage only become more apparent with the crisis.

There was a time when one of the therapies recommended, at least by the lay counselor, for an unstable marriage or an unhappy marriage was a baby—"There is nothing wrong with your marriage that a baby would not cure." This is now considered to be a dangerous solution if indiscriminately applied. It may be the solution, but empirical evidence demonstrates that a baby might be the straw that breaks the camel's back rather than the solution.

We now recognize such counsel as a type of reductionism, that is, if your marriage isn't working, try becoming a family. The trouble is that a marriage does not become a family; the marriage still persists even if the couple does decide to become a family. And rather than resulting in a happy marriage it may only result in an unhappy marriage plus an unhappy family. There is no doubt that, since the principal power structure in the family will be the same as it is in the marriage, the marriage has a good prospect of spoiling the family rather than the family redeeming the marriage. Other possibilities are that happy family life might bring about a happy married life, or it might be possible to experience a happy family and at the same time have only an average or unhappy marriage.

The small vs. the large family. There is no right number

of children to have, as we have pointed out with statements by specialists whose job it is to help people clarify what is right. Also, there is no best or optimum number of children.

The notion that a large family is somehow right and best has persisted in our folk culture even during a time when the number of children per family has been persistently downward. One manifestation of this folk culture is the persistence of the practice of applauding in public gatherings when a couple is presented to the group, for some reason or other, and the master of ceremonies announces that they are "the proud parents of seven children!" For some reason this seems to call for more applause than if they are the proud parents of one or two children.

One of the arguments has been that a large family is better for the personality growth of the children. There are supposedly advantages to be gained from the greater number of contacts that the child has and the give and take that he experiences. The hypothesis that family size is directly correlated with good personality adjustment of children has recently been tested by Hawkes *et al.* with a sample of 256 children.

It seems clear from the data obtained in this investigation that the large family does not necessarily provide the child with a more favorable environment for personality development as compared with the family in which there are only two or three children. The advantages of the large family in providing the child with a play group, thus aiding in his socialization process, may be offset by feelings of rivalry and jealousy which may develop in the large family. Certain economic problems may be generated in the large family which create threatening situations for the child. This would be particularly important in the child's peer culture where conformity in dress, ability to have things, et cetera, are strongly stressed and where the child from a large family might not be able to successfully "keep up" financially with children from smaller families. In our urban-industrial society, a large family presents economic limitations if not difficulties for many parents. Of course, these points run counter to the ideal description of the large, usually rural, American family. However, they may be more relevant for the present-day American family living in an industrial and urbanized setting.

The other side of the argument, the possible detrimental effect of the small family, usually hinges about the argument of over-protection or indulgence of the child. It is possible that jealousies among children are more likely where there are just two children seeking recognition and attention from their parents than where there are more children present.[8]

But to say that both the large and the small family have contributions to make to the life of children and to the life of parents is not the same thing as saying that the large and the small family are the same or identical. They are not. It is at this point that the couple may want to decide whether or not a large or small family is the thing for them. For the size of family tends to effect directly the way in which the family will be organized and the way in which it will function. We will illustrate by indicating some of the characteristics implicit in a family with one or two children compared with a family with a larger number of children.

There is no question but that when more persons are added to a group the activity multiplies and the organization of the group becomes more complex. This is true whether one is talking about persons in a family or in any other group setting. But multiplying the numbers in a family has its special complications since each new member comes into the group as an unsocialized being in need of being taught how to get along in a social setting. Each new member represents a separate "barbarian invasion" while the number of relatively "civilized" members—father and mother —remains constant. Hence it means that with each addition to the family the possibility of father and mother planning,

[8] Glenn R. Hawkes, Lee Burchinal, and Bruce Gardner, "Size of Family and Adjustment of Children," *Marriage and Family Living*, Vol. XX, February 1958, p. 68.

supervising, and controlling the activities of the family decreases, unless the additions are widely spaced. What this comes to mean is that in the small family the parents can offer the advantages, as well as the disadvantages, of intensive parenthood to their children, whereas the parents of a larger family must offer more "extensive" parenthood to their children.

In the small family, the parents can give a great deal of personal attention to each child; he can be personally taught, counseled, and allowed free expression, and punishment can be tailored to fit him and his crimes. In the large family, on the other hand, there are many more problems, crises, needs, etc., and there are still only two adults to minister to them. As a result each individual must of necessity be given less attention. The parents must try to do what is good for all and a number of situations and activities must remain unsupervised by them personally because of lack of time and energy. This means, in part, that rules may have to replace personal attention. It may also mean that each child will have to be somewhat more on his own, that the children will have to settle some of their own disputes and handle their own problems without consultation with a parent, and that children will hence be enlisted to help with the control, discipline, and supervision of their siblings. In many instances they will naturally supervise each other in the give and take of the home.

It is a matter for the couple to decide what kind of family they want. If they feel the need to work very closely with each of their children and to give each much personal attention and guidance, they might well decide on a small family. If they, on the other hand, like the spontaneity, the unpredictability, and the general verve of interacting children and are not so concerned with the careful guidance of each, they might well decide upon a larger family. For the couple willing and eager to have children, either family type can provide satisfactions both for children and for parents.

Regarding the spacing of the children, there are several possibilities for the couple to consider. One plan is to have the two or four, or whatever number of children they want, closely spaced so that they will have the advantages of each other's company and association as they grow up and also so that the couple may restrict the familial phase to a shorter and more concentrated period of time. An opposite plan is to space the children well apart so that each can be carefully attended and enjoyed and appreciated according to his own needs and for himself. There are, of course, many other variations on these general plans that the couple may want to consider as best suiting their needs and conditions and the interests of their children.

The amount of interest and energy to invest in family. We pointed out in an earlier context that each of the couple members will have to decide how much of himself he wants to invest in his spouse and his marriage In a similar manner, each spouse and the partners together will have to determine how much of themselves and their marriage they want to invest in family. The wife, more than the husband, will want to evaluate herself on this score, for more of the integrative and expressive roles in the family fall to her while her husband must of necessity concentrate more of his attention on outside tasks, particularly the task of providing for the family. She will have to ask herself to what extent she is a mothering type with strong maternal, loving, caressing, protecting, serving tendencies and interests.

The couple will also want to consider how much of the integrative and expressive tendencies are a part of the husband's make-up and interest. Will the wife have to carry the heavy responsibility of the home alone while her husband pours all of his energy into his extrafamilial roles— work, sports, business, fraternal associations, etc.?

These are questions the couple will want to ask. If most of the answers are in the negative, they would do well to consider a small family or even no children at all.

But perhaps the major interests of both marriage partners are primarily familial. If their shared goals call for a secure job with a reliable company, regular hours of work, and a lot of free time of at-home togetherness, they would be regarded as essentially familial in their interest and activity patterns. If, on the other hand, they share goals calling for more stringent extrafamilial activity—the life of the missionary, the crusader, the creative genius, the statesman or politician—family interests may suffer, because these activities call for most of one's time and energy twenty-four hours a day. Society needs both kinds of people—the crusader and the man who is satisfied with the static job and rich family life—but in planning their family it is good for the couple to decide which they want out of life.

Being familial or extrafamilial in orientation does not determine the family size, however. The family oriented couple may reason, "In the light of this let's have a small family so that we can really get to know each one and give them the best in life," or they may reason, "In the light of this let's move out to the suburbs and get a big house and have a big happy family." The crusader and his wife (or his crusading wife) might reason, "Our responsibility is to society, to posterity; we must be free to devote all our time and energy to it; hence, we must have a small family." Or they may reason, "We are extremely able people, and therefore we have a responsibility to pass our genius and enthusiasm on to the next generation; let's have a good-sized family."

No specific factors are determinative in deciding family size, but it is important for the marriage partners to consider them in advance rather than in retrospect.

None of the major marriage models prescribes an ideal family size; however, much attention is given to the question in the Roman Catholic version of the Judaic-Christian model. Its emphasis is on the larger family size.

The popular, rationalistic view of family size seems to favor a smaller number of children. The major reasons given are that the parents can then continue to have something of a life of their own—companionship and self-realization— and the children have opportunities for more parental attention and more of the things that money can buy—adequate diet, fine clothing, good education, etc.

Summary

Couples should give some thought to children before marriage, particularly to the basic question, "Do they desire a family?" Most persons who marry seem to desire, or at least accept, children. Hence, if a person has a strong aversion to being a parent, his future spouse should know about it in advance of marriage.

Things to decide before planning the first baby are: how soon after marriage do they want a baby; the health of both but particularly the prospective mother's health; their social and economic readiness for parenthood; the adequacy of their living quarters and community for child-rearing.

At some time early in marriage the couple may also want to make some plans concerning family size and spacing of children. The plan should be a tentative one for several reasons: parenthood is not completely voluntary; they may like a "trial run" to see what child-rearing is like; and they cannot foretell the future. Present conditions may change, making it advisable to alter the planned number and spacing.

The small family—as the ideal family—is not as prevalent a model today as it once was, even among the middle and upper classes. There has been at least a slight shift in emphasis toward the desirability of larger families. Generally speaking, small and large families differ in character because of the difference in number of persons involved. The young couple planning a family will want to consider a family size which seems most consistent with their values and their personal desires.

QUESTIONS AND PROJECTS

1. What are some prevalent misconceptions about the Roman Catholic view on family planning?
2. What things concerning future offspring should couples decide before they marry?
3. What specific plans regarding offspring should be made after marriage but prior to conception?
4. Why should the family plan be kept on a tentative basis?
5. What does it mean to say that couples are more romantic about parenthood than they are about marriage?
6. Make parallel columns. In one list the characteristics of the small family system and in the other the characteristics of the large family system. Which appeals to you? Why?

SUGGESTED READINGS

Bossard, James H. S., and Eleanor Stoker Boll, *The Large Family System*, Philadelphia: University of Pennsylvania Press, 1956.

Christensen, Harold T., and Robert E. Philbrick, "Family Size As a Factor in the Marital Adjustment of College Couples," *American Sociological Review*, Vol. 17, June 1952, pp. 306–312.

Hawkes, Glenn R., Lee Burchinal, and Bruce Gardner, "Size of Family and Adjustment of Children," *Marriage and Family Living*, Vol. XX, February 1958, pp. 65–68.

Jaco, E. Gartley, and Ivan Belknap, "Is a New Family Form Emerging in the Urban Fringe?" *American Sociological Review*, Vol. 18, October 1953, pp. 551–557.

LeMasters, E. E., "Parenthood As Crisis," *Marriage and Family Living*, Vol. XIX, November 1957, pp. 352–355.

Loth, David, "Planned Parenthood," *The Annals*, Vol. 272, November 1950, pp. 95–101.

Rose, Arnold M., "Factors Associated with the Life Satisfaction of Middle-Class, Middle-Aged Persons," *Marriage and Family Living*, Vol. XVII, February 1955, pp. 15–19.

24 *The First Baby*

A couple may have sentimental reasons for wanting their baby born within a specific season or month of the year. They may desire to have their child born on or near the birth date of one of the parents or of a favorite relative, or at a season of the year that has some special meaning for the couple. In earlier times it was not uncommon to regard superstitiously various days and seasons as invested with good or bad omen for the child born at that particular time, and, in some instances in primitive societies, babies born on evil days were exposed or put to death.

Today, the couple might have important reasons for wanting the birth of the child to come in a certain season. With the advent of reliable conception-control methods, the fertile couple may, within limits, select the birth date of their baby. They may select the year, the season of the year, and perhaps even the month of the year when the baby is to be born—granted, however, that some luck might be necessary to accomplish the latter. In fact, there are a number of considerations that the couple might weigh in deciding on a best birth date.

"She keeps saying, 'It's the most natural thing in the world.'"
Reproduced courtesy of *Ladies' Home Journal*
C. P. Co. 1958.

Choosing the Baby's Birth Date

The convenience and comfort of the mother presents several considerations that enter into the choice of birth date. The expectant mother might choose to be in the late stages of pregnancy during a season of the year when pregnancy and confinement would be least unpleasant. The warmest months of the year are commonly regarded as least comfortable months for pregnancy and confinement.

On the other hand, her extrafamilial careers may be a deciding factor in choosing a birth date. If she has a business or professional career which she plans to interrupt only temporarily, she will want to choose a date for birth when her career as a mother and her business or professional career will each suffer the least. An obvious example is the married school teacher who chooses to have her baby during the summer months when school is not in session. Not all women are career women in the business or professional sense, but most have some career or careers outside of the home that they might want to consider in choosing a birth date; for instance, a woman may choose to have the baby during a slack season in her voluntary and club activities.

A second person to consider in choosing a birth date is His Highness, the baby. He cannot speak for himself, but he may, nevertheless, have ideas on when he would most like to be born. This may seem to be carrying child-centeredness too far, but there are factors to consider.

There are several seasons in the year when it is more difficult to be a baby, particularly in climates where there is great variation in temperature throughout the year. Though we have been more successful in overcoming summer diseases of babies than winter diseases, summer can still be an unpleasant time to be small. A newborn baby is immobile, cannot express his needs and desires in any specific sense, and cannot protect himself. For these reasons the hot sun may burn his tender skin, excessive heat and sweating create rash, and flies and mosquitoes treat him as fair game for a meal.

At the other extreme, the dead of winter may be even a less desirable time to be tiny. Respiratory diseases can be especially traumatic for the little baby, for he is immobile, he cannot snuffle, he cannot blow his nose, and he cannot clear away congestion through coughing. He can be altogether miserable without being able to do anything about it and he might even be set back in his development.

If the baby were to choose his own birth date he would likely choose to be a tiny baby in the spring or fall.

Last, but not necessarily least, some consideration should be given to the expectant father and his extrafamilial roles. It is not uncommon in the democratic family for the couple to plan the birth and confinement to coincide with the husband's vacation, or vice versa, so that he can be with his wife during this period—the idea being that the couple may want to enjoy this experience without the presence of an outsider as helper in the home. For the couple just getting a start, the reason for coordinating birth and husband's vacation may be primarily an economic one, however.

If the husband's occupation requires the wife's active participation either as a partner or as a companion and hostess in entertaining business and professional associates, certain seasons of the year will require more of her time than others.

If we have given the impression that the baby must fit everyone's convenience in picking a time to be born, this is not our intention. For the couple planning a family, the birth of the baby should be so important that they are willing to make any compromises necessary to insure a successful period of pregnancy and the birth of a healthy, welcome baby. The point is that, through careful planning, it may be possible to have the joys of parenthood without completely disrupting the other careers of husband and wife.

Conception and Pregnancy

Physiologically, the expectant father has nothing to do with the process of pregnancy. His involvement is only a momentary one at the time in orgasm when the sperm cells are deposited in the vagina. Physiologically, this event is no different than any other time when semen is deposited in the vagina during intercourse, and with this event (conception) the husband's part in the long process which eventuates in the birth of the baby is at an end.

392

The event of coitus ending in impregnation may have been different for the couple, psychologically, from other cases of sexual intercourse because of the conscious purpose involved. At this time coitus is engaged in with the awesome desire to produce a new life that will be a part of each of the parents and hence a very special creative event in their love life. The procreative function is brought into play in only a small number of occasions in the sex life of the planned, small family and hence becomes a special time for the couple in love.

The period after conception and prior to birth is the prenatal period. If the preconception examination revealed no complications, medical care received during the pregnancy will be more or less routine and preventive in nature and will include instructions in proper diet, activity, etc., during the pregnancy.

It is commonly regarded as good practice for the wife to make her first postconception visit to the doctor shortly after having first missed menses. She makes this visit to the doctor whether she senses a need for medical care or not. An older custom was for the woman to see a doctor during pregnancy only if there were complications. Otherwise she saw the doctor, or he saw her, for the first and only time when he came to deliver the baby. Frequently, of course, even the delivery was attended by an untrained midwife rather than by a doctor.

To some—husbands especially—it may seem unnecessary for the wife to make periodic visits to the doctor during pregnancy. But one need only point to the drastic reduction in maternal and infant mortality rates to make the point for adequate medical attention during and following pregnancy. Regular visits to the doctor are reassuring to the couple, and especially to the wife, during the first pregnancy. Hence, medical counsel at this time can serve an important psychological as well as medical function.

The couple that has an opportunity to attend classes for

expectant couples is even more fortunate. Such classes are not universally available, but when they are they can serve to lower tensions and channel anxieties into study, reading, and other preparations for receiving the new baby.

The Expectant Father

Marriage is for mature or relatively mature persons. It is perhaps even more true that parenthood is for mature or relatively mature couples.

The importance of maturity becomes apparent with pregnancy and the birth of the first baby. The mature husband can be expected to receive the news that his wife has conceived with pride and joy. He has demonstrated his manliness through his ability to impregnate, and he now has the opportunity to show his willingness and capacity to care for dependents—his wife and the new baby.

It is apt to be the insecure, immature husband who contemplates his wife's pregnancy with misgivings and ambivalence. If he feels a need to be mothered himself rather than a desire to care for dependents, he will see the child as a threat to the attention he has been receiving from his wife. And he has reason to fear, for it is certain that he will have to share, or even take second place in, his wife's ministrations for a while.

Pregnancy is clearly one of those periods in family living when the needs of one spouse, in this case the wife, take priority over the needs of the other. In this period, especially in the late stages of pregnancy, the husband's roles in the family tend to become the supportive ones in adjustment to the expressive roles of the wife. Not that we indulge the pregnant woman as deliberately today as we once did, but it is a good part of manly chivalry for the husband to be attentive to his wife's needs and to treat her with special tenderness during this period. She gets more than her share of the responsibility with the pregnancy, and the only way he can obviate some of this disparity is through additional considerateness, attentiveness, and helpfulness.

The Expectant Mother

For the wife, conception is only the beginning of a chain of physiological functions that ends with the birth of the baby. Sociologically, motherhood becomes the major career. For the father, on the other hand, the occupational career takes on even greater relative importance as each additional dependent is added to the family.

There are differences in response to pregnancy on the part of mature and immature women. If the wife feels secure about the relationship between herself and her husband, it will help much to give her the reassurance she needs as she willingly enters a dependent role. Nevertheless, marked physical changes take place to which she must adjust. In a few months' time she takes on physical characteristics considered least desirable for the modern woman. The fashionable woman is flat-abdomened either by nature, by exercise, by diet, or with a strong assist from ingenious supportive garments. The pregnant woman, on the other hand, loses her shapely figure and takes on characteristics of an older person. She becomes less agile, less mobile, and short of breath. Along with this, many women during pregnancy are bothered by nausea and other discomforts.

These are facts of life that the expectant mother must accept. The mature woman not only accepts the changes but, with a little planning and effort—carefully chosen hairdo, make-up, and clothing—retains her charm and attractive appearance during the period of pregnancy.

The immature woman may become unduly fretful over her condition, let her appearance go, and react in a childish way to her changing anatomical features and the curtailment of certain activities in which she has indulged in the past. In a recent study of 212 wives, a question was asked about "felt emotional upset" in five periods of their married life, including the period before conception, the trimesters of pregnancy, and the period after the birth of their first child. The highest ratings of emotional upset for the total sample occurred during the early part of pregnancy when 56.2 per cent of the wives admitted to some or frequent upset.[1]

Emotional reactions were found to be closely related to intent, however. Those who were experiencing a planned pregnancy reacted more favorably to the knowledge that they had conceived, had less emotional upset, and were happier in the earlier part of pregnancy than were the wives in the group that neither tried to avoid nor tried to effect pregnancy and the group who tried to avoid pregnancy.

From Marriage to Marriage Plus Family

Pregnancy naturally affects the relationship between the pair and the roles that each will play from then on. In fact, both husband and wife, consciously or unconsciously, choose new statuses and new roles when they determine to become parents.

A question that normally comes to the fore is, What will happen to the sex life of the couple during and following pregnancy? Must they discontinue coitus with the onset of pregnancy? These are questions the couple may want to

[1] Shirley and Thomas Poffenberger and Judson T. Landis, "Intent Toward Conception and the Pregnancy Experience," *American Sociological Review*, Vol. 17, October 1952, p. 618.

raise with their doctor, but, generally speaking, if there are no complicating factors normal coitus continues during pregnancy. The doctor may caution the couple to take care at certain periods in the pregnancy, and coitus may cease altogether in the weeks preceding birth. All through the later months of pregnancy consideration of the condition of the wife will be a factor in techniques and activities in intercourse.

In the study of 212 pregnancies, information was secured on the change in sex desire of husbands and wives during the first pregnancy. Half of the wives and three out of four of the husbands saw no change in sex desire during the first trimester, but through the next two trimesters the desire of both decreased noticeably. More than one-fourth of the wives noted a marked decrease in sex desire with the onset of pregnancy, and less than one in five noted an increase in desire.[2]

If the wife has confidence in the conception control method being used, indications are that pregnancy and birth are no deterrent to good sex adjustment after the birth of the baby, and the couple can normally resume sex relations within a few weeks after the birth of the baby.

Pregnancy is not only process; it is also the condition that becomes the natural rite of passage to a new status as the couple with their immanent addition come to regard themselves and to be regarded by others not just as a marriage or a married couple but as a marriage and a family.

Children may not notice a pregnant woman and adolescent boys may regard the pregnant woman as a subject for wisecracks, but married friends and acquaintances treat the expectant couple with understanding and sympathy. Everyone loves a lover, and everyone has warm and empathic feelings toward the couple expecting their first baby. The expectant couple is surrounded with good will and a spirit

[2] Judson T. and Mary G. Landis, *Building a Successful Marriage*, New York: Prentice-Hall, Inc., 1958, pp. 522–523.

of helpfulness. Close friends and relatives have free and well-meaning advice for the couple yet uninitiated to parenthood. Even the expectant father's business associates and friends are somewhat lenient with the expectant father in a good-humored way as he momentarily awaits the arrival of his first-born. He gets truly congratulatory greetings when he passes the cigars, particularly if the first-born is a son!

Hence, in many little ways, the young couple by easy stages gradually move in their own eyes and in the eyes of the community from the simple structure and functions of the marriage to the complex structure and functions of marriage plus family and the intricate interaction through wife, mother, husband, father, and child roles.

> Couple members begin to prepare for the new parental roles, both consciously and unconsciously, even before the birth and employ some psychological techniques for mitigating the feelings of uncertainty and anxiety that may accompany pregnancy.
>
> The curiosity about the baby's sex and appearance leads the couple to endow the fetus with a sex, a personality, and response patterns. Indeed, it is not uncommon to give it a name or nickname, implying thereby its hoped-for sex. Unusual names, unlikely to be used later, such as Atlas, Mr. X, Toby, Fritzy, or Li'l Abner, may reflect, in some instances, the couple's attempts to cover up their fears that the infant will not be normal by attempts at humor, which in turn help to minimize the attachment to the unborn.[3]

Incorporating the New Baby into the New Family

As Duvall and Hill have pointed out, there are at least three stages in getting used to a new baby. First, there is the "flowers and pink ribbons" stage. The new mother is in the

[3] Willard Waller and Reuben Hill, *The Family: A Dynamic Interpretation*, New York: The Dryden Press, 1951, p. 382.

hospital receiving solicitous care; someone other than herself is preparing her meals; she is getting enough sleep; and skilled nurses care for the baby. The room is filled with the color and fragrance of flowers, and each day brings gifts and greetings. And, now that everyone is "doing fine," the young father is relieved of tensions caused by loss of sleep and concern over the delivery and can also bask in the glory accompanying their joint accomplishment.

But the first stage is too good to last. Mother and baby come home from the hospital, relatives and friends turn to other concerns, and the inexperienced couple are left with the problem of incorporating their undisciplined little barbarian into a new routine for him and for them—a family routine. During this anomic stage, home life may be chaotic and marked by some dissolution and depression until a new routine incorporating baby's schedule—and lack of schedule —is worked out. In the third stage life takes on some semblance of order and routine again. A new family has been launched and is on its way.

But we would not want to leave the impression that the family routine is identical with or even similar to marriage routine. In fact, it is hardly correct to speak of family routine, for life is never routine so long as there are growing children in the home. The spontaneity and unpredictability of babies and small children account for one of the major changes that comes into the ordered life of the married couple.

Another major change is that one or both parents— generally the mother—must live every hour, day and night, alert to the dependent child's needs and ready to discontinue any other activity to respond to them. The marriage partners learn to live with each other in mind, but the needs, demands, and desires of the spouse do not compare with the restrictions on personal freedom which the young child places on the activities of the parent. It is not an exaggeration to say that no parental activity—not even sleep

—can be planned without taking the baby and his needs into account.

But obviously the popularity of babies among married couples cannot be explained on these grounds. They want babies. Even with reliable contraception, couples are having them and having them of their own free choice.

"That's our song!"

Reprinted from *Love and Hisses* by Brant House.
Copyright 1956, Ace Books, Inc.

Young couples may be overly romantic over the prospects of having a baby of their own; nevertheless, there are rewards in having a baby. There is the sense of accomplishment and fulfillment, the feeling of being needed by someone, the pride in one's own, the appealing activities of an innocent and growing child.

Summary

Relatively speaking, it is only within recent decades that specific family planning has become a possibility. With this awesome prospect of being able to plan, it behooves the married couple to think seriously regarding the best time for the birth of a baby. There are at least three persons to be considered in the decision. The mother may want to choose a time of the year when late stages of pregnancy and confinement will be most pleasant—or least unpleasant—for her, both from the point of view of her comfort and from the point of view of other responsibilities or careers that she pursues.

Seasons of the year make a difference to the newborn baby, especially in climates where there are marked seasonal variations in the weather. The heat of summer and the cold of winter are least comfortable for the baby. The hazards of these seasons are also to some extent reflected in infant mortality rates.

Father's season of heaviest occupational involvement and his normal vacation period are also factors to consider in choosing the birth date of the baby.

Besides the immediate family members the medical doctor plays an important role in the planning of the new addition. If some time has passed since the premarital physical examinations, preconception examinations may be in order. Later there is prenatal care, delivery, and postnatal care.

Father and mother roles are not added to husband and wife roles with the birth of the baby. They begin to emerge between the time of conception and birth of the baby. The new role for the husband is more in the nature of a new psychological status. For the wife marked physiological changes, as well as a new psychological status, mark the beginning of the parental role.

With the birth of the first baby a new family is launched. Marriage and family are not the same. Just as marriage has its responsibilities and rewards, so family has its own responsibilities and rewards, as remaining chapters on the family bear out.

QUESTIONS AND PROJECTS

1. What factors should the couple consider in choosing the birth date of the first baby? Of subsequent babies?
2. What changes take place in the psychological and social statuses of couple members during the gestation period?
3. What effect does the first baby have upon marriage routine?
4. What characteristics of the newborn infant make of him a routine breaker?
5. In conversation with two or more "new" fathers or mothers ask what the baby has done to married life. How do their answers compare with the account given in this chapter?

SUGGESTED READINGS

Cavan, Ruth Shonle, *The American Family*, New York: Thomas Y. Crowell Company, 1956, Chapter 18.

Duvall, Evelyn M., *Family Development*, Chicago: J. B. Lippincott Co., 1957, Chapters 6, 7, 8.

————, and Reuben Hill, *When You Marry*, New York: D. C. Heath and Company, 1953, Part 3.

Fishbein, Morris, and Ruby Jo Reeves Kennedy (eds.), *Modern Marriage and Family Living*, New York: Oxford University Press, Inc., 1957, Part 4.

Himes, Norman E., and Donald L. Taylor, *Your Marriage*, New York: Rinehart & Company, Inc., 1955, Chapter 20.

Poffenberger, Shirley and Thomas, and Judson T. Landis, "Intent Toward Conception and the Pregnancy Experience," *American Sociological Review*, Vol. 17, October 1952, pp. 616–620.

Waller, Willard, and Reuben Hill, *The Family: A Dynamic Interpretation*, New York: The Dryden Press, 1951, Chapter 18.

25 *Guiding the Growing Child*

The Nature of Human Nature

Parenthood stands out as an awesome responsibility today, for natural experiments and researches in the social sciences have clearly demonstrated that the human traits of human beings are learned rather than inborn or instinctive. And, basically, it is the parents who must teach.

Social scientists are frequently misunderstood when they speak of the human baby as a creature that is not born human, but, rightly understood, this is quite correct. This is not to say that he is born some creature other than a human being, but that human beings are not born with the peculiar instincts or built-in response patterns that characterize other mammals. Like other creatures, the human fetus is "pure organism." After birth other creatures remain almost "pure organism," while birth for the human offspring signifies a significant change in character as he becomes a learning, valuing being with a budding ego that will make of him a supra-organic creature.

Humans are born with an original organic nature that is unique, but human nature as we know it in the actions of men in society is acquired after birth. Man has an original organic nature and an acquired human nature. Man is born

"Stop growing."
Reproduced courtesy of Chas. Cartwright.

man, but he is so adaptable that he can take on a variety of human natures, depending upon the way in which he is brought up—the historical setting in which he finds himself. On the other hand, the dog, for instance, is born dog and essentially behaves like a dog in any historical setting.

Students reading about so-called primitive peoples for the first time—the Eskimo for instance—are likely to regard some of their actions as more "animal" than "human." To eat "rotten" fish and birds or to expose one's baby or one's grandmother to the elements to freeze to death or to be eaten by polar bear hardly seem to the ethnocentric, fastidious, moralistic American to be actions "natural" to human beings. To be sure they are not natural actions but particular types of learned activity in a particular social and historical setting.

Man by original nature is wonderfully and marvelously made, endowed with potentialities beyond even his own comprehension. He never ceases to stand in awe of what he can accomplish—guided missiles, automation, space travel. But he becomes this marvelous creature—human nature—only within an environment of proper care and adequate motivation. The responsibility for getting him off to a good start is the awesome task of his parents.

That the job of getting the child started toward acceptable human responses is an important one and one that must become a major career of someone—usually the mother—is apparent in the following striking study of children in two separate institutions for children.

The institutions differed in one single factor. This factor was the amount of emotional interchange offered. In institution No. 1, which we have called "Nursery," the children were raised by their own mothers. In institution No. 2, which we have called "Foundlinghome," the children were raised from the third month by overworked nursing personnel: one nurse had to care for from eight to twelve children. Thus, the available emotional interchange between child and mother formed the one independent variable in the comparison of the two groups. . . .

While the children in "Nursery" developed into normal healthy toddlers, a two-year observation of "Foundlinghome" showed that the emotionally starved children never learned to speak, to walk, to feed themselves. With one or two exceptions in a total of 91 children, those who survived were human wrecks who behaved either in the manner of agitated or of apathetic idiots.

The most impressive evidence probably is a comparison of the mortality rate of the two institutions. "Nursery" in this respect has an outstanding record, far better than the average of the country. In a five years' observation period during which we observed a total of 239 children, each for one year or more, "Nursery" did not lose a single child through death. In "Foundlinghome" on the other hand, 37 per cent of the children died during a two years' observation period.

The high mortality is but the most extreme consequence of the general decline, both physical and psychological, which is shown by children completely starved of emotional interchange. . . .

The results of this study caused us to focus our attention on the mother-child relation in all our further research on infants. We strove to examine whether in less spectacular conditions also it was truly such an all-important influence. Closer investigation bore out this impression. We could establish, in the course of our further research, with the help of statistical methods, that the regularity in the emergence of emotional response, and subsequently of developmental progress both physical and mental, is predicated on adequate mother-child relations. Inappropriate mother-child relations result regularly either in the absence of developmental progress, emotional or otherwise, or in paradoxical responses.

This is not a surprising finding for those who have observed infants with their mothers; during the first year of life it is the mother, or her substitute, who transmits literally every experience to the infant. Consequently, barring starvation, disease or actual physical injury, no other factor is capable of so influencing the child's development in every field as its relation to its mother. Therefore this relationship becomes the central ecological factor in infant development in the course of the first year. On the other hand, development, particularly in the emotional sector, provides an extremely sensitive and reliable indicator of variations in the mother-child relationship.[1]

[1] René A. Spitz, "The Role of Ecological Factors in Emotional Development in Infancy," *Child Development*, Vol. 20, September 1949, pp. 147–151.

Evidence such as the above demonstrates that parent-hood during the early stages of the life of the child is a 24-hour-per-day career. It cannot be ignored if the child is to develop up to his potential. Care can perhaps be delegated if the parents find someone who is willing to put forth the effort and devotion needed to give dedicated service. If it cannot be delegated, it falls largely to the mother and she might advisedly consider setting aside thought of any other career of consequence until the youngest child is in school. The hours of time spent talking to the child, smiling at him, "kitchy-kitchy-cooing" him is not idle pastime. These may be vital in getting the child started—setting his motivation to be human in gear. Experiences stimulate his mind and the hours spent holding, fondling, stroking, soothing, and singing to the child may be the things he needs to develop his emotional nature on a sound basis in the preverbal years.

How to Raise Children

Every conscientious couple is concerned to do the right things for their child—to raise him in such a way that he will be a credit to his parents, himself, and the larger community. How can this be done? What is the right and best way to rear a child?

On the basis of all we know today about human nature and nurture one might expect that we would be articulate on the right and proper ways to raise children. But nothing is much farther from the truth. We have very limited empirical proof that any of the common-sense methods of child care or the "brilliant clinical insights and hunches" are confirmed as right or best ways to raise children.

The situation has been complicated by the fact that expert advice has been subject to dramatic changes within past decades. In 1928, John B. Watson was telling parents who were literate and imbued with the idea that one asks the specialist—not one's mother or grandmother—how to rear a child:

> There is a sensible way of treating children . . . let your behavior always be objective and kindly firm. Never hug and kiss them, never let them sit on your lap. If you must, kiss them once on the forehead when they say goodnight. Shake hands with them in the morning.[2]

But the child of the above parents, reared according to Watson, might when her own child came along secure a copy of Bowlby, *Maternal Care and Mental Health,* and read:

> For the moment it is sufficient to say that what is believed to be essential for mental health is that the infant and young child should experience a warm, intimate, and continuous relationship with his mother in which both find satisfaction and enjoyment.[3]

Insofar as these authors are representative of expert opinion, it would appear that we have reversed our point of view in the brief space of twenty-five years. Interestingly enough neither view is inconsistent with the American ideal.

At the time that this is being written permissiveness as the best way of raising children is shading off into the developmental orientation. In 1955, Paul H. Landis wrote in a permissive vein:

> The democratic family can best be differentiated from the authoritarian family of the past by recognizing its focal point. In almost every aspect of its pattern of living the modern home is child-centered rather than adult-centered. It assumes that the needs of the child are paramount to those of the father and mother. Parents do not consider that their children "owe" them anything—

---

[2] As quoted in Glenn R. Hawkes, "The Child in the Family," *Marriage and Family Living,* Vol. XIX, February 1957, p. 46.
[3] As quoted in *Ibid.*

either love, respect, gratitude, or repayment for their own work and worry in the child's behalf. They hope, however, that by their own attitude of unselfish devotion they can arouse and develop similar attitudes in their off-spring.[4]

This permissive view has come to be regarded by the developmental school as too child-centered. It may be that the parents were too dominant in the traditional—"Honor thy father and thy mother"—days, but, they argue, permissiveness goes too far in the direction of child-centeredness. The developmental family is person-centered. "The developmental orientation is dynamic, for people are ever changing and growing. Parents who put developing persons first in their concerns tend to be flexibly capable of change, ready to adapt and readjust as both their children and they themselves develop through the months and years. This point of view is of the twentieth century." [5]

The developmental orientation is not the only view of the twentieth century, however. It in turn has been challenged by the recent emphasis on adjustment—belongingness and to-getherness—as the goal of life. But adjustment is also under attack, and suggestions that personality may develop better "under fire" with some trauma and discontinuities have recently been made. In this connection, the old discipline controversy which seemed so deeply buried some years ago is rearing its ugly head again—only its head does not appear to be so ugly anymore. In summary, so far as the researchers are concerned, the issue of what is best for the child is anything but closed.

Where does this leave the parent? He does not have a large number of children on whom he can or wants to experiment with various philosophies of child care. He has a few precious offspring to raise—and that right now. He can-

---

[4] From *Making the Most of Marriage* by Paul H. Landis. Copyright © 1955, Appleton-Century-Crofts, Inc., p. 440.
[5] Evelyn M. Duvall, *Family Development*, Chicago: J. B. Lippincott Company, 1957, p. 62.

not wait until the day when the optimum techniques for child-rearing have been developed, if the day ever comes.

Perhaps the picture is not as hopeless a one as the previous discussion would lead one to believe. Here are some things to consider:

1. Children are perhaps not as fragile, psychologically speaking, as we once in our application of psychoanalytic theory regarded them to be. The biographies of great men, and the not-so-great, indicate that there is room for some error in child care without ruining the child's chances for adjustment to life. There is a considerable body of opinion favoring the view that more important than the techniques used in rearing the child are the attitudes toward people and toward life that prevail in the marriage and in the family.

2. If the marriage partners are able to transfer to the offspring attitudes of acceptance, respect, and desire for growth that they hold toward themselves and toward each other, they will perhaps have established a milieu for child development in the home that will be difficult to destroy, regardless of inadequacy in their child-rearing philosophy or techniques. This means making the family a community of love as the marriage is a community of love. The process is not an automatic one. Marriage partners who treat each other with acceptance, respect, and permissiveness do not automatically have the same relationship to their children. For the husband-wife relationship and the parent-child relationship are not equivalent. During the impressionable years of the child's early life—impressionable for the parents, that is—the relationship of the parent and the child is a relationship of a superordinate and a subordinate person. The change to a status of equals may require effort, particularly on the part of the parents, for the superordinate-subordinate relationship becomes firmly established. In other words, parents have difficulty recognizing their child as an emerging adult and accepting him as such.

3. The offspring has to learn certain basic techniques and

skills regardless of the brand of child psychology accepted by the parents. Many of these he acquires without conscious effort on the part of the parent to teach, or even in spite of their efforts. The latter is true of language—children brought up in an English-speaking family speak English. They not only speak the English the parents may have consciously tried to teach them, but they may pick up the dialect of the parents, perhaps in spite of the parents' attempts to help them speak without it.

The child is not very old before he begins to learn the way of life of his family and community. This will at first be taught mostly by his mother but also by father, brothers, and sisters as he grows away from bassinet, crib, and play pen. He begins to learn what the American way of life is and how to deal with people and things within it. There are —besides toys—chairs and tables, wallpaper, light plugs, floor lamps on long unsteady poles, dishes that break when dropped, and domesticated dogs that bite if treated in too violent a manner.

He learns to deal with people other than his long-suffering mother. There are possessive brothers and sisters, father who wants his evening paper intact, Mrs. Smith who always has candy, Mrs. Jones who doesn't appreciate having little children pick her tulips.

By experience, by imitation, by precept he learns the basic skills of communicating with others and getting along in society as a responsible member. This important process of socialization of the child is largely the accomplishment of the home and is accomplished by most parents with reasonably good success, using a variety of techniques beyond the inevitable experiencing and imitating.

4. The child must learn a basic acceptance of and respect for people, both himself and others. The parents must realize that good child training results in a product that can eventually get along without its teacher. It takes maturity in the parent to accept this. It is essential then that parents teach

the child to accept and respect himself and to gain some appreciation of the areas in which his talents lie. On the latter the school gives an important assist.

Since a successful launching is the final stage in child-rearing, the parents will want to encourage independence as the child is able to use it—independence to do things for himself, to decide for himself.

5. The desire to achieve on the part of the growing child must always be tempered by a constrained concern for others. This involves treating others as equals, but it also involves a respect for those in superior positions and in positions of authority. It is a part of learning to get along with others to learn the meaning of status and authority in society. Within the democratic tradition of our society, it is not uncommon to find children reared in an atmosphere of lack of respect for parents or others in authority. Respect for status and authority can first be taught through teaching the child respect for parents. "Honor thy father and thy mother" need not involve autocratic decrees; it may be a part of wisdom even in a democratic society. A child need not have any less of a sense of respect for himself if he learns that there are other persons who because of their wisdom, experience, or station in life merit respect and deference. To recognize the legitimate authority of others and to be able to accept it without chafing is not a sign of weakness but a sign of maturity.

6. As the parent communicates to the child by precept and example what his attitude should be toward things, people, and himself, the parent is teaching the child a way of life, a set of ethical and moral standards that the parent believes to be right and proper. Beyond this informal teaching of values, however, the parents must provide satisfactory answers to the ultimate questions as they arise out of the thinking and experience of the child. A child is not very old before he asks the great philosophical questions of man—questions relating to man's existence. Since man can relate

to the past, the present, and the future and has the capacity to evaluate himself in terms of these, he soon asks questions like: Where did I come from? Why am I here? What will happen to me in the future? What will become of me after I die? The so-called great religions as well as secular thought have answers to these questions; it is up to the parents to communicate the answers which they regard as valid.

Some parents in an attempt to be democratic and progressive feel that it is not right to teach religion. Believing the child should have the right to develop his own philosophy of life, they attempt to leave these questions unanswered. The child, however, develops some philosophy of life—a religion—whether the parents teach him or not. They may prefer that he learn a way of life that has come to have meaning for them and for other adults.

7. Parents will also need to teach the child about himself—his body, its functions, and its proper care. Common standards of sanitation, cleanliness, and health make his life more enjoyable and make him a more acceptable person. Parents experience no difficulty in teaching these things; but they commonly experience difficulty when it comes to teaching the child the peculiarities of his own sex and the difference between the sexes. This is an important area of life. Because of taboos, warped attitudes, and inadequate knowledge on the part of many parents, this matter deserves discussion. It will be considered in the following chapter.

Summary

Systematic study of human nature provides knowledge and insights into the job to be done by parents in guiding the growing child to maturity. This is not to say, however, that common-sense experiences plus the researches of the experts resolve themselves into a clear-cut blueprint for raising children.

Some hunches and insights for child-raising are to be gained by deliberating on the implications of the American ideal and the empirical research data. One is led to conclude that (1) human nature is learned, and hence teaching and experience are crucial; (2) certain basic skills must be learned by every human being if he is to get along with himself and with society, and this is true regardless of the teaching methods employed in transmitting them; (3) the American ideal calls for training that instills respect for self and respect for others; (4) the American ideal calls for an environment of care and motivation that provides maximum opportunities for the child to develop to the limit of his capacities and talents; (5) according to the American ideal man is free but also responsible and must have opportunity to acquire an adequate value orientation or philosophy of life to guide his actions in a satisfying and responsible way.

QUESTIONS AND PROJECTS

1. What do we mean when we say that human offspring are not born human?
2. Why is mother care—or care by a substitute mother—essential to the development of human traits in babies?
3. What characterizes the permissive school of child-rearing? The developmental school?
4. What is the difference between a child-centered and a person-centered family?
5. Regardless of the lack of evidence in support of any particular child-rearing pattern, there are certain things every child must learn to get along in a society. What things would you include besides those discussed in this chapter?

SUGGESTED READINGS

Aldous, Joan, and Leone Kell, "Child-rearing Values of Mothers in Relation to Their Children's Perceptions of Their

Mothers' Control: An Exploratory Study," *Marriage and Family Living*, Vol. XVIII, February 1956, pp. 72–74.

Blood, Robert O., "Consequences of Permissiveness for Parents of Young Children," *Marriage and Family Living*, Vol. XV, August 1953, pp. 209–212.

———, "A Situational Approach to the Study of Permissiveness in Child Rearing," *American Sociological Review*, Vol. 18, February 1953, pp. 84–87.

Commission on Education, Lutheran World Federation, "The Responsibility of the Family for Christian Education," *Commission on Education Report 1952–1957*, Geneva: The Lutheran World Federation, 1957, pp. 1–104.

Duvall, Evelyn M., *Family Development*, Chicago: J. B. Lippincott Co., 1957, Chapters 9, 10.

Hawkes, Glenn R., "The Child in the Family," *Marriage and Family Living*, Vol. XIX, February 1957, pp. 46–51.

Kirkpatrick, Clifford, *The Family: As Process and Institution*, New York: The Ronald Press Company, 1955, Chapter 19.

LeMasters, E. E., *Modern Courtship and Marriage*, New York: The Macmillan Co., 1957, Chapter XXV.

Martin, William E., "Effects of Early Training on Personality," *Marriage and Family Living*, Vol. XIX, February 1957, pp. 39–45.

Spitz, René A., "The Role of Ecological Factors in Emotional Development in Infancy," *Child Development*, Vol. 20, September 1949, pp. 145–155.

26 *The Adolescent in the Home*

The human offspring spends only slightly more than a decade as a child in the family before signs of emerging adulthood begin to appear. Almost before the parents realize it, the emerging adult period comes as a new experience to both the parents and the child. This period of emergence is commonly referred to as adolescence, or "the teens."

The adolescent, or emerging adult, needs sympathetic understanding from his parents; the parents need sympathetic understanding from the adolescent, too. But it would be asking too much of the child, even in the person-centered democratic family, to expect him to have the maturity and perspective that the parents might be expected to bring to the situation. Nevertheless, parents who have insisted throughout the childhood of the adolescent that adults, too, are people with needs, interests, and desires can expect the adolescent to attempt to provide part of the understanding as they learn to cope with each other.

In a study of 528 high-school students, problems concerning the use of automobiles, the student's diet, and concern about school work headed a rather long list of problems which students regarded as serious disturbances in their rela-

"Someday, son, all this will belong to you."
Reproduced courtesy of Frank O'Neal.

tionships with their mothers. These and other seriously disturbing factors in the relationship between adolescents and their mothers are shown in Tables 24 and 25.

TABLE 24 *Percentage of Boys Who Checked Each Item That Was a Seriously Disturbing Factor in Their Relationships with Their Mothers*

Won't let me use the car	85.7
Insists that I eat foods which I dislike but which are good for me	82.4
Scolds if my school marks aren't as high as other people's	82.4
Insists that I tell her exactly what I spend my money for	80.0
Pesters me about my table manners	74.8
Pesters me about my personal manners and habits	68.5
Holds my sister or brother up as a model to me	66.9
Objects to my going automobile riding at night with boys	65.7
Won't let me follow a vocation in which I am interested	64.5
Complains about my hands or neck or fingernails being dirty	55.7
Won't give me a regular allowance	54.1

Teases me about my girl friends	51.3
Insists that I take my sister or brother wherever I go	50.5
Brags about me to other people	50.1

SOURCE: Paul H. Landis, *Understanding Teen-Agers*, New York: Appleton-Century-Crofts, Inc., 1955, Table 7, p. 114.

TABLE 25   *Percentage of Girls Who Checked Each Item That Was a Seriously Disturbing Factor in Their Relationships with Their Mothers*

Objects to my going automobile riding at night with boys	87.4
Scolds if my school marks aren't as high as other people's	85.9
Insists that I eat foods which I dislike but which are good for me	83.8
Insists that I take my sister or brother wherever I go	82.3
Insists that I tell her exactly what I spend my money for	81.2
Spends most of her time at bridge parties, etc., and is rarely ever at home	78.0
Holds my sister or brother up as a model to me	75.8
Won't let me use the car	70.8
Pesters me about my personal manners and habits	70.0
Insists that I go with friends of her choice	69.7
Nags about any little thing	66.4
Objects to my going automobile riding during the days with boys	66.4
Teases me about my boy friends	65.7
Fusses because I use lipstick	64.6
Pesters me about my table manners	63.9
Worries about my physical health	58.8
Objects to my going to dances	58.8
Insists that I be a goody-goody	57.8
Won't let me take subjects I want in school	56.1
Refuses to let me buy the clothes I like	55.6
Won't let me attend the church I wanted to attend	53.4
Won't let me entertain at home	53.1
Won't give me a regular allowance	52.3
Insists upon nagging me regarding what I wear and how I dress	50.9

SOURCE: Paul H. Landis, *Understanding Teen-Agers*, New York: Appleton-Century-Crofts, Inc., 1955, Table 8, p. 115.

Adolescence As a Physical Phenomenon

Roughly speaking, adolescence begins with the more rapid physical development and the climactic first menses for the girl and the somewhat later appearance of certain bodily changes in the boy. For both sexes early adolescence is a time of rapid growth and change in bodily characteristics.

In the girl, changes appear in the structure of the pelvic bones, menarche, development of the breasts, and appearance of pubic hair. It is during this period that the mature ovaries for the first time begin to release eggs capable of being fertilized; adolescence marks a period in which the girl develops the capacity to conceive.

In the boy, along with the appearance of pubic hair and the general growth in height and weight, there is enlargement of the genitals and accompanying development of the testes and other glands. As semen containing sperm cells is produced, nocturnal emissions—the discharge of seminal fluid during sleep—give evidence of sexual maturity; the male is capable of impregnating.

These physical changes in the boy and girl have psychological and social consequences. This is markedly true, of course, in regard to the ability to reproduce, but the adolescent himself may be more aware of the psychological and social consequences of other physical changes. For instance, growth during adolescence is extremely variable from person to person. The fact that one is unusually small or large for one's age, unusually strong (if a boy), or well developed (if a girl) has psychological and social consequences.

The parent needs to be aware of and sympathetic to the problems of adjustment presented by these changes. The unusually small or skinny adolescent is apt to be the butt of many a good-natured or unkind word; the unusually tall and well-developed boy receives undue attention from downtown quarterbacks thirsty for a winning football team; the well-developed girl has the undue attention of innumerable men. The adolescent needs sympathetic understanding.

The Facts of Life—Sexual and Otherwise

Parents commonly find themselves tongue-tied by their own inhibitions and taboos or by a lack of knowledge about the facts of life. The knowledge can easily be gained since any good library has an adequate selection of books on the facts of sex for the parent willing to put in the reading time. They will also have books indicating the questions children commonly ask with some representative answers.

As shown in Table 26, in a recent study involving over

TABLE 26 *Sources of Sex Information of 5500 High School Seniors*

Source of Information	Boys Per Cent	Girls Per Cent
Parents and adults at home	38.2	64.6
Church, Sunday school, minister	3.2	2.5
Older kids, magazines, movies	52.3	26.7
Class and supervised discussion	10.5	20.8
An adult counselor	8.7	6.4

SOURCE: L. J. Elias, *High School Youth Look at Their Problems,* The College Bookstore, State College of Washington, Pullman, Washington, January 1949.

5000 high school seniors, only the girls listed the home as the major source of their sex information (64.6 per cent).

Boys received more of their information from "older kids, magazines, movies" (52.3 per cent).

For the person with twenty or thirty years of inhibition behind him, acquiring proper attitudes toward open discussion of sex matters is much more difficult than acquiring adequate knowledge. Learning a proper technical vocabulary and using it instead of the terms of the street or the baby talk used by one's mother will help. One professional woman learned the proper vocabulary and then practiced talking about sex aloud to herself as she drove her car from client to client to help her in talking with ease about sex matters to her children! It would be better still to use an adult vocabulary from the time of the birth of the first baby, for the baby will grow up knowing the correct terminology and the parents will be accustomed to using it.

Answering the child's first sex questions with a correct but simple answer will help the parent get started, too. Mother may be upset by the question, but the child will not be, and he will likely not detect mother's nervousness unless she falters too badly in her answers. To know that "the baby grows in its mother's tummy" may be all that the child is interested in for some time. The child is usually quite old before he becomes concerned about the father's part in reproduction, though he may want to know why mothers and fathers do not take turns having babies. To reassure him that while mother is bearing and rearing babies father must be providing for the family will satisfy the child and will not be a dishonest answer.

By the time the child approaches adolescence, if the questions have not come up before this, the parent should take the initiative in setting the stage for the explanation of reproduction and the father and mother roles in it. No adolescent should enter the fertile period himself without knowing the facts of human reproduction. For a girl not to know where babies come from until her own pregnancy forces the facts of life upon her is the gravest kind of injustice, but this happens even in our own day.

Parents may want to have illustrated books on human anatomy and physiology available in the home for the older children. It will be better if the parents can explain matters in a conversational way, since it is not reassuring to find that the parents know so little about sex and reproduction that they have to refer the child to books. But parents have found that it works fairly well to have such books around the house so that the child can read for himself when his curiosity is aroused.

Apart from the knowledge of coitus, the child of each sex must know what is happening to him before adolescence begins. With the fine literature available today, there is no reason for a daughter to arrive at first menses without an explanation in advance not only of the facts but also of the attitudes she should take and how she should take care of herself. Since there are products sold in connection with this physiological function, manufacturers provide simple and well-written free literature on the subject. The public library is also a source of literature.

With the boy there is no product sold and hence there is no readily available supply of free literature. But the boy should not have a seminal discharge without knowing what it means. The boy may get some kind of an explanation from his peers, but it is apt to be inaccurate or misleading. On the occasion when the father tells him about nocturnal emissions he may also want to discuss masturbation as well as the new power that he possesses and his responsibility to the other sex.

The young person may have been taught from early childhood to respect other people and not to exploit them for his own purposes; now the parent will want to apply these attitudes specifically to the matter of sex exploitation which is so widely approved in the male subculture. "All's fair in love and war" has a host of adherents in our society.

Child—Adolescent—Adult

In many primitive societies the emergence of adulthood is signalized and made socially significant with initiation rites or rites of passage. In these simpler societies—that is societies in which less formal training is necessary before adult roles are assumed—the initiation rites may symbolize the abrupt passage of the individual from childhood to adulthood without an intervening stage. In other words, the initiation is not a rite of passage from childhood to "teenhood" but from childhood to adulthood. In these societies the child may reach not only physical maturity but also psychological and social maturity before his fifteenth birthday. From then on he will be treated and expected to behave in an adult way in adult roles.

Our society has no such specific rites of passage from childhood to adulthood; nor should it, for the child in our society enters adolescence, not adulthood, at puberty. In other words, though some societies are characterized by two major life stages, childhood and adulthood, modern society is characterized by three stages—childhood, adolescence, and adulthood. The simpler society has one stage of dependency and development and one of independent performance. Our society has two stages of dependency and development—childhood and adolescence.

This prolonged period of dependence creates complications. Though the child matures sexually at puberty, as he does in all societies, our society is not prepared to grant any large measure of responsible participation to him either in terms of marital or premarital sex involvement.

The emerging adult is required to live in sort of a make-believe world—not the dependence of childhood and not the independence of adulthood. This somewhat artificial life is lived primarily in the family of procreation and in the school. The adolescent is denied significant roles in the life of the society; in fact, he is by law excluded from most of the economic roles of the society, even though he is quite capable of performing many of them. The family, the school, the church, and other agencies and organizations have attempted to keep life meaningful for him without giving him any significant roles in the ongoing society. He sometimes rebels by making a shambles of the school, raping the neighbor's daughter, or planning the strategy for a gang war, but most of the time he accepts the role of a dependent without disrupting the smooth functioning of the society. Parents must appreciate and try to be helpful to him in his plight.

The Emerging Adult As a Continuing Member of the Family of Procreation

During the period when parents are helping the adolescent to get ready to fly from the home nest into the world of independent activity, they also have the responsibility of maintaining the family as a satisfying group for him. He will vacillate in his own thinking and acting between rejection of his home and desire to be a dependent within it. Parents who have developed a relationship of acceptance, respect, and trust during the childhood period of their offspring will be able to keep the channels of communication open during this period of vacillation, provided they do not take offense at the adolescent's lack of consistency in his responses to them. Parents must be prepared to accept periods of secretiveness, moodiness, expansiveness, signs of independence, and signs of complete dependence. If they can take these in their stride, the adolescent will appreciate knowing that when he does have a need for his parents they are ready to accept him and his need as worthy of serious adult attention.

A family that has gotten in the habit of doing things together will want to continue to plan activities together, incorporating the interests of the emerging adult insofar as this is possible. Often he will not want to share in the planning of family activities and may reject the family activity without a moment's hesitation. But to stop planing group activities is hardly the answer to the problems of the vacillating adolescent. In fact, the parents may want to incorporate this emerging adult into the planning of family activities more and more as he proceeds in maturity and good judgment. Democratic planning can be started long before puberty, but the adolescent's understanding of the problems and the significance of his contributions to their solution can be expected to increase with age and maturity.

Helping the Adolescent Become a Self-Respecting Self

At the same time that the family tries to make home life as attractive as possible for the adolescent, they must realize that the motive for doing this should not be a possessive one. In other words, it is their responsibility to help him become a self-respecting person capable of standing on his own feet. He will have taken over much in the way of personality traits and value orientations from his parents, but as he moves out of the family and begins to transfer his loyalty from parents to peers he will for the first time become seriously objective about his home and what he has been taught in it. The freedom he seeks is not real independence but the right to enter groups of his own choosing. He will still be extremely culture bound, but more and more it will come to be the culture of his peers, not of his parents.

He will test out his own personality and his philosophy of life as he has opportunity to associate with different persons in his age groups. Does he find an athletically minded group most to his liking? A church group? A group in complete rebellion from parental authority? A group sowing its wild oats? He will see his own personality, his standards, and his values mirrored as he feels at home or does not feel at home in various groups.

He will also find out in groups whether he is a leader or a follower, the group wit or the group philosopher. Since he is apt to be extremely self-conscious at this stage, he will be carefully evaluating how others react to him.

The school helps tell him who he is. What subjects does he like? What extracurricular activities does he like? What vocational possibilities appeal to him? These help point to his future career. They also help tell him who he is.

Concerns of adolescents are reflected in the responses listed in Table 27. In the study of 5500 high school seniors

TABLE 27 *Percentage of 5500 High School Seniors Checking Certain Vocational Problems, Arranged by Order of Frequency Checked by Boys*

Vocational Problem	Per Cent of Boys Checking	Per Cent of Girls Checking
Choosing a vocation	30.9	19.3
What job best suited for	26.9	21.8
Concerned about the future	25.7	26.4
Making something of myself	25.4	27.1
Don't know what I really want	22.5	23.9
Whether to go to college	22.2	17.0
Don't know what I want to be	20.9	18.3
Don't want to depend on anyone	14.9	14.9
Want advice to choose vocation	13.0	10.4
Do not know my abilities	11.5	11.1

Vocational Problem	Per Cent of Boys Checking	Per Cent of Girls Checking
Need for vocational training in high school	10.4	8.3
Afraid I won't succeed	8.0	12.1
Worried about getting a job	7.5	11.5
Growing up	5.0	10.5
Choosing marriage or a career	2.8	16.8

SOURCE: L. J. Elias, *High School Youth Look at Their Problems,* The College Bookstore, State College of Washington, Pullman, Washington, January 1949.

previously referred to, students were asked to check items in a list of thirty common questions concerning vocation which were problems for them. The items most frequently checked are arranged in order of frequency checked by boys. As one might anticipate, boys showed somewhat greater concern over vocation than did girls, with girls showing concern over the marriage-career dilemma.

The Adolescent and Larger Loyalties

The adolescent is apt to be religious, idealistic, and altruistic. The family that has been close to the church throughout the adolescent's childhood will probably find the adolescent choosing to identify with the church during this period of his life, particularly if he has learned and been encouraged to rely on resources beyond himself and his parents as he grows up. The child that has learned to rely on powers outside himself may in the highly emotional period of adolescence find occasions for religious experience as he feels insecure in himself, in his parents, in his peer group. The church can be a good place for him to give vent to his altruistic feelings, also. If he has been encouraged to give of his time, talent, and money during childhood he can easily relate these things to adolescent life. Adolescents are apt to like the big, the challenging, and the dramatic. An adolescent may not only like to give, he may want to give sacrificially. He may take on service projects or seek outlets for giving himself and plan on a career as a public servant, missionary, social reformer, doctor. He may "get over" this stage and not enter such work, but there is no particular merit in curbing his enthusiasm or his idealism. There is always room in society for inspired servants of mankind.

Summary

Adolescence is the period between childhood and adulthood. As society becomes more complex, as new discovery and accumulation in the arts, science, and technology add to the complexity of life, greater and greater competence is required of young persons before they can assume responsible adult roles in society. Adolescence is a period marked by lack of directly productive work; it is a period with emphasis on education—preparation for life—and much leisure and recreation. Often the ends of this preparatory period seem remote and unreal, and the adolescent finds it difficult to retain his enthusiasm and motivation. Even the person who is motivated to prepare for adult life is often bewildered by the variety of values and norms and the variety of vocational pursuits open to him.

Some of the most important decisions in life are made during adolescence or the "teens"—courses of study, types of companions with whom to associate, moral and religious values. The adolescent needs and deserves the sympathetic understanding and active support of parents and all agencies concerned with human values and the quality of the next generation of adults.

Parents must help the adolescent prepare for a life independent of them and at the same time make him feel that he remains and will always remain an integral part of the family in which he spent his childhood and youth—the family of orientation.

QUESTIONS AND PROJECTS

1. At what age should the child's sex education begin? At what age should it be discontinued? Elaborate.
2. Describe the period of adolescence as distinct from childhood and adulthood.
3. In what respects is it correct to say that some of life's most important decisions are made during adolescence? How can the home help the adolescent make wise choices in these areas of decision?
4. How do you account for the greater concern on the part of boys than of girls in choosing a career?

SUGGESTED READINGS

Baber, Ray E., *Marriage and the Family*, New York: McGraw-Hill Book Co., 1953, Chapter 9.

Crow, Lester D. and Alice, *Adolescent Development and Adjustment*, New York: McGraw-Hill Book Co., 1956.

Elkin, Frederick, and William A. Westley, "The Myth of Adolescent Culture," *American Sociological Review*, Vol. 20, December 1955, pp. 680–684.

Hacker, Helen M., "The New Burdens of Masculinity," *Marriage and Family Living*, Vol. XIX, August 1957, Chapter 11, pp. 227–233.

Havighurst, Robert J., and Hilda Taba, *Adolescent Character and Personality*, New York: John Wiley & Sons, Inc., 1949.

Landis, Paul H., *Adolescence and Youth*, New York: McGraw-Hill Book Co., 1945.

Truxal, Andrew G., and Francis E. Merrill, *Marriage and the Family in American Culture*, New York: Prentice-Hall, Inc., 1953, Chapter 20.

Warnath, Charles F., "The Relation of Family Cohesiveness and Adolescent Independence to Social Effectiveness," *Marriage and Family Living*, Vol. XVII, November 1955, pp. 346–348.

Winch, Robert F., *The Modern Family*, New York: Henry Holt & Co., Inc., 1952, Chapter 10.

———, and Robert McGinnis, *Selected Studies in Marriage and the Family*, New York: Henry Holt & Co., Inc., 1953, Chapter 9.

27 *Family Living*

Each member of the family except the very young child has tasks to perform outside the home. The husband typically goes to work each morning, the children go to school, and the wife may go shopping. Hence the family is a dispersed unit throughout much of each day; each day it sends at least some of its members out to perform tasks in the community.

What does or should the family do for each individual in preparing him to carry out his particular out-of-home tasks?

First of all, the family, unlike any other social unit, has the responsibility of helping each member to develop competence in dealing with himself and in getting along with others. This is especially true for the children since their most impressionable and formative years are spent in the home. But even husband and wife, with their most plastic years behind them, should show signs of growth in personal competence and competence in getting along with others.

The impact of the home on members when they are outside the home is empirically demonstrated in two recent studies. In a study of 64 ninth grade boys in a New York town, Warnath concludes that boys who are held in esteem by their classmates generally report more activities with other members of their families, give more instances of warm and friendly feelings of family members for each other, are permitted to participate more freely in activities outside the home, and conduct themselves more like adults than do their classmates. According to Warnath, the home appears to be a seat of learning for the development of social skills and perhaps for the desire to participate in activities with others.[1] Hollingshead reports from the Elmtown study that family culture was the most powerful factor conditioning a child's continuation in or withdrawal from school.

Closely related is the fact that the social class of the family gives the individual status outside the home. To be so-and-so's wife or so-and-so's child ascribes some status to the individual irrespective of his own merit. The status of the family in the community provides entree to groups and activities in the community if the status of the family is respectable or it becomes the barrier to participation if family status is low. This was one of the most striking findings of the Hollingshead study of youth in Elmtown.

There is a functional relationship between the class position of an adolescent's family and his social behavior in the community. Therefore, we can conclude with confidence that adolescents who have been reared in families that possess different class cultures may be expected to follow different behavior patterns in their responses to

[1] Charles F. Warnath, "The Relation of Family Cohesiveness and Adolescent Independence to Social Effectiveness," *Marriage and Family Living*, Vol. XVII, November 1955, p. 348.

situations they encounter in their participation in the community's social life. Furthermore, this study, if it has done nothing else, has demonstrated clearly that, for a complete cross section of a relatively homogeneous age and sex group in one community in contemporary America, the home an adolescent comes from conditions in a very definite manner the way he behaves in his relations with the school, the church, the job, recreation, his peers, and his family.[2]

As the child emerges as an independent person, the status of his family will not be so important to him, but in the early stages a family with a good reputation can be mighty reassuring to a person starting out on his own.

But the home is not only a launching pad, sending its members forth into the community and into the larger world. As it launches its members each morning so later in the day and on days when there are not outside tasks to perform, it gathers its members again, closes the door, and the unit which had been so inviolably public during the day, while its members were away performing tasks, becomes inviolably private when the door is closed and the "no-trespassing" sign is out.

A good home is not only a good place to be from but a good place to come back to. One of the major functions of the homemaker is to provide a pleasant, restful haven for the weary breadwinner and the child home from the competitive American school. To have a home to come to that is quiet, tastefully decorated, restful, and where peace and love reign is one of the greatest gifts to the family member.

The Family Per Se

In a society such as ours in which we think of the individual as the measure of all things, we are apt to evaluate the

[2] Reprinted with permission from August B. Hollingshead, *Elmtown's Youth*, copyright 1949, John Wiley & Sons, Inc., p. 441.

family only in terms of how well it serves individuals. Are the husband and wife (as individuals) happy with their marriage? Are the parents doing all that they should be doing for their children?

But the family as it regroups at noon, at the end of the day, or on weekends, is, or can be, more than the sum of its parts; if it is, it serves functions other than those which are purely centered on the individual career. What do we see if we view the family not as the sum of its out-of-home parts but as an inviolably private entity not reducible to its parts? It is in this way that marriage is viewed when referred to as a unity. It is possible to think of the family in this way —father, mother, and the children as one—*a* family.

It has been said that it takes a baby to make a family out of a marriage. This is true biologically, and it is true statistically, but it is not a definition of family from a sociological or psychological point of view. Something must happen to the individuals in relation to one another before the three or more persons become a family; the responsible members —the leadership coalition of husband and wife—must resolve to give themselves to this entity, the family, not only for what they will get out of it but also for the good of the children and for the good of the family per se. In other words, the parents must possess values favorable toward family unity—not only toward marriage unity—and these values will in interaction filter down from the leadership coalition to other members of the family and will become the prevailing norms for interaction. Values favorable toward family unity provide the setting par excellence for children to experience the most demanding kind of socialization of all, namely, learning to compromise one's own desires and wishes for the good of others and for goals outside of and higher than oneself—learning to function out of chosen values of cooperation rather than purely selfish and personal motives.

The rural farm family was a natural setting for such

intimate interaction, because the breadwinning function of the family was so well integrated with other family functions. The following examples related by Loomis and Beegle demonstrate the strong sense of family unity that often developed in connection with joint productive enterprises on the farm.

The author remembers that when he was a boy of seventeen, his family put up three cuttings of about one hundred acres of alfalfa hay. His father, without question the leader in this set event, worked with him on the hay stack. . . . The younger brother, who was nine years of age, drove the stacker team that lifted the hay. A brother fifteen years old and the mother bucked the hay in on top of the stacker head, each using a two-horse buck rake. There remained a sister of twelve who sometimes drove the stacker team or prepared meals and carried water and lunch to the stacking crew. If any one had not fulfilled his role according to expectations, the interaction equilibrium of the whole crew would have been disrupted. This was family teamwork, the nature of which few non-agricultural families . . . ever experience as a productive unit. . . .

Not only does childhood in the agricultural environment present opportunities to participate in sets under workaday conditions, but team activities must be carried on under crisis situations as well. Among the author's most vivid memories are several occasions when the hay stacking, threshing, beet harvesting, and other set activities were broken up by the severe rain or hail storms which often come up on short notice in the Great Plains. There were times when the whole family tried to corral livestock, repair washed-out ditches, or prevent the crops from being destroyed by pests. Such events are carried on with intense physical activity accompanied by intense emotional interaction, because every activity is of tremendous importance to each member as well as to the family unit.[3]

[3] Charles P. Loomis and J. Allan Beegle, *Rural Social Systems*, pp. 43–44. Copyright 1950 by Prentice-Hall, Inc., Englewood Cliffs, N.J. Reprinted by permission of the publisher.

At such times the individual is not acting on his own behalf but in the interests of the whole family, whose interests are his interests because of the consensus existing among the members.

It is generally conceded that children who came out of such training experiences knew both what it was to accept the authority of another—the authority of the family and the authority of the father as its recognized head—and what it meant to make strictly individual interests subservient to those of a group. But we cannot turn back the clock; we cannot go back to the "good old days" of the rural farm family. Modern urban living is not as conducive to integrated family living. It does not come about as naturally. The husband and wife as responsible leaders of the family must want it badly enough to make it work. So, family unity and rich family culture for families in an urbanized, segmented society begins with a decision that it shall be so.

What conditions are essential to the development of a rich family culture and family unity? There are at least five conditions: (1) a high value placed on family living by the leadership coalition; (2) people in interaction; (3) a setting in which to interact; (4) a closed door; (5) communication under conditions indispensable to interaction. We have discussed the first of these in the preceding paragraphs.

Family Members in Interaction

A second necessary condition is a continuing intimate relationship among a number of individuals, a sufficiently large number to allow for building up an organization of some degree of complexity but not so large as to prevent full communication. Each addition to the family adds to the complexity of the interaction pattern. Compared to family interaction in a family with several children, the interaction of husband and wife without children presents a simple pattern. As demonstrated by Bossard's Law of Family Interaction, "with the addition of each person to a family or primary group, the number of persons increases in the simplest arithmetic progression in whole numbers, while the number of personal interrelationships within the group increases in the order of triangular numbers." [4] In a marriage (two persons) there is one relationship; with husband, wife, and two children there are six relationships; and with four children there are fifteen relationships. Other things being equal, the greater the number of interaction patterns within the family, the greater the opportunity for developing family culture and interdependence between family members.

A Setting in Which to Interact

A helpful condition for culture growth is that the group be attached to a fixed position on the earth's surface. This is not only an aid in the preservation of the continuity of the culture but tends to create an intimacy with the natural environment so that at length the ways of living of the individuals of the group become adapted to and even expressive of their habitat. The physical environment is then a common basis for sentiment as well as for traditional behavior. [5]

With single-family dwellings and home ownership on the increase, there is the growing possibility of families having fixed positions on the earth's surface. According to a study by Thomas P. Monahan, about twice as many families were doubling-up in 1947 as in 1955.

[4] James H. S. Bossard, "The Law of Family Interaction," *American Journal of Sociology*, Vol. 50, January 1955, p. 292.
[5] Margaret Park Redfield, "The American Family: Consensus and Freedom," *American Journal of Sociology*, Vol. 52, 1946, p. 178.

All but 3 or 4 per cent of married couples maintain a home of their own, that is, they either rent or own a home, but close to half of the persons with broken marriages share the homes of others.

Living in a single-family dwelling is not quite synonymous with having a fixed position on the face of the earth, however. We are a mobile people and it is common for families to follow the demands of the breadwinner's job wherever it may lead them; it is also not uncommon today to sell the old house and get a new one as is done with automobiles. So, even though the home is owned, it may be a home in different communities or parts of the country over a period of years so that the ways of living of the individuals of the group may not become adapted to and expressive of their habitat.

The Closed Door

For a family to acquire a distinctive form and culture that is its own, a certain amount of isolation from outside influences is required. The American family has shown at least some inclination to face outward, as is witnessed by the front porch, the unenclosed back yard, the picture window facing the street, and the informality in modern suburbia.

Trends in American home planning at present show a somewhat greater concern for privacy. The large picture window overlooking the garden on the rear of the house, the patio, the fence and plantings to give privacy all attest to such a trend. The architecture of the house, the placement of the house on the lot, and the accompanying landscaping can all be planned in such a way as to provide privacy in family living even in an urban setting.

Communication Under Conditions Indispensable to Interaction

Communication is basic to the development of family unity and family culture. It is not only necessary that family members speak a common language but also that they keep the channels of communication open. In this regard, the family may find that their lives become richer and more stimulating as the children grow older precisely because of their greater ability to communicate on a level that is meaningful and stimulating to the parents and because this more advanced ability to communicate means a more sophisticated culture. When they can enjoy music and literature together, for instance, their culture may be more enriching for all than when they could only enjoy the grosser aspects of culture together.

Keeping the channels of communication open is basic to the smooth functioning of the family and the growth of family culture and its enjoyment. Such communication can best be maintained on a pattern of equality between the participants. This needs a little explanation, for it is a particular kind of equality. It does not mean that they are equal in capacity, in achievement, or in status. What it means is that each is equally respected, accepted, trusted, believed in. This is all that is necessary. It would be an injustice to the child to have him believe that he at six years of age has as good judgment or as great a wealth of experience to draw upon as his father or mother. Each must be respected as he is. All differences involved must be allowed for, and each must be encouraged to make his peculiar contribution to family life.

Communication is dependent not only on a language for

communication and a willingness to regard each family member as equal but also on a considerable area of values held in common. Basic are the values of mother and father. Their interaction since the time of marriage and until the children are old enough to contribute seriously to the stock of values of the family adds to their stock of common values. By the time the children are incorporated into family discussions, the husband and wife present a fairly solid front of basic values which the children take over in an uncritical way. These values are taught by example and by precept. In fact, the very time for teaching will often come when members of the family are deciding something as a group. Mother or father may say, "We don't believe in treating people in that way," or "We believe in sharing, don't we?"—thus instructing and reminding the child at the same time. No family discussion will get far without agreement on basic values.

In summary, there must be communication based on common language, respect for each other, and some agreement on basic values before development of a rich and unique family culture is possible.

In the family as in the marriage, different interests must be recognized and permitted. The family might achieve unity by denying or overruling all differences in personality and interests between the members, but this is not a type of unity consistent with the American ideal. The family must provide a delicate balance between individual interests and those of the group. Since each member of the family, including mother, is following an individual career, there will be clashes of personality and clashes of interests. This is not unfortunate, though it may at times make the communication out of which family culture grows temporarily unpleasant. These differences are grist for the mill.

For family culture and family unity to be rich and growing, account must be taken of personality and interest differences of its members, and the family must not be so isolated—an unlikely occurrence in an American community—that it does not receive stimuli and irritants from the outside that make it grow and adapt to the interests of its members and the needs of the community and society.

Basic to this whole consideration is the acceptance by family members of the family as vital to each. Each must accept the fact that, except for his most vital private concerns, he is able to willingly compromise in the interest of maintaining and developing the family. If the destruction of the family as an entity is not regarded as one of the alternative ways of resolving differences, a compromising nature is essential. For this to be a wholesome attitude and a positive one, each member of the family should feel that the family is important to him and to his life. The compromising posture may grow out of a sense of duty. Because of a sense of responsibility or convictions drawn from the Judaic-Christian marriage model or the rationalistic marriage model, family members may feel that it is their duty to maintain the family even though it is not always to their best interests individually.

Family Activities

What types of family activity contribute to this development of family culture and family unity? Before we discuss specific types of activities it is best to point out that one of the most important things contributing to family unity is simply the living together in good faith under one roof for so many hours out of each day, so many days out of each year, and so many years out of each life. This forced intimacy is bound either to cause a mighty eruption—not uncommon in the early years of marriage—or to result in a smoothly operating system.

Now we will discuss some of the specific activities that might contribute to family culture and family unity.

The daily meal. Although in many families it will be difficult to get together for even one meal in the day, the meal can be a very satisfying occasion for family communication. At the end of the day when the major activities have been laid aside, it is rewarding to sit down to a meal with healthy appetites and much to share from the day's expe-

"*It's an ancient custom from before television known as eating at the table.*"
Reproduced courtesy of *Ladies' Home Journal*
C. P. Co. 1958.

riences. Support for each other can be given here, joys and disappointments can be shared, and some of the next day's or week's activities can be planned. Many families begin or end this meal in a mood of reverence or thankfulness by saying grace—a custom that is not as obsolete as some writers have believed.

Routine family work. Most of the family activities are carried on because they have significance in themselves and not primarily because they create family unity. This is not true of the family work. There was a time when one of the most natural occasions for family activity centered around work. Now it is one of the least natural occasions. This is true in two respects. In the first place, when the children are small their assistance with the routine work of the family may very definitely not have value in and of itself. Any father who has had his little son insist on helping push the lawnmower, or the mother with a young daughter who wants to bake a cake, knows what patience it takes and how little it adds to the accomplishment of the task. By and large, it becomes a situation wherein "two heads—or pairs of hands—are not better than one," and mother or dad tolerates—or even encourages—such cooperative activity precisely to develop the "we" feeling in the children and, perhaps, in the hope that a pattern will develop which will continue until the time when the child is truly helpful. Secondly, in the urban, highly mechanized home, there may not be enough work to give everyone a meaningful task, and mother and father may have to hold their efficient selves in check so that their children may feel that they are necessary to the work of the family.

There are possibilities, of course, for increasing the work. Mother may take on more home projects or more community or church volunteer work. Also, the children may be enlisted to do jobs for which the family might otherwise hire outside help. Father and son might take on a project such as raising rabbits or building a boat, or the child might be encouraged to take a paper route or mow the neighbor's lawn and in that way share in work activity. Work for all in the modern family is not natural, and if a family regards it as an important part of developing "we" feeling, they will have to make an effort to find or make work.

Perhaps it would be more realistic, however, to accept Foote's observation that family living has come to consist almost entirely of play, at least in the suburbs. Play might then be used as a positive force for building family unity and family culture.

Recreational activities. One hardly needs to tell fun-loving Americans about the values in recreational activities. Some activities promote more "we" feeling than others, however. Purely spectator sports perhaps result in the least whereas participation activities give a maximum of "we" feeling. Participation activities can be found that minimize

"*. . . and so the Tolson family bid farewell to beautiful Lake Wamaragh.*"

Drawing by Robt. Day, copr. © 1957
The New Yorker Magazine, Inc.

differences in status between the members of the family. Picnics, fishing, auto trips, boating, etc., allow for much interaction between members around activities that are not so specialized that one must be highly proficient to participate. These are mainly out-of-home activities. There are, of course, at-home recreational activities that can be enjoyed as a family, such as singing and playing instruments, parlor games, cook-outs in the back yard, etc.

Family events. Days that are special only to the family can be made the occasion for much family activity. Birthdays for children are quite commonly celebrated with parties involving peers of the child. Many families, however, make the whole day an occasion for focusing on the "birthday baby" with special honors, freedom from household chores, breakfast in bed, gifts, and a special meal to meet the specific delights of the honored one.

Baptism and confirmation, school graduation, discharge from the army, and many other occasions can be made occasions in which one family member "stars" while the others play supportive roles.

Family reunions and celebration of events in the lives of family members outside the immediate family help the members, especially the children, to appreciate the meaning of a larger unit of relatives than just the immediate nuclear family.

Holiday and holy day celebrations. The year is rich in occasions for special ritual and celebration not only for the larger community but also for the immediate family. Christmas, Easter, Thanksgiving, and other religious and secular holidays are pregnant with meaning and opportunities to deck the home with symbolism that makes home life exciting and helps bring home to the members the meaning of various seasons and events.

The family council. Some families find that a formal meeting of the family on specified occasions is fun and helpful in planning events for the family, focusing on the career of one of the members, solving critical problems, or preventing a crisis by planning in advance. In the family council, someone presides and the formal organization may be carried to the point of utilizing a secretary and a treasurer, if the family takes to this and the children find it to be fun or impressive. Members bring up any plan, problem, or gripe, and, growing out of a free discussion, a solution is reached. Also, last week's decisions may be reviewed to see if a follow-up is necessary or if the action taken proved to be satisfactory.

Some families like this more formal organization. Others claim to accomplish the same thing by always being ready to discuss matters as they come up, perhaps in connection with the family meal. A family which discusses only when there is a crisis and when tempers are high might try a regular time for discussion and avoid some of the "heat" by providing some of the "light" in advance of the event.

The family altar. The term family altar refers to a practice in many homes—Jewish, Protestant, and Catholic—of having some form of religious worship in addition to grace at meals and bedtime prayers, in which all members of the family participate. There are many plans. They may involve merely a longer grace at meals where the prayers involve other aspects than the giving of thanks for food and drink, or they may be quite elaborate with candles, the reading of holy writ, songs, prayers, and blessings.

We are not concerned here with the form of the worship but with its function as a part of the Judaic-Christian marriage model. When a family worships together they are asserting their common belief in a God and in the sacred teachings. They are asserting common answers to the ultimate questions of man's existence. They may ask for guidance for the careers of each as well as for the family.

Family worship, then, places the individual and the family in a perspective. It has a leveling effect as father and mother—who may seem at other times to know all the answers—also bow before a higher power, admitting inadequacies and seeking strength, wisdom, and guidance.

For some families, worship will be formal; for others it serves its most useful function if kept simple and informal, especially in families with smaller children. Some families combine the weekly or daily worship and the family council, thereby putting family planning into a perspective before God.

These are some of the activities engaged in by families that may contribute to a feeling of unity and to the building of family culture as well as being useful in their own right. Some defenders of the American ideal fear that family unity might call for too great a compromise of freedom and individuality on the part of family members. This is a danger;

but, as Redfield has pointed out, living in a society always involves limitations on one's actions, and those whose personality has not been shaped by intimate attachments appear to be more vulnerable and less human than those who have been caught up in such attachments.

Summary

The democratic family—like the democratic marriage—is characterized by unity, togetherness, and self-realization.

In chapters on childhood and adolescence we have discussed what husband and wife and the home can contribute to the self-realization of the child as he grows through childhood, into adolescence, and is finally launched from the home. In the present chapter we have discussed oneness or family unity and family culture in terms of the conditions and the activities that contribute to its development. It was suggested that husband and wife might even create tasks to give the child a sense of belonging and a feeling of being important in the effective functioning of the family and the home.

There are certain conditions which tend to facilitate the development of a unique culture for the family and contribute to the growth of family unity. These conditions are a high value placed on family culture and family unity, a number of persons in interaction, a stable and familiar setting in which to interact, privacy, and communication free of status barriers between family members.

A few of the great variety of family activities that contribute to and are an outgrowth of family culture and unity are briefly discussed in the chapter. These activities include the family meal, family tasks, recreation, celebrations on special days, the family council, and the family altar.

QUESTIONS AND PROJECTS

1. How are experiences in the home reflected in the out-of-home activities of family members?
2. Under what conditions do husband, wife, and children become a family psychologically and sociologically?
3. What does it mean to develop a family culture?
4. What is the significance of shared values to family unity?
5. What kinds of family activities contribute to family unity?

SUGGESTED READINGS

Beasley, Christine, "How Can the Family Breed Democracy," *Marriage and Family Living*, Vol. XV, August 1953, pp. 201–205.

Bell, Wendell, "Familism and Suburbanization," *Rural Sociology*, Vol. 21, pp. 276–283.

Bossard, James H. S., and Eleanor S. Boll, *Ritual in Family Living*, Philadelphia: University of Pennsylvania Press, 1950.

Collier, K. G., "Authority, Society and Education," *The Journal of Educational Sociology*, Vol. 30, February 1957, pp. 283–288.

Connor, Ruth, Theodore B. Johannis, Jr., and James Walters, "Family Recreation in Relation to Role Conceptions of Family Members," *Marriage and Family Living*, Vol. XVIII, November 1955, pp. 306–309.

Dornbusch, Sanford M., and David M. Heer, "The Evaluation of Work by Females, 1940–50," *The American Journal of Sociology*, Vol. LXIII, July 1957, pp. 27–29.

Duvall, Evelyn M., *Family Development*, Chicago: J. B. Lippincott Co., 1957.

Dyer, William G., "A Comparison of Families of High and Low Job Satisfaction," *Marriage and Family Living*, Vol. XVIII, February 1956, pp. 58–60.

Elder, Rachel Ann, "Traditional and Developmental Conceptions of Fatherhood," *Marriage and Family Living*, Vol. XI, Summer 1949, pp. 98–100, 106.

Folkman, Jerome D., "Stressful and Supportive Familial Interaction," *Marriage and Family Living*, Vol. XVIII, May 1956, pp. 102–106.

Foote, Nelson N., "Family Living As Play," *Marriage and Family Living*, Vol. XVII, November 1955, pp. 296–301.

George, Gordon, "The Sociology of Ritual," *The American Catholic Sociological Review*, Vol. XVII, June 1956, pp. 117–130.

Mogey, J. M., "A Century of Declining Paternal Authority," *Marriage and Family Living*, Vol. XIX, August 1957, pp. 234–239.

Monahan, Thomas P., "The Number of Children in American Families and the Sharing of Households," *Marriage and Family Living*, Vol. XVIII, August 1956, pp. 201–203.

Redfield, Margaret Park, "The American Family: Consensus and Freedom," *American Journal of Sociology*, Vol. 52, 1946, pp. 175–183.

Schmidt, John F., and Wayne C. Rohrer, "The Relationship of Family Type to Social Participation," *Marriage and Family Living*, Vol. XVIII, August 1956, pp. 224–230.

Strodtbeck, Fred L., "The Family As a Three-Person Group," *American Sociological Review*, Vol. 19, pp. 23–29.

Westcott, Regina H., *The Family Lives Its Religion*, New York: Harper & Brothers, 1954.

Whyte, William H., Jr., *The Organization Man*, Garden City, New York: Doubleday & Company, Inc., 1957, Part VII.

28 The Family
and the Larger Community

ii ii

The marriage-family system is a unit of the larger society. Each marriage and each family has interpersonal roots in the past, for both spouses are the offspring of historical families. Each has contemporary interpersonal ties as relatives and others become the associates of family members. Marriage and the family have emerged as differentiated social systems and continue to exist as functioning systems or units in any community. The marriage-family system must be placed in context to be understood. In-laws, friends, the neighborhood, the school, the church, and the state are all a part of this context.

In-Laws

Each marriage partner comes from a different family and brings a different history of family life with him. In marriage, whether the marriage partners are aware of it or not, two family traditions are joined as two families are joined. Couples may not be aware of the importance of wider family contacts during dating days, but as they enter serious engagement and particularly as they approach marriage, the families from which they come loom larger in the consciousness of each.

In the Chicago study by Burgess and Wallin, roughly one-third of the couples said they always agreed as to ways of dealing with their families, another one-third almost always agreed, and slightly less than a third disagreed. A considerable proportion of men and women agreed that they were sensitive about their own families and the families of the engagement partners.

That in-laws can be problems should come as no surprise to anyone, for whenever relationships are close, interpersonal or interfamily tensions can arise.

According to the American stereotype, the person who is most apt to be the source of friction is the mother-in-law. Some recent research bears this out. In a study of 7000 Catholic couples, Thomas reports that more marriages were broken in the first year because of mother-in-law trouble than by any other cause. And Duvall states that among couples indicating in-law problems, the mother-in-law was reported as the cause of the difficulty far more frequently than any other family member, with the sister-in-law in second place.

On the other hand, as many couples will attest, the in-laws are frequently a part of their solution, not a part of their problem. In-laws can be of help in a number of ways, not the least of which is in helping the young couple who need assistance with financing.

Tense relationships between the marriage partners and the in-laws in America are not without their normative support. We are inclined to regard in-laws as superfluous and unimportant to the married couple. We have the mistaken

"*Mother just loves to crochet, and the very least you can do is be a good sport about it!*"

Reprinted from *Love and Hisses* by Brant House.
Copyright 1956, Ace Books, Inc.

notion that once the couple is married they can, if they like, move away from and forget the in-laws. We stress the fact that emancipation of the child from his family of orientation is good and that once he marries he should transfer loyalty from parents to spouse. Lastly, we have the notion that children, not parents, are most important. The parents are to live for the children, not the child for his parents or his family.

In accordance with these norms, mother-in-law receives

an unusually bad press in America. No kinship role has been the butt of more jokes than that of mother-in-law.

In regard to relationships with relatives, the young couple is well-advised even before marriage to give thought to the part that relationships with in-laws will play in their marriage and family relationships. Even in a mobile and segmented society such as ours, in which the kinship ties are relatively insignificant in any formal sense, the marriage partners do not break the emotional or the social ties with marriage. Rather than divorcing oneself from the family of orientation at marriage, one in effect becomes a part also of a second family of orientation—that of one's spouse. Recent studies have shown that even in a large urban center with its mobile population, it is not unusual to have relatives in the same metropolitan area and to visit them with some frequency.

Even though the mother-in-law stereotype is well entrenched in our culture, Duvall reports a definite trend toward rejection of the stereotype by young urban couples. Over half of the couples had no mother-in-law complaints. In contradiction to the mother-in-law stereotype and the wide disregard of kinship ties in the popular culture, many young couples find that getting to know the relatives of each spouse and cultivating the relationships can provide continuing and mutually rewarding experiences. Older persons— the parent and the grandparent generations—enjoy having younger acquaintances to cheer and inspire them. Such relationships are enriching to young people as well, particularly the relationships with persons who have lived longer and possess some of the wisdom of years.

A new day may be in sight for the relationship existing between the generations. Older people have not recently in our history received the favorable attention they are increasingly being accorded. Even the three-generation household— parents, children, and grandparents—is more and more to be observed.

The Family and Its Friends

Besides its relationships with its relatives, the immediate family and the larger community are in contact through friends of the members of the family.

In an interesting research project, Zimmerman has shown that the family tends to pick its friends according to the same principle that husbands and wives use in picking each other. Couples that succeed in marriage tend to be made up of partners who selected each other on the basis of similarity in values and beliefs; the family becomes a unit guided by a leadership coalition—husband and wife—with homogeneity of values. The members believe, think, and act alike.

Zimmerman hypothesized that couples wishing to maintain and develop their value system would choose as close friends persons who were in sympathy with their way of life, for families, as well as individuals, are reluctant to trust persons they do not understand and with whom they are not already in close agreement.

In accord with the hypothesis, Zimmerman found that friends are like the family in religious faith, regional background, and economic class, among other things, and that the first family friend—the most intimate one—is more like the family than are other family friends.

Thus family friend groups are like layers of woolen blankets on a bed when one is sleeping in a cold room. Those with many blankets may feel cold, but if so the feeling is from some other reason than the penetration of cold through the protective layers.

We may speak of the family friend groupings as the protective socio-psychological envelopes around the individual family member.[1]

[1] Carle C. Zimmerman and Lucius F. Cervantes, *Marriage and the Family*, p. 112. Copyright 1956 by Henry Regnery Company.

In other words, the family members may receive inspiration and enrichment of life through associations with persons outside the home, but the family who wish to perpetuate their unique family culture choose these associates very carefully and make of them a buffer between themselves and aspects of community and societal life of which they do not approve.

The Family and the Neighborhood

High on the list of factors operative when a married couple choose a part of the country in which to live is the economic factor. A major question is, Can the breadwinner find work there? Within this general framework, the family chooses the neighborhood in which to locate and the community facilities it will support and utilize.

The choice of a neighborhood and the choice of a home within it are partially but not entirely guided by economic considerations. In choosing a neighborhood, just as in choosing friends, the marriage partners search for a neighborhood that will provide congenial acquaintances and friends for members of the family. High on the list of factors considered are the right school for the children, a church for the family, adequate recreational facilities, etc.

The ease and success with which the family maintains and promotes its chosen way of life will in large measure depend on the complexion of the neighborhood in which they establish residence. This has been pointed out in a dramatic way in Whyte's studies of family and neighbor life in modern suburbia. He found that each court in the suburban housing development produced a different pattern of action, and whether newcomers become civic leaders, bridge fans, or churchgoers was influenced to a large extent by the interests and concerns unique to that particular court or neighborhood.

The Family and the School

The family, to the extent that it performs its socializing function, is the basic educational agency in the life of the child. But the school is the formal ally, instructing the child in skills which the parents have neither the time nor, perhaps, the ability to teach. It is the school that prepares a child to participate in and enjoy the culture of his society and helps him to choose a vocation in life.

Because the school helps socialize and teach the child, parents who are concerned about maintaining a particular set of values and way of life take an interest in the school, what is being taught, and how it is being taught. In the larger urban centers the family may have the opportunity of choosing between several public, private, and parochial schools, and in this way the family may extend its influence and utilize the school in promoting the way of life in which it believes.

The Family and the Church

No other agency in society has considered itself as closely allied with the family as has the church in the Judaic-Christian tradition.

The church is a major agency in society attempting to satisfy a person's need for meaning. All of the questions regarding man's existence as a consciously finite being are answered in the teachings of the major religions.

Besides giving meaning to life, the Judaic-Christian tradition has provided values and norms for social life. Love of neighbor is a general principle for social life in family, community, and all other relationships.

At the heart of the church's concern are regular worship services plus occasional services ministering to particular crisis situations in the lives of individuals and families. We have already spoken of the marriage ceremony. There are also baptism and confirmation services, home dedication services, and burial services, among others.

Religious groups offer help and encouragement to the family as it attempts to maintain itself as something of a formal religious group as well; family prayers, devotions, grace at meals, etc., are fostered. St. Augustine, for instance, referred to the homes as little churches and addressed fathers in the homes as "Fellow Bishops."

The State and the Family

Both in its control and service functions the state is an ally of the family. Families benefit in a special way from numerous facets of the protection offered by law, the police, and the courts.

Besides the general areas of control and justice, many of the programs administered by the state are designed precisely to be of assistance to families and their dependents. This is true of much of the social welfare legislation. Social welfare programs include care of dependent children whether inside or outside the home, care of the physically and mentally handicapped, compensation for the unemployed, financial assistance and care for the aged, family counseling services, and many others.

This is not to say that the state always acts as a friend

of the family. In time of litigation and in times of war when the state calls for able-bodied men to fight, the friendship between the state and particular families becomes strained.

Summary

The family is an integral part of the social order; it does not operate in a vacuum but is constantly influencing and being influenced by the environing society.

Throughout the book we have emphasized the influence of the three marriage models as well as the general American ethos on the actions of individuals in marriage and in the family. In this chapter we have indicated briefly some of the specific ties of the family with the larger community of relatives, friends, neighborhood, and social systems, such as the school, the church, and the state.

There is always tension between a social entity which tries to retain and build some unique cultural characteristics, such as is true of many families, and the environing society. By choosing friends, a neighborhood, and institutional associations that are relatively congenial, the uniqueness of the individual family can be maintained and fostered even as its members participate daily outside the home in the life and activities of the larger community.

QUESTIONS AND PROJECTS

1. How do you account for the lack of prestige of mothers-in-law and other relatives outside the immediate family in American society?
2. Is there any similarity in the way families choose friends and in the way marriage partners choose each other? Elaborate.
3. In what way are friends a buffer between the family and the rest of society?

4. In what ways do other agencies in the community serve the family? In what ways does the family serve the other agencies?

SUGGESTED READINGS

Albrecht, Ruth, "Intergeneration Parent Patterns," *Journal of Home Economics,* Vol. 46, January 1954, pp. 29–32.

————, "Relationships of Older Parents with Their Children," *Marriage and Family Living,* Vol. 16, February 1954, pp. 32–35.

Anders, Sarah F., "Religious Behavior of Church Families," *Marriage and Family Living,* Vol. XVII, February 1955, pp. 54–57.

Duvall, Evelyn M., *In-Laws: Pro and Con,* New York: Association Press, 1954.

Greth, Morris S., "The Christian Family and the Community," *The Lutheran Quarterly,* Vol. II, May 1950, pp. 3–18.

Jaco, E. Gartley, and Ivan Belknap, "Is a New Family Form Emerging in the Urban Fringe?" *American Sociological Review,* Vol. 18, October 1953, pp. 551–557.

Parsons, Talcott, and Robert F. Bales, *Family, Socialization and Interaction Process,* Glencoe: The Free Press, 1955, Chapter VI.

Reuss, Carl F., "Research Findings on the Effects of Modern-Day Religion on Family Living," *Marriage and Family Living,* Vol. XVI, August 1954, pp. 221–225.

Sussman, Marvin B., "The Help Pattern in the Middle Class Family," *American Sociological Review,* Vol. 18, February 1953, pp. 22–28.

Thomas, John L., "The Social Web of Marriage," *Social Order,* Vol. VI, May 1956, pp. 199–204.

Ward, William, "The Christian Family and Its Community," *The Seminar on the Family and Christian Education,* St. Olaf College, Northfield, Minnesota, August 5–9, 1957, Vol. XV, pp. 1–19 (mimeographed).

Whyte, William H., Jr., *The Organization Man,* Garden City, New York: Doubleday & Company, Inc., 1957, Part VII.

Williams, Robin M., Jr., *American Society,* New York: Alfred A. Knopf, Inc., 1951, Chapter 13.

Zimmerman, Carle C., and Lucius F. Cervantes, *Marriage and the Family,* Chicago: Henry Regnery Co., 1956, The Present Crisis.

In Summation—
Marriage and
the American Ideal

Much has been said about values in this book, particularly values inherent in three contemporary marriage models and in the overarching core of ultimate values—the American ideal. Even with this emphasis on values, however, the book is not an apology for any particular marriage model or for the American ideal per se.

Rather than defend a particular way of life, we have accepted a way of life and asked: What meaning does it have for the individual in marriage and the family? We have taken the basic core of ultimate values and examined it, as well as aspects of it embodied in the three marriage models, in terms of what adherence means for persons in the society.

We have used the data of social science, and particularly the data of family sociology, to illuminate as well as to evaluate critically the ideal as it finds expression—or does not find expression—in the prescriptions and proscriptions of the three marriage models. In relating values and actions of people, we have concentrated on three areas of human action and interaction—dating, marriage, and family life. What do the model values mean in each of these areas of life?

In random dating, the American value system calls for equal status between the sexes in deciding whether or not to date, equal status between the sexes on the date, and general respect for self and for each other. Another person—in this case one's date—cannot be used for personal advantage at his expense or to his detriment. In a society of free men, using another person becomes indefensible.

In serious dating, as in random dating, the American ideal calls for equal rights for each partner in choosing whether or not to date seriously, to become engaged, to accept proposals of marriage. As the dating system works itself out—in accordance with the basic nature of the sexes and in accordance with long accepted procedure—there is a difference in the roles played by each sex, however. The man plays the more aggressive role and the woman the more submissive role. But the man does not assume the aggressive role as a right, for the double standard, insofar as it exists, is sub rosa. It is never explicitly advocated as an ideal of our culture. In fact, the double standard is antithetical to the very core of values at the center of American culture. According to the high value placed on freedom and equality, neither person shall by fraud, duress, or coercion become the master of the other.

Marriage

In marriage the basic core of values again calls for freedom and equality. More than this, love becomes the essential and only basis upon which a relationship consistent with the American ideal can be consummated. But, one might ask: Can't a person contract to be the spouse of another without being in love? The answer is "Yes," but such a marriage falls short of the ideal. Mutual love—the free giving of oneself to another who also freely gives himself— is the only acceptable basis for marriage in a society of free and inviolable individuals.

In a society of free men who freely choose each other as marriage partners, love and fidelity are the only basis for a lasting marriage consistent with the ideal. If love is genuine and the partners act in good faith, they can expect love to be the binding force that will make for lasting marriage. But if love is not genuine, or if either partner does not act in good faith, the only thing that can hold a marriage together in a society of free men is fidelity—the acceptance of the responsibility of remaining true to one's vows and to the person to whom one made the vows. In a free society, the person can choose to be faithful, even at personal sacrifice, but he cannot be forced to be faithful. To freely sacrifice himself is one of his rights as a free man. Hence, if there is to be lasting marriage, love and fidelity become the only basis for it.

In regard to married life itself, the American ideal resolves itself into three specific values or goals—oneness, togetherness, and self-realization. To belong is apparently a universal desire of man and a need basic to his humanity, as was shown in the chapter on childhood. Togetherness is a more recently emerged value or goal of marriage, but it is consistent with a democratic division of labor among equals. It is the self-realization goal, however, that gives American marriage its peculiar, tenuous character. In a marriage of two inviolable, free individuals, each partner must have a chance to grow and develop within the marriage—and at times even at the apparent expense of the marriage—for Americans take the inviolable character of the individual seriously. The individual is regarded as too sacred to suffer, or to be allowed to suffer, violation. This in large part explains the prevalence in American society of divorce as an exit from marriage for one who asserts that his marriage no longer suits his best interests. Divorce is antithetical to marriage, antithetical to the stable family which church and state strive toward, but a way out for the inviolable, free individual who feels that he wants to or must break the marriage agreement.

The extent to which the belief in the free and inviolable man has permeated our thinking is seen in the empirical data on divorce actions. The popularity of cruelty as a stated grounds for divorce is a good illustration. Over one-half of all divorces granted in the United States specify cruelty as the grounds.

The rank order of causes of divorce and the percentage of divorces for each cause is shown in Table 28.

In most states cruelty refers to physical cruelty, but in some states mental cruelty is also a ground for divorce. Mental cruelty as grounds reflects the limits to which we have been willing to carry the American ideal to insure personal freedom. A person has a right to peace of mind as well as physical well-being.

Divorce and the increase in divorce in recent decades—except for the last decade—is a source of grave concern in our society. For example, the ratio of children to divorces has increased from 85 children per 100 divorces in 1953 to 95 children per 100 divorces in 1956. The estimated number

TABLE 28 *Causes of Divorce and Percentage of Divorces for Each Cause*

Cause of Divorce	Per Cent
Cruelty	51.8
Desertion	15.8
Drunkenness	1.8
Nonsupport	1.5
Adultery	1.3
Conviction of crime	0.6
Fraud	0.3
Bigamy	0.3
Insanity	0.1
Under age	0.1
Other	26.5

SOURCE: U. S. Department of Health, Education, and Welfare, National Office of Vital Statistics, *Divorces and Annulments: Detailed Statistics for Reporting Areas*, Vital Statistics—Special Reports, National Summaries, Vol. 48, No. 2, March 25, 1958, p. 34.

of children reported increased from 330,000 to 361,000 in 1956. This increase in the number of children involved in divorces is due partly to an increase in the proportion of divorced couples with children and partly to an increase in the average number of children per couple. The proportion of divorces with children in 22 reporting states and the average number of children involved in these divorces is shown in Table 29.

How to preserve the stable family and at the same time guarantee the rights of the individual is a problem that has no easy solution. The conflicting ends of marriage—marriage integration and self-realization—are at the heart of the problem.

Year	Per Cent Divorces with Children Involved	Children Per Divorce
1956	48.9	1.93
1955	48.1	1.92
1954	47.8	1.88
1953	45.5	1.86
	Per Cent Change	
1953–1956	7.5	3.8
1955–1956	1.7	0.9
1954–1955	0.6	1.8
1953–1954	5.1	1.1

SOURCE: U. S. Department of Health, Education, and Welfare, National Office of Vital Statistics, *Divorces and Annulments Detailed Statistics for Reporting Areas*, Vital Statistics— Special Reports, National Summaries, Vol. 48, No. 2, March 25, 1958, p. 31.

The problem is viewed differently depending on the marriage model one is considering. Those who follow the romantic marriage model hold no brief for marriage. If the partners are unhappy with each other, let them separate. The protagonists of the rationalistic model—by and large a socially responsible group—see the solution in mate selection. The marriage partners must be so carefully selected, on a rational basis, that marriage will be successful and the partners will remain true because they are happy and adjusted in marriage and do not want to separate. The protagonists of the Judaic-Christian model encourage or insist upon fidelity to spouse and marriage even, at times, at the expense of personal freedom or self-realization. If the weight of evidence seems to call for it, however, all Judaic-Christian marriage models permit a break in the marital relationship—annulment, separation, or divorce.

The paradox is a continuing one. If self-realization continues to be a goal within marriage, then accomplishment of it is not a threat to marriage. In other words, in a marriage of equals, oneness or unity—which on a cursory view might appear to be the ultimate goal in marriage—must take its place alongside self-realization as a goal. Unity and self-realization become the major goals in a marriage that is consistent with the American ideal, even though there is often tension between these two goals.

Family

Within the family per se, the goals of the American ideal become the goals of unity and self-realization, also. To belong is an essential quality of humanness. That is, man is not human except in association with other humans, particularly in his formative years. The family is an ideal structure for drawing out the human potentialities in the child and for giving him a sense of oneness with his fellows and with the rest of mankind.

But in family living, as in marriage, there is tension because of the second goal of family living—self-realization. Each member of the family—the parent as well as the child—has the right to opportunities for self-realization even while immersed in family life. This is not to suggest that family is only a threat to self-realization. It can be a channel for self-realization. This is true for the husband-father and the child but even more true for the wife-mother who chooses marriage and family as her major career.

For the young person who accepts the values inherent in the American ideal—dignity, freedom, and the right to personal growth on the part of every man—preparation for marriage becomes a search for specific values and patterns for action that will give maximum self-realization to each member of his proposed marriage-family system—himself, his spouse, and their offspring. To achieve self-realization is an honorable but idealistic goal and one that will require all the resources at his command.

In pursuing self-realization, one might choose to commit himself to his beloved, to marriage, and to family. Such commitment may well become the channel for his self-realization, and in no sense constitute an abrogation of his freedom.

SUGGESTED READINGS

Bailey, Derrick S., *The Mystery of Love and Marriage*, New York: Harper & Brothers, 1952, Chapters VI, XI.

Becker, Howard, and Reuben Hill, *Family, Marriage and Parenthood*, Boston: D. C. Heath & Company, 1955, Chapter 26.

Bernard, Jessie, *Remarriage*, New York: The Dryden Press, Inc., 1956.

Burgess, Ernest W., and Harvey J. Locke, *The Family*, New York: American Book Company, 1953, Part IV.

Fishbein, Morris, and Ruby Jo Reeves Kennedy, *Modern Marriage and Family Living*, New York: Oxford University Press, Inc., 1957, Chapter 33.

Goode, William J., *After Divorce*, Glencoe: The Free Press, 1956.

Himes, Norman E., and Donald L. Taylor, *Your Marriage*, New York: Rinehart & Company, Inc., 1955, Chapter 26.

Kane, John, *Marriage and the Family: A Catholic Approach*, New York: The Dryden Press, Inc., 1952, Chapter 12.

Landis, Paul H., *Making the Most of Marriage*, New York: Appleton-Century-Crofts, Inc., 1955, Chapter 32.

U.S. Department of Health, Education, and Welfare, National Office of Vital Statistics, *Divorces and Annulments: Detailed Statistics for Reporting Areas*, 1956, Vital Statistics —Special Reports, National Summaries, Vol. 48, No. 2, March 25, 1958, pp. 27–46.

Appendix: Marriage and Family Finances

In a society based on a money economy rather than on a subsistence economy, marriage and the family must be financed. A very few farm families may still pursue a subsistence economy—producing their own food, clothing, and shelter—but for most families the means of support will come in the form of dollars. Usually these dollars are earned as wages and are in turn translated through spending into the things that satisfy the needs and values of the family.

The crux of the problem of financing for the majority of families is to discover the most efficient way to translate cash into goods that bring maximum satisfaction to the family members. In answering this question each family must decide in accordance with its own values what things it is willing to save, budget, or go in debt for.

We cannot decide the values for the family, but here are some guidelines that might help in getting the most for one's money.

Planning

Any kind of planning makes sense. This is a generally believed and probably irrefutable principle. It is certainly true when applied to family finances, because the family income of few families is adequate to meet all reasonable desires of the family members.

As late as 1957, 37 per cent of family incomes were below $4000 per year, and 14 per cent were less than $2000 per year. The average, however, was $6130 per year.[1] Most families feel that they could use more money, and some feel that it would be the answer to their most pressing problems.

The particular type of financial plan will vary from family to family, but any plan includes some record of income and expenditures with some attempt to plan anticipated expenditures in terms of anticipated income.

Whether the family wants to budget or to use a less formal type of financial planning will vary with individual tastes. In any event, they will benefit from keeping orderly records of expenditures, income, anticipated expenditures, and anticipated income. Stationery stores or bookstores commonly carry financial record books specifically designed to help the family in keeping such records.

The family financial plan reflects and helps make objective the values of the family members. For this reason a family should not use someone else's breakdown of income and expenditures so far as amounts or percentages are con-

[1] U.S. Bureau of the Census.

cerned. For instance, there is no right amount to budget for food, for clothing, for savings, etc. The right amount is the amount that the family finds to be best for them and in accord with their values and way of life.

For the family deciding to budget their income, it is well to find out where the money "naturally" goes before amounts for each major category are set up. There will be certain fixed costs—rent, income tax, etc.—but there are some highly variable costs—entertainment, travel, luxury items— that can be adapted more readily to income and anticipated income.

After keeping records of income and expenditures for a time the marriage partners may ask themselves: Is this where we want our money to go? Is this where it must go? In answering these questions the family, and particularly the leadership coalition, will become more aware of the cost of their way of life.

Does having a new car each year mean so much to us that we are willing to invest heavily from our limited budget? Shall we "eat well"? Or shall we go a little more to the hamburger or ring bologna side and buy a book or record or attend a ball with the money we save?

Couples may not think of budget discussions as discussions of values, but they are. It will help clear the air and hold down the tempers if they realize that they are having a realistic discussion on what they want out of life rather than an argument over money.

Life (or Protection) Insurance

It is true that no family can provide for all of its needs or desires, financially speaking. On the other hand, a family can have too much security in that they may be carrying a heavier burden in protection (insurance) against financial crisis than is reasonable for their budget.

The purpose of insurance is basically twofold—protection and a means of saving money. Early in the marriage the couple will hardly be in a position to save but will need to protect themselves against the financial problems that would result if they or particularly the major breadwinner, were to die. It is important that the newly married couple do some careful thinking about insurance programs.

First, how much life insurance do they need? Ideally speaking, there are few couples who can afford all the insurance they need in the event of death of one of the spouses. If the breadwinner should die and leave a young wife and child, how much insurance would they need? Likely they could not afford to carry enough insurance to provide a living for the wife and child until the child was through school. But it would seem reasonable for them to think in terms of enough insurance so that the wife could make the transition to widowhood without immediate financial crisis. This might involve enough insurance to cover the cost of a refresher course in school for the wife before she returned to work, enough to pay the mortgage on the house, enough to meet current expenses.

Secondly, they might want to vary the amount of protection with changes in the family cycle. In general, the more obligations you have, the more protection you need. In other words, the couple heavily in debt to pay for a house need more protection than when the house is paid for. The couple with three small children need more than the couple whose children are grown. For these reasons the couple may want to keep the plan flexible by having some protection coverage for the lifetime of the parent or parents and some that will cover them during the period of greatest financial responsibility—term insurance.

Thirdly, the insurance should be carried on the parent who has the major share of the financial responsibility in the family. Since the little children are already economic liabilities, the couple may not want to make them even greater liabilities by having yearly insurance premiums to pay. Should they die the economic loss would be relatively inconsequential; should the father die the economic consequences could be catastrophic. It is better to carry the insurance on the father than on the baby.

In the fourth place, the same policy may vary some in cost from company to company. Therefore, it is a good idea to shop around before buying. Generally speaking, if someone else—employer, U. S. Government, etc.—is willing to pay part or all of the premium, one can hardly go wrong on purchasing the insurance so provided.

Health Insurance

No young couple planning a family can afford to be without health or medical insurance. Not only is it necessary to cover costs of hospitalization and surgery but also to pay maternity costs. Most policies provide for maternity benefits, and no couple planning to have children should consider a policy without this feature. The policy must be in force before the baby is conceived, however.

Other Insurance

The young man with a car has had experience with the absolute need for automobile insurance. Such insurance becomes ever more vital as the couple acquire more property.

In buying or building a house, the couple will need to make sure that insurance is in effect at the moment the purchase is made or the moment building is begun. Such protection is needed to cover loss from fires, storm, or other hazards.

The couple will also want to investigate the merits of carrying liability insurance as well as insurance on personal property and contents of the home.

Savings and Installment Buying

There are a number of ways to save money. From childhood one may have regarded putting money in the bank at interest as *the* way to save. This is a good and secure way to save with a modest return in the form of interest. But for the young couple there may be other and perhaps more practical ways of investing money. If it does not involve too hazardous or expensive financing, the couple may want to build up equity in some capital item such as a house that can be liquidated (turned into cash) if need be, but which can be used and enjoyed while equity is being built up.

Many couples think in these terms and live entirely on credit rather than on current income and savings. Within reason this can be a real blessing. If someone else has money and is willing to permit the use of it at a reasonable rate of interest, it is possible for him to get a return on his money and for the young couple to have the things they want now rather than having to wait until they can save for them. The family can live beyond its means in a sense if the monthly payments plus the interest are not outside the budgetary possibilities and the liabilities are met by adequate protection in the form of insurance.

The system of buying now and paying later seems to have largely replaced older systems, as pointed out by Whyte and others. Budgetism—buying now and paying later—has replaced budgeting—saving now and buying later. Whyte points out that budgetism has operated to put people more in debt, but that it need not. The added debt results from the couple's desire to regulate their finances by having control and discipline placed with someone else. They are more trusting of others than they are of themselves when it comes to financial matters.

Contributions

Many persons use gifts in money as a way of showing their concern for others, for sharing with the less fortunate, and for financing movements and causes they believe in. This is very common within the Judaic-Christian tradition and within our culture generally. In Old Testament times, under Mosaic law, the person was expected to give a tithe— a tenth—of what he received in wages and produce to support religious and charitable causes.

In our society we have planned and organized our charities within the structure of the state so that by paying taxes we also contribute to meeting the needs of others. Many charities, however, are not so organized; they depend on the good will of the people and their voluntary contributions.

Though we are discussing contributions as the last item to be discussed in the family financial planning, many religiously oriented persons place it first, thereby symbolizing their trust in God rather than in material things. They set aside first the portion for the "Lord's work" and live on what remains. Many make this giving a proportional matter, as has been practiced since Old Testament times, with the proportion ranging below, above, or at the tenth—"according as the Lord has prospered them."

Economic Factors and Family Happiness

A number of the empirical studies of marital adjustment have dealt at least in a superficial way with the relation between economic factors and adjustment. Results have not been consistent or conclusive, but by and large, the empirical data support the belief that economic factors do play a part in marriage and family adjustment.

This is no startling discovery since common sense would dictate that in a society where families are maintained in large part by money brought into the home from the outside, a regular and reasonably adequate supply of dollars would be essential to the maintenance of the family. Also, in a society where money and material things give status and prestige the amount and the regularity of supply is crucial. Furthermore, wealth enables one to enjoy greater educational, social, and cultural opportunities.

In summary, in a society such as ours—based on a money economy and almost limitless opportunities to spend money for desirable items—few families have all the money they can use. But by deciding on some goals in life and by carefully budgeting available resources to meet these goals, most families in our economy of abundance can live successfully within their means.

SUGGESTED READINGS

Bigelow, Howard F., *Family Finance*, Philadelphia: J. B. Lippincott Co., 1953.

Himes, Norman E., and Donald L. Taylor, *Your Marriage*, New York: Rinehart & Company, Inc., 1955, Chapters 14, 15, 16, 17, 18, 19.

Kyrk, Hazel, *The Family in the American Economy*, Chicago: University of Chicago Press, 1953.

LeMasters, E. E., *Modern Courtship and Marriage*, New York: The Macmillan Co., 1957, Chapters XIX, XX.
Whyte, William H., Jr., *The Organization Man*, Garden City, New York: Doubleday & Company, Inc., 1957, Chapters 23, 24.

Index

Index

479

Freedom, of man, 4, 5
Friends, of family members,
454-455
Frigidity, 328-329
Fromm, Erich, 11, 103

G

Gardner, Bruce, 383, 388
Gartenberg, Max, 65
Gebhard, Paul H., 35, 218,
243, 333, 334, 342
George, Gordon, 449
Glick, Paul C., 305, 345
Glover, Leland E., 16
Goode, William J., 325, 467
Greenberg, Joseph H., 370
Greth, Morris S., 459
Group, importance of the, 7-8

H

Hacker, Helen M., 312, 429
Hamblin, Robert L., 243, 342
Happiness,
as goal of marriage, 56-62
family finance and, 475
Harmony in marriage, 263-294
Hartel, Frank J., 243
Havighurst, Robert J., 429
Hawkes, Glenn R., 382-383,
388, 408, 415
Health, as personality trait, 278
Health insurance, 472
Heer, David M., 305, 311, 448
Heinecken, Martin J., 325
Herman, Robert D., 81
Herrera, Lee F., 364, 370
Hill, Reuben, 59, 64, 65, 143,
146, 183, 214, 262, 266,
288, 294, 307, 366, 369,
398, 402, 467
Himes, Joseph S., 131
Himes, Norman E., 285, 402,
467, 475
Hoffman, D. K., 312
Hollingshead, August B., 74-

75, 81, 184-185, 223-
224, 250-251, 432-433
Homogamy,
in personality characteristics,
124-126
in physical traits, 120-121
in social characteristics, 121-
124
Honesty, as a character trait,
282
Honeymoon, 257-261
Howard, David H., 214, 219,
259, 262
Human nature, 403-405
Humor, sense of, 279-280
Husbands, kinds of, 304-305

I

Ideal, American, the, 5-8
as overarching core of ultimate values, 460
child-rearing and, 408, 414
defined, 4-5
divorce and, 463-464
engagement and, 190, 198,
204-205
family unity and, 440, 446-
447
freedom of roles in marriage
and, 305-306
importance of being some-
one and, 102-103
investment of self in marriage and, 314
love as basis of mate selection and, 98-99, 101-
102
marriage and, 462-466
marriage educator and, 15-17
marriage models and, 55, 61,
64
motives for marriage and,
148-149
premarital sexual intimacy
and, 242

essential elements of, 51-54

family size and, 361

functions of marriage under, 54

origin and historical development of, 48-53

sex expression in marriage and, 356-357

Marriageability,

acceptance of self and, 149-150

adaptability and, 175-179

age and, 157-160, 171-172

expectations and, 149

knowledge of self and, 149-150

knowledge of the other and, 161-162

love of the other and, 162-163

personality traits and, 150-157

racial differences and, 166

religious differences and, 166-171

revelation of self to beloved and, 155-157

unity sought and, 173-177

Martin, Clyde E., 35, 218, 243, 333, 334, 342

Martin, William E., 415

Martinson, Floyd M., 114, 151

Mate, ideal, image of the, 117-118

Mate selection,

dating and, 98

desire for intimate association in, 119-120

influence of associates in, 126-127

love as basis of, 98-99, 101-102

parental image in, 118

personality characteristics and, 124-126

physical traits and, 120-121

propinquity and, 128

reason in, and the American ideal, 146, 180

religion and, 166-171

social characteristics and, 121-124

timing and, 128-129

Maupassant, Guy de, 104-105

McGinley, Phyllis, 81

McGinnis, Robert, 351, 430

Mead, Margaret, 35

Men, see Husbands; Man

Merrill, Francis E., 429

Mihanovich, Clement S., 65, 342, 373

Miles, Catharine Cox, 33

Models, see Marriage models

Mogey, J. M., 449

Monahan, Thomas P., 214, 449

Mother-child relationship,

disturbing factors in, 417-418

importance of, 405-407, 408

Mother-in-law, see In-laws

Motivation and interests, sex differences and, 31-34

Mowrer, Harriet, 288, 307

Munroe, Ruth, 128, 337

Myrdal, Gunnar, 6, 18

N

Neighborhood, the, family and, 455-456

Neptune, Donna, 184, 214

Niebuhr, Reinhold, 55

O

Other-directedness, 7

Overstreet, H. A., 101

Ovid, 49

P

Parental image, in mate selection, 118

Parenthood, 407

Westcott, Regina H., 449
Westoff, Charles F., 364, 369
Whelpton, P. K., 364, 370
Whyte, William H., 7, 316, 325, 449, 459, 473-474, 476
Williams, Robin M., Jr., 18, 22, 35, 325, 459
Winch, Robert, 126, 132, 351, 430
Winter, Gibson, 295
Wives,
  corporation, 316
  working, 305-306

Women,
  married, incidence of orgasm in coitus among, 334
  nature of, 19-34
  rights of, and the American ideal, 23
  roles of, 21-34
Wood, Leland F., 114, 295
Wylie, William P., 144

Z

Zimmerman, Carle C., 18, 35, 38, 42, 65, 298, 454, 459